The Illustrated Directory of

Dogs

Johnson

The Illustrated Directory of

Dogs

JULIETTE CUNLIFFE

Colin Gower Enterprises

Dedication

"Buy a puppy and your money will buy
Love unflinching that cannot lie."

To all our wonderful dogs: Fritz, Otto, Sidney, George, Freddie, and Alfie.

"Brothers and sisters, I bid you beware
Of giving your heart to a dog to tear."

Rudyard Kipling

Colin Gower Enterprises ltd.,
Cordwainers, Caring Lane,
Leeds, Maidstone, Kent ME17 1TJ
United Kingdom

© 2007 Colin Gower Enterprises Ltd.

ISBN: 0-681-63616-5

Designed by Cara Rogers
Photography by Carol Ann Johnson, J.P.Bell
Color Reproduction by Wyndeham Graphics
Printed and bound in Indonesia

Contents

Johnson

Introduction

For those of us who really love dogs, our canine friends are truly a part of our lives. Just as we, as humans, vary enormously, so do dogs. They come in all shapes and sizes with a variety of different hair styles, and they vary in temperament too. For these reasons, it is essential that we choose a breed of dog that fits in well with our lifestyle. If we live in a tiny apartment, a Saint Bernard is probably not a wise choice, and if we want to go out hunting rabbits, a Pekingese will simply not fit the purpose.

It is essential therefore to do our homework before purchasing a new pet. In the pages that follow, readers will find information about numerous different breeds, some of them well known to almost everyone, others that are rarely seen and may be difficult to find. It is very important not to rush into buying a dog. If the breed you know will suit you best is not available when you want it, it is best to wait a while, rather than to opt for another breed, just for convenience sake or because you can't wait to have a new four-legged friend in your life. Many of the

Above: Children can build up a great rapport with their pets.

really good breeders have waiting lists for their puppies, and that wait will probably be well worthwhile. After all, on average a dog's life can vary between about 8 and 15 years, so you want to be certain you have made the right choice, so that you will live happily together for the duration.

Another thing to consider is when your pet will join you and your family. Everyone knows that 'a dog is for life, not just for Christmas', the implication being that a dog is not just something to be discarded after the novelty wears off. However, there are other reasons not to buy during the festive season.

When introducing a new dog to your family, this needs to be done when you have time to devote to his socialization and care. He will need to get used to you and your close

Below: It's good if children and dogs can grow up together.

Above: A dog is a friend for life.

family before meeting loads of new faces, so no overly-busy time of year is right. Likewise, if you have vacation scheduled, you will not want your dog to arrive with you just two or three weeks before your departure, then to have to be put into kennels while you are away. When your new pet arrives, everything will be strange to him, so he will need to take things one step at a time. He must feel comfortable and thoroughly secure before he is moved to a new environment, albeit temporarily. If he is a puppy he will be away from his siblings and dam for the very first time; if he is older, he will not realise why he has been parted from people he probably loved and on whom he had come to depend. Just think of the situation from his point of view, and you will know when the time is right.

Preparing for the homecoming

There will be loads to do in preparation for the arrival of the new dog in your life. Planning his sleeping arrangements, play area and feeding routine are not things that can be left until the very last moment.

Firstly think where you would like your dog to sleep. You will have to start as you mean to go on. If you allow him to sleep on your bed from the very first night, he will expect to sleep there for the rest of his life, and this may not always be convenient! Every dog needs to have a "safe place", somewhere he considers as his own little area, where he can go and have a nap when the fancy takes him. This should ideally be somewhere in a fairly quiet spot, particularly if you

have a puppy, for he will need a lot of rest during the growing stage. Dogs can become rather protective of their own personal space, even with family members. This is quite understandable, so do not allow children to constantly go to the bed to disturb your dog while he is asleep.

Another very important thing you will need to organise before his arrival is that your yard area is fully secure. Dogs have a canny way of escaping though even the tiniest gap

Below: A dog can greatly help a wheelchair user.

Above: Your dog will adore a special place of his own.

Below: Even baby puppies can be great climbers.

down too far to eat and drink. This is an important aid to digestion and can help greatly in avoiding gastric torsion, otherwise known as bloat. If you have a young puppy that still has a lot of growing to do, you may need to buy one at a suitable height for his arrival, then a higher one when he is fully grown. Such stands can be simply functional, or can be almost a piece of furniture, so look carefully to decide what suits you best.

Before moving on, you will notice that throughout this book I have referred to dogs as "he". That may be rather sexist, but far better than

if they see or hear something interesting on the other side. Bear in mind too, that some breeds are diggers, whilst others are expert climbers, in which case your fencing will have to be adjusted to suit.

Then there is diet to consider. It is no good bringing your new dog home only to find that you don't have his special kind of food ready and waiting, and maybe the local store doesn't stock that particular brand. If you have bought from a reputable source, you should have been given a diet sheet, giving full details of the type of food, quantities fed and frequency of meals. In time you will be able to change this to suit your own circumstances, but any change must be done gradually, otherwise your dog will almost certainly get an upset tummy, which is not ideal for him or for you!

If yours is one of the taller breeds, you may need to get a stand for feeding and water bowls, so that your dog does not have to bend

Johnson

calling a dog an "it", don't you think? Of course your own dog may be male or female (dog or bitch), and this something else you will have to consider very carefully before making your purchase.

There are various differences between the two sexes, and the amount of noticeable difference varies according to the breed. Often males are larger than bitches, though this is not always the case, particularly in Toy breeds. Dogs often have rather more coat and they can be more dominant in nature, especially if they have been used at stud. Bitches, of course, come into season (on heat), usually every 6 to 7 months, but some breeds, such as the Tibetan Mastiff, only come into season once a year. Unless you have elected to have your bitch spayed, you will need to keep her confined in your own home and yard at this time, and if you have male dogs in your household they will have to be kept apart from her. A season generally

Left: Tiny pups can grow into very large dogs.

lasts around 23 days, so at that time you will almost undoubtedly have to alter your routine.

Grooming and general maintainance

Grooming demands vary considerably according to the breed, so it is impossible in a book of this nature to be specific about what you should and shouldn't do. Dogs have so many different coat types and even within one breed, there can sometimes be more than one variety. The Dachshund is a prime example; not only are there two different sizes in this breed, but three coat types, smooth, long and wire. Each of these needs different care and grooming techniques. Looking after the coat of a smooth coated Whippet is understandably less demanding than the coat of an Afghan Hound, but for some people half the fun of owning a dog is the pleasure derived from grooming the coat and presenting it to absolute perfection.

But however long or short the coat, whatever its texture, it still demands regular care. Even the shortest coat needs a regular brushing to keep not only the coat healthy and clean, but the skin also. Some breeds have coats that only require infrequent baths, maybe just a dry shampoo even, but others need bathing on a regular basis, every couple of weeks, or maybe even more frequently if they are exhibited in the showring.

If yours is purely a pet, you will probably decide to take your dog along to a professional grooming parlor once in a while, to get him looking his best. But between times his coat must never be neglected, so you will need a suitable brush and comb and if you have a smooth coated dog a "hound glove" will also be a great help. This is usually shaped like a mitten and has chamois leather on one side and velvet on the other. After a thorough brush and comb, a quick rub over with the leather, followed

Below: Teaching a dog to lie over for grooming is a great help.

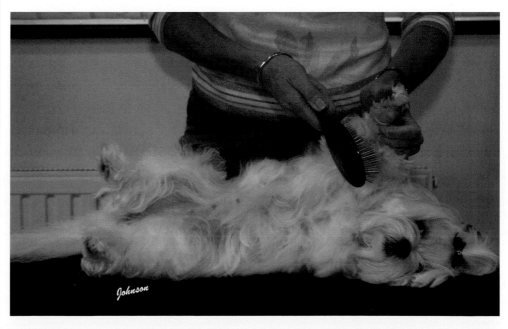

Johnson

Above: *Tying up the hair on a long coated breed.*

by the velvet will leave a cracking good shine of the coat, and your dog will feel a million dollars!

If you decide to bath your dog at home, especially if you have a long-coated breed, you will need to invest in a special canine hairdryer. These are not cheap, but will give you many years of good service and will speed up the drying process no end. If you have a long coated dog, you will simply not get a good finish to the coat following a bath unless you have suitable drying equipment. Many of the better quality machines also have a blaster attached, to blow out the bulk of the water, before drying normally. It is also far better to use canine shampoos and conditioners rather than those designed for human use, and a good little tip is never to groom a long coated dog without using a spray to moisten the coat; this will avoid the ends of the coat breaking.

Some of the long coated breeds have their head hair tied up, both to give the dog stylish good looks and also to keep it tidy. Some of the smaller long coated breeds, such as the Yorkshire Terrier and Maltese, sometimes have their coats kept in wraps to prevent hair breakage and stimulate growth. This is really not necessary unless they take part in conformation competition, but some owners like their pets to look their very best anyway.

Another way of protecting the coat is to wear a little outfit. Some of these are designed just for fun, but others have a practical side them for they prevent the hair from dragging on the ground which would cause it not only to break, but also to get dirty. Even smooth coated breeds can sometimes benefit

Above: Keeping a Poodle's pom poms clean on a muddy day.

from a coat, not to protect the coat itself but to protect the dog from the elements. Most Whippets, for example, have a wardrobe of outdoor clothes, a warm jacket for when it's cold and a raincoat for wet weather days.

Some of the more difficult breeds to get looking in tip-top condition are the wire coated breeds, such as Terriers. Some of them need to be hand-stripped to get them looking their best, but this is something that can take years of practise, so you may be best to leave this to a professional, unless you are prepared to learn properly from someone who already has years of experience. Of course, many breeds that are hand stripped for the showring are simply clippered if they are kept purely as pets.

Brief information about specific grooming needs is included on the pages that follow, but of course

Right: Clipping toenails.

there are certain aspects of coat care that apply to all breeds. Toenails should always be regularly kept in trim. If your dog visits a parlor frequently this will hopefully be looked after as a matter of course, but if not you will have to cut the nails yourself. This is not usually difficult to do, proving your dog has been trained from puppyhood. Always be careful only to trim off a small amount of nail at a time, to avoid making it bleed. This would cause your dog discomfort and he may never be patient again when it's time to trim his nails. In case of emergency, it is wise to keep a styptic pencil with your grooming equipment; this will quickly stem any bleeding in case the worst happens!

Keeping the ears clean and free from infection should also be a matter of routine, on a weekly or fortnightly basis. Dogs that have drop ears, hanging down by the side of the head, are more prone to picking up infection than those

whose ears are exposed, such as the Pharaoh Hound. Long coated breeds also usually have at least some hair growing inside the ear, which can trap dirt and germs inside the canal. The hair should be very carefully removed, either using special canine ear tweezers, or gently by hand, using the thumb and forefinger. Be sure never to delve too deeply into the ear as this can cause damage. This will usually need to be done about once a month, but more or less frequently depending on the density of hair growth.

Another important aspect of canine care concerns the teeth. Apart from a feeding a healthy diet, which will assist in keeping teeth in good order, the teeth should also be cleaned on a fairly regular basis. There are now plenty of canine toothpastes available, with special toothbrushes too. Although your dog is sure to take a little time to get used to this procedure, with a little patience you will win him over.

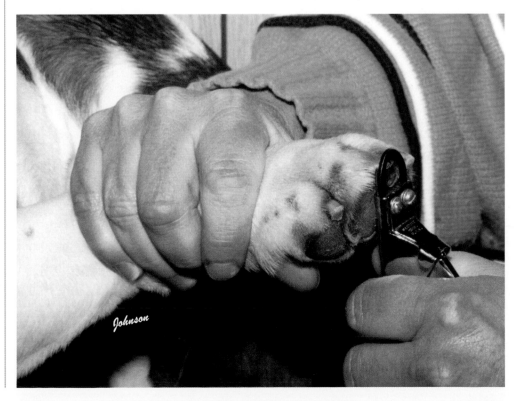

Johnson

could cause your dog to limp.

When a dog has been exercising in the snow, ice balls are likely to build up between the pads of the feet. These can easily be removed by bathing with luke warm water upon returning home. Again, it is important to dry off the feet thoroughly after bathing.

Diet

Today there are an infinite number of diets available for dogs and the type of diet that is fed depends a lot upon the type of dog and its lifestyle, not to mention the owner's convenience and ultimate selection.

Dogs naturally enjoy meat, for this is what they would have eaten in the wild, but in fact they are omnivores so are both willing and able to eat various types of food, including vegetables and fruit. Although a dog can survive perfectly well without any variety in his diet, this must be very boring, so some variation is always appreciated.

Whether choosing to feed one of the many complete diets or feeding fresh foods, the diet must be well-balanced, containing both protein and carbohydrates. A dog does not require such a high protein content as a cat, and a dog that lives an active life needs a higher protein content that one that live a more sedentary life. A certain amount of fatty acids, vitamins and minerals are also needed for healthy skin and coat, as well as for a variety of bodily functions. Fruit and vegetables are always beneficial to a

Some dogs even enjoy a tooth-cleaning session, especially if they like the taste of the paste!

Eye care is also important; again this has a twofold purpose, both for the health of the eye and for cosmetic reasons. Eyes should always be carefully cleared of any stickiness which may have built up in the inner corners. There are several different ways of doing this but the safest is to use a clean piece of moistened tissue or a soft cotton bud. The type of coat will determine how frequently this needs to be done. White dogs such as Maltese and Bichon Frisé can very easily get soiling below the eye, but good pet stores will sell grooming products that help this.

Lastly, keeping the nether regions of a dog clean is also an important part of coat care and maintenance. Especially if you have a long-coated breed, soiling can occur below the anal region, which can not only be uncomfortable for the dog, but can also cause infection to set in. For this reason it is absolutely essential

to check the area carefully each day and to clean up as necessary, always drying the coat thoroughly if it has been necessary to moisten the hair.

Another little area than needs to be checked frequently on male dogs is the penis. It must always be kept clean and in breeds that grow substantial coat here, the hair may need to be trimmed a little. However, it is important never to trim the coat too short or it can get trapped inside the sheath, causing irritation and infection. It is wise to leave at least half an inch of hair at the end, a little more on large dogs.

Lastly, the feet and pads should be checked regularly. This is especially important if a dog has been running on rough land or walking on tarmac, especially in warm, dry weather. Always check between the pads to be sure nothing has become trapped. If hair grows between the pads in most breeds it is usual to trim this out with small blunt-ended scissors so that knots do not form between the pads, which would make life very uncomfortable and diet, and for a convalescent dog, boneless chicken or fish, mixed with boiled brown rice are highly digestible, as well as being nutritious.

Owners of overweight dogs should watch calorie intake, giving a healthy raw carrot or two to pad out a meal, something that also helps keep teeth clean. Large dogs can usually cope with a complete carrot and will enjoy crunching it up, but smaller dogs should be fed manageable sized pieces.

All ready-prepared foods contain a comprehensive list of ingredients and these should be studied very carefully before making your selection. Prepared foods also vary considerably in price, but often (though not always) the higher priced foods need to be fed in slightly lower quantities, so this is also worthy of consideration. You will also have to select a brand that is regularly available in your local store, unless you plan to buy in bulk. Dried foods that are bought in quantity should always be stored securely so that they cannot attract vermin.

A change from one food product to another should never be made suddenly as this will cause loose motions. Any change made should be done gradually over a period of a few days, mixing one the new product in with the old, and gradually increasing the proportions. Any fresh or tinned foods that is left uneaten should always be removed and disposed of, but dried food can be left available all day. Adult dogs usually require one main meal daily, with a light snack given at the other end of the day. However, some people prefer to feed two meals of equal quantity. This routine is particularly suitable for dogs that are prone to bloat.

Dogs should never be allowed to exercise energetically within an hour either side of a meal, and as has already been mentioned, tall dogs should have their food bowls raised from the ground. These precautions will play a large part in avoiding the occurrence of bloat, which can be fatal. Cooked bones can be highly dangerous for dogs, and one should even take care with uncooked ones. Marrow bones are usually safe, but must be removed immediately if they start to splinter or break up.

Water must be available at all times, and changed frequently. Dogs that are fed a ready-prepared dried food, will drink more water than those fed on a diet of fresh foods. Stainless steel bowls are the most hygienic both for food and for water, and non-spill bowls are available from good retail stores; these are especially beneficial when travelling.

Avoiding obesity

The most common reason for obesity in dogs is over eating, exacerbated in many cases by insufficient exercise. Some breeds are more prone to gaining weight than others, the Labrador Retriever and Cocker Spaniel being two well known examples. Even a Whippet

Below: Trimming hair from between the pads.

Johnson

Left: A puppy's first set of teeth, showing a scissors bite.

can become overweight, but at least in a smooth-coated breed the owner can easily see the extra inches beginning to creep on! If a dog has a weight problem, you must be sure that he only eats what you give him. If other people in your family, or visitors to the home are likely to feed him tid-bits between meals, make sure they know that this is forbidden. Sometimes there can be a medical reason for a dog carrying excess weight, in which case this must be discussed with your veterinarian before introducing a diet. Indeed some special diet foods are available only through veterinary outlets.

If fed an especially enjoyable meal, a dog may eat more than he might otherwise have done, but if appetizing meals are fed regularly, intake will be reduced accordingly. So it is possible to feed tasty, sensible food all the while. Social factors also have a bearing on a

dog's food intake. Puppies fed in a group will, on average, eat more than if they are fed individually without any element of competition. The same rule applies in adulthood too.

In general, dogs that are choosy about their food have fewer problems with obesity, but those who eat anything that is placed before them are understandably more likely to put on excess weight. Hormonal problems can also affect a dog's weight. A bitch that has been spayed, or a dog that has been castrated, undergoes hormonal changes that are likely to alter the weight-regulating mechanism.

In cold weather, a dog's appetite will often increase. This being the case, it is prudent to increase bulk without increasing calories; vegetables are very useful for this. Remember, too that the majority of dogs enjoy fruit, so apples,

chopped in bite-sized pieces are always a welcome addition to a diet. Grapes, though, can cause cancer, so should never be fed to dogs. Human chocolate also has a carcinogenic effect, so must never be given, although special "doggy chocs" are perfectly alright to feed – but watch the weight!

General health care

Immediately after buying your dog it is wise to take him along to your veterinarian for a health check. This way no problems will go undetected from the outset. Dog owners must, however, realize that even healthy dogs can get sick. May different problems can arise, some of them more serious than others, but the following are some of the more common ailments of which you should be aware.

Abscess – An abscess is very painful and in long-coated breeds may go undetected until it has reached an advanced stage. The abscess should be gently bathed in a warm saline solution. This will bring it to a head so that it bursts and the pus content is released and drained. Even after it has burst, bathing must be continued because it must be allowed drain completely before the skin heals over. Should the abscess not burst, of if another appears, a veterinarian must be consulted and a course of antibiotic treatment will probably be prescribed.

Anal Glands – Situated on either side of the anal opening, these glands cause discomfort when full. A sign of this is the dog scraping his bottom along the ground in an endeavour to alleviate the aggravation. The gland can easily be emptied by your vet, but this is something most owners are able to do themselves provided that have be taught exactly how to do so (otherwise damage can be caused).

Constipation – Usually caused by diet, constipation can frequently be rectified by altering a dog's feeding program. Offer soaked biscuits rather than completely dry food, with lightly cooked green vegetables too. A teaspoon of olive oil, fed orally, can also help to clear out a blockage.

Dandruff – This may indicate that more fat is needed in the diet. You can try adding a little vegetable oil to the food, or supplement the diet with some canine oil capsules.

Diarrhea – Often caused by a change of diet or a slight chill, diarrhea can usually be rectified by starving a dog for 24 hours. This will allow the stomach to empty and settle. However, fresh drinking water must always be freely available. Feed a light diet for the next few days, before going back into routine feeding. If there is any sign of blood in the motions, or if the diarrhea is coupled with vomiting or other symptoms, veterinary advice must be sought without delay.

Ear Infections - Build up of wax and ear mites can give rise to canker. Signs of this are a dog scratching at the ear or shaking the head, or holding it on one side. Usually there is a foul-smelling discharge, which is usually dark brown in color. Special ear drops will usually rectify the problem, but if the ears are hot, or if the dog shows any other signs of being unwell, veterinary attention is required immediately.

Eye Problems – These are many and varied and some breeds have hereditary problems, for which testing services are usually available.

Below: Cleaning an adult dog's teeth with a toothbrush.

Above: A novel way of transporting your toy dog.

For breeds in which there are genetic disorders, such as Progressive Retinal Atrophy (PRA), both sire and dam must be tested prior to mating being carried out. Purchasers of puppies should always ask to see certification prior to purchase, and the certificate must not be more than one year old. Any dog can suffer an eye injury, but some breeds are more prone than others, usually if the eyes are rounded and prominent. At any sign of ulceration, or if there is an unusual bluish-color in the eye, veterinary advice must be sought immediately to avoid irreparable damage. Another problem that can sometimes occur is what is known as "cherry eye", which is actually an enlargement of the nictitating membrane in the inner corner of the eye. This often occurs in both eyes and is usually apparent within the first few weeks of life, but can sometimes not appear until adulthood. This is something that requires veterinary treatment, but is not a problem that impairs vision. However, later in life, dry eye may occur as a result as the lacrimal glands are likely to have been affected. This problem can usually be alleviated with the use of "artificial tears", or ointment obtainable from a veterinarian.

Heart Problems – Although it is fairly rare to find a dog having a sudden heart attack as we know it in humans, dogs can suffer from heart disease, especially when there is either a gradual or sudden obstruction to the flow of blood to the brain. This causes a dog to become limp and collapse, often becoming unconscious. Frequently the dog recovers in a matter of seconds, when he should immediately be given fresh air. In coronary cases caused by poor blood supply to the heart muscle, the type of collapse is different; the limbs usually remain stiff and the dog does no lose consciousness. In either case veterinary help must be sought without delay.

Hay Fever – Dogs can have allergies to pollens, just as some humans do. This is displayed by excessive watering of the eyes and sneezing, due to inflammation of the mucous membranes within the nose. Finding the best form of relief can be difficult but, using trial and error, a veterinarian or homeopath can often find a way of easing the problem.

Heat Stroke – All dogs must always have access to shade and must never be left in a car, especially in warm or hot weather, even with the windows open. Heat builds up exceptionally quickly and death soon results as body temperature rises. Symptoms of heat stroke include vomiting, diarrhea and collapse. To reduce body temperature as quickly as possible, submerge the affected dog up to the neck in cool water, even in a stream if one is handy. If water is restricted, pour over the dog whatever is available. In any event immediate veterinary help must be sought.

Inguinal Hernia – Although not common, inguinal hernias can be found in both dogs and bitches and can be either in one groin, or in both. Sometimes they are not apparent until a dog is well into adulthood. Veterinary advice should always be sought immediately such a hernia is noticed; your veterinarian will decide whether or not surgical intervention is necessary.

Intolerance to Dairy Products – A few breeds seem to have a particular intolerance to a surfeit of dairy products. This can cause a rash on the belly or under the legs, appearing either in patches or as spots. If diary products are fed, it is best to reduce or eliminate them, to determine whether or not this is actually the cause of the rash. Although several breeds can be affected in this way, this intolerance seems particularly prevalent in Tibetan and Oriental breeds.

Kennel Cough – Vaccinations are available to prevent kennel cough, which is highly contagious. In the early stages a dog attempts to clear the throat, appearing to have something stuck. This soon develops into a hoarse cough. An affected dog must be isolated, as kennel cough is airborne and can easily be passed on to other dogs in the vicinity. Veterinary attention must be sought at the very first sign. Usually the problem it rapidly rectified with medication, but the dog must not be allowed in public places until the specified period of time has elapsed; the veterinarian will offer advice about this. Most dogs recover easily, but kennel cough can be dangerous in the very young, old and infirm.

Kidney Failure – Frequent urination may indicate a kidney problem, especially if this is coupled with accelerated breathing and premature ageing. Veterinary advice is essential.

Liver Diseases – All liver problems are serious and require immediate veterinary attention at the very first sign. A noticeable symptom is jaundiced yellowing of the white of the eye, and of the membranes lining the eye and mouth. A yellowing on the underside of the ear flap might also be noticed, but this is less easy to detect under artificial light than in daylight. Other symptoms include vomiting, loss of appetite, constipation and infrequent passing of highly colored urine.

Pyometra – This is a serious problem caused by a bitch's uterus filling with pus, often initially noticed by high temperature and increased thirst. There are two forms of pyometra, one with vaginal discharge and one without, the latter being even more dangerous. However, both are life threatening and death can occur in a matter of hours. Veterinary help must be sought immediately and often the only solution is for the

Below: Something interesting here.

Johnson

Right: Socialisation is important, This puppy Lhasa Apso and Deerhound enjoy a great game together.

bitch to be spayed.

Spinal Disorders – Especially in the short-legged, long-backed breeds, owners should be on the alert for back problems. Care should be taken, especially with youngsters and older dogs; they should not be allowed to jump on and off furniture, and in an ideal world they should not climb or descend stairs. At any sign of spinal injury a vet must be consulted at once. Sometimes a dog can recover completely, but in other cases at least partial paralysis is a result. Occasionally dogs thus affected can get around reasonably well using a

two-wheeled cart to support the back end, but of course they lose much of their independence in doing so. Supervised swimming in a hydrotherapy pool can be a useful means of exercise following injury and some people use an experienced animal chiropractor to good effect.

Travel Sickness – Many dogs never from motion sickness at all, but others do so as puppies. Most grow out of this as they mature, but this is always an inconvenience and can put a puppy off car rides. Take your veterinarian's advice as to which travel sickness tablets to use and the appropriate dose. Always read the instructions carefully and be sure to give the tablets well in advance of a journey, to give them time to take effect.

Umbilical Hernias – Breeding lines within some breeds of dog seem prone to umbilical hernias; these appear as a lump on the umbilicus and, if present, will be evident when a puppy is purchased. Hernias can vary in size and are usually soft, but should be checked by a veterinarian so see if surgery is appropriate. If an umbilical hernia becomes hard it can strangulate, requiring urgent surgery. Umbilical hernias can occasionally be caused by trauma at birth, probably by the bitch tugging at the umbilical cord; these usually disappear within a few weeks.

Undescended Testicles – Male dogs should have both testicles descended into the scrotum. They are usually clearly evident before the age of 4 or 5 months, but can occasionally come later. If neither, or only one appears, veterinary consultation is important, because if present, there is risk of a tumor forming.

Breed specific problems

Each of the breeds described in this directory has a few words about health problems in the breed. Readers should, however, note that although details given vary in quantity and complexity, this is often because more research has been done in some breeds than in others. A breed with a number of illness listed very probably indicates that careful monitoring of health issues has been carried out by breed clubs and that, for the good of the breed, all illnesses discovered have been reported upon. This is often the case for some of the more popular breeds, for which there are more clubs and, correspondingly, more owners willing to report any problems they encounter. Conversely, less well known breeds may have had little health research carried out, so there is less documentary evidence of problems that can arise.

Parasites

Dogs can be affected by internal or external parasites so regular worming and flea control programs are important.

Internal - There are various different internal parasites, some more prevalent in certain countries and areas than in others. It is vitally important that a thorough worming program is commenced while puppies are still with the breeder and that this is continued afterwards. Worming is carried out every few weeks during the early stages of a dog's life (keeping to a strict regime according to the product used), then in adulthood worming should be carried out every six months. Always purchase worming agents from your veterinarian, rather than though a retail outlet, for the latter are usually less effective.

Worms that can affect dogs are roundworms, prevalent in dogs universally, tapeworms (universal), hookworms (America), whipworms (common in North America), threadworms (South-western US and Gulf Coast) and heartworms. All internal parasites are debilitating. Sometimes they are present without any signs at all, and can easily be passed from dam to puppies prior to whelping, all the more reason to take especial care.

Because the flea is an immediate host to the tapeworm, it is absolutely essential that the worming routine is up-to-date if your dog has fleas.

External – A sign of external parasites is scratching, so immediately this is noticed your dog should be thoroughly checked over. Of course there are other reasons for scratching too, such as allergies, but you must determine the cause. A dog can even have an allergic reaction to fleas.

Fleas are small reddish-brown insects that thrive on blood and are not easy to see as they move quickly through the coat and can jump great distances. The presence of flea dirt looks like small black grains of

Left: Firmly guiding a dog into the sit position.

Above: Paper training a puppy.

sand; this is a sure sign your dog has fleas! A wide variety of insecticidal agents is available, but they should not be mixed, so seek your vet's advice as to what should be used, particularly in view of the fact that you will probably also have to treat your dog's bedding and other areas of your home.

Lice are also biting insects but they move more slowly and do not jump, so are easier to detect and eradicate. They tend to accumulate on ears and neck.

Harvest mites can be cleared by using an appropriate shampoo, bought for your vet's surgery. They look like tiny grains of orange sand and form clusters between the toes and sometimes also collect above the eyes.

Ticks are blood-sucking insects that attach themselves to the skin and are usually found in sheep and deer country. When they first attach they are difficult to see, but enlarge in size as they become engorged with blood. They need to be removed with great care because if the head is left in the dog, this can very easily become infected. There are various ways of removing ticks, perhaps the safest is to smother the tick in oil to prevent it breathing.

Emergency first aid

Any accident is distressing for a dog and always needs to be dealt with as a matter of urgency. However, it is important to realise that even the most docile of dogs can be dangerous to handle when injured, especially if the dog has been trapped during the accident.

Obviously major accidents need to be dealt with by a vet as quickly as possible, and if you are able to take your injured dog to a veterinarian,

Below: A male can ruin your plants but a bitch will mark your lawn.

Left: Encouraging a puppy to come with a tid bit.

telephone en route to warn him that you are coming. At the same time, give him as much information as possible about what has happened, so that he can be as well prepared for your arrival as possible. It will help him to know anything relating to heartbeat, breathing, gasping, major haemorrhage, pale gums, inability to stand and any possible fractures.

It is important that you do not panic. Approach the dog cautiously but reassuringly, restraining him if possible with a lead. If necessary a muzzle can be improvised, perhaps from a scarf. Tie this around the muzzle and then around the back of the head. But if there is any sign of chest injury or difficulty in breathing, under no circumstances apply a muzzle. A muzzled dog must never be left alone. If moving an injured dog, this must be done

Right: Teaching Sit and Stay without a lead

carefully, being on the alert for any sign of him going blue or having difficulty breathing. He should be transferred to a blanket if available, which can be used as a stretcher. If two other people can assist you, it will be possible to support his head, back and pelvis, although obviously moving a small dog is rather easier.

Thankfully not all injuries are serious and some minor problems can be dealt with at home.

Bites – Initially clean the wound by bathing in warm water. If the skin's surface is broken a vet should check this in case antibiotic treatment or sutures are needed.

Bleeding – Small cuts usually stop bleeding after a few minutes, but if this continues, or if blood pumps out from an artery, immediate professional help is required. An emergency compress can be made from clean material soaked in water, applied with enough pressure to arrest the bleeding.

Burns – Initially apply plenty of cold water to the burned area. Minor burns can be treated with a proprietary burns ointment, but serious burns need veterinary attention as they are always accompanied by shock.

Collapse - Urgent veterinary attention is imperative. Meanwhile, create an airway by clearing mucus from the throat and pulling the tongue forward. If necessary,

Above: Listening and learning

stimulate the dog's respiratory system with firm compressions to the chest wall, every 10 seconds.

Foreign bodies lodged in the mouth – A dog that appears to have difficulty closing his mouth, or constantly paws at the face, probably has something wedged between his teeth, or even across the roof of the mouth between the molars. It may be possible to dislodge this with relative ease, but if not a vet must be contacted at once.

Fur balls – Particularly in long- or heavily-coated breeds, furballs are occasionally vomited without any

sign of illness or discomfort, but they should never be regarded lightly as they can cause choking. The hair will have been ingested by the dog having licked the coat over a period of time.

Grass seeds – These can penetrate any part of a dog, the long barbs causing them to move further and further into the coat. They can cause irritation, infection or an abscess, so often need removal by a veterinarian. Grass seeds can also be trapped in the nostril, usually indicated by fits of sneezing.

Lameness – There are many different reasons why lameness can occur, but the most likely cause is damage or discomfort to the pad of the foot. A cut will be easily noticed and will require veterinary attention. Sometimes, however, the cause is not evident. There could have been a bite, which may show some swelling, or the dog may have trodden on something sharp, such as a thorn, which has embedded itself. In long-coated breeds, a knot many have been formed by long hair growing between the pads; this can be removed with relative ease using blunt ended scissors. Any lameness that is not corrected quickly needs veterinary investigation.

Poisoning – This takes several different forms, so needs correspondingly varied treatment. Initial signs may include vomiting,

Above and below: Agility trials

Above: Flyball.

muscular spasm and bleeding from an exit point, such as the gums. If possible, you must tell your vet the likely source of poison so that an appropriate antidote can be administered. When initially telephoning your veterinarian, ask if vomiting should be induced or not, for sometimes this is not appropriate. Keep your dog warm and quiet, with access to plenty of fresh air.

Stings – Stings inside the mouth can be very dangerous, so dogs that tend to snap at flying insects should be discouraged from doing so. An anti-histamine injection will be required immediately. Keep your dog cool and pull the tongue forward, leaving the airway clear. Stings on the pad or elsewhere are less serious and antiseptic lotions can bring some relief. Bee stings

Below: Obedience teams competing from all over the world at a major event.

should be removed with tweezers and bicarbonate of soda applied.

Training techniques

To get the best out of your relationship with your dog, at least some training is important. You may not wish to take training to extremes, but basic training is essential if you are to have a well behaved dog who is a pleasure to live with. Leash training is absolutely essential, for when you are both away from home, it may neither be suitable nor safe to have you dog running free.

Basic obedience

Before you allow your dog off the leash in a public place, you must be certain that he will come back to you upon command. Not everyone likes dogs, so you dog must be taught not to jump up at passing strangers.

Your dog will soon pick up simple commands; 'No' is absolutely essential, and 'Come', 'Sit', 'Down', 'Wait' and 'Stay' are all highly useful too. Training classes are especially good as an introduction to basic obedience, and those who wish to take things a stage further may like to compete for certificates, which can be challenging, but lots

of fun too.

Training often involves the use of tid-bits and clicker-training is now also widely used. Your dog should never be treated harshly, but must learn to earn your respect for all the right reasons. Some breeds absorb training more easily than others, but all can learn a little if given time and attention.

It is important also to socialize dogs from a young age if they are to grow up to be well-adjusted adults. They need contact with other dogs and of course with humans too. When being introduced to children they should always be under close supervision.

Toilet training for puppies

A puppy arriving at its new home may or may not already have become house trained to a greater

Above: Agility – through the tunnel

or lesser extent, but in his new home everything will be different, so lessons will have to begin all over again.

Without fail, when a puppy awakes from a long sleep or has had a meal, he should be taken outside and encouraged to relieve himself. Initially it is best to carry him out quickly, for he will not know where to find the door and will very probably get caught out on the way there! Stay with your puppy, or keep a careful eye on him from a window, but do not play games with him or he will forget his reason for going outside.

Paper training is also a useful method, especially for tiny puppies, who will generally prefer to urinate on paper than on the floor. Puppies

actually like to keep their sleeping area clean, but will very probably have gotten used to doing their "pees" and "poohs" on the paper that lined the floor of their play area. Now that he is living in his new home, you can place several sheets of paper on the floor, progressively moving them closer and closer to the door, until the paper is actually outside. During training, some owners like to leave a little soiling on the paper, so the puppy associates this with where he is meant to urinate next time around.

Giving reward

When a dog has done something good, it is essential that he is rewarded. This need not necessarily be a reward in kind, but may simply be plenty of praise. This will give your dog great pleasure and will encourage him to do the same "good deed" on a future occasion.

Tid-bits may be given in training, but these must be small and suitable, not in any way causing a dog to become obese. On the other hand, a dog that does a lot of physical work during training will easily burn off the odd extra calorie.

When punishment is needed

A dog who misbehaves will need to be punished, so that he knows he has done wrong. However, it is important that punishment is only meted out when he has actually been caught in the act. If punished subsequent to a misdeed, he will simply not associate the two and will wonder why he is being reprimanded. This applies both to puppies and to adults.

Verbal reprimand is usually quite sufficient, and at no time should a dog be treated violently. The simple words, 'Bad dog', or 'No', will usually suffice. Afterwards do not pet him for a while, or again you will cause confusion in his mind. .Most dogs also respond to a direct look in the eyes, combined with verbal reprimand. Of course an owner must take great care not to get bitten in the process, but especially for a small breed, if held securely at the back of the neck (never taking his weight off the ground or other surface), this often does the trick.

Leash training

While some young dogs take to leash training like ducks to water, for others it can be a very trying time. To begin with, a puppy should just be allowed to get the feel of a collar around his neck, before

Johnson

Left: Standard poodle moving in show ring.

attaching a leash. Initially the collar should just remain around the neck for a moment or two (always under supervision), the time factor then gradually being increased. Eventually the puppy will stop trying to scratch it off!

When the lesh is attached the puppy should be taken somewhere safe, ideally in your yard or garden; if possible this should not be an area than he associates with play. Different owners have different methods of leash training, and a lot depends on the size of dog and his personality. With small breeds, I always like the puppy to "take" me along to begin with; I hold the lead very lightly so that the puppy hardly knows that anyone is attached at the other end. Then, slowly, I start

to take control, usually with some resistance form my canine companion! Larger dogs generally seem more amenable to leash training so one should be able to assert one's authority from the start.

Initially a dog should always be trained to walk on the left but later, especially if a dog is destined for the showring, he will also need to be able to walk on the right occasionally. It is absolutely essential that your dog is unable to slip his collar by accident, so careful consideration must be given to this important part of his outfit.

Teaching a dog to stay

Although there are different methods of training a dog to sit and stay, this exercise will need a long

leash for first of all you will get the dog to sit, then you will move away slowly, repeating the command

Above and below: Heelwork to music.

'Stay'. Initially, you will keep the leash in your hand, without putting any pressure on it. A hand signal can be used to reinforce the verbal command. If the dog moves, verbal reprimand is in order and the dog should be placed back in the sitting position. The exercise is then repeated.

Gradually the distance between dog and owner is increased and when the dog responds well, the owner returns to the dog, rather than the other way around. When your dog is comfortable with this exercise you will be able to call the dog to you, though initially this should be done on the same, long leash. You will tug gently on the leash, using the word, 'Come'. When your dog is proficient at the commands, 'Sit', 'Stay' and 'Come', the time will have come when you can work without a leash, though always in a safe place away from traffic.

Rewards will have been important throughout the training process and soon you will be able to build up to more advanced obedience training. 'Down' and 'Fetch' are usually the next lessons to be learned. Again the trainer will initially need to give assistance, gently pushing or placing the dog into the required lying position. When this has bee accomplished the time during which the dog can be left will be increased slowly, with the handler moving further and further away, possibly even out of sight. To do this it is important that the dog has complete trust in his trainer, and vice versa.

When teaching a dog to fetch and retrieve, it is often difficult at the outset to get your dog to drop the object as requested. Tid-bits can come in handy here, as usually the dog will willingly give up his prize in exchange for a tasty morsel!

Training can indeed be both fun and rewarding for both dog and owner, and although I have never succeeded in getting my own dogs to perform their toilet on command, some owners apparently teach them to do this too – maybe you will be one of the lucky ones!

Activities for you and your dog
There are many different kinds of dog owner, some want their dogs purely as pets, others need a dog to perform a service for them, and still others like to enter into some competitive sport with their dog. Of course, if a dog is first and foremost a pet, the other skills learned may be part and parcel of pet ownership, merely serving to enhance an owner's rapport with the dog.

Already we have touched on obedience work, which can be taken to higher and higher levels as a dog's proficiency increases. Competitive obedience can be interesting to do and gives a great sense of achievement to an owner

Below: Obedience demonstration team under the spotlight.

who has worked hard with his dog, usually over a long period. Other dogs are entered into conformation shows, but this usually means that a puppy will have been selected specifically for this purpose, for to win high honors in the showring it needs to be an extremely high-quality specimen in terms of its conformation to the breed standard. Many show dogs owners travel enormous distances with their dogs, often crossing continents to challenge competition overseas.

Any enthusiastic dog and owner, though, can take part in agility or flyball competition, or even frisbee. Owners may be able to join a local team and although there is a highly competitive element to this, everyone, including the dogs, have great fun. Sometimes at conformation shows, an area is set aside for this element of the dog fraternity and the ringside audience marvels at the skill of the dogs as they carry out their allotted tasks. The spirit of camaraderie is truly great.

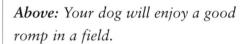

Other ways of enjoying your dog's company is to take part in "Heelwork to Music", or "Dancing With Dogs". This is particularly suitable if your dog is already obedience trained and if you have a flair for dance yourself. Together you and your dog will make a wonderful partnership. This is always particularly enjoyable for spectators to watch too and is admired by many, even though they may have no particular desire to

Above: Your dog will enjoy a good romp in a field.

participate themselves.

In recent years many a dog has become the close companion of someone who is physically challenged. Dogs have long been used as guides for the blind, but in recent decades more and more have been used as hearing dogs for deaf people and in various types of therapy work. Some are taken along to hospitals and homes for the elderly, where they provide tremendous interest and companionship to people who are no longer able to live at home, where they would probably choose to have a dog of their own.

Of course some dogs are working animals and they perform all sorts of useful tasks, far too many to mention here, but several types of work they do be are mentioned in relation to specific breeds in the pages that follow.

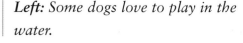

Left: Some dogs love to play in the water.

A
B
C
D
E
F
G
H
I
J
K
L
M
N
O
P
Q
R
S
T
U
V
W
X
Y
Z

Affenpinscher

Average height: 9.5-11.5 inches
Average weight: 7-8 pounds

Johnson

BREED NOTES

SIZE	GROOMING
✓	✓✓

EXERCISE	LIFESPAN
✓	✓✓

Appearance

The Affenpinscher's rough, harsh coat is short and dense in some parts and shaggy in others. In the USA black, gray, silver, red, black and tan, or belge (a mixture of red, black and white hairs) are all acceptable colors, but in many countries only black is allowed. The hair on the head stands away from the skull and frames the dark, sparkling eyes, nose and chin, giving a perfectly quaint and monkey-like appearance. This breed is an absolute charmer!

Characteristics

Absolutely oozing with character and mischief, the Affenpinscher is often called "The Black Devil".

Left: The Affenpinscher is a thoroughly appealing breed, simply oozing with character.

Johnson

Full of self-confidence and with a lively temperament, there is said to be a certain comic seriousness about him. He is a loyal companion, but watchful of strangers and despite his small size shows no fear when confronted with an adversary.

Origins and History

Originating in central Europe during the 17th century, the Affenpinscher is one of the oldest of the Toy breeds. This was one of a

Above: This little 'Black Devil' looks ready to take on the world!

number of small terriers kept as ratters in stores and on farms. Bred down in size, they became companions inside the home where

A
B
C
D
E
F
G
H
I
J
K
L
M
N
O
P
Q
R
S
T
U
V
W
X
Y
Z

they earned their keep by controlling the mouse population. Eventually the area around Munich in Germany became the centre for Affenpinscher breeding and this breed has become a major influence in the development of other small, rough-coated dogs. The

Below: This Affenpinscher is clearly proud to be in the show ring.

Affenpinscher was accepted by the American Kennel Club (AKC) in 1936.

Health Issues

Although a Toy breed, the Affenpinscher is not delicate in any way, however, tests are recommended for hip dysplasia and luxating patella (slipping stifles). Eyes should also be checked.

Exercise and Grooming

An active breed, the Affenpinscher will create his own exercise around your yard, but walks on a leash are also important. Because he shows no fear of dogs larger than himself, take care when exercising him in public places. The Affenpinscher's is not a difficult coat to manage and a correct coat needs little attention

Johnson

and no trimming. The face is sometimes scissored to create a round shape, and pet owners often like to cut the beard shorter to help keep the mouth area clean. A slicker brush can be used to remove dead hairs, added to which you will need a fine- or medium-toothed comb and a small bristle brush. The Affenpinscher is meant to look shaggy, so don't attempt to make him look too neat and tidy!

Above: The breed has a monkey-like appearance.

Right: 'How dare you even think I did that!'

A
B
C
D
E
F
G
H
I
J
K
L
M
N
O
P
Q
R
S
T
U
V
W
X
Y
Z

Afghan Hound

Average height: dogs – 26-28 inches; bitches – 24-26 inches
Average weight: dogs – 60 pounds; bitches – 50 pounds

Appearance

The sight of a well-groomed Afghan Hound is quite spectacular, for this is surely one of the most glamorous of the larger breeds. With the long coat and profuse trouserings, silky topknot, slightly Roman nose, punishing jaw and that wonderful Eastern expression that looks both at and through you, you cannot fail to be impressed. The tail should have a typical ring or curve at the end, and along the back the hair is short and close, known as a "saddle". All colors are acceptable but white markings, especially on the head, are undesirable.

BREED NOTES

SIZE	GROOMING
✓	✓
✓	✓
✓	✓
EXERCISE	**LIFESPAN**
✓	✓
✓	✓
✓	

Characteristics

The Afghan typically combines speed with power. Renowned for a proud carriage of head, the eyes gaze into the distance as if in memory of ages past. A true "king of dogs", the Afghan is considered more noble than the common dog and is highly prized by tribesmen. Temperament is dignified and aloof.

Origins and History

Bred to hunt by sight, essentially two different "types" of Afghan evolved in Afghanistan, that which lived on the plains being more rangy and more sparse in coat than the hound from the hills. The breed

Left: The Afghan Hound is always on the alert

World War, but Major and Mrs Bell-Murray and Miss Jean Manson took some to Scotland in 1920. These they had acquired in Baluchistan, which is today part of Pakistan. The breed first appeared in the USA in 1926 but it was not until 1940 that the Afghan Hound Club of America was admitted to AKC membership.

Health Issues

The Afghan Hound is reputed to be a fairly healthy breed, but some genetic disorders have been known to occur, such as cataracts,

Left: This breed comes in a fine array of stunning colors.

Below: Providing the coat is kept in good condition and is well groomed, the Afghan always looks elegant.

Johnson

A
B
C
D
E
F
G
H
I
J
K
L
M
N
O
P
Q
R
S
T
U
V
W
X
Y
Z

to occur, such as cataracts, demodicosis, hip dysplasia and hypothyroidism. Like all of the sight hound breeds, Afghans can be sensitive to certain antibiotics, so it is essential to discuss this with your vet prior to an operation. Bloat (gastric torsion) is something else to be aware of in any deep-chested

Opposite: The Afghan has a special way of looking "at and through you".

Left: This highly successful show dog displays all the qualities of his breed.

Below: This Best in Show winner shows the ringed tail, which is so characteristic of the breed

Johnson

A
B
C
D
E
F
G
H
I
J
K
L
M
N
O
P
Q
R
S
T
U
V
W
X
Y
Z

Johnson

Exercise and Grooming

A reasonable amount of free and controlled exercise is a necessity. Because of the splendid long coat, grooming is an essential part of Afghan care. Even pet Afghans need regular baths, and those that are shown are always bathed immediately prior to a show so that they look their very best. A professional canine hairdryer is an important part of any Afghan owner's grooming equipment, as is a good solid grooming table and high quality combs and brushes, the latter often made of pure bristle.

Opposite: The Afghan puppy looks very different from the mature adult

Above: This Champion's coat is in full bloom.

Below: One of the author's early Afghans, "Ami", always enjoyed taking his ease.

A
B
C
D
E
F
G
H
I
J
K
L
M
N
O
P
Q
R
S
T
U
V
W
X
Y
Z

Airedale Terrier

Average height: dogs – 23 inches; bitches – slightly less
Average weight: 44-50 pounds

Appearance

A large Terrier breed that is sturdy, well-muscled and well-boned, the Airedale is often called "the King of Terriers". Always on the lookout for something exciting to happen, the breed has small dark eyes and a keen expression. The wiry coat is hard and dense, but not so long as to appear ragged. Some of the hardest coats are crinkling or just slightly waved and under this outercoat is a softer undercoat. The colour is always tan, with dark markings of black or dark grizzle.

Characteristics

The Airedale's sweet disposition is probably inherited from the hound blood in its ancestry, but there is also a certain dignified aloofness. This is a wonderful family dog, always ready to join in with the children's games and is suitable for either town or country. Airedales will usually stand their ground if challenged.

Origins and History

Named after the River Aire in Yorkshire, UK, the breed was

BREED NOTES

SIZE	GROOMING
✓ ✓ ✓	✓ ✓
EXERCISE	**LIFESPAN**
✓ ✓	✓ ✓

A
B
C
D
E
F
G
H
I
J
K
L
M
N
O
P
Q
R
S
T
U
V
W
X
Y
Z

Opposite: Airedale Terrier pups are always ready for a good game.

Right: Thinking what to do next!

developed in the mid-nineteenth century by local otter hunters who needed a dual-purpose dog that could not only work otters and vermin but was also sufficiently large to protect the home. A descendent of the Black and Tan Terrier, which is now extinct, the blood of the Otterhound and Irish Terrier also run through his veins, and maybe that of the Welsh Terrier too. Considered the patriarch of the breed is Ch Master Briar (1897-1906), one of whose sons, Ch.

Caption: 'I'm listening very careful to what my owner says.'

A
B
C
D
E
F
G
H
I
J
K
L
M
N
O
P
Q
R
S
T
U
V
W
X
Y
Z

Above left:: It is easy to see why the Airedale is often called "the King of Terriers".

Above right: There always seems something better on the other side of the fence!

Opposite: 'Don't you wish she'd let us off our leashes?'

Clonmel Monarch, was exported to the USA where he formed the cornerstone of the breed here. Airedale Terriers have been used on large game in Africa, India, Canada, and America, and in Europe they have been used for police and wartime duties, employed both as guards and messengers.

Health Issues
Although this is a relatively healthy breed, the following genetic disorders have been known to occur: hip dysplasia, hypothyroidism, von Willebrand's disease and Progressive Retinal Atrophy (PRA).

Exercise and Grooming
Do not be deceived by the Airedale's relatively short coat. Like most Terriers, the coat needs careful attention and to present this breed in show condition, professional grooming expertise is essential. Stripping is important, especially at coat-shedding time. Give your dog a daily brush and comb to keep him looking smart. A reasonable amount of exercise should be given daily,

Right: This breed has small dark eyes and a keen expression

A
B
C
D
E
F
G
H
I
J
K
L
M
N
O
P
Q
R
S
T
U
V
W
X
Y
Z

Akita

Average height: dogs – 26-28 inches; bitches – 24-26 inches
Average weight: dogs – 100-130 pounds; bitches – 70-100 pounds

Appearance

Large, powerful and alert, the Akita is a substantial breed with heavy bone structure and a massive head with square, powerful jaws. The large, full tail is set high and carried over the back or against the flank. This is a double-coated breed, with a thick, soft undercoat that is shorter than the outercoat. Any color is acceptable, including white, brindle or pinto. It is important that the colors are brilliant and clear, and that markings are well balanced.

Characteristics

The Akita, whose name derives from the province of Akita in Japan, is dignified, courageous and aloof, with a tendency to show dominance over other dogs. Sensible training and careful handling is therefore essential. In the breed's homeland the Akita is affectionately

Opposite: Color patterns vary greatly; this Akita has no facial mask.

Below: A friendly greeting between Akitas.

BREED NOTES

SIZE	GROOMING
✓	✓
✓	✓
✓	

EXERCISE	LIFESPAN
✓	✓
✓	✓
✓	

A
B
C
D
E
F
G
H
I
J
K
L
M
N
O
P
Q
R
S
T
U
V
W
X
Y
Z

Below: The Akita is a substantially made dog

considered a loyal companion and pet. He offers protection to the home and is a symbol of good health. When a Japanese child is born the family will usually receive a small statue of an Akita, signifying health, happiness and a long life.

Origins and History

With origins that can be traced back to other spitz-type dogs from the polar regions, the Akita was developed in Japan around 300 years ago. Initially used as a fighting dog, later the breed was employed to hunt bear, wild boar and deer, especially in the mountainous region of northern Japan. It is one of seven Japanese dogs designated as a National Monument. Helen Keller brought the first Akita to the USA in 1937 and the Akita Club of America was founded in 1956. Not until 1973 was the breed admitted to the AKC Stud Book, receiving regular show classification the following year.

Health Issues

The Akita is generally a healthy dog but hip dysplasia is known within the breed, so screening both sire and dam before breeding is necessary. Nervous and auto-immune diseases are also known, as are dwarfism and entropion (ingrowing eyelashes).

Above: An Akita pup of just a few days old will still fit almost fit into the palms of your hand.

Below: Young puppies always like to snuggle up together for comfort.

A
B
C
D
E
F
G
H
I
J
K
L
M
N
O
P
Q
R
S
T
U
V
W
X
Y
Z

Johnson

Exercise and Grooming

An Akita's coat should be kept well groomed in order to present it to its best. A serious grooming session once a week will usually suffice, except during a heavy moult. Most owners use a metal, double-toothed comb. This breed needs a lot of exercise to keep it well muscled, though an Akita will not usually complain if he has to miss the occasional walk. Because this is a hunting dog, great care should be taken when allowed to run free.

Left: A successful show dog showing all the power of this breed.

Below: A high quality Akita youngster, showing a typical outline in profile.

Johnson

Alaskan Malamute

Average height: dogs – 25 inches; bitches – 23 inches
Average weight: dogs – 85 pounds (but can weigh even 100 pounds); bitches – 75 pounds

Appearance

With its substantial head, powerful, heavy bone and broad, deep chest, the Alaskan Malamute is a dog admirably constructed to pull heavy loads and to survive in Alaskan temperatures. The outer coat is thick and coarse; the undercoat dense, from one to two inches, oily and woolly. Malamutes' coats are less dense during the summer months. Coat color ranges from light grey through intermediate shadings to black, sable and shadings of sable to red. The only solid color allowable is white.

Characteristics

This is a self-confident, strong-willed, affectionate and friendly breed. Although not a "one man" dog, he is a loyal and devoted companion and gets along well with other people too. Although usually tolerant of his family's pets, he is less tolerant of other animals with which he comes into contact, especially if they are dogs of the same sex. The Alaskan Malamute seldom barks.

Johnson

Left: The Alaskan Malmute has powerful, heavy bone, and a broad, deep chest.

BREED NOTES

SIZE	GROOMING
✓	✓
✓	✓
✓	✓

EXERCISE	LIFESPAN
✓	✓
✓	✓
✓	

A
B
C
D
E
F
G
H
I
J
K
L
M
N
O
P
Q
R
S
T
U
V
W
X
Y
Z

Johnson

Origins and History

The Alaskan Malamute is one of the oldest Arctic sled dogs and is named after the Mahlemut Innuit tribe that settled along the shores of Kotzebue Sound in the upper-western part of Alaska. The breed was originally also used for hunting seals and was set loose in packs to course polar bears. It is likely that when Alaska became settled by white men the native breed may have been mixed with others, but in the USA, from 1926 onward, there was an interest in developing a pure strain, in part due to the increasing popularity of sled dog racing. Apart from the breed's legendary freighting on polar expeditions, it also served the Military during both World Wars. The Alaskan Malamute was recognised for AKC registration in 1935. This breed is a cousin to Russia's Samoyed and to the Siberian Husky and the Eskimo dogs of Greenland and Labrador.

Health Issues

Because the Alaskan Malamute has

Above: The breed is suitably constructed to pull heavy loads.

Opposite: A stunning head on Alaskan Malamute youngster.

a wide gene pool, the breed is free of many inherited. Problems that do sometimes occur include bloat, cataracts, dwarfism, hip dysplasia and hypothyroidism.

Exercise and Grooming

The Alaskan Malamute needs roughly an hour each day of hard

Johnson

exercise. Some owners join sledding clubs to provide this. The breed does have a tendency to run off, so should always be well controlled and supervised. The coat should be given some attention on a daily basis, even if just a five minute brushing. They tend not to have any doggy odour so don't need to be bathed frequently.

Opposite: A "baby gate" is useful for keeping dogs out of the dining room when you are eating.

Right: The Alaskan Malamute's dense coat offers protection against the elements.

Below: A perfect example of sound, typical movement

Alpine Dachsbracke

Average height: 13-16.5 inches
Average weight: 33-40 pounds

BREED NOTES

SIZE	GROOMING
✓ ✓	✓ ✓

EXERCISE	LIFESPAN
✓ ✓ ✓	✓ ✓

Above: The Alpine Dachsbracke is also known as the Alpine Basset.

Appearance

A tough, hardy, solidly built scenthound the Alpine Dachsbracke is strong-boned and has firm muscles. His nose pigment and that around his eyes is black and his jaws meet in either a scissors or level bite. His ears are set on high, without folds; they hang broad and smooth and are of medium length, well rounded at the tips. Although he has short legs, they are not bowed. His body is long. Dark stag red is the ideal color, with or without black hairs lightly interspersed. However, he may also be black with clearly defined red-brown markings on his head. His short double coat consists of a very dense top coat and a dense undercoat.

Characteristics

An intelligent and fearless dog, the Alpine Dachsbracke is a friendly character. Although he is primarily a hunter, and therefore kept mainly by huntsmen, he is a good companion and is usually good with children and other family pets. He does, however, exhibit a strong prey drive so is unlikely to take kindly to other small animals.

Origins and History

The Alpine Dachsbracke, also known as the Alpine Basset, is a scenthound that was developed in the woodlands of the Austrian Alps, specifically to trail wounded game. Hunters did not wish their quarry to escape, thereby dying a long, painful death, so these short-legged hounds followed their blood trail to seek them out as quickly as possible. The breed came about by crossing Austrian Hounds with Dachshunds and has for generations been Austria's foremost coldtrailing deerhunter. The Alpine Dachsbracke is also useful for rabbit and fox, and sometimes boar. The breed was a favourite of Crown Prince Rudolf when he went on hunting trips, and even accompanied him to Turkey in 1881 and to Egypt in 1885. In 1932 the breed was recognised in Austria as the country's third scenthound breed. This breed has only rarely been seen outside its homeland.

Exercise and Grooming

This breed has a moderate to high energy level, so is best suited to a living situation in which there is plenty of activity. His coat is not difficulty to maintain, but should be thoroughly brushed about once a week.

American English Coonhound

Average height: dogs – 24-26 inches; bitches 23-25 inches
Average weight: Weight is in proportion to height

Appearance

This is a powerful dog with nothing exaggerated about him. He possesses the grace and attitude of a well-conditioned athlete. The body is strong, but racy; the chest deep with plenty of lung room and the back strong. Musculature is well-defined. The head is broad, the expression kind and houndy and the ears hang rather low. The hard, protective coat is red and white ticked, blue and white ticked, tri-colored with ticking, red and white, and white and black.

Characteristics

Because the American English Coonhound has been selectively breed, it has become the epitome of a swift, hot-trailing, competitive hound, used to track and hunt raccoons, opossums, cougars, deer, boar, bobcats and some species of bear. Used as a pack hunter or a single-hound hunter, the breed is super-charged with tremendous speed and excellent voice but has a pleasant, confident temperament and is sociable with humans and with dogs.

Origins and History

The American English Coonhound evolved as a descendent of the English Foxhound, which was known in the New World as the Virginia Hound. Bred to adapt to rougher terrain, they were originally were used to hunt fox by day and coon by night and were actually named the English Fox and Coonhound. To complicate matters, the breeds we now know as the Treeing Walker and the Bluetick were also called English Coonhounds at one time, but in 1945 they were declared separate breeds. The American English Coonhound has been recorded in the Foundation Stock Service since 1995.

Health Issues

The American English Coonhound is considered a healthy breed, but hip dysplasia is not unknown.

Exercise and Grooming

This breed is a natural hunter and this should always be borne in mind when taking the regular exercise that is needed. Apart from walks and free running, swimming is often enjoyed too. Baths should not be given too frequently, but brushing is needed to keep the coat clean.

Below: The American English Coonhound is a well-conditioned athlete.

BREED NOTES

SIZE	GROOMING
✓✓✓	✓

EXERCISE	LIFESPAN
✓✓✓	✓✓

American Eskimo Dog

Average height: Three separate size divisions:
toy, 9-12 inches; miniature over 12 inches up to 15 inches; standard, over 15 inches up to 19 inches
there is no preference for size within each division
Average weight: No weight is specified

Appearance

Presenting a picture of strength, agility, alertness and beauty, the American Eskimo Dog is a small to medium sized Nordic-type dog. The face and head are typical of such Spitz breeds; the ears erect and triangular in shape. The double coat, with dense undercoat and longer guard hair growing through, is white, which is the preferred color, or white with biscuit cream. The richly plumed tail is carried loosely on the back.

Below: A typical profile showing the abundant double coat.

Characteristics

The American Eskimo Dog is a loving companion and loyal family member, renowned for his gentleness when playing with children. This is an energetic breed, alert and highly intelligent. Protective of his home, he is an excellent watch dog and will sound a warning bark to announce the arrival of strangers.

Origins and History

The American Eskimo is a member of the Spitz group of breeds, which is one of the most ancient dog families. The "Eskie" as he is frequently known, was specifically bred to guard people and property and is closely related to the white German Spitz, white Keeshond, white Pomeranian and the Volpino Italiano, which is also white. After the Second World War it is likely that some Japanese Spitz blood was also introduced on the West Coast. In the 19th century, small, white spitz-type dogs were commonly found in communities of German immigrants to the USA and in the latter part of that century these dogs were used in trick-dog acts in traveling circuses, helping to popularize the breed. The American Eskimo Dog Club of America was formed in 1985 and in 1993 their

BREED NOTES

SIZE	GROOMING
✔ ✔	✔ ✔
EXERCISE	**LIFESPAN**
✔ ✔	✔ ✔

Opposite: This cute little puppy has already been trained to stand on the table.

Left: The American Eskimo Dog is a picture of alertness and beauty.

registry was transferred to the American Kennel Club, gaining full recognition in 1995.

Health Issues

In general this is a very healthy breed, but some genetic problems have been found, including Progressive Retinal Atrophy (PRA) for which Eskis should be tested. Take extra care of eyes and tear ducts.

Exercise and Grooming

An active breed, the American Eskimo Dog certainly needs exercise, but will create much of this for himself if given the right situation. He loves walks with his owner. The stunning coat needs to be kept scrupulously clean and trimming is never permitted, except to neaten the feet and rear pasterns. At least two good brushings are needed each week, with a firm, bristle brush.

A
B
C
D
E
F
G
H
I
J
K
L
M
N
O
P
Q
R
S
T
U
V
W
X
Y
Z

American Foxhound

Average height: dogs – 22-25 inches; bitches 21-24 inches
Average weight: 65-75 pounds

Appearance

The American Foxhound has a fairly long skull, slightly domed at the occiput and the moderately low set ears are long and fine in texture. The breed has a hound-like expression, soft and pleading. The tail is set moderately high and carried gaily with a slight curve. It has a very slight brush. Any color is acceptable for the breed's close, hard coat. Hips and thighs are strong and muscled, providing an abundance of propelling power.

Characteristics

Mild tempered and easy going, the American Foxhound can also be rather stubborn and independent. He is an ideal choice for those living on farms or in rural areas. This is an exceptionally athletic breed that is always willing to work. Because the Foxhound hunts in packs, he usually gets along well with other dogs.

Origins and History

The American Foxhound's history dates back to the early 17th century in Virginia, Maryland and Tennessee. In the middle of that century, more hounds were brought from England and France to further develop the breed. The hound that was being developed had four major functions; as a field trial hound, a hound for hunting fox with a hunter, a trail or drag hound and as a pack hound. Eventually it was the Walker, Trigg and Goodman

Foxhounds that made up the major portion of the breed today. In 1770 George Washington imported a number of hounds from England and a number of French Foxhounds from the Marquis de Lafayette followed in 1785. Carefully bred, they essentially became the founders of the modern American Foxhound.

Health Issues

This is generally a very healthy breed but cases of thrombocytopathy have been reported. Blood testing is recommended for this.

Exercise and Grooming

Plenty of exercise is necessary for this breed with access to plenty of space, as the American Foxhound likes to run and to follow scents. Daily walks, and ideally jogging trips, will prevent him from becoming restless. The short, smooth coat is easy to maintain, with occasional brushing and shampooing, primarily to remove dead hair during the moulting season.

Below: This American Foxhound, living in Canada, loves being out on the hunt but also enjoys the comforts of the home.

BREED NOTES

SIZE	GROOMING
✔ ✔ ✔	✔

EXERCISE	LIFESPAN
✔ ✔ ✔	✔ ✔

American Staffordshire Terrier

Average height: dogs – 18-19 inches; bitches – 17-18 inches
Average weight: should be in proportion to height, averaging 50-75 pounds

Appearance

The American Staffordshire Terrier gives the impression of great strength for his size. Muscular, and yet both agile and graceful, he should be stocky, not racy in outline, with forelegs set rather wide apart to allow for his deep, broad chest. The medium length head has very pronounced cheek muscles and a broad skull. The

Below: This young American Staffordshire Terrier is a real charmer!

strong underjaw has biting power and the nose must be black. Ears may be cropped or uncropped, but there is a preference for the latter. The low set tail is relatively short and tapers to a fine point. Any color, solid, parti, or patched is permissible.

Characteristics

This courageous dog is keenly alive to his surroundings, an intelligent breed that is an excellent guardian. Although his ancestry goes back to fighting dogs, he has also been used for farm work and for hunting large game such as wild pigs and bears. Well-bred American Staffordshire Terriers, like other similar breeds, share a natural love for people.

Origins and History

The American Staffordshire Terrier owes its origins to England's Staffordshire Bull Terrier which in turn goes back to England's old-style Bulldog and one of England's early Terrier breeds, possibly the white English Terrier, or the Black-and-Tan Terrier; maybe even the Fox Terrier. Breeders in England were attempting to create a breed that had the courage and tenacity of the Bulldog combined with the terrier's spirit and agility. These dogs found their way to America in 1870 under various different names and in 1936 were accepted for registration in the AKC Stud Book as Staffordshire Terriers. In 1972 the breed became called the

BREED NOTES

SIZE	GROOMING
✔ ✔	✔
EXERCISE	**LIFESPAN**
✔ ✔	✔ ✔

American Staffordshire Terrier.

Health Issues

The genetic health problems associated with this breed are: Spinocerebellar (hereditary ataxia), heart disease, hip dysplasia, elbow dysplasia, hypothyroidism and Progressive Retinal Atrophy (PRA).

Exercise and Grooming

The American Staffordshire Terrier's short, close, stiff coat is easy to manage and therefore requires little grooming. This being a strong, muscular breed, exercise is important but owners should keep their dogs under close supervision when exercising in public places. This is an inquisitive, intelligent and determined breed and if allowed to become bored can easily damage home and property. Early obedience training is therefore essential.

A
B
C
D
E
F
G
H
I
J
K
L
M
N
O
P
Q
R
S
T
U
V
W
X
Y
Z

American Water Spaniel

Average height: 15-18 inches for either sex but bitches tend to be slightly smaller
Average weight: dogs – 40-50 pounds; bitches 24-40 pounds

Appearance

An active, muscular dog that is solidly built, the American Water Spaniel has a closely curled or moderately waved coat with sufficiently dense undercoat to protect him from the elements. Hair on the forehead is short and smooth, without a topknot. The head is in proportion to the overall dog and the nose must be wide enough with well-developed nostrils to enable good scenting power. The eyes are round, but should not protrude; their color harmonises with the coat which is either solid liver, brown or dark chocolate. A little white on toes and chest is permissible. Long, wide ears extend to the nose and toes are closely grouped, webbed and well-padded. The lively tail has moderate feathering.

Characteristics

With an intelligent demeanor, the American Water Spaniel is friendly

Below: This American Water Spaniel is the epitome of his breed.

BREED NOTES

SIZE	GROOMING
✓ ✓	✓ ✓

EXERCISE	LIFESPAN
✓ ✓	✓ ✓

Rosie

Above: Well developed nostrils give the breed good scenting powers.

Below: Always happy when at the water's edge.

Bottom: And thoroughly at home in the water too!

and eager to please. The breed has great energy and eagerness for the hunt, and yet is controllable in the field. This is a breed that is physically and mentally tough enough to withstand the cold water of the Great Lakes and yet sufficiently small to launch himself from a boat and to climb back in again with ease! In addition to being an excellent sporting dog, he is an efficient watchdog that fits agreeably into the family circle.

Origins and History

The origin of the American Water Spaniel is something of a mystery, but the breed was developed mainly in the Mid-West of the United States as an all-around hunting dog, bred to retrieve from skiff or canoes and to work ground with relative ease. It is likely that the Irish Water Spaniel, Curly-coated Retriever and old English Water Spaniel lie somewhere in his background.

Appreciated by sportsmen in many parts of the USA, this was initially purely a working gundog but has now found its way into the showring. The breed was recognised by the AKC in 1940.

Health Issues

Like all breeds, the American Water Spaniel can encounter some health problems, amongst which are hip dysplasia, hypothyroidism, epilepsy and eye diseases.

Exercise and Grooming

This is a working gundog and as such is very active, so requires regular exercise. The coat may be trimmed to present a well-groomed appearance and the ears may be shaved, but it is perfectly acceptable to do neither of these things. It is however important to keep the coat clean and in tidy condition. The oily coat requires brushing on a weekly basis, but baths should only be given when necessary.

Below: A puppy in training.

Anatolian Shepherd Dog

Average height: dogs – 29 inches upward; bitches 27 inches upward
Average weight: dogs 110-150 pounds; bitches 80-120 pounds

Appearance

A large Turkish guarding breed, the Anatolian Shepherd Dog displays impressive power and possesses great endurance and agility. He has good bone, a well-muscled torso and strong head. General balance is considered more important than size. The moderately long neck is slightly arched, powerful, and muscular, with a protective ruff and more skin than elsewhere on the body The strong, broad thighs are heavily muscled. Coat is short to rough (between one and four inches), with a thick undercoat. Feathering may occur on the ear fringes, legs, breeching, and tail. All color patterns and markings are equally acceptable

Characteristics

Not considered a "glamor breed", the Anatolian Shepherd Dog is fiercely loyal, independent and hardy. Utterly faithful to his job, he is highly intelligent and responsive to his master though his independent nature means he can be slow to respond to commands. Calm and observant of his surroundings, when properly trained he can be bold without showing aggression. Although loyal and affectionate to his owners, he is suspicious of strangers and of anything new entering his domain. This is a working guard dog without equal!

Below: This impressive dog has great endurance when working.

BREED NOTES

SIZE	GROOMING
✓ ✓ ✓	✓ ✓

EXERCISE	LIFESPAN
✓ ✓ ✓	✓ ✓

Origins and History

This guardian breed has its origins in Turkey where it is still used today to protect livestock from predators. The breed is thousands of years old, developed to withstand the county's harsh climate, living a nomadic lifestyle with shepherds. Of the same size and color as the livestock it guards, it can fit in among the flock undetected by predators. The Anatolian Shepherd Dog first came to the USA in the 1950s and breed club was formed in the 1970s. Not until 1995 was it entered on the American Kennel Club's registry, moving to the Working Group in 1998. It is important to note that Anatolian Shepherds are also known as Goban Köpegi or Anatolian Karabash.

Health Issues

The breed has few serious health

problems but the following issues have been seen: hip dysplasia, hypothyroidism, some forms of cancer and bloat (gastric torsion) which can occur in any deep-chested dog and is a life-threatening emergency when it occurs. Cases of entropion have also been recorded.

Exercise and Grooming

A large, powerful and active breed, the Anatolian needs plenty of space to exercise freely in an enclosed area. When in public places, owners must be extremely sensible and in absolute control. Early training is of great importance. Coat care is relatively simple, but should be kept clean at all times and groomed out more thoroughly at moulting time.

Above: On the lookout!

Below: Displaying the true character of this Turkish guarding breed.

A
B
C
D
E
F
G
H
I
J
K
L
M
N
O
P
Q
R
S
T
U
V
W
X
Y
Z

Appenzeller Sennenhunde

Average height: 19-23 inches
Average weight: 48-55 pounds

Appearance

The rarest of the Swiss breeds, the Appenzeller Sennenhunde is a muscular dog, but not massive. Although short-coated, there is a thick undercoat. His head is fairly refined and he carries his tail curled over his back. The most common coat color is a tri-color, with a black ground coat and rich rust and white markings. Occasionally a base coat of Havannah brown is found in the

Below: This bitch and dog await instructions from their owner.

breed. The nose is black or brown, in-keeping with coat color.

Characteristics

As a breed the Appenzeller is active and outgoing but somewhat suspicious of strangers. His group and protective instincts are strong, making him very loyal and devoted to family members, home and property. He is intelligent and easily trained.

Origins and History

The Appenzeller Sennenhunde is one

BREED NOTES

SIZE	GROOMING
✓✓	✓
EXERCISE	LIFESPAN
✓✓✓	✓✓

of four Swiss breeds and was originally bred as a livestock guardian and cattle herding dog, controlling a wayward cow by dashing in to nip at its heel. In 1897 it was recognised as a breed requiring preservation. At this time dogs were scattered on Swiss farms, where they were also used for general farm work. A breed club was set up in 1906 and a standard drawn up in 1914. Like the other Swiss breeds, the Appenzeller is believed to be descended from the Roman Molossers, these having been crossed with some of the native dogs of the lower Alps. Others are of the opinion that the breed descend purely from dogs

Above: 'Don't look at me that way!'

Below: An impressive head and an equally impressive collar.

A
B
C
D
E
F
G
H
I
J
K
L
M
N
O
P
Q
R
S
T
U
V
W
X
Y
Z

Above: A fine example of the different color combinations in this breed.

Left: Taking a moment's well-earned relaxation

native to the region. Although still not popular in the USA, at least one was recorded in the country in the 1950s. The breed was recorded in the KC's Foundation Stock Service in 1998.

Exercise and Grooming

A particularly high energy breed, the Appenzeller Senennhund needs plenty of exercise, both mental and physical. The means that this really not a suitable breed for everyone; perhaps the reason why it has not yet become popular here. The coat is easy to care for but needs regular attention, because it is a double coat. The coat does shed, the short hairs sticking tenaciously to clothing and upholstery.

Below: Attired in a harness, in readiness for work.

A
B
C
D
E
F
G
H
I
J
K
L
M
N
O
P
Q
R
S
T
U
V
W
X
Y
Z

Argentine Dogo

Average height: 23.5-27.5 inches
Average weight: 80-100 pounds

Appearance

The Argentine Dogo gives an instant overall impression of great power. Heavily-boned and smooth-muscled, he has a massive head, strong neck and a deep, broad body. The white coat is short, smooth, thick and glossy, its colour expelling heat from the body. Any spot of color on the body is a disqualifying point, but small spots on the head are acceptable. Eyelid rims should be black, giving a lively, intelligent look, but with marked firmness.

Characteristics

Alert, determined and intelligent, this is a fearless breed, frequently used for cattle protection and police work. Correctly raised and trained, this is a friendly, outgoing dog with an excellent temperament. Despite the fact that in the UK he is considered "a dangerous breed" and is therefore not allowed in that country, he is generally good with children, gentle with other animals

Below: A mature Argentine Dogo displaying the substance of the breed.

BREED NOTES

SIZE	GROOMING
✔ ✔ ✔	✔
EXERCISE	**LIFESPAN**
✔ ✔ ✔	✔ ✔

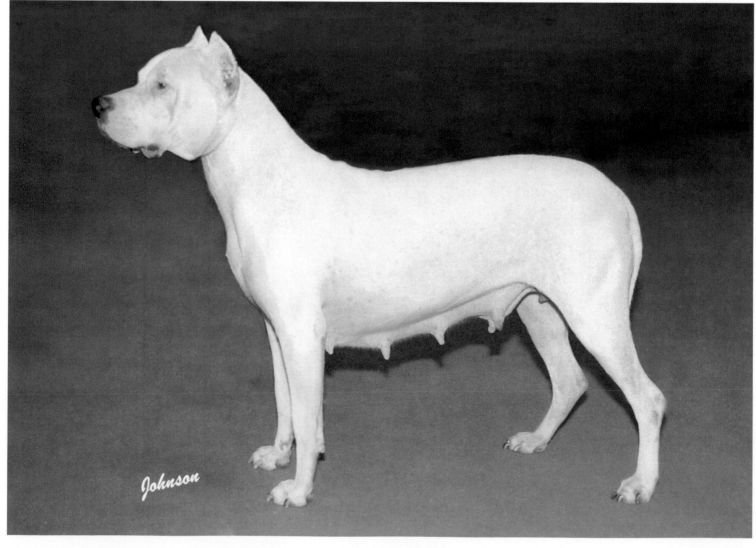

Johnson

and easy to train. However, the Dogo is a natural guardian and will defend any family member whom he considers to be threatened. It is therefore necessary that introduction of visitors is carefully supervised, and that training begins at an early age.

Origins and History
The Argentine Dogo is the only internationally recognised dog breed from Argentina. Developed by the Martinez brothers in the mid-1920s, it was bred as a fearless hunter capable of hunting large game, including the mountain lion and boar. To the now extinct Fighting Dog of Cordoba, founders of the breed added the blood of the Pointer, Boxer, Great Dane, Bull Terrier, Bulldog, Irish Wolfhound, Dogue de Bordeaux and also the Great Pyrenees to help develop the white coat, and the Spanish Mastiff for his power. What an incredible mélange, but so very well worthwhile!

Health Issues
Although generally a healthy breed, as in all breeds of dog, some genetic disorders can occur. The Argentine Dogo is susceptible to hip dysplasia and like other primarily white dogs, to deafness. The breed may be born either partially or completely deaf so

Above: A wonderful example of a Junior Dogo bitch, living in Moscow and judged by the author in Estonia.

it is important that all dogs of this breed are tested.

Exercise and Grooming
A physically strong and agile dog, the Argentine Dogo should be given plenty of exercise to keep him in good bodily condition. When exercised in public places, owners should take the breed's protective nature into consideration and exert sensible supervision. The breed's short coat is easy to keep in good order.

A
B
C
D
E
F
G
H
I
J
K
L
M
N
O
P
Q
R
S
T
U
V
W
X
Y
Z

Australian Cattle Dog

Average height: dogs – 18-20 inches; bitches – 17-19 inches
Average weight: 33-50 pounds

Appearance

A strong, compact herding dog, the Australian Cattle Dog is built to work. The combination of substance, power, balance and hard, muscular condition conveys the impression of great agility, strength and endurance. This breed's strong head is in balance with the rest of the dog, with a broad skull and muscular cheeks. As the Australian Cattle Dog is required to move difficult cattle by heeling or biting, teeth which are sound and strong are very important. Eyes express alertness and intelligence. The coat is smooth, straight and hard and lies flat to resist water. There is also a short, dense undercoat. Coat color may be either red or blue speckle; even markings are desirable on the head.

BREED NOTES

SIZE	GROOMING
✔✔	✔
EXERCISE	LIFESPAN
✔✔	✔✔

Characteristics

This breed is agile, alert, watchful, courageous and protective, with the ability and willingness to carry out his allotted task however arduous. As his name implies his prime function is the control and movement of cattle in both wide open and confined areas; he seems to possess remarkable reasoning powers. He is always alert, extremely intelligent, watchful, courageous and trustworthy, with an implicit devotion to duty and to his family. Although naturally suspicious of strangers, he must be amenable to handling.

Origins and History

The Australian Cattle Dog was developed in Australia from the

Left: The puppy already shows the alertness that he will display in adulthood.

1840s onward. The aim was to produce a silent worker that would be able to control livestock in wide-open spaces as well as in the stockyard. It is believed that the native Australian Dingo was used in the breed's formation, as well as the Dalmatian, the Bull Terrier and the Australian Kelpie. Today the breed is recognised for aptitude in herding trials, agility and competitive obedience.

Health Issues

The Australian Cattle Dog is a relatively healthy long-lived breed; in fact one reportedly lived to be 29 years, but 12-15 years is average. The breed is known to encounter occasional problems with deafness but its genetic mode of inheritance is not yet known. Other problems to watch out for in this breed are hip dysplasia and Progressive Retinal Atrophy (PRA).

Exercise and Grooming

This is a high energy breed that is extremely active so both mental

Above: A highly typical specimen of the breed, showing power, balance and hard, muscular condition.

and physical stimulation are essential. Herding abilities are natural to the Australian Cattle Dog but the breed also excels at such sports as flyball, agility and frisbee competition. Coat care is important, but by no means difficult. Especial care should be taken to remove dead coat during the moulting season. Baths may be given as needed.

A
B
C
D
E
F
G
H
I
J
K
L
M
N
O
P
Q
R
S
T
U
V
W
X
Y
Z

Australian Shepherd

Average height: dogs – 20-23 inches; bitches – 18-21 inches
Average weight: 35-70 pounds

Appearance
A well-balanced dog of medium size, males are more masculine in appearance, without being coarse; bitches are more feminine, but not fine in bone. The eyes are very expressive and come in a variety of hues. The weather resistant, medium-length coat comes in a wide variety of colors: blue, merle, red merle, black, liver or red, with or without tan markings. He may have a natural bobbed tail, or else it is docked.

Below: This top winning show dog portrays all the character of the breed.

Characteristics
The Australian Shepherd is very alert and intelligent, possessing great eagerness and strong herding and guarding instincts. A good-natured breed, he is never shy and not aggressive towards animals or people but is protective of his home and family. Loyal to his family, he is a great companion, always eager to

Opposite: This American Champion travelled all the way to Britain to compete at Crufts Dog Show, taking home the award for Best in Show.

please his loved ones. He is also easy to train, and training is important, as is socialization.

Origins and History
Despite its name, the Australian Shepherd was developed in the USA, not, as might be expected in Australia! The breed has been in the USA for over a century, possible a lot longer as native American Indians have often given accounts of them. This is an all purpose farm/ranch dog and still works as a stock dog today. In our modern world the Australian Shepherd is also now found working as a guide dog, service dog and doing therapy work. The breed is also used for search and rescue, works with the

Johnson

police and is employed as a narcotics dog.

Health Issues

The Australian Shepherd is a fairly healthy breed, but several problems have been encountered, amongst them deafness, epilepsy, eye problems, hip dysplasia and osteochondritis desicans (OCD), which is a degeneration of bone underlying the cartilage of joints. This always shows up during the growing phase. This breed has been noted to be sensitive to invermectin.

Below: Even when relaxing, the Australian Shepherd is always alert.

A
B
C
D
E
F
G
H
I
J
K
L
M
N
O
P
Q
R
S
T
U
V
W
X
Y
Z

Exercise and Grooming

Because this is a high energy dog, he enjoys having work to do so it is essential to provide him with plenty of physical and mental exercise. He enjoys taking part in all kinds of activities and dog sports, so owners of Australian Shepherds should be prepared to spend plenty of time with their dogs. Although his coat is very attractive, it does not need too much work to keep it in good condition. A weekly brushing is important to remove mats, tangles and dust. During the moulting season a slicker brush will help to remove undercoat.

Above: These three Australian Shepherds make a pretty picture sitting on their owner's garden bench.

Below: Australian Shepherds always seem happy and ready to please their owners.

***Opposite:** The breed comes in the most wonderful array of colors, and this is a particularly fine example of the breed.*

Johnson

Australian Terrier

Average height: 10-11 inches
Average weight: 14-16 pounds

Appearance

This small, sturdy breed is a medium-boned working Terrier, rather longer than he is high and somewhat "hard bitten" in appearance, keen and intelligent. He has a strong, powerful muzzle and his small, pricked ears are set high on the skull and yet well apart. This spunky little fellow's topknot protects his eyes when working and his neck is well-furnished with hair, forming a protective ruff. The harsh, straight coat is straight and mostly about 2.5 inches long and its colour is blue tan, solid sandy or solid red. The topknot is silver or a lighter shade of the body coat.

Characteristics

With his strong personality, the

Below: A good example of mature Australian Terrier displaying the blue-tan color.

Opposite: The "Aussie" has a keen, intelligent expression with pricked ears.

BREED NOTES	
SIZE	GROOMING
✔	✔ ✔
EXERCISE	LIFESPAN
✔ ✔	✔ ✔

Johnson

Johnson

A
B
C
D
E
F
G
H
I
J
K
L
M
N
O
P
Q
R
S
T
U
V
W
X
Y
Z

Australian Terrier is a very active little dog and believes himself to be much larger than he actually is. He is keen, intelligent and self-assured but also both friendly and affectionate, making him an excellent companion. The 'Aussie', as he is familiarly known, is a natural watchdog, so you can expect him to sound the alarm by barking at the approach of any stranger, human or canine.

Origins and History

Bred originally by the British in Australia early in the nineteenth century, the Australian Terrier was developed to hunt rats and snakes, which he killed by springing into the air and landing behind the snake's neck. He has an inborn urge to chase little things that move, be they squirrels, rabbits or cats! The breed arose from a blend of Terriers that had been imported to Australia from England and Scotland, so he carries the blood of many different Terrier breeds. The English Kennel Club did not decide to accept this breed until1936, and in America it did not gain recognition until 1958.

Health Issues

A fairly healthy breed, the

Left: A high quality specimen of the breed.

Opposite: This young pup shows all the signs of growing up to be as good as the adult he is pictured with.

Australian Terrier has few health problems, although diabetes, patella luxation and Legg-Perthes disease have been observed.

Exercise and Grooming
The lively Australian Terrier needs plenty of exercise, but much of this he will create for himself. Take care when exercising him in public places that he does not scamper off after a squirrel, or someone's stray cat! The harsh coat is relatively easy to care for by Terrier standards but the hair around ears and eyes needs careful trimming and occasional plucking. Bathing should be limited to once a month.

Right: The "Aussie" is always on the alert!

Below: Like mother like child.

A
B
C
D
E
F
G
H
I
J
K
L
M
N
O
P
Q
R
S
T
U
V
W
X
Y
Z

Azawakh

Average height: dogs – 25-29 inches; bitches – 23.5-27.5 inches
Average weight: dogs – 44-55 pounds; bitches – 33-44 pounds

Appearance

Leggy and yet elegant, the Azawakh gives a distinct overall impression of great finesse. Muscles can be seen under the skin and coat on chest and abdomen is minimal, so as to be virtually devoid of hair. All four legs have white "stockings" and there is a white bib and white tip to the tail, which was sometimes painted by hunters so that they could distinguish their own dogs. The short coat can be any shade of fawn, from light sable to dark fawn, with flecking limited to the extremities. There may or may not be a black mask on the head.

Characteristics

This is an independent breed, attentive and alert and the Azawakh is usually reserved with strangers. With those he knows he is very gentle and can be affectionate. It is said that this remarkable breed is fleet-footed enough to catch animals such as hares and gazelle, courageous enough to ward off large predators, untiring like a camel and beautiful, like an Arab horse.

Below: The Azawakh gives a distinct impression of finesse

BREED NOTES

SIZE	GROOMING
✔	✔
✔	
✔	

EXERCISE	LIFESPAN
✔	✔
✔	✔
✔	

Below: This is a sighthound, as is eminently clear from the expression.

Origins and History

The Azawakh is an African sighthound originating in Mali, for hundreds of years the companion of the nomads of the southern Sahara, who know the breed as the Tuareg Sloughi. The Azawakh is used by cattle breeders to protect their cattle, people and camps from predators and other intruders. Working in a pack, it also hunts prey, bringing it to exhaustion and then to the ground until the master arrives. At the beginning of a hunt the hound is seated in his master's saddle and only slipped when prey is sighted. He can reach speeds over 40 miles per hour, and can course for as long as five hours. The Azawakh first appeared in Europe in 1970 but was not registered by the American Kennel Club until 1999, when it was recognised on the Foundation Stock Service.

Health Issues

Like most other members of the sighthound family, the Azawakh can be sensitive to anaesthetics. It is therefore essential to discuss this issue with your vet prior to any surgery taking place. Bloat is another problem that has been known to occur in the breed.

Exercise and Grooming

Like all sighthounds, the Azawakh should be given the opportunity to have plenty of exercise, for he needs to stretch those long, elegant legs! His coat is so short that it is easy to care for, but an occasional rub over with a chamois leather is always useful, and a piece of velvet can be used to put the final touch.

Below: The Azawakh has white "stockings" on all four legs.

A
B
C
D
E
F
G
H
I
J
K
L
M
N
O
P
Q
R
S
T
U
V
W
X
Y
Z

A
B
C
D
E
F
G
H
I
J
K
L
M
N
O
P
Q
R
S
T
U
V
W
X
Y
Z

Basenji

Average height: dogs – 17 inches; bitches – 16 inches
Average weight: dogs – 24 pounds; bitches – 22 pounds

Appearance
Lightly built and finely boned, the Basenji is an aristocratic-looking dog. His dark, almond-shaped eyes are far-seeing and have a rather inscrutable expression. The small, erect ears are slightly hooded and wrinkles appear on the forehead when the ears are erect. With his definite waist and tightly curled tail, the Basenji presents a picture of Gazelle-like grace. The short, fine coat comes in chestnut red, tricolour or brindle. This breed's skin is very pliant.

Characteristics
The Basenji is famous as a 'barkless dog', but is by no means silent, uttering its own special noise, somewhere between a chortle and a yodel. This is an athletic dog, fast

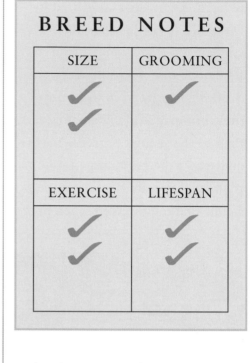

BREED NOTES

SIZE	GROOMING
✓ ✓	✓
EXERCISE	**LIFESPAN**
✓ ✓	✓ ✓

Johnson

Left: This Best in Show winner is happy to pose on the podium.

and agile, and rather cat-like in his mannerisms. He is frisky and agile and cleans himself very much as a cat does. An intelligent, somewhat independent breed, the Basenji is very affectionate and highly alert. Although rather aloof and cautious when amongst strangers, he is gentle and loving with friends and family.

Origins and History
One of the oldest breeds, the Basenji developed from a diversity of canid types, and is probably closely related to the pariah. Its distant ancestors were those depicted on Egyptian rock carvings, dating back some 5,000 years. Over time the Basenji has been described as terrier and a spitz breed, but now it falls into the hound group, hunting both by sight and by

Johnson

Left: The Basenji has an inscrutable expression.

dog and is sadly often fatal, however thanks to modern treatment, some affected dogs now survive. Another concern for this breed is Pyruvate Kinase (PK) deficiency, an inherited deficiency causing anemia.

Exercise and Grooming

It should always be kept in mind that the Basenji is an exceptionally good jumper and the translation of a familiar name for the breed in Africa is the 'jumping-up-and-down-dog'. This is a high energy breed that needs plenty of exercise, enjoying lure coursing, tracking, conformation, obedience and agility. The Basenji seems quite happy to groom himself, but he does shed a little hair, so this should be brushed out occasionally.

Below: A classic profile showing well carried ears and good tail set.

scent. The breed bears a close resemblance to the Kufu dog, the first domestic dog known in Egypt. Because of its lack of voice, hunters in Africa tie around its neck a dried gourd, filled with pebbles. In 1943 the American Kennel Club accepted the breed for registration and approved the breed standard.

Health Issues

Amongst the health problems encountered by the Basenji are Progressive Retinal Atrophy (PRA), hypothyroidism and Fanconi syndrome. The latter is a kidney disease that strikes the middle-aged

Johnson

Basset Hound

Average height: 14 inches (over 15 inches disqualifies)
Average weight: 60-70 pounds

Appearance

There can be few who do not recognise the Basset Hound, with his loose, folding skin, short legs yet substantial frame. For his height, he is heavier in bone than any other breed of dog. The velvety ears are long, the eyes soft and rather sad in

Johnson

BREED NOTES

SIZE	GROOMING
✓ ✓	✓
EXERCISE	LIFESPAN
✓ ✓ ✓	✓ ✓

that large, well-proportioned head, creating an aristocratic intelligent expression. This hound's dense coat offers protection from thorny shrubs; it is usually black, white and tan, known as tricolour, or lemon and white, called bicolour, but any hound colour is permitted.

Characteristics

Despite the shape of his frame, the Basset Hound is capable great endurance in the field and is not at all clumsy; his movement is, quite simply, deliberate. Extremely devoted to his family, he is mild-mannered and never sharp or timid. A laid back, sociable and affectionate sort of chap, he is

Left: The Basset Hound is a big dog on short legs. Just look at the size of these feet!

used to hunt in packs, using his long ears to stir up the scent, then driving the prey into open spaces. The breed was exported to England in 1866 and eventually to America in 1893 and 1894 where the Basset Hound Club of America was created in 1935.

Health Issues

In general, this is a healthy breed, but common disorders sometimes encountered are glaucoma, hip and elbow dysplasia, hypothyroidism, patella luxation, von Willebrands disease and thrombopathia. The latter is a disorder of small blood cells and dogs with this problem are more susceptible to bruising and hemorrhage than other dogs.

Left: *The best of friends.*

Below: *This top-winning hound does the breed proud.*

intelligent, but also has an independent nature so doesn't always choose to obey commands. He is great with children and generally gets along well with other dogs.

Origins and History

Originating in France in the fifteenth century, the Basset Hound was bred as a scenting hound, so has a particularly keen nose. Slower than his cousin the Bloodhound, he proved useful to huntsmen on foot when pursuing small game. This hound has been

A
B
C
D
E
F
G
H
I
J
K
L
M
N
O
P
Q
R
S
T
U
V
W
X
Y
Z

Exercise and Grooming

A Basset Hound will enjoy a game or a daily walk, and may like quite a lot of exercise. However, reasonably mild exercise can prevent excessive strain on his front legs. Extended periods of time outdoors can keep him happy and fit but when indoors he can be rather idle! Wiping his ears should be done regularly, and toenails often need attention. Shampooing, though, should only be done when needed and a few minutes' brushing with a hard bristle brush will keep the coat in good order.

Left: An excellent example of a Basset Hound's head.

Below: The long ears cup the scent.

Bavarian Mountain Hound

Average height: Up to 20 inches
Average weight: 55-77 pounds

Appearance

The Bavarian Mountain Hound has a very short, thick, shiny coat that is hard to the touch; there may be a small ridge on the back of the neck. The color may be all shades of black-masked fawn or brindle, often with a burnished look. He is comparatively light for a bloodhound and relatively short on the leg, but is a well-muscled dog, especially designed to hunt on mountain slopes where, if he were of a heavier build, the going would be too hard.

Characteristics

This is a quiet, calm breed, very poised and attached to his master and his master's family. He is usually kept by foresters and game wardens. An intelligent dog, when hunting he is hard, single-minded and persistent. His work is highly specialized and he must be worked consistently to bring out the best of his talents. This is not a breed for the casual hunter, nor for the novice dog owner.

Origins and History

The Bavarian Mountain Hound is a Schweisshund, literally meaning "bloodhound", a generic term for a dog that follows a blood trail. In this case it is the trail of small game, which can travel many miles before dying a slow, agonising death. Dogs for the trailing of wounded animals are common on the Continent, the honor code of the German huntsman obliging him to locate all shot game, either dead or wounded. Sometimes there may be only a few drops of blood, several yards apart, so it takes a dog with an excellent nose and great cold-trailing ability; sometimes they need to trail for days before finding the game, dead or alive. Bavaria is a mountainous region in southern Germany, near the Austrian and Swiss borders. The Bavarian Mountain Hound, which has been around since the 19th century, is a finer version of the Hanoverian Hound, which was probably crossed with Tyrolean Hounds to create this breed. He is an elegant, athletic, sure footed hound that hunts for small game such as hare and fowl.

Health Issues

No hereditary health problems have apparently been reported for this breed.

BREED NOTES

SIZE	GROOMING
✓ ✓	✓

EXERCISE	LIFESPAN
✓ ✓ ✓	✓ ✓

Exercise and Grooming

The Bavarian Mountain Hound has bags of stamina and needs plenty of opportunity for exercise. He needs lead walking plus time off of the lead in a secure area. Very little grooming is required, just a weekly brush and check over.

Below: Happy when out working.

A
B
C
D
E
F
G
H
I
J
K
L
M
N
O
P
Q
R
S
T
U
V
W
X
Y
Z

Beagle

Average height: In the USA the breed is divided into two size varieties: up to and including 13 inches; over 13 inches but under 15 inches.
Average weight: 18-30

Appearance

A reasonably small, but toughly built hound, the Beagle has a wide, slightly domed skull, with a square muzzle, wide nostrils and long ears with rounded tips. The topline is straight and level. The most common coat colors are black, tan and white (tricolour), and tan and white, but the Beagle can be any hound color. The tight, firm feet are always white, and there is a white tip to the gaily carried tail so the hound is easier to follow in the field.

Characteristics

The Beagle is a wonderful family companion and is generally very good with children. Because this is a 'pack animal', companionship is essential; this can be provided both by humans and other dogs. He tends not to bond only with one person but enjoys being with the whole family. He is bright, friendly and outgoing, active and inquisitive. Because he has a highly developed sense of smell and a rather independent nature, he does have a tendency to roam.

Origins and History

The actual origin of the Beagle is not certain, but it may date back to 200 AD, when small game was tracked by scent. In England the breed was used as a hunting companion that could be followed on foot and in the nineteenth century small 'Pocket Beagles' came into fashion too. Although dogs of this general type

BREED NOTES

SIZE	GROOMING
✔✔	✔
EXERCISE	**LIFESPAN**
✔✔✔	✔✔

Left: This Champion expresses great typicality.

Caption: Puppies need time for both rest and play.

Caption: A great family companion.

were known in the USA prior to the 1970s, it was then that the Beagle as we know it today arrived from England and breed type was established. The English Beagle was used to track fox, but the smaller American type was used for rabbits. The National Beagle Club was formed in 1888 and interestingly Lyndon B Johnson owned three Beagles, named 'Him', 'Her' and 'Edgar'.

Health Issues

This is generally considered a very

A
B
C
D
E
F
G
H
I
J
K
L
M
N
O
P
Q
R
S
T
U
V
W
X
Y
Z

A
B
C
D
E
F
G
H
I
J
K
L
M
N
O
P
Q
R
S
T
U
V
W
X
Y
Z

Johnson

Johnson

Opposie top: This puppy has made herself very comfortable on the sofa.

Opposite: Profile of a typical hound.

Above and right: The Beagle's head from various angles.

healthy breed, but inherited problems that have been known to occur are epilepsy, thyroid abnormalities, hip dysplasia, eye disorders and disc disease. This is a long-lived hound that usually makes 14 years, but 17 years is not unusual.

Exercise and Grooming
The Beagle is an energetic breed, so daily outdoor exercise is essential. A healthy-paced walk on a leash is

A
B
C
D
E
F
G
H
I
J
K
L
M
N
O
P
Q
R
S
T
U
V
W
X
Y
Z

always appreciated; additionally he should spend plenty of time in an outdoor yard. Shedding is minimal and many say that the Beagle has no doggy odour. Brushing once or twice each week is recommended to keep the coat healthy and clean, but ears can be prone to infection so need to be checked and cleaned regularly.

Right: *Patient but alert.*

Below: *Working Beagles at a Hound Show.*

Bearded Collie

Average height: dogs – 21-22 inches; bitches – 20-21 inches
Average weight: 35-55 pounds

Appearance

Combining strength with agility, the Bearded Collie has a long, harsh, straight outercoat, suitable for repelling rain and snow. In contrast the undercoat is soft, furry and close. All 'Beardies' as they familiarly known, are born dark, but as they grow older the coat changes to black, brown, blue or fawn, with or without white markings. Eyes are large and expressive; their color should generally tone with the coat, as does pigmentation.

Characteristics

Because he is a herding dog, instinct has a habit of taking over and the Bearded Collie may well decide to herd whatever he considers to be his flock! Energetic and enthusiastic, he is by no means hyperactive. Ideal as a family dog, he loves the company of children and also gets along well with other family pets. This is an intelligent, friendly and fun-loving breed, but he is an independent

Below: Showing all the attributes of the breed in profile.

BREED NOTES

SIZE	GROOMING
✔ ✔ ✔	✔ ✔ ✔
EXERCISE	**LIFESPAN**
✔ ✔	✔ ✔

Johnson

A
B
C
D
E
F
G
H
I
J
K
L
M
N
O
P
Q
R
S
T
U
V
W
X
Y
Z

Above: Veterinary bedding is very suitable when bringing up puppies.

thinker and can be a little stubborn when it takes his fancy.

Origins and History

One of Britain's oldest breeds, the Bearded Collie originated in Scotland. It is generally believed that the breed came about by crossing the Polish Lowland Sheepdog to the local herding dogs found in Scotland in the 16th century. Some believe the Komondor from Hungary may have played a part in his make-up. He was used as a tireless sheepdog and cattle drover but did not become familiar in other parts of the world until the 1940s, since when he has

Right: Expressive eyes that tone with the coat color.

become very popular. The breed became popular in Canada before the USA where it was accepted by the American Kennel Club in 1976.

Health Issues

This is generally a very healthy breed with a life expectancy of up to 14 years. However some eye problems are cause for concern and Addison's disease is not unknown.

Exercise and Grooming

This is a breed that is happiest when kept busy, so exercise is important to him. Well-suited to agility, herding, obedience, tracking and conformation, he often works as a Therapy dog. The Bearded Collie's long coat needs to be brushed regularly, so owners should allow about an hour each week. When the coat changes from a puppy to adult coat, more time will be needed for grooming. Sometimes older dogs are kept in short coat.

Above: A family group

Below: Best of Breed winner striding out well in the show ring.

A
B
C
D
E
F
G
H
I
J
K
L
M
N
O
P
Q
R
S
T
U
V
W
X
Y
Z

Beauceron

Average height: dogs – 25.5-27.5 inches; bitches – 24-26.5 inches
Average weight: dogs – up to 100 pounds; bitches – 80-90 pounds

Appearance

This well constructed, strong dog is also quick and agile, with smooth, powerful, effortless movement. The texture of the short coat is rough and coarse, with a fine, soft undercoat. Around the neck the hair is somewhat longer. In the American showring the accepted colors are black and tan, black or grey, black and tan (Harlequin), but other colous such as tawny gray or gray and black can be found in the working dog. His tail is long and left uncropped, but ears may or may not be cropped. This breed has double dew-claws on the hind legs.

Johnson

BREED NOTES

SIZE	GROOMING
✔	✔
✔	✔
✔	
EXERCISE	**LIFESPAN**
✔	✔
✔	✔
✔	

Left: A highly expressive head. Notice the rather longer hair around the neck.

Characteristics

An athletic and versatile breed, the Beauceron is renowned for his excellent memory and his natural guarding instinct. Although he is sociable with dogs he knows, his territorial instincts may cause him to be intolerant of others. A breed that is always willing to work; he is fearless, vigilant, obedient, calm, courageous and patient. Training is important from an early age. Because this is a strong-willed dog he must be taught to know his place in the family pack. Rather boisterous, the Beauceron can be a bit clumsy until the age of about two years, so is not ideally suited to a family with very small children

Above and right: Examples of Beauceron with cropped ears (above) and uncropped ears (below), displaying different color patterns.

Origins and History

Dating back to the 16th century, this is a French shepherd dog that was used extensively on farms, as a livestock herding dog and as a guard. The Beauceron was used mainly with sheep, but also with cattle. In both world wars hewas employed by the military to carry messages, detect mines, find the wounded, as well as to carry food

Johnson

Johnson

Opposite: "Vigilant, and obedient."

and ammunition. Today he is still widely used for herding and protection of livestock and by police forces for search and rescue, prison security, apprehension of criminals and narcotics detection.

Health Issues
Health problems that have been encountered in the Beauceron are progressive retinal atrophy (PRA), hip dysplasia and bloat, which is also known as gastric torsion.

Exercise and Grooming
Because the breed is so active mentally and physically he needs plenty of stimulus and is certainly not content to lie around the

Above: This breed is a good livestock protector.

house all day. He needs firm handling and does not like being left alone for long periods. His coat is easy to manage and provided dead coat is removed with a slicker brush, it is no trouble to keep him looking smart.

A
B
C
D
E
F
G
H
I
J
K
L
M
N
O
P
Q
R
S
T
U
V
W
X
Y
Z

Bedlington Terrier

Average height: dogs – 16.5 inches; bitches – 15.5 inches
Average weight: 17-23 pounds

Appearance

The Bedlington Terrier is truly unique in his appearance with his woolly coat, tasseled ears and arched back. Although lightly made and graceful, he is not weedy or shelly, but strong, hard and muscular. His head is pear-shaped and he has a long, rat tail. The weather resistant coat is crisp to the touch but not wiry, created by a blend of hard and soft hair that has

Below: Two adorable littermates, of different colors.

a tendency to curl. Coat color, which lightens with maturity, can be blue, sandy, liver, blue and tan, sandy and tan or liver and tan. The topknot is lighter than the body coat.

Characteristics

The Bedlington is more sensitive than other terriers and much quieter, due undoubtedly to his Whippet ancestry. However, once roused he is full of terrier spirit. Highly reputed for his speed and endurance, this is a breed that is easily trained and

BREED NOTES

SIZE	GROOMING
✓ ✓	✓ ✓

EXERCISE	LIFESPAN
✓ ✓	✓ ✓

excels in obedience. A loyal companion for people of all ages, he loves to play and is graceful, alert and entertaining.

Origins and History

The Rothbury or Northumberland Fox Terrier came from the north of England where it was kept to control vermin. From the late 18th century, it became popular with coal miners who cross-bred the Rothbury to the Whippet so creating the Bedlington that is familiar to us today. The crossing produced one of the gamest terriers, capable of swimming down an otter, coursing a rabbit and also fighting in the pit. The Dandie Dinmont is also believed to be closely connected with this breed.

Left: This Bedlington puppy has liver pigmentation.

Below left: A liver adult.

Below Right: A lovely profile showing characteristic topline.

A
B
C
D
E
F
G
H
I
J
K
L
M
N
O
P
Q
R
S
T
U
V
W
X
Y
Z

Above: These new-born puppies are still very dark, but their color will lighten as they mature.

Left: Being a veteran warrants your own personal little sofa!

The National Bedlington Terrier Club was formed in 1875.

Health Issues
Copper Toxosis is the most significant hereditary problem found in the Bedlington Terrier. This is an inherited defect in the metabolism of copper and is known to cause chronic hepatitis which leads to slowly progressive liver disease. Retinal dysplasia is an eye condition that can also affect the Bedlington.

Above: An expertly presented "pear-shaped" head.

Exercise and Grooming

This is an active breed, enjoying plenty of exercise and play. The coat is virtually shed-proof and needs to be combed frequently. Trimming is necessary roughly every two months. Occasional bathing will clean the coat without making it limp, but Bedlingtons exhibited in the showring will need greater attention to their coats.

A
B
C
D
E
F
G
H
I
J
K
L
M
N
O
P
Q
R
S
T
U
V
W
X
Y
Z

Belgian Laekenois

Average height: dogs – 24-26 inches; bitches – 22-24 inches
Average weight:

Appearance

An elegant, square well-balanced dog, the Belgian Lakenois has a proud carriage of head and gives the impression of depth and solidity, without bulkiness. Males are rather more grand and impressive than females, which have a distinctly feminine look. It is the coat that primarily sets the breed apart from its close cousins, the Belgian Shepherd, Belgian Malinois and Belgian Tervuren. The texture is rough and coarse, giving a disorderly, tousled look. Hair is about 2.5 inches all over the body, but head hair must not be in excess, hiding the eyes or the lines of the head. A beard is always present. All shades of red or fawn to grayish tones are acceptable. Traces of black appear mainly on the muzzle and tail, which should not form a plume.

Characteristics

The Belgian Lakenois reflects qualities of intelligence, courage, alertness and devotion to his master. With his inherent aptitude as a guardian of flock and field, he is understandably protective. Always in motion when not under command, he is attentive and watchful; Although observant and vigilant with strangers, he is not apprehensive, showing no shyness, fear or viciousness unless provoked.

Left: A highly typical example of the breed.

BREED NOTES

SIZE	GROOMING
✓	✓
✓	✓
✓	
EXERCISE	**LIFESPAN**
✓	✓
✓	✓
✓	

With family and close friend the Lakenois is affectionate and friendly.

Origins and History

Considered by most authorities to be the oldest of the four varieties of Belgian Shepherd, the breed's history can be traced back to the fawn wire-haired Vos I de Laeken, born in 1885. In the 19th century he proved his worth in the flax fields of Flanders where he was employed to guard the fields. The breed became a favourite of Queen Marie Henriette when she noticed the dogs used by a shepherd in the grounds of Laeken Castle. In both World Wars it was used as a liaison dog and in the 1920s was used by the Brussels police. The Laekenois

arrived in the USA in 1956 but numbers are still fairly few.

Health Issues

Because of this breed's low fat to body weight ration, the breed can be more sensitive to anaesthesia than many other breeds. Progressive Retinal Atrophy (PRA) is another problem encountered, as well as epilepsy.

Exercise and Grooming

Like other Belgian Shepherd varieties, this is a breed that must be trained and kept fully occupied, for as a flock guardian he is always ready to work and on the alert. His tousled coat is perhaps surprisingly easy to care for.

Left: Perhaps he knows he is the oldest of the four Belgian Shepherd breeds?

Below: The coat of the Lakenois sets it apart from the other Belgian Shepherd breeds.

A
B
C
D
E
F
G
H
I
J
K
L
M
N
O
P
Q
R
S
T
U
V
W
X
Y
Z

A
B
C
D
E
F
G
H
I
J
K
L
M
N
O
P
Q
R
S
T
U
V
W
X
Y
Z

Belgian Malinois

Average height: dogs – 24-26 inches; bitches – 22-24 inches
Average weight: dogs – 7-8 pounds; bitches – 7-8 pounds

Appearance

Well balanced and square in profile, with a exceedingly proud carriage of head, the Belgian Malinois is one of the less well known of the four varieties of Belgian Shepherd dogs. The clean-cut head is strong, but without heaviness and the brown, almond shaped eyes have a questioning, intelligent gaze. Compared with the breed's close cousins, the coat is relatively short. It is short, straight and hard enough to be weather resistant, with a dense undercoat. Hair on the head, ears and lower legs is very short, but longer around the neck, forming a collarette, on the tail and on the backs of the thighs. The basic coloring is rich fawn to mahogany, with black tips on the hairs. Mask and ears are black.

Characteristics

This is a confident breed, exhibiting neither aggressiveness nor shyness in new situations. Although the Malinois can be reserved with strangers, he is affectionate to those he knows and loves. Although naturally possessive of his owner and his owner's property, he is not overly aggressive. Quick and responsive to his owner's commands, the Malinois possesses a strong desire to work.

Origins and History

One of the first short-coated Belgian Shepherds was Charlot, born in 1891; she was used as a model of the Belgian Malinois by the artist, A Clarys. The breed shared its origin with the other varieties of Belgian Shepherd dogs butsoon established itself as an identifiable type. It was bred primarily around the city of Malines, hence the name. In Belgium it is said to be the favourite of the Shepherd dogs, because of its excellent working character. The first Malinois came to the USA in 1911 but the enthusiasm for the breed waned and not until new importations in 1967 did popularity start to rise again.

Health Issues

Watch out for Progressive Retinal Atrophy (PRA), epilepsy, hip dysplasia and thyroid problems. The Malinois can be more sensitive to anaesthesia than many other breeds.

Exercise and Grooming

A hard working breed, the Belgian Malinois is used for conformation, obedience, schutzhund, herding, sledding and tracking. He needs plenty of exercise, both physical and mental. The coat is easy to care for, but undercoat needs to be removed during the moulting season.

BREED NOTES

SIZE	GROOMING
✓ ✓ ✓	✓ ✓

EXERCISE	LIFESPAN
✓ ✓ ✓	✓ ✓

Belgian Sheepdog

Average height: dogs – 24-26 inches; bitches – 22-24 inches
Average weight:

BREED NOTES

SIZE	GROOMING
✓ ✓ ✓	✓ ✓

EXERCISE	LIFESPAN
✓ ✓ ✓	✓ ✓

Appearance

Strong, agile and well-muscled, the Belgian Sheepdog is elegant in appearance and square in outline, with a very proud carriage of head and neck. The male is usually rather more impressive and grand than the female. Bone structure is moderately heavy in proportion to height so that he is neither spindly and leggy, nor cumbersome and bulky. His head is clean-cut and strong and he has an intelligent, questioning gaze. Ears are triangular, stiff and erect. The coat color is black, or may be black with a limited amount of white in specified areas. The abundant guard hairs are long and straight, of a medium harsh texture. There is an extremely dense

Left: With a proud carriage of head and neck, the Belgian Sheepdog's ears are triangular, stiff and erect.

A
C
D
E
F
G
H
I
J
K
L
M
N
O
P
Q
R
S
T
U
V
W
X
Y
Z

Johnson

Opposite: A lovely example of the breed showing excellent coat quality.

Above: These pups have been put to bed in their whelping box, to keep them out of mischief!

Left: This young Malinois, has chosen this full-grown Belgian Shepherd as a firm companion.

undercoat making him adaptable to climatic extremes.

Characteristics

Important qualities of the Belgian Sheepdog are his intelligence, courage, alertness and devotion to his master. He is always ready to protect. Loving and tolerant toward children, provided he has been raised with them, the Belgian Sheepdog can make a good family pet. Affectionate and friendly, he can also be quite sensitive, but is active and easy to train.

A
B
C
D
E
F
G
H
I
J
K
L
M
N
O
P
Q
R
S
T
U
V
W
X
Y
Z

Origins and History

In many parts of the world the Belgian Sheepdog is known as the Groenendale. His origin can be traced back to the 1800s and late in the 19th century a club was formed to determine if there was a true Belgian shepherding breed. Once recognised, interest in the Belgian Sheepdog increased, partly because of his capability of performing many different functions. The Paris police used the breed, as did the New York police who imported four Belgian Sheepdogs to work alongside the American-bred Groenendale. Belgian customs officers also used this dog for border patrol, and of course the

Above: The Belgian Shepherd has a low fat to body ratio, a lot of the apparent "bulk" you see is his abundant coat.

Left: As with many breeds, the dog is more masculine than the bitch.

Right: This veteran's coat color is giving away his age.

breed was useful as a herder and watchdog. The Belgian Sheepdog was used on battle fields during the war years, even pulling machine guns. In 1959, the American Kennel Club decided that only the Groenendale could be registered as a Belgian Sheepdog.

Health Issues

This breed can be more sensitive to anesthesia than others, because of its low fat to body weight ratio. Health problems to look out for in the Belgian Sheepdog include Progressive Retinal Atrophy (PRA), epilepsy, hip

A
B
C
D
E
F
G
H
I
J
K
L
M
N
O
P
Q
R
S
T
U
V
W
X
Y
Z

dysplasia and thyroid problems.

Exercise and Grooming

A breed that needs plenty of physical activity and mental stimulation, the Belgian Sheepdog is particularly suited to the following activities: obedience, tracking, schutzhund, herding and even sledding. Their skills can also be employed in police work, search and rescue, and as guide and therapy dogs. The coat needs to be brushed twice weekly, more frequently when it moults. Careful, discrete clipping is done, primarily at the extremities of the ears and between toes.

Right: This breed needs lots of mental stimulation

Below: Two lovely head studies.

Belgian Tervuren

Average height: dogs – 24-26 inches; bitches – 22-24 inches
Average weight:

Appearance

The rich fawn to russet mahogany coat with its black overlay gives the Belgian Tervuren and most striking appearance. His medium harsh coat is not silky or wiry and the guard hairs are long, close-fitting, straight and abundant. The undercoat is very dense, especially during the colder months of the year. The face has a black mask and the ears are mostly black. Like his close cousins, the Tervuren stands squarely on all fours and is a well-balanced, medium-sized dog. He is elegant in appearance and the males should appear unquestionably masculine, whilst the females have a distinctly feminine look about them. The triangular ears are well-cupped, stiff and erect.

Characteristics

Vigilant with strangers, the Belgian Tervuren is an observant dog, but not apprehensive, showing no fear or shyness. He does not show viciousness

Below: The Tervuren's coat colour is different from his cousin, the Belgian Sheepdog.

BREED NOTES

SIZE	GROOMING
✓	✓
✓	✓
✓	

EXERCISE	LIFESPAN
✓	✓
✓	✓
✓	

A
B
C
D
E
F
G
H
I
J
K
L
M
N
O
P
Q
R
S
T
U
V
W
X
Y
Z

Below: This top-winning Champion has a magnificent coat.

Above: A young puppy, not yet wearing his mature adult coat.

Right: The friendly Tervuren

without unprovoked attack. He should stand his ground and be prepared to meet overtures, without making them himself. Affectionate with those he knows well, the Tervuren is friendly and thoroughly enjoys the attention he is given.

Origins and History

In its homeland, the Belgian Tervuren is distinguished by its coat length and color, "long-haired other than black". The breed owes its name to the village of Tervuren, which was the home of Mr F Corbeel, an early devotee of the breed. Before the Industrial Age, the farmers of Belgium needed a general purpose herding and guard dog, providing security for farm and family. From the establishment of the Belgian

Johnson

Above: The rich fawn to russet mahogany coat always has a black overlay.

Shepherd Dog, only a few people were interested in producing the Tervuren, but interest increased as the century progressed. The first American Kennel Club registration for this breed was in 1918, but there followed a lull until the 1950s and in 1959 the Belgian Tervuren was classified as a distinct breed.

Health Issues

Problems to be alert for include Progressive Retinal Atrophy (PRA), epilepsy, hip dysplasia and thyroid problems. Because of the low fat to body weight ratio, the Tervuren can be more sensitive to anesthesia than other breeds.

Exercise and Grooming

A physically active breed that also needs mental stimulation, apart from the many activities suited to his close cousins, long walks and energizing play sessions will also be much appreciated by the Tervuren. The coat needs to be brushed thoroughly at least twice each week, more frequently during the moulting season.

Bergamasco

Average height: dogs – 22.5-24.5 inches; bitches – 21-23inches
Average weight: dogs – 70-84 pounds; bitches – 57-71 pounds

Johnson

BREED NOTES

SIZE	GROOMING
✓	✓
✓	✓
✓	✓

EXERCISE	LIFESPAN
✓	✓
✓	✓

Appearance

A heavily boned, herding dog, the Bergamasco has a large head and a thick tail that hangs down and curves upward slightly at the end. Perhaps the most notable feature of the breed is the abundant coat which covers the entire dog and forms 'flocks' or loose mats, offering protection from weather and predators. Even the hair on the head is long and hangs over the eyes. The hair is made up of three coat types, an oily undercoat forming a waterproof layer against the skin, 'goat hair', which is long, straight and rough, and a woolly outercoat. Colors are solid gray or gradation of this color including Isabella and fawn, to black, though it should not be shiny or lustrous. In profile the breed is compact, but just slightly longer than tall.

Cunliffe

Top: A fine example of a mature adult.

Above: The Bergamaso can be found in various colors.

Above: Moving out in the show ring.

Above right: Ever attentive to their owners.

Below: The remarkable flocked coat.

Characteristics

A vigilant guard, with a strong protective instinct, the Bergamasco is naturally stubborn and will persevere with a task until done, having the ability to think for himself. A very intelligent animal, he is courageous but not aggressive without cause. He has a patient nature, is quiet and eager to please, making him an excellent companion.

Origins and History

Believed to trace its origins back to Persia, this is an Italian sheepdog that travelled with nomadic shepherds, taking their dogs to the Alps. There is became called the Bergamasco. The dogs worked closely with their shepherds, guarding and protecting flocks. They were trained to be problem solvers, working out what needed to be done and finding a solution without being given specific direction. Following the Second World War, when the need for shepherding dogs declined, the breed became close to extinction, surviving only due to dedicated breeders. The Bergamasco was first imported to the USA in the 1990s.

Health Issues

Generally a very healthy breed, the breed may be susceptible to some heath problems, including hereditary disorders. Owners should be aware of the possibility of hip dysplasia and eye disorders.

Exercise and Grooming

This is an active agile breed that requires a lot of space and ideally needs a daily walk, as well as freedom in an enclosed area. The Bergamasco's puppy coat is similar to that of the Old English Sheepdog, but as he grows older the 'goat hair' and 'wool' begin to appear, when it need 'ripping' into mats. This is only done once but for the next six months a weekly check is needed to be sure the mats have not grown back together. Following this they stay apart naturally. The flocks are never groomed out so no brushing is required and it is a surprisingly easy coat to maintain. When bathed occasionally, this should be done in the summer for the coat takes at least a full day to dry out.

A
B
C
D
E
F
G
H
I
J
K
L
M
N
O
P
Q
R
S
T
U
V
W
X
Y
Z

Berger Picard

Average height: 21-25.5 inches
Average weight: 50-70 pounds

Appearance

The Berger Picard has an enchanting rustic, tousled look about him, with his distinctively shaggy, rough, double coat. It is a weatherproof coat, harsh and crisp to the touch and falls into two basic colors, fawn and gray, with a wide range of shade variations in between. Eyebrows are thick, but they do not shield this dog's dark, frank eyes. Ears are of moderate size, broad at their base and set rather high. The tail is natural and is carried with a slight J-curve at the tip.

BREED NOTES

SIZE	GROOMING
✓ ✓ ✓	✓ ✓

EXERCISE	LIFESPAN
✓ ✓ ✓	✓ ✓

Johnson

Characteristics

The Berger Picard is a very devoted dog and can be rather comical. This is a people oriented dog that is very loyal and can make a great family pet. However the breed needs sensible training and socialization. Lively and intelligent, the Berger Picard has a rather sensitive and assertive disposition that responds quickly to obedience training. Although a laid-back sort of a dog, he can have a stubborn streak and can be reserved toward strangers. He is not an excessive barker.

Origins and History

This is believed to be one of France's oldest herding breeds but

Left: He has an enchanting, rustic, tousled look.

with World Wars I and II both being fought in northern France, the Berger Picard almost became extinct; indeed it is still rare today with only around 3,500 dogs in its homeland.. Although shown at a dog show in Paris in 1863, the breed was not officially recognised in France until 1925. It was the release of the move Because of Winn Dixie that the breed was introduced to America; the producers needed a dog that looked like a mutt, but they needed several that all looked alike so selected this little known breed. Some believe the Berger Picard is related to the Briard and

Right: *A dark gray.*

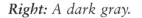

Left: *This fawn colored dog is a devoted companion.*

Beauceron, whilst others consider that the Dutch and Belgian shepherding breeds have closer ties.

Exercise and Grooming

This is a quiet breed that is more suited to an outdoor life than an indoor one. He needs to be given enough exercise to release his energy. Around the house the Berger Picard is a quiet dog. The coat does not require special care to produce its rustic appearance. Brushing should only be done once a month and bathing is rare. No trimming should be done, except perhaps around the edges of the ears. This breed does not shed very much and has no doggy odor.

A
B
C
D
E
F
G
H
I
J
K
L
M
N
O
P
Q
R
S
T
U
V
W
X
Y
Z

A
B
C
D
E
F
G
H
I
J
K
L
M
N
O
P
Q
R
S
T
U
V
W
X
Y
Z

Bernese Mountain Dog

Average height: dogs – 24.5-27.5 inches; bitches – 22.5-26 inches
Average weight: dogs – 85-120 pounds; bitches – 65-100 pounds

Appearance

Large, sturdy, strong and yet agile, the Bernese Mountain Dog is tri-colored, with a heavy double coat and distinctive markings. The ground colour is jet black and the russet and white markings are in specific places, such as on feet, tip of tail, and over each eye. His is a weather resistant coat, with a natural sheen.

Characteristics

This is a breed with a wonderful temperament, dependable, consistent and always eager to please. He has a special way of always appearing to be in command of the situation. He loves human companionship and is a devoted, faithful and affectionate friend. He certainly does not like to be left outdoors, but he prefers to be included as a family member. His calm, gentle disposition makes him

Below: Although large and strong, the Bernese is agile.

Opposite: A beautiful head study showing the tan markings over each eye

BREED NOTES

SIZE	GROOMING
✓ ✓ ✓	✓ ✓
EXERCISE	**LIFESPAN**
✓ ✓ ✓	✓

Johnson

Johnson

A
B
C
D
E
F
G
H
I
J
K
L
M
N
O
P
Q
R
S
T
U
V
W
X
Y
Z

Above: The Bernese is the only Swiss Mountain Dog with a long coat.

Opposite: This breed has a calm, gentle disposition.

good with children and other animals. Although he may appear to be rather aloof with strangers, he is never aggressive or timid.

Origins and History

One of four breeds of Swiss Mountain Dog, this is the second largest and the only one with a long coat. Ancestors of these breeds were Mastiffs, taken to Switzerland over 2,000 years ago. The Mastiffs were interbred with local farm dogs, creating a smaller animal, but still very trustworthy. The Bernese Mountain Dog was originally used to drive livestock and to pull carts, mainly in the town of Berne. The breed came to America in the mid-1920s and was officially recognised

Left: This trio clearly shows their russet and white markings on a black ground.

Johnson

A
B
C
D
E
F
G
H
I
J
K
L
M
N
O
P
Q
R
S
T
U
V
W
X
Y
Z

Johnson

IVESHEAD

by the America Kennel Club in 1937. Today the breed is still used for farm work and for herding, tracking, and search and rescue.

Health Issues

The Bernese Mountain Dog is sadly a breed with a relatively short life expectancy averaging 7 to 8 years, although some certainly make it into double figures. A heart-warming Swiss saying is, 'Three years a young dog, three years a good dog, and

three years an old dog... all else, a gift from God'. Some health problems known to affect this breed are hip and elbow dysplasia, cancer, bloat, sub-aortic stenosis, autoimmune diseases, thyroid disorders, eye diseases and skin and coat problems.

Exercise and Grooming

Despite its large size, the Bernese does not need a great deal of exercise but enjoys a daily walk. As with other large breeds, care should be taken not

Above: The Bernese is a carting breed and now competes in colourful competition

to over exercise during the growth stages of puppyhood. At this time exercise should be restricted to your yard. The Bernese Mountain Dog requires occasional baths and frequent brushing. During seasonal moults, it sheds a lot of the undercoat so will need more attention at this time.

Bichon Frisé

Average height: 9.5-11.5 inches
Average weight: 10-18 pounds

Appearance

The Bichon Frisé is described as a white powder puff with black eyes, eye rims, halos, lips, nose and footpads. With his soft, dark-eyed, inquisitive, alert expression, his dark, round eyes look directly forward. The texture of a Bichon's coat is of the utmost importance; a soft, dense undercoat and a topcoat of coarser, curlier texture. The two textures combined give a soft but substantial feel, something like plush velvet. When patted, it simply springs back. In colour the Bichon Frisé is always white, though there may be shadings of buff, cream or apricot around the ears or on the body.

Characteristics

The Bichon Frisé loves to play, but is not overly energetic, although he has a delightfully entertaining personality. He is gentle mannered, sensitive and affectionate and his cheerful attitude is a hallmark of the breed, his jaunty tail expressing his happiness. Although by no means a guard dog, he will certainly announce the arrival of strangers.

BREED NOTES

SIZE	GROOMING
✔	✔
	✔
	✔
EXERCISE	LIFESPAN
✔	✔
	✔

Johnson

Left: A white powder puff with black eyes.

A
B
C
D
E
F
G
H
I
J
K
L
M
N
O
P
Q
R
S
T
U
V
W
X
Y
Z

Origins and History

Descended from the Barbet or Water Spaniel, all members of the Bichon family originated in the Mediterranean area. The Bichon travelled greatly, often used by sailors as an item of barter. So it was that these little dogs moved from continent to continent. It is generally believed that Spanish seamen took them to Tenerife. In the 14th century Italian sailors rediscovered the Bichon, taking it

Right: A beautifully balanced Bichon.

Below: They are this little girl's pride and joy!

back to Italy where the breed became a great favourite, especially amongst the nobility. At that time, in the Italian courts, they were often cut "lion style". By 1800 the Bichon had become a common dog, roaming the streets, often accompanying organ grinders and performing tricks in circuses and fairs.

Left: All Bichon puppies enjoy playing with a safe toy.

Below: An agile breed, this Bichon can easily jump the breakers on the sea front.

129

A
B
C
D
E
F
G
H
I
J
K
L
M
N
O
P
Q
R
S
T
U
V
W
X
Y
Z

During the early part of the 20th century the breed obtained official recognition in France and the first litter in the USA was whelped in 1956.

Health Issues

This is generally a healthy little breed with a good life expectancy of 14 to 16 years, sometimes longer. The oldest recorded Bichon in the USA died of natural causes at 21! Health concerns to watch out for include patella luxation, ear infections and eye diseases. Skin allergies, dental trouble, bladder infections and bladder stones, can also give cause for concern.

Exercise and Grooming

The Bichon is not over-demanding, but loves a good walk with his owner and enjoys plenty of games. The coat is trimmed to reveal the natural outline of the

Above: *This baby Bichon loves the company of his larger Tibetan Terrier friend.*

Left: *A top quality Bichon makes a stunning picture.*

body, but it is always rounded off and never cut so short as to present an overly trimmed picture. It is left sufficiently long to give the powder-puff look that is so characteristic. Trimming is an art and needs a dedicated owner to keep it in tip-top condition. Because the coat does not shed it mats, so regular grooming is imperative. Regular bathing is also essential.

Black and Tan Coonhound

Average height: dogs – 25-27 inches; bitches – 23-25 inches
Average weight: dogs – 60-100 pounds

Appearance

With an alert, friendly and eager expression, the head of the Black and Tan Coonhound is cleanly modelled, with no folds in the skin. The long, low set ears are well set back, hanging in graceful folds and giving this hound a majestic appearance.

The Black and Tan Coonhound has moderate bone and good muscle tone, males being heavier in bone and muscle than females. The coat is short but dense to withstand rough going and he has been selectively bred, not only for his skills, but also on the basis of color: coal black with rich tan markings above eyes, on sides of muzzle, chest, legs and breeching, with black pencil markings on toes

Characteristics

Even tempered, outgoing and friendly, this is a powerful, agile and alert dog, but not aggressive to other dogs or to people. As a working scent hound, must be able to work in close contact with other hounds. Not particularly fast, the Black and Tan trails rather like a Bloodhound, entirely by scent, with

Right: This Black and Tan Coonhound's head clearly shows resemblance to the old Talbot Hound that lies in his ancestry. This one is taking his ease, making use of the "arm rest", in typical hound-like fashion!

his nose to the ground and giving voice when he locates quarry.

Origins and History

A descendant of the old Talbot Hound that was known in England in the 11th century and subsequently the Bloodhound and American Foxhound, the original work of the Black and Tan Coonhound was to trail possum and raccoons. One of many tracking breeds that have been developed in the USA, six different Coonhounds have been developed here. He has the courage and stamina to hunt deer, bear and mountain lion, hunting by scent and working the trail with determination. This breed was accepted for American Kennel Club Registration in 1945 and since 1995

has been recorded under the Foundation Stock Serve Programme.

Exercise and Grooming

This breed needs lots of outdoor activity.

BREED NOTES

SIZE	GROOMING
✔ ✔ ✔	✔
EXERCISE	LIFESPAN
✔ ✔ ✔	✔ ✔

A
B
C
D
E
F
G
H
I
J
K
L
M
N
O
P
Q
R
S
T
U
V
W
X
Y
Z

Black Russian Terrier

Average height: dogs – 25.5-28 inches; bitches – 25-27 inches
Average weight:

Appearance
This breed has massive bone structure and well-developed muscles, with tight, elastic skin that shows no folds or dewlap. The coat is black, but can carry some grey hairs. It is rough, hard and very dense. With a moustache on his upper lip, a beard on his lower one and eyebrows that are rough and bristled, he is a very commanding fellow indeed.

Characteristics
An energetic breed with stable temperament, the Black Russian should never be timid, fearful or over excitable. He is confident, enduring and courageous, intelligent and assertive. He is, though, wary of strangers and has strong protective instincts. Owners of this breed should have plenty of experience in handling dogs and be willing and able to train the dog sensibly whilst still in its youth.

Origins and History
The Black Russian Terrier was born of dire necessity, for Russia suffered great losses to the dog population at the close of World War II. Many different breeds were involved in the make-up of this breed, including the Giant Schnauzer, Newfoundland, Rottweiler and Airedale Terrier, as well as some local breeds. By 1955, second and third generation Black Russians were exhibited. The Russians had succeeded in creating a sturdily built military dog that was hardy and strong. He was used by the Red Army to guard military installations, border troops and prison camps, and was also used by the police. Now he carries out many functions including guard duty and search and rescue work. The breed was admitted to the American Kennel Club as recently as 2004.

Health Issues
Health problems that can affect the Black Russian Terrier are hip and elbow dysplasia and if not checked regularly, the ears may be susceptible to otitis.

Exercise and Grooming
This breed needs a good amount of exercise to keep its muscles in tone and to keep the breed's lively mind active. When Black Russians are

Left: A fine specimen of a correctly constructed, well-presented Black Russian.

BREED NOTES	
SIZE	GROOMING
✓ ✓ ✓	✓ ✓ ✓
EXERCISE	LIFESPAN
✓ ✓ ✓	✓ ✓

Johnson

A
B
C
D
E
F
G
H
I
J
K
L
M
N
O
P
Q
R
S
T
U
V
W
X
Y
Z

being exercised in public places, owners should be sure that they are in full control. The Black Russian Terrier needs to be groomed each week, but professional grooming is necessary at least every six weeks and trimming is necessary at least twice each year.

Above: Massive bone structure and well developed muscles make this a commanding breed.

Bloodhound

Average height: dogs – 25-27 inches; bitches – 23-25 inches
Average weight: dogs – 90-100 pounds; bitches – 80-100 pounds

Appearance
With his incredible sense of smell, the Bloodhound is perhaps the most easily recognizable of any of the scenthound breeds. The Bloodhound is notable for his sad expression and long, low-set ears, giving him a dignified, noble expression denoting solemnity, wisdom and power. His skin is

BREED NOTES

SIZE	GROOMING
✓	✓
✓	
✓	

EXERCISE	LIFESPAN
✓	✓
✓	
✓	

Left: The Bloodhound's sense of smell is extremely sensitive.

extremely loose, especially so around the head and neck, hanging in deep folds. Colors are black and tan, liver and tan or red. He may also have a small amount of white on the chest and on the tip of the tail.

Characteristics
This is a very affectionate dog with a gentle, sensitive nature. He gets along well with other dogs and seems especially fond of children. Although he can be a little shy he is wonderfully loyal and a great family companion. He does respond to commands, but in a leisurely, deliberate way.

Origins and History
It is difficult to ascertain how far

back the history of the Bloodhound reaches, but some authorities believe the breed was known prior to the Christian era. In the third century AD a dog was described that was unrivaled for its scenting powers and determination to stay on the trail until the quarry was located. Certainly the Bloodhound appeared in Europe long before the crusades. The English elite were at the forefront of developing the breed for use when hunting on horseback.

First used to hunt stag, the breed later became legendary as a hound used to track down criminals, fugitives and those who had simply got lost. He is a tireless tracker. The breed has been established in America for over a century and testimony of a Bloodhound's man trailing results is acceptable in almost any court.

Health Issues
The Bloodhound is considered

Above: Mother and baby.

relatively free from inherited health problems, but is susceptible to joint problems which are especially likely to occur if this hound becomes too heavy, or if he is over-exercised at a young age. Hip and elbow dysplasia can also occur. Eyes and ears need special attention as they easily gather dust and debris, which can lead to infection.

A
B
C
D
E
F
G
H
I
J
K
L
M
N
O
P
Q
R
S
T
U
V
W
X
Y
Z

Above: The Bloodhound has a thoroughly stately air.

Left: This super Bloodhound beat all other exhibits in the Hound Group at Crufts!

Exercise and Grooming

A high energy breed, a Bloodhound needs at least two hours of exercise each day, except during the growth stage of puppyhood when too much exercise is detrimental. Any exercise area should be well fenced, for because this hound is so good at tracking, it will wander off in pursuit of a scent if not restrained. Regular brushing is needed to maintain his smooth, short coat. Eyes should be wiped daily and ears checked regularly, especially during warm weather.

Bluetick Coonhound

Average height: dogs – 24-30 inches; bitches – 23-28 inches
Average weight: dogs – 55-100 pounds; bitches – 45-80 pounds

Appearance

Strong and deep-chested with a typically houndy expression and fairly long ears, the Bluetick Coonhound combines power with agility and endurance. He has a pleasantly pleading expression and almost round, dark brown eyes. The square muzzle is well-proportioned with width of the skull. The chest is large and very deep, with a girth of some 26 to 35 inches in males, and in bitches 23 to 32 inches. The smooth, glossy, medium coarse coat lies close to the body and the dark blue, mottled coat color is impressive. More blue than black is preferred and blue ticking should predominate over white in the body coat. There are tan dots over the eyes and on the cheeks, with dark red ticking on other parts of the body and legs.

Characteristics

The Bluetick is kind and self-assured. This is an intelligent, pleasing hound that is an equally fine companion for a day at home or a night of hunting. He makes for an excellent family pet and shares a lot of characteristics in common with the Black and Tan Coonhound.

Origins and History

The Bluetick Coonhound was created by crossing French hounds, foxhounds, curs and English Coonhounds. Its color indicates that the Grand Bleu de Gascogne was one of the various French hounds used. Ancestors that had come over to America were thought by the hunters to be too slow for the trail, but when cross-bred with American hounds their hunting abilities increased. In 1945 the Bluetick broke away from the other hounds,

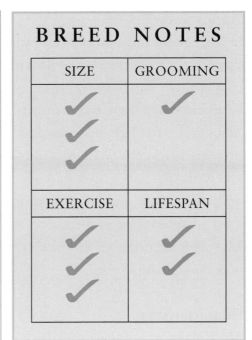

BREED NOTES	
SIZE	GROOMING
✔✔✔	✔
EXERCISE	LIFESPAN
✔✔✔	✔✔

creating a reputation of its own. This is a cold-nosed hunter that trees hard and long, and is admired for its endurance on the trail. A famous owner was George Washington who likened the breed's musical voice to "the bells of Moscow".

Health Issues

Although a relatively healthy breed, health problems of which owners should be aware include eye problems, hip dysplasia, bloat, hypothyroidism and luxating patella.

Exercise and Grooming

This breed's energy levels are fairly average, so a 40 minute walk each day should suffice. However, the Bluetick will also need plenty of free exercise each day in a safe, fenced area. Grooming the Bluetick is not difficult, but the coat should be brushed regularly

A
B
C
D
E
F
G
H
I
J
K
L
M
N
O
P
Q
R
S
T
U
V
W
X
Y
Z

Bolognese

Average height: dogs – 10.5-12 inches; bitches – 10-11 inches
Average weight: dogs – 3-5 pounds

Appearance

Small, square and compact this little breed has a long, pure white flocked coat without curl. It covers the entire head and body and is shown in natural state. Lips, eye rims and nose are black, the eyes large, round and dark. The ears are set on high and are long and pendulous, giving a broad appearance to the head. The tail is carried over the back but may drop when at rest.

Characteristics

The Bolognese is a delightful Toy dog that is an excellent companion being vivacious and playful. An intelligent breed that simply loves the company of his family and gets along well with children, he can be rather reserved with strangers. This is a very serious, enterprising breed that can be jaunty and happy, or calm and apparently rather melancholy when the mood takes him. Although this is not a "yappy" breed, because their hearing is so acute, they will bark at strange or unfamiliar noises.

Origins and History

The Bolognese, one of the Bichon group, was valued in Italy as early as the 11th and 12th centuries, becoming a favourite of the nobility during the Renaissance, because of his grace and charm. The breed was developed in Bologna. In 1668 Cosimo de Medici sent eight Bolognese to Belgium where they were to be given as gifts to several of the wealthy and influential families of Brussels. There have been well-known owners in various countries, amongst them Catherine the Great of Russia (1729-1796), Madame De Pompadour (1721-1764) and Empress Maria Theresa

BREED NOTES

SIZE	GROOMING
✔	✔ ✔ ✔
EXERCISE	LIFESPAN
✔	✔ ✔

Opposite: A bundle of fun, with striking black lips, nose and eye rims.

Below left: The coat of the Bolognese covers the entire head and body.

Below: Three Bolognese are small enough to walk together.

of Austria. In time the breed became virtually extinct but recently a few dedicated breeders have restored the Bolognese to its current popularity. The breed was first shown in England in 1990 and in America it has been recorded in the Foundation Stock Service since 1999.

Health Issues

The Bolognese is generally a healthy breed but can be hypoallergenic.

Exercise and Grooming

This is an intelligent little dog that is fairly easy to train and loves to please. The Bolognese therefore enjoys human companionship and enjoys a lead walk or an energetic game. The single coat is never trimmed or clipped, but left natural. This is a single coat (without undercoat) and is not-shedding, so requires regular grooming to prevent mats forming. The occasional bath is necessary to get the Bolognese looking in tip-top condition.

A
B
C
D
E
F
G
H
I
J
K
L
M
N
O
P
Q
R
S
T
U
V
W
X
Y
Z

Border Collie

Average height: dogs – 19-22 inches; bitches – 18-21 inches
Average weight: dogs – 30-65 pounds

Appearance

As can be seen from its wide weight range, bone structure in this breed varies considerably; bone must be strong, medium being correct, but lighter bone is preferred over heavy. The weather-resistant coat of the Border Collie has a top coat that can be straight or wavy, with a soft, short, dense undercoat. There are two coat types, rough (which is medium length without being excessive) or smooth. The color seen most usually is black and white, but other colors include red and white, Tri-color, liver, blue merle, red merle, yellow or white, with small amounts of brown, black or red. Eye color also differs, from amber to dark brown and sometimes even blue.

Characteristics

The highly intelligent Border Collie is very suitable for training, possessing single-mindedness for the task in hand. Although

Below: Working on the farm.

BREED NOTES

SIZE	GROOMING
✔ ✔	✔ ✔
EXERCISE	**LIFESPAN**
✔ ✔ ✔	✔ ✔

affectionate to owners and friends, he can be reserved with strangers. A well-trained Border Collie can be a wonderful companion, but it should never be forgotten that this is essentially a working dog.

Origins and History

Established around a century ago in the countryside of the English/Scottish border, the Border Collie has since developed into a remarkable breed, capable of working long days on rugged terrain. The breed has remarkable instinct and an uncanny ability to reason. Known throughout the world as the premier sheepherding

Right: A Border Collie is always ready for action.

Below: A show Border Collie, whose coat is in tip-top condition.

Below right: Relaxing in the garden.

A
B
C
D
E
F
G
H
I
J
K
L
M
N
O
P
Q
R
S
T
U
V
W
X
Y
Z

dog, the Border Collie is used in many different countries to great advantage. The breed obtained full recognition with the American Kennel Club in 1995.

Left: This little pup will soon mature into a worthy companion.

Below: Playing is such fun when you're young!

Opposite: Enjoying a frolic.

Opposite bottom left: This puppy will grow up to be a good friend for his young mistress.

Opposite bottom right: This unusual coat coloring is highly attractive.

A
B
C
D
E
F
G
H
I
J
K
L
M
N
O
P
Q
R
S
T
U
V
W
X
Y
Z

Health Issues

Although this is a hardy breed they can be susceptible to allergies and to skin conditions, as well as hip dysplasia, osteochondrosis dissecans (OCD), eye diseases, epilepsy, deafness and ceroid lipofuscinosis (CL). The latter is also known as 'Storage Disease' and is a rare inherited condition that affects the body's nerve cells; this normally displays itself at between one and two years of age.

Right: A working partnership.

Below left: All dressed up in his bow tie for a special event.

Below right: This Border has dark brown eyes, but eye color can vary in this breed.

Because this is such an active breed, it can also be prone to athletic injuries.

Exercise and Grooming

The Border Collie has to be kept active, both mentally and physically, otherwise it is all too easy to have a difficult dog on your hands! Activities the Border Collie enjoys are agility, flyball, obedience work, herding and even dancing to music. His is an easy coat to maintain with regular combing and brushing to keep it in good condition. At moulting time, extra care is needed, especially in the removal of the soft, thick undercoat.

Left: Stainless steel feeding bowls are hygienic and easy to clean.

Below: Two very different coat colors.

A
B
C
D
E
F
G
H
I
J
K
L
M
N
O
P
Q
R
S
T
U
V
W
X
Y
Z

Border Terrier

Average height: 11-16 inches;
Average weight: dogs – 13-15.5 pounds; bitches – 11.5-14 pounds

Appearance

An active terrier with medium bone, the Border is strongly put together, displaying endurance and agility. He is rather narrow in shoulder, body and quarters. The otter-like head is distinctive and his keen eye is dark hazel, full of fire and intelligence. The moderately broad skull is flat and his V-shaped ears drop forward. Teeth are strong in proportion to overall size. The Border Terrier has a weather-resistant, close-fitting, coat that repels dirt with its hard, wiry outercoat and soft undercoat. The color is red, grizzle and tan, blue and tan or wheaten.

Characteristics

Good tempered, affectionate and easily trained, the Border is the most popular of the Terrier breeds. Always on the alert, he is active, agile, determined and fearless. Providing they are introduced at a young age, Border Terriers can generally get along well with the family's other dogs and even cats. However the situation is likely to be different with birds and other small animals such as hampsters, guinea pigs and rabbits. A Border

BREED NOTES

SIZE	GROOMING
✓	✓ ✓
EXERCISE	**LIFESPAN**
✓ ✓	✓ ✓

Below: Waiting for a game.

Above: *A well proportioned, successful show dog.*

Right: *Young pup ready to tackle the world*

may also not appreciate the neighbor's cat!

Origins and History

Coming from the border land between England and Scotland, on either side of the Cheviot Hills, the breed was developed by farmers to hunt fox, otter and vermin. Still the Border Terrier's most important characteristics are those necessary for his performance. With sufficient leg length to follow a horse, he is also small enough to follow a fox to ground, either going underground to bolt the fox, or to remain with the fox, barking to indicate location. A useful dog for controlling vermin, in

A
B
C
D
E
F
G
H
I J
J
K
L
M
N
O
P
Q
R
S
T
U
V
W
X
Y
Z

A
C
D
E
F
G
H
I
J
K
L
M
N
O
P
Q
R
S
T
U
V
W
X
Y
Z

Opposite: 'This is a great vantage point we've found!'

Right: Relaxing in the shade

the 18th century these dogs were expected to find their own food, so had to be good hunters to survive. The English Kennel Club recognised the breed in 1920, but it had existed at least since the nineteenth century. The first breed registration in the USA was in 1930.

Health Issues

This generally a healthy breed but some genetic problems can occur. These include hip dysplasia, Progressive Retinal Atrophy (PRA), juvenile cataracts and seizures. Other concerns are heart defects, allergies and undescended testicles. Anesthesia can also be problematic, so this should be discussed with a vet prior to surgery.

Exercise and Grooming

Plenty of play and exercise is essential for this active breed, and a thirty minute walk is also appreciated by this game little fellow. Activities he enjoys are flyball, agility, earthdog tests, tracking and obedience classes. Although not a high maintenance breed, the Border Terrier needs regular grooming. The coat does shed, so thorough brushing should be done each week. Stripping, ideally by hand or otherwise with a stripping tool, needs to be done twice a year.

Left: The Border Terrier has an otter-like head.

A
B
C
D
E
F
G
H
I
J
K
L
M
N
O
P
Q
R
S
T
U
V
W
X
Y
Z

A
B
C
D
E
F
G
H
I
J
K
L
M
N
O
P
Q
R
S
T
U
V
W
X
Y
Z

Borzoi

Average height: dogs – 28 inches (minimum); bitches – 26 inches (minimum)
Average weight: dogs – 75-105 pounds; bitches – 55-90 pounds

Appearance

This elegant, aristocratic member of the dog world has a graceful curve over the loin, making the Borzoi capable of great speed and agility.

Males are generally larger than bitches with a longer, more profuse coat, which can be any color or combination of colors. On the head, ears and front of legs, the coat is

BREED NOTES

SIZE	GROOMING
✓ ✓ ✓	✓ ✓

EXERCISE	LIFESPAN
✓ ✓ ✓	✓ ✓

Johnson

short and smooth. The Borzoi has remarkable muscular power. His skull is slightly domed, long and narrow, inclined to be Roman-nosed. Jaws are long, powerful and deep, whilst the dark eyes show and intelligent but rather soft expression. His long, low-set tail is carried in a graceful curve.

Characteristics

The Borzoi has a quiet, gentle nature and dignified manner. Although aloof with strangers he is devoted to his family, being affectionate and loyal. Highly prized for his beauty, intelligence and gentle nature, this breed makes a wonderful companion. Calm and quiet indoors, he is great lure courser and enjoys long runs and

Left: All the distinctive attributes of a sighthound.

Above: '*I had a great game in the water, but now I feel a bit of a mess!*'

cold weather. Although he generally gets along well with children he is not an ideal playmate for youngsters.

Origins and History
Known until 1936 as the Russian Wolfhound, the Borzoi originated in the 17th century when the Russian aristocracy crossed Arabian greyhounds with a heavily-coated Russian breed. The first breed standard was drawn up in 1650. A member of the sighthound family, the Borzoi was bred to course hare, fox and wolves on open terrain. It is believed that the first Borzoi that came to America was brought over from England in 1889 and in 1903 three visits were made to Russia to import hounds from the Perchino & Woronzova kennels. In Western states the Borzoi is still used by farmers to control coyote populations.

Health Issues
A very healthy breed in general, like

A
B
C
D
E
F
G
H
I
J
K
L
M
N
O
P
Q
R
S
T
U
V
W
X
Y
Z

Above: The Borzoi has remarkable muscular power.

all other breeds some genetic disorders raise their heads from time to time. These include Progressive Retinal Atrophy (PRA) and Osteocondritis dissecans (OCD). Borzoi owners should also be aware that bloat can affect this deep-chested breed and, like other sighthounds, the Borzoi is sensitive to a number of anesthetics, so it is important to discuss this with a vet prior to surgery.

Exercise and Grooming

The Borzoi needs plenty of space outdoors to run around in a safe, fenced yard, ideally with a daily walk on a leash too. Running loose near busy roads or streets can be dangerous. The Borzoi enjoys racing games and outdoor activities, as well agility events and lure coursing. Regular grooming is needed each

Opposite top: He is inclined to be Roman-nosed.

Opposite left: In the showring.

Opposite right: Elegantly taking his ease.

day to remove loose hair and dirt from the coat. The Borzoi is not generally bathed very frequently. Hair between the pads of the feet should be carefully trimmed.

A
B
C
D
E
F
G
H
I
J
K
L
M
N
O
P
Q
R
S
T
U
V
W
X
Y
Z

Boston Terrier

Average height: dogs – 15-17 inches
Average weight: Three weight divisions: Under 15 pounds; 15 pounds and under 20 pounds; 20 pounds and not exceeding 25 pounds.

Appearance

The Boston Terrier has distinctive features; a square skull, flat on top, free from wrinkles, flat cheeks and an abrupt brow. The expression is kind and alert, indicating a high degree of intelligence. Large, round, dark eyes are set well apart and the small ears, carried erect, can be either natural or cropped. Length of leg must balance with the length of body to give the Boston Terrier its square appearance. A sturdy dog, the Boston must not appear to be either spindly or coarse and bone and muscle are in proportion to weight and structure. The short, smooth coat is bright and fine in texture, its color black, brindle or seal (appearing black but with a red cast when viewed in bright light), with white markings.

Characteristics

Nicknamed 'the American gentleman', this is a friendly, lively dog, noted for his excellent disposition and high intelligence. Kind, gentle and affectionate, the Boston Terrier is a devoted

BREED NOTES

SIZE	GROOMING
✔	✔
EXERCISE	**LIFESPAN**
✔ ✔	✔ ✔

Miniature Bulldog and the French Bulldog, the Boston Terrier is native to the USA. In 1889, fanciers formed the American Bull Terrier Club (the former name of Boston Terriers), but because of opposition from both Bulldog and Bull Terrier fanciers, the name was changed in 1891. Recognised by the American Kennel Club in 1893, between 1929 and 1935, this was the most popular breed in the country.

Health Issues

Health problems encountered in this breed include hypothyroidism, eye diseases, patella luxation, deafness and demodetic mange. Because of the Boston Terrier's short head it can be

Left In the early 1930s this was the most popular breed in America.

Below: It's easy to see why the Boston is nicknamed "the American gentleman"

Opposite: The Boston Terrier is a sturdy dog, neither spindly nor coarse.

companion to adults and children, and usually gets along well with other dogs and pets. A natural watchdog, although not a fighter he is able to take care of himself. It is important to note that Boston Terriers must be kept indoors. Their short, sleek coats do not protect them from the cold and in hot weather their short muzzles make them susceptible to heat distress.

Origins and History

The result of cross-breeding between the Bulldog and now extinct White English Terrier, subsequently the

A
B
C
D
E
F
G
H
I
J
K
L
M
N
O
P
Q
R
S
T
U
V
W
X
Y
Z

Above: A distinctive feature is the square skull, flat on top.

Above right The best of friends.

Right: In training.

affected by brachycephalic airway obstruction syndrome (BAOS); apart from snuffling and snorting, some may experience increasingly noisy breathing, coughing, gagging and collapsing episodes, with a decrease in tolerance to exercise. In time, this causes increased strain on the heart.

Exercise and Grooming

The Boston Terrier loves to play and enjoys competing in obedience, agility, flyball and tracking events. However, his exercise needs are moderate and no long walks are necessary. The short, smooth coat does not require a lot of attention, just occasional brushing.

Above: The short, smooth coat is bright and fine.

Above right: In the US, ears may be natural or cropped.

Below: Good profile showing the thick, muscular neck.

A
B
C
D
E
F
G
H
I
J
K
L
M
N
O
P
Q
R
S
T
U
V
W
X
Y
Z

Bouvier des Flandres

Average height: dogs – 24.5-27.5 inches; bitches – 23.5-26.5 inches
Average weight: dogs – 77-88 pounds; bitches – 60-77 pounds

Appearance

The harsh, double coat of the Bouvier des Flandres protects him in all weathers and gives him his notably rugged appearance. The outer hairs of the top-coat, which is about 2.5 inches long, are rough and harsh; the undercoat is fine and dense. Powerfully and compactly built, he is strongly boned giving the impression of great strength without heaviness or clumsiness. Colour is from fawn to black, through salt and pepper, gray or brindle. The Bouvier's head is impressive in size, accentuated by mustache and beard.

Characteristics

The Bouvier does well in most environments for he enjoys human companionship. This is a versatile breed that is intelligent, alert and agile, making him suitable for many forms of activity, including farm work, for which he was bred. The Bouvier is mentally very alert and has a fine sense of smell. He is even tempered and should never be shy or over-aggressive. This is a

BREED NOTES

SIZE	GROOMING
✔	✔
✔	✔
✔	✔

EXERCISE	LIFESPAN
✔	✔
✔	✔
✔	

Left: The Bouvier's head is of impressive size.

Opposite: This breed is suited to many activities, including farm work.

A
B
C
D
E
F
G
H
I
J
K
L
M
N
O
P
Q
R
S
T
U
V
W
X
Y
Z

calm, rational dog that is prudently bold, playful and outgoing with people he knows.

Origins and History

The Bouvier des Flandres originated, as his name implies in Flanders, Belgium and literally means "cow dog of Flanders". This is because the breed was used for herding and driving cattle and most of the early breeders were farmers, butchers or cattle merchants who simply needed a dog suitable to help

Left: This playful puppy still has a lot of growing to do.

Below: This Champion displays all the attributes of the breed.

not established until 1963

Health Issues

Heath problems of which owners should be aware in this breed are hip dysplasia, which is prevalent health concern in the Bouvier, bloat or gastric torsion, eye problems such as cataracts and glaucoma, and thyroid problems.

Exercise and Grooming

With highly capable mental and physical ability, the Bouvier needs to be kept active. He enjoys many activities including obedience competition, agility, carting, herding and tracking. The Bouvier has also been successfully used as guide dog for the blind. The coat may be trimmed slightly to accentuate the body line, but he should not be overarrimmed. Weekly grooming with a brush and comb is needed.

Left The Bouvier is suited to most environments.

Below: This is an even tempered breed.

them with their work. This resulted in early Bouviers not being uniform in size, weight or color. Things began to move forward in 1910 and by the time the First World War broke out the Bouvier was making great progress, but few people succeeded in keeping their dogs during the war. In those troubled times he had been used as an ambulance and messenger dog. The Bouvier was recognized by the American Kennel Club in 1929 and accepted to its Stud Book in 1931 but the American breed club was

A
B
C
D
E
F
G
H
I
J
K
L
M
N
O
P
Q
R
S
T
U
V
W
X
Y
Z

A
B
C
D
E
F
G
H
I
J
K
L
M
N
O
P
Q
R
S
T
U
V
W
X
Y
Z

Boxer

Average height: dogs – 23-25 inches; bitches – 21.5-23.5 inches
Average weight: dogs – 70 pounds; bitches – 60 pounds

BREED NOTES

SIZE	GROOMING
✓	✓
✓	
✓	

EXERCISE	LIFESPAN
✓	✓
✓	✓
✓	

Left: The Boxer's muzzle appears slightly pushed in.

Opposite: 'We have everything we could wish for in our garden.'

on the forehead to display expressions of curiosity, excitement, happiness, surprise or even sadness. In America ears are customarily cropped, but may be left uncropped. The short, shiny coat fits tight to his body and comes in varying shades of fawn and brindle. This is surely a breed that combines strength, agility, elegance and style.

Characteristics

Alert, dignified and self-confident, the Boxer is also energetic, playful and fun-loving, both with family and friends. Indeed this is an even-tempered, loyal and loving family companion. However, his wariness

Appearance

A squarely-built dog, the Boxer's nose is broad and the top of his muzzle appears slightly pushed in, leaving the jaw undershot. The

markings on the face enhance the Boxer expression. His twinkling black eyes give evidence of his intelligence and emotion and when the eras are erect, wrinkles appear

A
B
C
D
E
F
G
H
I
J
K
L
M
N
O
P
Q
R
S
T
U
V
W
X
Y
Z

of strangers makes him an excellent guard. Due to his stubbornness at times, early training in obedience is highly recommended.

Origins and History

The Boxer was developed in Germany using various different breeds, amongst them the Bulldog, Great Dane and the Brabant Bullenbeisser, which is a mastiff-type dog. Originally bred to hunt and to hold prey, the breed was later used as a guard dog. The first American Kennel Club registration

Below: Markings on the face enhance the expression.

Opposite top left: Baby puppy whose feet indicate how big he will grow.

Opposite top right: Cropped ears.

Opposite bottom: A high quality show specimen.

A
B
C
D
E
F
G
H
I
J
K
L
M
N
O
P
Q
R
S
T
U
V
W
X
Y
Z

of a Boxer was in 1904, but not until about 1940 did people in America take a real interest in the breed, since when popularity has risen enormously. Boxers are now often used to do search and rescue and therapy work. Because of his natural guarding instincts, the Boxer is also sometimes trained as a Schutzhund.

Health Issues

The Boxer can be prone to heart disease, which can be inherited or caused by bacterial, viral or parasitic agents. Cancer has also occurred in the breed, and brain tumors can cause seizures later in life. Other conditions that can affect this breed include dysplasia and

Right: Wearing a harness, suited to a dog who pulls on the leash when out walking.

Left: Crop-eared Boxers of different colors.

hypothyroidism. The Boxer is sensitive to temperature extremes and does not enjoy draughts, summer heat, or cold.

Exercise and Grooming

Exercise should be provided in a safely fenced are or on a leash. The Boxer enjoys work and enjoys competing in obedience, tracking and agility. The short, smooth coat can be kept in good condition by brushing occasionally, but he has a natural tendency to keep himself clean. Bathing can be done occasionally.

Opposite: A well earned rest.

A
B
C
D
E
F
G
H
I
J
K
L
M
N
O
P
Q
R
S
T
U
V
W
X
Y
Z

Boykin Spaniel

Average height: dogs – 15.5-18 inches; bitches – 14-16.5 inches
Average weight: dogs – 30-40 pounds; bitches – 25-30 pounds

Appearance

The Boykin Spaniel has a medium coat that is flat to somewhat curly; its color is solid, rich liver, or dark chocolate. Light feathering is acceptable on legs, feet, ears, chest and belly, but a short, straight coat without feathering is also acceptable. The head is impressive, not heavy nor snipey, and is in balance with the rest of the dog. The forehead is covered with short, smooth hair. In keeping with this breed's coat color, the eyes are yellow to brown and the nose is dark liver, with well-opened nostrils for good scenting. Jaws are of sufficient length to allow the dog to carry game and a close scissors bite (in which the lower teeth touch behind the upper incisors) is preferred. An even bite (teeth meeting edge to edge) is acceptable, but not an over or undershot jaw.

Characteristics

An excellent companion, hunting dog and family friend, the Boykin Spaniel likes to join in with family life, but never looses his hunting instinct. Agile, intelligent and easily trained, he is always friendly, eager to please and gets along very well with children. Early socialization, though, is important. The breed is an instinctive swimmer and the often-heard expression "a Boykin

Right: An excellent hunting companion.

doesn't rock the boat" probably describes him in a nutshell!

Origins and History

Bred originally by hunters in South Carolina during the early 20th century, the Boykin Spaniel was developed as the ideal dog for hunting wild turkeys in the Wateree River Swamp. As time has progressed he has adapted beautifully to the dove fields and duck marshes with abilities both in retrieving and flushing. Apart from a stray dog found wandering near a Methodist church, said to be the forerunner of all Boykin Spaniels today, other early ancestors include the Chesapeake Bay Retriever, Springer Spaniel, Cocker Spaniel, and the American Water Spaniel. Today the breed is found throughout the USA, with a higher concentration on the Atlantic Seaboard. The Boykin Spaniel joins the American Kennel Club's Miscellaneous Group in 2008.

Health Issues

Some of the health problems encountered in the Boykin Spaniel are hip dysplasia, allergies and eye problems, amongst which the most commonly diagnosed is cataract.

BREED NOTES

SIZE	GROOMING
✔ ✔	✔ ✔
EXERCISE	**LIFESPAN**
✔ ✔ ✔	✔ ✔

Bracco Italiano

Average height: dogs – 22.75-26.25 inches; bitches – 21.75-24.5 inches
Average weight: 55-88 pounds

Appearance

A strong, well-balanced, powerful hunting dog, the Bracco Italiano has a noble appearance. He is almost square, well muscled and with a deep chest. His distinctive, sculpted head is chiselled under the eyes, which are fairly large, with a soft expression. Ear leathers extend to the tip of the nose and are supple, folded inward. The tail when docked covers the genitals and is thick at the base, straight and with a tendency to taper. When undocked it is slightly curved, but never held high or carried over the back. The short, dense coat is glossy, the skin tough, but elastic. Pigment is never black, but pale pink to dark brown, depending on the coat color.

Characteristics

The Bracco is reasonably easy to train, just so long as there is consistency and gentle firmness in the training regime. This is an intelligent, faithful and loving dog that gets along well with children and other dogs. He is ideally suited to a family that enjoys an outdoor

BREED NOTES

SIZE	GROOMING
✔ ✔ ✔	✔
EXERCISE	LIFESPAN
✔ ✔ ✔	✔ ✔

Left: The Bracco has a distinctive, sculpted head.

lifestyle and is a hardy and adaptable dog, gentle and even tempered.

Origins and History

The Bracco Italiano is believed to be one of the classic, ancient pointers, essentially from Italy's northern areas. The breed has certainly been around since the Middle Ages, and during the Renaissance Period became widespread. Held in high regard by the nobility, the Bracco was used by the aristocracy to hunt feathered game, a sport exclusive to people of this rank. The Gonzaga and Medici families bred Bracco Italiani and their puppies were highly sought after by nobles and royalty. Over the centuries the breed has developed so that instead of

A
B
C
D
E
F
G
H
I
J
K
L
M
N
O
P
Q
R
S
T
U
V
W
X
Y
Z

Above: Ever alert

hunting with nets, it became adapted to modern methods, using the gun. It is probable that the white and orange variety originated in Piedmont, this being somewhat lighter in frame than the brown and white from Lombardy. The translation of the breed's name merely means "Italian Pointer".

Health Issues
Some Bracco Italiani have been known to suffer from allergies and, conversely, a few owners have been discovered to have an allergic reaction to their dogs.

Exercise and Grooming
Now used as a Gundog and as a companion animal, the Bracco should have a couple of hours of exercise daily, some of it on a leash. The smooth, short coat is easy to care for, but dead hairs need to be removed with a comb once or twice each week.

Below: A fine profile example of the breed.

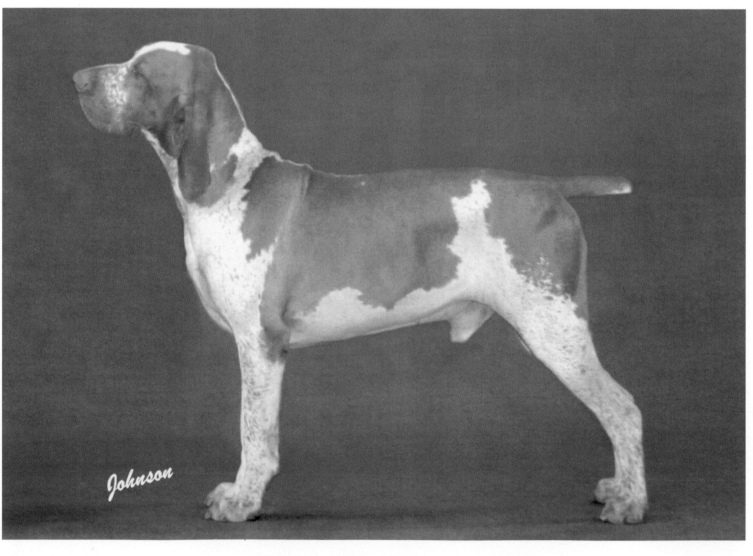

Brazilian Terrier

Average height: dogs – 13.75-15.75 inches; bitches – 13-15 inches
Average weight: 15-20 pounds (22 pounds maximum)

Above: The Brazilian Terrier is descended from Fox Terrier-types.

Appearance

In looks the Brazilian Terrier is typical of dogs descended from Fox Terrier-types. The skull is flat and triangular and the muzzle is moderately tapered. Ears are dropped and the neck rather long. His limbs have been developed for running and jumping, giving a clean-cut, sporty look. The body is a little on the square side, but the rounded edges rather complement this somewhat stocky look. The tail may be docked or left natural, in which case it is curved. The short, smooth coat is tri-colored; predominantly white with head and saddle markings of black and tan, but brown and blue are also accepted.

Characteristics

He is perky, alert, intelligent and frisky; he loves to play and when with his owner will do this all the time! The Brazilian Terrier also enjoys barking and digging, and is a great ratter! This is especially useful on rural ranches in Brazil, where he tracks rodents before the kill. This breed is absolutely fearless and highly spirited. Although obedient, he needs an owner who is as strong willed as he is himself, for he needs firm, experienced training. This breed is very good at figuring out how to get what he wants! He is friendly and generally kind to children, but cannot be trusted with other animals. He is unlikely to take kindly to strangers, so when house guests visit, the dog must be made aware that this is an invited guest before he impedes on the dog's territory.

Origins and History

The Brazilian Terrier came about by combining several small breeds including the Fox Terrier and Jack Russell, which was taken to Brazil from Europe in the 19th century. The Miniature Pinscher and large Chihuahuas are also thought to have been involved. Although it is popular in Brazil, the breed is almost unknown outside its homeland. This terrier has been around for around 100 years, but was not registered until 1973. It is a hunter, used in a pack and also as a single hunter; when in a pack these game little dogs surround their prey and terrorize it into exhaustion. He is also an excellent vermin catcher.

Health Issues

Little is documented about health issues for this breed, but the average life expectancy is 12 to 14 years.

Exercise and Grooming

The Brazilian Terrier needs both mental and physical activity if he is to be happy. Without the opportunity to exercise his muscles and his brain he can become restless and destructive. Because he loves to explore and has a strong hunting instinct, he should not be let off the leash in an open place unless he has been fully trained. His short, smooth coat is easy to care fore, needing just a quick brush and comb every now and again.

BREED NOTES

SIZE	GROOMING
✔ ✔	✔
EXERCISE	**LIFESPAN**
✔ ✔ ✔	✔ ✔

A
B
C
D
E
F
G
H
I
J
K
L
M
N
O
P
Q
R
S
T
U
V
W
X
Y
Z

Briard

Average height: dogs – 23-27 inches; bitches – 22-25.5 inches
Average weight: 70-90 pounds

Appearance
Vigorous , alert and powerful without coarseness, the Briard is strong in bone and muscle. The Briard's substantial head is covered with hair that arches into eyebrows and forms a beard under the chin. Ears may be left natural, in which case they are lifted slightly when alert, or they may be cropped. Occasionally blue-grey is seen, but the most usual coat colors are tawny or black. The long outer coat is coarse, hard and dry, lying flat against the body but forming a slight wave. Below this is a fine, tight undercoat. All uniform colors are permitted except white The Briard's toes are strong, well-arched and compact and two dewclaws are required on each rear leg.

Characteristics
The Briard has been described as 'a heart of gold wrapped in fur', a lovely picture painted in words. Intelligent, loyal and eager to please he is naturally protective. In the home he is calm, but can work all day without tiring. He is devoted to home and family, especially children and although an independent thinker he is obedient, with an excellent memory. This breed is also an excellent guardian and watchdog. He can be somewhat

BREED NOTES

SIZE	GROOMING
✔	✔
	✔
	✔
EXERCISE	**LIFESPAN**
✔	✔
✔	✔
✔	

Below: An excellent specimen with natural ears

breed's numbers. Today the breed is a versatile herding dog, used to fetch, drive and to do boundary work, an ideal partner for the shepherd. He works quietly, circling, always eager and alert.

Health Issues

The Briard Club of America recommends testing for the following genetic disorders: hip dysplasia, Progressive Retinal Atrophy (PRA), von Willebrand's disease, hypothyroidism and night blindness. Bloat is another problem encountered by this breed.

Exercise and Grooming

As a working breed, the Briard always enjoys having a job to do so herding, guarding, agility, tracking or carting are suitable forms of exercise. He will enjoy a country walk, running ahead of you and then checking back to be sure you are still there! Dirt and water do not readily cling to the coat and if it is well-groomed it sheds very little. A coat kept in good condition requires about two hours' work on it each week.

aloof toward strangers and early training is strongly recommended.

Above and below: Show dog with cropped ears.

Origins and History

An ancient French herding breed that dates back to the 8th century, both Napoleon and the Emperor Charlemagne were believed to have owned Briards. The breed has been used to guard flocks and as a herding dog for many a long year, and was the official dog of the French army, used to carry supplies to the frontline, to search for wounded soldiers and as sentry dogs. Sadly many Briards were lost in both word wars, depleting the

A
B
C
D
E
F
G
H
I
J
K
L
M
N
O
P
Q
R
S
T
U
V
W
X
Y
Z

Britanny

Average height: 17.5-20.5 inches
Average weight: 30-40 pounds

Appearance

A compact, medium-sized dog, the Britanny is quite leggy, so as well as being agile he is a good ground coverer. He is strong, vigorous and energetic and a very quick mover. The dense coat is flat or wavy, but never curly. Ears carry a little fringe and the legs have some feathering. The skin is fine and fairly loose so that it rolls with briars and sticks. Colors are orange and white or liver and white, either clear or roan.

Below: The Brittany is a wonderful shooting dog.

Characteristics

The Brittany is recognized as a superb shooting dog and show dog, in addition to being a wonderful house dog and companion. He is typically friendly, alert and easy to please, loyal, obedient, very energetic and yet gentle. He is never mean or aggressive and thrives on love and attention. He works in the same manner as the Pointer, but without the range, pointing and

BREED NOTES

SIZE	GROOMING
✔✔	✔
EXERCISE	**LIFESPAN**
✔✔✔	✔✔

Johnson

Above: Pup pondering on what life holds ahead.

holding his game. In addition he retrieves both on land and on water and is said to absorb training more easily than some of the other pointing breeds. He has a keen nose and a very biddable disposition.

Origins and History

The Brittany originated as early as 150 AD in the French province of the same name. It is likely that dogs of Brittany and Wales shared their ancestry and developed similarly; indeed there is a remarkable resemblance between the Brittany and the Welsh Springer Spaniel. The Irish Setter as well as the French land spaniels are also thought to have played their part in the breed's make-up. Dogs of Brittany–type appeared in 17th century paintings and tapestries. The first tailless ancestor of today's Brittany is believed to have been bred in Pontou in the mid 19th century. The breed first came to the USA in 1931 and received approval from the American Kennel Club three years later. In France this breed is still used on fur and feather and in America is generally used on upland game.

Health Issues

Brittanys appear to have fewer

Above: He has a keen game sense.

genetically inherited diseases than many other breeds, but hip dysplasia, epilepsy, skin allergies and eye problems are not unknown.

Exercise and Grooming

This is a high energy sporting dog so needs at least an hour of good exercise every day. Hunting keeps him happy. Just taking a Brittany for a walk on a leash is insufficient. Coat-wise he is not high maintenance; a good brushing with a slicker brush once or twice each week is usually enough. This will take out any dead hair that has accumulated.

A
B
C
D
E
F
G
H
I
J
K
L
M
N
O
P
Q
R
S
T
U
V
W
X
Y
Z

Brussels Griffon

Average height: No height specified
Average weight: 8-10 pounds

Appearance

The Brussels Griffon has a delightful flat face, prominent chin and large, wide-set eyes giving him an almost human expression. This breed is undershot, meaning that the incisors of the lower jaw protrude over the upper incisors. The lower jaw is prominent, rather broad with an upward sweep but neither teeth nor tongue should show when the mouth is closed. His body is square and sturdy; the forelegs

Below: High quality black smooth male.

BREED NOTES

SIZE	GROOMING
✔	✔
	✔
EXERCISE	**LIFESPAN**
✔	✔
	✔

set moderately wide apart and he has strong, well muscled thighs. There

Below: A top winning Champion smooth.

are two coat types in this breed, rough and smooth. The rough coat is wiry and dense, the harder and more wiry the better, whilst the smooth coat is straight, short, tight and glossy, with no trace of wiry hair. Colors are red, belge, which is black and reddish brown mixed, black and tan, and black. The high-set tail is docked to about one-third.

A B C D E F G H I J K L M N O P Q R S T U V W X Y Z

A
B
C
D
E
F
G
H
I
J
K
L
M
N
O
P
Q
R
S
T
U
V
W
X
Y
Z

Characteristics

Intelligent, alert and sensitive, this breed is full of self-importance. The Brussels Griffon gets along well with children and other pets, always enjoying company. He is curious, mischievous, playful and can be easily trained in obedience.

Origins and History

During the early years of the 19th century coachmen in Belgium kept small wire-coated, terrier-type dogs in their stables as ratters. These dogs had developed from the German Affenpinscher and general street

Above: Moving to perfection.

Left: The Brussels Griffon has an almost human expression.

dogs, but other breeds were also used, amongst them the Pug, King Charles and Ruby Spaniel. This resulted in two coat types emerging on what was to become the Brussels Griffon. These were rough and smooth, the latter known also as the Brabancon in honor of Belgium's national anthem. The breed is now rarely used as a stable worker, but instead is a much loved companion dog, first recognised by the American Kennel Club in 1910.

Health Issues

The National Brussels Griffon Club recommends screening for hereditary eye defects, patella luxation and hip dysplasia.

Exercise and Grooming

This lively little breed likes plenty of play and will appreciate a walk on a leash. The smooth variety clearly has the easier coat to mange. This just needs a regular brush to keep it looking fresh and healthy. During the moulting season, more regular brushing and baths will be needed. For the rough, apart from regular brushing, the coat needs to be hand-stripped or trimmed about every three months. Hand-stripping (without scissors or clippers) is essential if a dog is to be shown.

Below: Black rough, curious, mischievous and playful.

Johnson

A
B
C
D
E
F
G
H
I
J
K
L
M
N
O
P
Q
R
S
T
U
V
W
X
Y
Z

Bull Terrier

Average height: 19-20 inches
Average weight: 45 pounds

Appearance

A strongly built, muscular dog, the Bull Terrier is symmetrical and active, with a keen, determined, intelligent expression. His egg-shaped head is very distinctive. It is long, strong and deep right to the end of the muzzle, but not coarse; the distance from the tip of the nose to the eyes should be perceptibly greater than that from the eyes to the top of the skull. Teeth meet in either a level or a scissors bite. The small, thin ears are placed closely together and must be capable of being held stiffly erect. The Bull Terrier's well-sunken eyes have a piercing glint and should never be blue. The tail is short, set on low, tapering to a point, and ideally should be carried horizontally. The Bull Terrier has a tight-fitting, short, flat coat, harsh to the touch and with a fine gloss. Color divides this breed into two varieties. Markings on the heads of white Bull Terriers are permissible, but not elsewhere on the coat. The colored variety is the same as the white and can be any color other than white, or any color with white markings. Amongst the colored variety, brindle is preferred.

Characteristics

Although the Bull Terrier is full of fire, he has a sweet disposition and

BREED NOTES

SIZE	GROOMING
✓ ✓	✓

EXERCISE	LIFESPAN
✓ ✓	✓ ✓

Below: A good example of the color variety.

Johnson

is amenable to discipline. People who do not know the breed may not realize that he is exceedingly friendly and thrives on affection. Still known as "the Gladiator of the canine world", this description belies his delightful nature. In general the breed gets along with other dogs, but un-neutered males may take aversion to dog of the same sex.

Origins and History

The breed dates back to around 1835 and it is generally believed that it was established by mating a Bulldog to the now extinct white English Terrier, resulting in what became known as the "bull and

Left: Ears should be held stiffly erect

Caption: Young pups need to be kept warm and snug.

A
B
C
D
E
F
G
H
I
J
K
L
M
N
O
P
Q
R
S
T
U
V
W
X
Y
Z

terrier." Later Spanish Pointer blood was introduced to increase size. Around 1860 fanciers decided that an entirely white dog would be more attractive, so James Hinks produced an all white Bull Terrier, which was considered highly fashionable. This was a dog for men who partook in dog fights and frequented the rat pit and was

Left: This puppy already shows the distinctive head shape.

Below: He has a thoroughly delight-ful nature.

Above: Distinctive egg-shaped head.

Right: A keen, determined, intelligent expression.

taught to defend himself and his master with great courage. He liked to provoke a fight and became known as "the white cavalier". The colored Bull Terrier was voted a separate variety of the breed in 1936.

Health Issues

The Bull Terrier is generally free of genetic diseases, but deafness is known to occur in the breed, so puppies should always be examined. Other problems include skin allergies and lameness, which occurs in puppies up to one year old due to a combination of weight, density of muscle and rapid growth.

A
B
C
D
E
F
G
H
I
J
K
L
M
N
O
P
Q
R
S
T
U
V
W
X
Y
Z

A
B
C
D
E
F
G
H
I
J
K
L
M
N
O
P
Q
R
S
T
U
V
W
X
Y
Z

Above: 'I'm really enjoying this!'

Left: A much loved pet

Opposite top: Moving with head held up (l) and pulling too much on the lead (r).

Opposite: A wonderful example of a Best in Show winning White.

Exercise and Grooming

This muscular breed needs plenty of exercise to stay fit; he loves playing and enjoys going for long walks. Young dogs should not be encouraged to jump or strain their joints and ligaments. This is a low maintenance breed with minimal grooming requirements, but at moulting times loose hair should be removed daily, using a rubber glove.

A
B
C
D
E
F
G
H
I
J
K
L
M
N
O
P
Q
R
S
T
U
V
W
X
Y
Z

Bulldog

Average height: 12-16 inches
Average weight: dogs – 50 pounds; bitches – 40 pounds

Appearance

The Bulldog has a very distinctive appearance and the reason for him looking so different from most breeds is that every point of his structure was designed to aid or protect him while fighting the bull, or even the bear. He is heavy, thick-set with a low-swung body, wide shoulders and sturdy limbs. The topline is distinctive, the spine rising above the loin. His massive short-faced head has massive jaws, very broad and square and his dentition is undershot, the lower jaw projecting considerably in front of the upper jaw and turning up. The head and face are covered with heavy wrinkles and there are loose, pendulous folds at the throat. The gait of the Bulldog is a loose-jointed, shuffling, sidewise motion, giving the characteristic "roll." His short coat of various colors is straight, flat, close, and with a fine texture, smooth and glossy.

Below: A well-constructed Bulldog, showing the breed's distinctive

Characteristics

The Bulldog is calm, kind and even

BREED NOTES

SIZE	GROOMING
✔ ✔	✔
EXERCISE	**LIFESPAN**
✔ ✔	✔ ✔

Johnson

Above: These pups are just a few days old, their eyes are still closed.

Right: Heavy and thick set, with sturdy limbs and wide shoulders.

in disposition with a dignified manner. He is resolute and courageous but not vicious or aggressive. He loves children and although his appearance may be rather intimidating for some, actually he does not make a particularly good watchdog. The Bulldog's calm temperament makes him an ideal candidate to work as a therapy dog.

Origins and History
The Bulldog is believed to have evolved from the Molossian dog, first taken to England by Phoenician traders in the 6th century BC. The

Johnson

A
B
C
D
E
F
G
H
I
J
K
L
M
N
O
P
Q
R
S
T
U
V
W
X
Y
Z

Above: Showing the character of the Bulldog breed.

Left: A youngster moving well

name "Bull" was used because of the breed's use in the cruel sport of bull-baiting. The sport necessitated an extremely savage dog to compete with the ferocious bull, but the Bulldog has come a very long way since then, both its temperament and appearance having been modified considerably. Bull-baiting became illegal in England in 1835

and was eventually eliminated, so the breed's usefulness was past, but some enthusiasts set themselves the task of preserving the Bulldog.

Health Issues

Because of the breed's facial structure, the Bulldog is susceptible to snuffling, snorting and snoring. The most common breathing disorder is caused by an elongated soft palate. Hypoplastic (narrow) trachea causes a shortness of breath, gurgling sounds and wheezing; but many with this condition live long, happy lives, provided it is monitored. If a Bulldog has pinched nostrils, thus allowing insufficient air to pass through the nose, this can usually be corrected with

Above and right: The Bulldog has unmistakable head features.

A
B
C
D
E
F
G
H
I
J
K
L
M
N
O
P
Q
R
S
T
U
V
W
X
Y
Z

surgery. Other concerns in the breed include internalized tail, entropion, ectropion, distichiasis, elbow dysplasia, cherry eye and patella luxation. Caesarean deliveries are often needed. An experienced Bulldog vet is always your best choice.

Exercise and Grooming

The Bulldog has a relatively low activity level and although he appreciates a daily outing, cannot tolerate hot, humid weather. Do not expect him to jog or walk long distances. Coat care is not difficult but daily care must be taken to keep the wrinkles free from dry skin.

Left and below: This young puppy shows great promise.

Opposite: *Investigating in the garden.*

A
B
C
D
E
F
G
H
I
J
K
L
M
N
O
P
Q
R
S
T
U
V
W
X
Y
Z

Bullmastiff

Average height: dogs – 25-27 inches; bitches – 24-26 inches
Average weight: dogs – 110-130 pounds; bitches – 100-120 pounds

Appearance
The Bullmastiff is a symmetrical dog showing great strength and endurance with a keen, alert, intelligent expression. He is powerfully built but active with a

Below: This breed shows great strength and endurance.

wide, muscular and slightly arched loin. The V shaped ears are carried close to the cheeks, set on wide and high, giving a square appearance to the skull. His short, dense, coat gives good protection against the weather and the color is red, fawn, or brindle; a dark muzzle is preferable The bite is preferably

BREED NOTES

SIZE	GROOMING
✔	✔
EXERCISE	LIFESPAN
✔✔✔	✔✔

level or slightly undershot. Except for a very small white spot on the chest, white marking is considered a

Below: 'When will someone come and play?'

fault. The tail is high-set, strong at the root and tapering to the hocks; may be straight or curved.

Characteristics

The primary use of the Bullmastiff today is as a firm, dependable and warm family dog who is very loving with his owners and generally gets along with children and family pets. He is fearless and confident, yet docile, combining reliability, intelligence, and willingness to please. He is a natural guardian of the home and will not back down from a fight, so early training and socialization are important. With

Left: The skull has a square appearance.

Below left: This youngster has a good black muzzle.

Below: A Bulldog showing symmetry

A
B
C
D
E
F
G
H
I
J
K
L
M
N
O
P
Q
R
S
T
U
V
W
X
Y
Z

Above: *This youngster already shows bodily substance.*

Below: *Just waiting.*

strangers he is rather standoffish.

Origins and History

Originating from the Mastiff and the Bulldog, references to this combination of breeding were found in many early manuscripts, several in the latter half of the 18th century. These dogs were used to solve England's eternal problem of keeping large estates and game preserves free from poachers. The Bulldog became a fearless breed that would silently attack on command, knock down a man and hold him without mauling or biting. Dogs of dark brindle color were preferable to work at night for they were less easily seen and were often called "Night Dogs". The English Kennel Club recognized the Bullmastiff as a purebred dog in 1924 and the

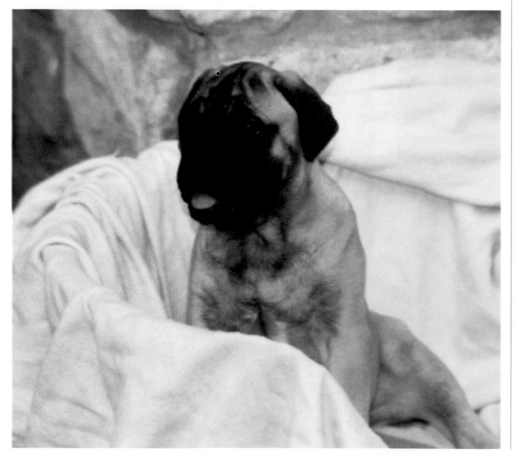

Above and below: Young puppies love to investigate the garden, which must be safely enclosed.

American Kennel Club followed suit in 1933. This breed has been used as a police and army dog, and in South Africa has been used by diamond companies as a guard.

Health Issues
Health concerns of especial importance in this breed are cancer and heart disease, bloat, hyperthyroidism, immune system dysfunction, allergies and joint problems including hip dysplasia, osteochondrosis dissicans (OCD) and panosteitis. Eye problems include entropion, ectropion and Progressive Retinal Atrophy (PRA).

Exercise and Grooming
The Bullmastiff is faster and more agile than his cousin, the Mastiff, and exercise is important to build stamina and prevent obesity. Because of the shortened muzzle, avoid over-exercising when it is hot or humid. Sufficient rest is also important for development of healthy bones, muscles, and joints, especially during the growing stage. The short, dense coat should periodically have dead hairs removed with a rubber brush.

Cairn Terrier

Average height: dogs – 10 inches; bitches – 9.5inches
Average weight: dogs – 14 pounds; bitches – 13 pounds

Appearance

Not so low to the ground as the Sealyham and Scottish Terrier, this is a very sturdy little dog with a strong body, giving the impression of strength and activity without heaviness. The pads of the Cairn's large feet are thick, the nails strong. His head is shorter and wider than any other terrier and is well furnished with hair, giving a foxy expression. The small,

Below: The Cairn's head is shorter and wider than that of other terriers.

pointed, erect ears are set wide apart, the tail carried gaily without curling over the back. The hard, double coat is weather resistant and may be any color except white.

Characteristics

A happy, outgoing, independent little dog, the Cairn Terrier thrives on human companionship. He is active, energetic and very inquisitive. Confident and fearless, many consider the Cairn to be a big dog wrapped in a small dog's body. The Cairn is extremely

BREED NOTES

SIZE	GROOMING
✔	✔✔
EXERCISE	**LIFESPAN**
✔✔	✔✔

Johnson

protective of his home and family, so makes an excellent watch dog. He will always alert his loved ones of any approaching stranger. Many Cairns have an affinity with children; indeed this is a very people-oriented breed. He loves to dig and will still give chase to anything he considers game. Early socialization with cats and other household pets is advisable.

Origins and History

The modern Cairn Terrier results from an attempt to recreate the old

Above: A lovely example of a successful show dog.

Left: His small, pointed, erect ears are set wide apart.

working terrier of Scotland's Isle of Skye. These old terriers had courage to bolt otter, foxes and other vermin from among rocks, cliffs, and ledges. Until 1873, the terriers of Scotland had been grouped together as "Scottish Terriers", but then they divided into two, the Scottish, West Highland White and Cairn, all classified as "Skye Terriers". All three could be found in the very same litter, only distinguishable by color. Towards the close of the 19th century and into the early years of the next, the three breeds were slowly divided up. Challenge certificates were awarded for Cairns in Britain in 1912 and in the USA the breed obtained official recognition in 1913

Health Issues

Some of the health concerns for

A
B
C
D
E
F
G
H
I
J
K
L
M
N
O
P
Q
R
S
T
U
V
W
X
Y
Z

the Cairn Terrier are allergic reactions (particularly to fleas), cataracts, heart defects, hypothyroidism, seizures and epilepsy.

Exercise and Grooming
A Cairn likes to explore and

Above: Feeding a tid bit.

enjoys lively games, but it is important to securely fence his exercise area as he is prone to digging! About an hour of brushing and combing each week will keep the Cairn's coat in

Oposite top: After a good game!

Opposite: Ever alert.

good condition. The longer hair around the feet and between the pads should be trimmed occasionally.

Canaan Dog

Average height: dogs – 20-24 inches; bitches – 19-23 inches
Average weight: dogs – 45-55 pounds; bitches – 35-45 pounds

Appearance

A medium-sized, square bodied dog, the Canaan Dog is without extremes, showing a clear, sharp outline. He moves with athletic agility and grace in a quick, brisk, ground-covering trot. He has a wedge-shaped head with low-set, erect ears that are broad at the base and slightly rounded at the tip. His expression is alert and inquisitive. The Canaan's double coat has a harsh, straight outercoat of .5 to 1.5 inches in length, longer on ruff and

BREED NOTES

SIZE	GROOMING
✔ ✔	✔
EXERCISE	LIFESPAN
✔ ✔	✔ ✔

back of thighs, shorter on head, body and legs. The bushy tail curls over the back when excited. There are two coat color patterns: predominantly white with mask and with or without additional patches of color or solid colored with or without white trim. Color ranges from black through all shades of brown, sandy, red or liver.

Characteristics

The Canaan Dog is reserved and aloof with strangers but with his family he is loyal, loving and very docile. He is also highly inquisitive, alert and vigilant. This is a highly territorial breed that serves as a responsive companion and natural guardian. He can be very vocal and persistent. The Canaan Dog is

Left: A very successful show dog.

easily trained, naturally clean and easy to housebreak. He is good with children and other pets when raised with them.

Origins and History

Originating in the Land of Canaan, this Israel's natural breed and dates back to biblical times. Dogs like this one guarded the camps and herded the flocks of the ancient Israelites. As the Hebrew population decreased many dogs sought refuge in the Negev Desert where, avoiding extinction, some lived with the Bedouins but most were undomesticated. Some were also guards for the Druze on Mount Carmel. In the 1930s the Drs Menzel were asked by the Jewish self-defense organization to re-establish this pariah dog as a breed, since when it has served as a sentry dog, messenger, Red Cross helper, mine detector and guide dog for the blind. The Canaan Dog was brought to the USA in 1965 and registered in the AKC's Stud Book in 1997.

Health Issues

The Canaan Dog is a seemingly healthy breed in general but hip dysplasia is something to be aware of and cryptorchids have been known.

Exercise and Grooming

This is an apparently tireless breed, a dog that is capable of trotting for hours, but he does not need an excessive amount of exercise. Grooming the Canaan is a simple matter, but dead hair must be regularly removed during the moulting season.

Above: A super example showing the wedge shaped head and low set, erect ears.

Below The Canaan Dog's ancestry dates back to biblical times.

A
B
C
D
E
F
G
H
I
J
K
L
M
N
O
P
Q
R
S
T
U
V
W
X
Y
Z

Cane Corso

Average height: dogs – 25-27.5 inches; bitches – 23.5-26 inches
Average weight: dogs – 92-120 pounds; bitches – 80-100 pounds

Appearance

The Cane Corso is a medium-large sized molosser breed, sturdy with large bones. He is muscular and athletic and a little longer than he is high. The head is large, with smooth, firm skin and when viewed from the top the skull has a square appearance. The Cane's expression is very alert and attentive. The ears, which are set well-above the cheekbones, may be cropped or left natural, in which case they are triangular and held tight to the cheeks. The preferred bites are slightly undershot or level, but a scissors bite is acceptable. Natural tails are accepted, but they are usually docked at the fourth vertebrae. Rear dew claws, if present, are always removed. The short, stiff, coat is shiny, adherent and dense with a light undercoat that becomes thicker in cold weather. Accepted colors are black, lighter and darker shades of gray, lighter and darker shades of fawn, and red. Brindling is allowed on all of these colors.

Characteristics

As a protector of property and his owners, the Cane Corso is unequalled and because he is strong and dominant the role of leader needs to be established early on. Early socialization and training are an absolute necessity for this breed. With his owner, family and children, he is loving and docile.

Origins and History

The Cane Corso is a direct ancestor of the old Roman Mollosian, Canis Pugnax but this is a lighter version,

Left: A splendid example of the breed from Moscow, given a high award by the author when judging in Estonia.

BREED NOTES	
SIZE	GROOMING
✔ ✔ ✔	✔
EXERCISE	LIFESPAN
✔ ✔ ✔	✔ ✔

used for hunting wild animals and as an auxiliary warrior in battles. For many a long year he has been a companion of the Italians, who have employed the Cane to protect property and cattle against large predators such as bears, and as a personal guard. In the hunt the Cane has been used against wild boar, stag and bear. The breed used to be common all over Italy but more recently, until 1988, it was only known in the south. The name is derived from the Latin, cohors, meaning "guardian" or "protector". The Cane Corso has been recorded in the AKC's Foundation Stock Service since 1996.

Health Issues
Heath problems to look out for

Right: *A very alert, attentive expression.*

Below: *The large head has smooth, firm skin.*

Below right: *The Cane is a little longer than he is high.*

A
B
C
D
E
F
G
H
I
J
K
L
M
N
O
P
Q
R
S
T
U
V
W
X
Y
Z

include demodectic mange, hip dysplasia, elbow dysplasia, epilepsy, thyroid problems, bloat and eye problems, especially entropion, ectropion and cherry eye. Heart disease is thought to be caused by a genetic factor; cardiomyopathy, sub-aortic stenosis and tricuspid valve dysplasia are of particular note.

Exercise and Grooming

An athletic and agile breed, the Cane requires a good amount of exercise to keep his muscles toned up. Amongst the activities he enjoys are weight pulling, carting, agility, herding and tracking. His coat is easy to care for and just needs a little extra attention at shedding time.

Above: This is a medium-large sized Molosser breed.

Below: When walking in the street, a Cane Cose should be well controlled.

Cardigan Welsh Corgi

Average height: 10.5-12.5 inches
Average weight: dogs – 30-38 pounds; bitches – 25-34 pounds

BREED NOTES

SIZE	GROOMING
✓ ✓	✓

EXERCISE	LIFESPAN
✓ ✓	✓ ✓

Appearance

Less well-known than his cousin, the Pembroke Welsh Corgi, the Cardigan has a full tail and is somewhat larger and longer in body. His ears are large and prominent in proportion to his size, and slightly rounded at the tip. He is low set with moderately heavy bone and a deep chest, his long silhouette culminating in a low tail set and fox-like brush. This is a handsome, powerful, small dog, capable of both speed and endurance. He is sturdily built but not coarse and his feet are rather large and rounded. The Cardigan's expression is alert and gentle, watchful, yet friendly. The medium length, weather-resistant coat is

Left: The Cardigan Welsh Corgi's ears are large in proportion to the breed's size.

A
B
C
D
E
F
G
H
I
J
K
L
M
N
O
P
Q
R
S
T
U
V
W
X
Y
Z

Above: A very worthy Champion.

Right: The expression is gentle and alert.

dense and double and comes in various colors: all shades of red, sable and brindle; black with or without tan or brindle points and blue merle, which is black and gray marbled, again with or without tan or brindle points.

Characteristics

With his steady, even temperament, this is an alert, intelligent, affectionate and adaptable breed. He makes a good family companion for he loves people and is always eager to please.

Origins and History

One of the earliest breeds of the British Isles, the Cardigan Corgi hails from Cardiganshire in Wales, where he arrived with the Celts from central Europe in about 1,200 BC. The breed is related to the Dachshund family. The Corgi was kept by Welsh hill farmers as an all-purpose farm dog; he drove, guarded and herded cattle by nipping at their heels. Today's Cardigan Welsh Corgi goes back to the old Bronant Corgi which had a slight infusion of brindle herder blood. Both types of Corgi (the Cardigan and the Pembroke) were classified as one breed in Britain until 1934. They have been in the USA since 1931 and the breed was admitted for AKC registration in 1935.

Health Issues

Although generally a healthy breed, there are a few problems of which owners should be aware. These include Progressive Retinal Atrophy (PRA), hip dysplasia, spinal disc problems, autoimmune diseases and cataracts.

Below: The Cardigan Corgi is found in various colors.

Johnson

A
B
C
D
E
F
G
H
I
J
K
L
M
N
O
P
Q
R
S
T
U
V
W
X
Y
Z

A
B
C
D
E
F
G
H
I
J
K
L
M
N
O
P
Q
R
S
T
U
V
W
X
Y
Z

Exercise and Grooming
The Cardigan Welsh Corgi requires plenty of outdoor exercise and enjoys conformation showing, obedience, herding, tracking and agility. He also makes a very good Therapy dog. Brushing is necessary a couple of times each week and the hair between the toes on the bottom of the feet should be trimmed occasionally.

Left: The tail is a fox-like brush.

Below: He is sturdily built, but not coarse.

Catahoula Leopard Dog

Average height: dogs – 22-26 inches; bitches – 20-24 inches
Average weight: 50-95 pounds, in proportion to height

Above: One of many unusual colors in this breed.

BREED NOTES

SIZE	GROOMING
✔✔✔	✔
EXERCISE	**LIFESPAN**
✔✔✔	✔✔

Appearance

This short-coated dog is well-muscled, but not bulky, giving an overall impression of agility and endurance. There are many unusual coat colors and patterns, as well as various different eye colors.

Characteristics

When working, the Catahoula Leopard Dog has a very serious temperament, and yet when off the job he might be described as "clownish". Although not aggressive or shy, he can be aloof toward strangers. It is in his nature to be protective, territorial and independent so the breed's temperament is not suitable for everyone. As a companion, he is affectionate, gentle and loyal, but may be aggressive towards other dogs, especially those of the same sex.

Origins and History

The Catahoula Leopard Dog originated in North Central Louisiana, around the Catahoula Lake. The word "Catahoula" is Indian in origin, meaning "sacred lake". The woods of Louisiana used to be full of wild hogs and these dogs were also indigenous to the area. The breed's instinct to work with wild hogs and cattle became evident, since when they have been bred by working oriented breeders. This dog is believed to be a cross between native American dogs, red wolves and other dogs taken to North America by the Spanish Conquistadors. He is equally capable of scenting, trailing and treeing game, making him very versatile, for he is also an excellent herding dog. This self governing instinct could easily be lost if the Catahoula is bred purely as a pet or show dog, without the working aspect being tantamount. Regardless of size, color, or color of eyes, the working instinct is the true test of purity. The breed has been recorded in the Foundation Stock Service since 1996.

Health Issues

Catahoulas are relatively free from disease but they are prone to hip dysplasia. Those that are predominantly white, or white faced with glass eyes, seem to have an 80% chance of deafness in either one or both ears. Another problem to watch out for is tunnel vision.

Exercise and Grooming

The Catahoula has a high energy level so is almost always happiest when they he has a job to do. He is good as a ranch or farm dog, but not suited to life as a family pet in a suburban household. Proper obedience training is important. Coat care is minimal.

A
B
C
D
E
F
G
H
I
J
K
L
M
N
O
P
Q
R
S
T
U
V
W
X
Y
Z

Caucasian Mountain Dog

Average height: dogs – not less than 25.5 inches (but can be up to 32 inches);
bitches – not less than 24.5 inches
Average weight: 70-160 pounds

Appearance

The Caucasian Mountain Dog is a powerful animal with strong muscle and bone, males being larger and more solid than bitches. The skin is thick but elastic, the coat natural and coarse with a lighter coloured undercoat. On the head and front of the limbs, the hair is short and close fitting. There are two coat types, longhaired, with a mane on neck and shoulders, "pants" and a thick bushy tail, shorthaired, which is still relatively thick, and a cross between the two (longhaired, but without mane, feathers and bushy tail). Colors vary and include grays, rust, straw, yellow, white, earth-colored, brindled, spotted or piebald. The head is solid, with a wide skull and strongly developed bones. The large, wide nose is black for preference, but may be brown in white or light colored dogs. The hanging ears are typically cropped short.

Characteristics

This is a strong dog, ever watchful and on guard, but with a calm nature if raised and trained

BREED NOTES

SIZE	GROOMING
✓	✓
✓	✓
✓	

EXERCISE	LIFESPAN
✓	✓
✓	✓
✓	

Cunliffe

Opposite: A successful show dog in Europe

correctly. His remarkable defence reaction will certainly be used if he considers it necessary. This breed is typically ferocious toward and distrustful of strangers. His faithfulness, protectiveness, and ferocity when called upon to defend are legendary.

Origins and History
The Caucasian Mountain Dog, known in most countries as the Caucasian Ovtcharka, is a large livestock guarding dog of robust constitution, indigenous to the mountain regions of the Georgian,

Armenian and Azerbaijani Union Republics. It functions as a guard and herding dog, and has historically been used as a fighting dog. Being such a hardy breed and with its tolerance for different climates, it has been used in almost all regions of the Soviet Union. The breed varies somewhat depending on its territory and use; those in the transcaucasus regions are more massively built, and those in the steppe regions are rangier in build and often short-coated.

Health Issues
This is generally a very healthy

Left: A young Caucasian working on a remote farm in Kazakhstan.

breed but breeding stock should be screened for hip and elbow dysplasia.

Exercise and Grooming
Being such a large, strong breed, it is essential to allow plenty of opportunity for exercise in a safely enclosed area. Well-trained Caucasians can be given additional exercise on a leash, and early training is of great importance. The amount of grooming required varies according to the type of coat, but some time should be allowed on a weekly basis.

Below: Even the show Caucasian is only for the experienced handler.

Cavalier King Charles Spaniel

Average height: 12-13 inches
Average weight: 13-18 pounds

BREED NOTES

SIZE	GROOMING
✓	✓ ✓
EXERCISE	LIFESPAN
✓ ✓	✓ ✓

Left: A Cavalier puppy is full of
energy.

Opposite top: But sometimes even a
puppy has to rest!

Opposite: This charming little breed
adores people.

Appearance

An active, graceful and well-balanced toy spaniel, the Cavalier has something of a "royal" appearance about him. With his sweet, gentle, melting expression, the Cavalier's large, dark, round eyes give a warm, lustrous, limpid look, the cushioning under the eyes contributing to the soft expression. From the slightly rounded skull his long ears fan slightly forward to frame the face. His coat is of moderate length, silky but free from curl, although there may be a slight wave. Feathering on ears, chest and tail is long; feathering on the feet is also characteristic. The splendid colors of this breed are Blenheim, which is rich chestnut markings well broken up on a clear, pearly white ground, tricolor, black and tan, and ruby, which is a whole colored red.

Characteristics

The Cavalier King Charles Spaniel is a charming little dog that adapts well to most living environments. He is wonderful with children and great company for senior citizens too. Intelligent,

A
B
C
D
E
F
G
H
I
J
K
L
M
N
O
P
Q
R
S
T
U
V
W
X
Y
Z

Johnson

Opposite: A successful Champion showing the gentle, melting expression.

Above: Grooming is easy, but important.

Below: A Blenheim.

A
B
C
D
E
F
G
H
I
J
K
L
M
N
O
P
Q
R
S
T
U
V
W
X
Y
Z

happy, playful, outgoing and always willing to please, he has a very sweet, affectionate nature. Because of his sporting and playful nature, he is apt to chase anything he considers fair game, so a secure exercise area is important.

Origins and History

His history goes back to the early Toy Spaniels of Europe that have appeared with aristocratic families in paintings and tapestries for centuries. During the Victorian and Edwardian eras the Cavalier became virtually extinct as

Right: He has an affectionate nature and is always eager to please.

Below: A pleasing profile showing long feathering on ears, chest and tail.

breed does have a tendency to become obese as a result of over-eating or lack of exercise.

Exercise and Grooming

Although small, this is an energetic breed so needs at least an hour of exercise daily. The Cavalier King Charles Spaniel has a very natural appearance, with no trimming or artificial sculpting, although hair growing between the pads on the underside of the feet may be trimmed. Coat care is fairly easy but a thorough brushing should be given at least once each week.

Left: This breed has a sporting and playful nature.

Below: A tri-color

shorter-nosed breeds were more in favour. Modern history really began in 1926 when American fancier, Roswell Eldridge made a concerted effort to buy the longer-nosed variety from Britain, offering cash prizes at Crufts to encourage their exhibition. In 1952 the first Cavaliers were eventually sent to America but not until 1996 did they enter AKC competition as the 140th recognized breed.

Health Issues

Generally a sturdy, healthy dog, health problems to watch out for are mitral valve disease (often with an early onset), syringyomelia, an inherited condition, eye problems and "episodic falling", also known as collapsing syndrome (often misdiagnosed as epilepsy). The

A
B
C
D
E
F
G
H
I
J
K
L
M
N
O
P
Q
R
S
T
U
V
W
X
Y
Z

Central Asian Shepherd Dog

Average height: dogs – 25.5 inches minimum; bitches – 23.5 inches minimum
Average weight: In proportion to height

Appearance

The Central Asian Shepherd Dog has great size, massive bone structure and powerful muscles, especially in males. His body is slightly longer than tall and his head is massive. Ears are normally cropped close to the head but when left natural they are small, triangular, pendant and set low. The skin of the neck is thick with well-developed and elastic subcutaneous tissue folds around the neck The high-set tail is thick at the base; when undocked it hangs down to the hock with a sickle shape. Two coat lengths are accepted (1?-2 inches or 2?-3 inches); both are double-coated and thick. Colors are white, black, gray, straw-colored, reddish brown, gray brown, brindle, parti-colored and ticked.

Characteristics

This is a territorial guardian, bred to guard people and their possessions. The Central Asian guards what ever is placed in his territory. Although very devoted to his family, he expects to be treated with respect and is inclined to be suspicious of strange people or dogs. Central Asians are steady, even-tempered dogs but when threatened, they react quickly and with complete seriousness. Slow to mature, they require extensive socialization and patient training techniques. This breed is hardy and able to adapt to a wide range of climates but is definitely not for the novice dog owner.

Origins and History

For thousands of years large, heavily-built dogs with cropped ears and tails have been used by nomadic tribes in Central Asia to

BREED NOTES	
SIZE	GROOMING
✔ ✔ ✔	✔ ✔
EXERCISE	LIFESPAN
✔ ✔ ✔	✔ ✔

J.C.

Left: Ears are normally cropped close to the head.

protect livestock from predators and other property. This is not a breed that was designed or created by any specific person or country, but came about as a result of harsh natural selection. Breed type differs depending on the terrain, so those found in the mountains of Mongolia are somewhat different from those from desert regions. The breed's history has merged with the civilization of man based around the ancient silk route; this remarkable dog has survived through extreme climates and against predators now extinct. Working Central Asian Shepherd Dogs are still found today in Afghanistan, Iran, Kazakhstan, Kirgyzstan, Tadjikistan, Turkmenistan, and Uzbekistan, where they guard families, horses and camels. A modern version of the breed has now been established in Russia so a difference in size, color and temperament is now emerging between modern cultivated and native dogs.

Health Issues

Due to its vast gene pool, this is generally a very healthy breed but hip and elbow dysplasia, crippling ACL and entropion have been known to occur

Exercise and Grooming

The Central Asian needs plenty of free exercise in a secure area. Sensible, early training is an absolute must. Some grooming is necessary, but is not too time consuming, though special attention should be given to the coat during the moulting season.

Above: This 4 month old puppy's ears have been left in their natural state.

Below: A particularly good Central Asian from Russia.

A B C D E F G H I J K L M N O P Q R S T U V W X Y Z

Cesky Terrier

Average height: 10-13 inches
Average weight: dogs – 16-22 pounds; bitches slightly less

Appearance

With drop ears and a long tail, the Cesky Terrier is longer than tall and has a soft, long, silky coat in shades of gray from charcoal to platinum. The breed is clipped all over except on the upper part of the head, legs, ribcage and belly, showing off the strong, muscled Cesky Terrier. All puppies are born black, black and tan, or brown, but during the first two or three years they change to their adult color. The Cesky's head is shaped like a blunt wedge and the almond-shaped eyes are slightly deep set, with a friendly expression. The bite may be scissor or level. Ears are set rather high and fall flat along the cheeks. He has a lean body and the rump is strongly developed with the hip bones often slightly higher than the withers.

Below: The head is shaped like a blunt wedge.

Characteristics

The Cesky Terrier has a balanced, non-aggressive character, but can be reserved toward strangers. He is not so excitable as other Terrier breeds, and yet always ready to give chase

BREED NOTES

SIZE	GROOMING
✔ ✔	✔ ✔
EXERCISE	**LIFESPAN**
✔ ✔	✔ ✔

to anything that captures his interest. He can work silently, but is right on target! Also able to work underground in burrows, the Cesky is ever keen and alert during the hunt but loyal to his owners.

Origins and History

The Cesky results from planned breeding in 1950 between a Sealyham dog and a Scottish Terrier. In doing this mating, Frantisek Horak a geneticist from Klanivce in what is now the Czech Republic aimed to develop a medium sized, well-muscled, light, short legged and well-pigmented hunting terrier, to work in packs. Despite an earlier export ban, the Cesky managed to become quite popular in Scandinavian countries and is now in most of Europ, the USA, Canada and Australia. Used

Above: A Cesky will always enjoy a ramble in a field

Below left: 'I've finished Mom!'

Below: Food left within reach is just too tempting!

A
B
C
D
E
F
G
H
I
J
K
L
M
N
O
P
Q
R
S
T
U
V
W
X
Y
Z

Above: Clipping shows off the breed's strong muscle.

to hunt fox, rabbit, duck, pheasant and wild boar, this is the most successful of the country's national breeds, having been featured on postage stamps, on television, in books and in a movie.

Health Issues

Because the Cesky Terrier is a fairly new breed, little is yet known about inherited ailments to which the breed is susceptible. However, rarely they suffer from "Scottie Cramp" that results in "bunny-hopping" when trotting. Like other Terriers, they may be prone to eye problems and to back problems, due to their body length, especially if overweight.

Exercise and Grooming

Approaching one hour of exercise each day is necessary; this may be a game in the garden, a walk in the woods or a ramble through the countryside. The Cesky's coat should be brushed at least once each week and clipped every six to eight weeks. Because the breed does not shed, regular grooming is important to keep the coat free from mats.

Left: Hip bones are often slightly higher than the withers.

Chesapeake Bay Retriever

Average height: dogs – 23-26 inches; bitches – 21-24 inches
Average weight: dogs – 65-80 pounds; bitches – 55-70 pounds

Appearance

The Chesapeake Bay Retriever has to be equally proficient on land and in water. This is reflected in his appearance for he must be able to function with ease and endurance. He is a strong, well-balanced, powerfully built dog with no tendency to weakness. His ribcage is barrel round and deep. With an intelligent expression, his eyes are a yellowish-amber. The Chesapeake's head is broad and round, his jaws of sufficient length and strength to carry game birds tenderly. The medium length tail is straight or slightly curved and the well-webbed hare feet are of good size with well-rounded, close toes. The short, thick, oily, slightly wavy coat is never over 1.5 inches long, and has a dense, fine, woolly undercoat. On face and legs the hair is very short and straight. There may be moderate feathering on hindquarters and tail. A Chesapeake's coat should resist the water in the same way that a duck's feathers do. The coat colour is as nearly that of its working surroundings as possible, any color of brown, sedge or deadgrass being acceptable.

Characteristics

This breed is valued for its bright

BREED NOTES

SIZE	GROOMING
✓	✓
✓	✓
✓	

EXERCISE	LIFESPAN
✓	✓
✓	✓
✓	

Below: All three colors in this breed.

A
B
C
D
E
F
G
H
I
J
K
L
M
N
O
P
Q
R
S
T
U
V
W
X
Y
Z

Johnson

and happy disposition, intelligence, quiet good sense and affectionate, protective nature. Used as a gundog and as a companion, the Chesapeake has courage and a willingness to work, coupled with alertness, nose and a love of water.

Origins and History

In 1807, survivors of an English ship-wreck off the coast of Maryland were two Newfoundland puppies that turned out to be wonderful retrievers. Many dogs used for

Above: The jaw can carry game birds tenderly.

retrieving in the area were bred to them, as were other outcrosses, such as the Otterhound, Flat- and Curly-coated Retrievers. By the time the

Left: Equally proficient on land and in water.

Health Issues

Some of the known health concerns are hip dysplasia, hypothyroidism, progressive rod-cone degeneration (a form of PRA) and bloat.

Exercise and Grooming

At least two hours' exercise a day is necessary, and if he has access to a pool or lake, all the better! Grooming is minimal and bathing is not advised. The coat needs to be brushed only when shedding.

AKC was established in 1884, a definite Chesapeake variety had been developed, known for its prowess in the rough, icy waters of Chesapeake Bay. This breed hunts waterfowl under the most adverse conditions, often having to break ice during the course of strenuous multiple retrieves. Frequently he must face wind, tide and long cold swims. The American Chesapeake Club, founded in 1918, held its first licensed retriever trial in 1932.

Below: Proud of his heritage.

Below: An intelligent expression, with yellowish-amber eyes.

A B C D E F G H I J K L M N O P Q R S T U V W X Y Z

225

A
B
C
D
E
F
G
H
I
J
K
L
M
N
O
P
Q
R
S
T
U
V
W
X
Y
Z

Chihuahua

Average height:
Average weight: Not to exceed 6 pounds

Appearance

This is a graceful, alert, swift-moving little dog, with a saucy expression, just slightly longer than he is high. He has a rounded, "apple domed" skull which may or may not have a molera (a soft spot on the skull). The full, luminous dark or ruby eyes do not protrude and the large erect-type ears are held more upright when alert. He may have a scissors or level bite and his moderately long tail is carried sickle-like. There are two coat varieties, smooth and long. Smooths have a soft coat, close and glossy, with a preference for furry hair on the tail. In Long Coats it is a soft texture, either flat or slightly curly, the tail plumed, with feathering on feet, legs and pants. A ruff is desirable for both coat types. The coat may be any color, solid, marked or splashed.

Characteristics

The Chihuahua can be very bold with dogs much larger than himself, so needs careful supervision. He can also be very protective of his family, being incredibly loyal and yet wary of strangers, making him a good

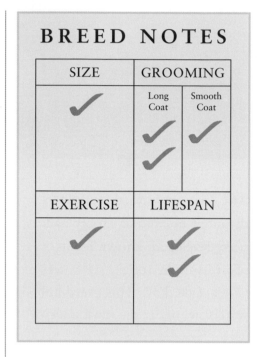

BREED NOTES

SIZE	GROOMING	
✓	Long Coat	Smooth Coat
	✓	✓
	✓	
EXERCISE	**LIFESPAN**	
✓	✓	
	✓	

Opposite: Smooth Coated Champion, a consistent winner even when a Veteran.

Left: Cute little puppy beginning to look like a grown-up.

watch dog. Although a Toy breed, he has certain terrier-like temperament qualities.

Origins and History

The progenitor of the Chihuahua is believed to be the Techichi, companion of the ancient Toltecs. Although no records are available prior to the 9th century, it is probable his ancestors were around even before the Mayans. It is likely that the Chihuahua was not only a popular pet, but also a religious necessity. Similar dogs have been found in materials from the Pyramids of Cholula and in

Johnson

A
B
C
D
E
F
G
H
I
J
K
L
M
N
O
P
Q
R
S
T
U
V
W
X
Y
Z

ruins of Chichen Itza on the Yucatan Peninsula. Mexico is considered the home of the Chihuahua and his appearance in Europe may be due to the travels of Christopher Columbus. The breed we know today is smaller than his ancestors and was first registered in the USA in 1904.

Left: *The UK's Long Coat breed record holder.*

Below: *Chihuahuas are happy in a safely enclosed yard, but enjoy their home comforts.*

Opposite: *Sitting in the lap of luxury!*

Opposite bottom: *Long Coat Chihuahua in full profile.*

A
B
C
D
E
F
G
H
I
J
K
L
M
N
O
P
Q
R
S
T
U
V
W
X
Y
Z

Left: Chihuahuas, though small, are agile.

Below: It sometimes pays off to beg so beautifully!

Health Issues

The Chihuahua is a long-lived breed, often living to 16 years and even longer. Health problems include patella luxation, eye problems, hypoglycaemia, heart disease and tooth and gum ailments. The presence of a molera is not a medical problem but is characteristic of the breed. Particularly tiny Chihuahuas may have more health problems than others.

Exercise and Grooming

Half an hour of exercise daily is quite enough for this tiny breed. Neither the long or short-coated variety takes a great deal of grooming; a good brush once a week should suffice.

Opposite: The Chihuahua is incredibly loyal.

A
B
C
D
E
F
G
H
I
J
K
L
M
N
O
P
Q
R
S
T
U
V
W
X
Y
Z

Chinese Crested

Average height: 11-13 inches
Average weight: No more than 12 pounds

Appearance

A fine-boned, elegant and graceful Toy dog, the Chinese Crested comes in two varieties, Hairless, with hair only on its head, tail and feet and Powderpuff, which is completely covered with hair. Both have an alert look about them with their uncropped ears large and erect and their cheeks tapering cleanly into the muzzle. Pigment varies according to coat and body colour. The Hairless variety frequently has missing teeth and this is not to be faulted. The slender tail tapers to a curve and is carried slightly forward, over the back, when moving. Hare feet, narrow with elongated toes, are typical. Wherever the body is hairless, the skin is soft and smooth, the head crest beginning at the stop and tapering off between the base of the skull and the back of the neck Hair on the ears and face is permitted on the Hairless and may be trimmed for neatness in both varieties. The double coat of the Powderpuff is soft and silky, straight and of moderate density and length. Both varieties may be any color or combination of colors.

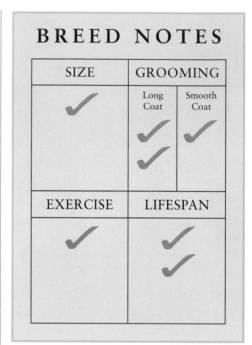

BREED NOTES

SIZE	GROOMING	
	Long Coat	Smooth Coat
✓	✓	✓
	✓	
EXERCISE	LIFESPAN	
✓	✓	
	✓	

Characteristics

The Chinese Crested is a loving companion, playful and entertaining with a gay, alert personality. This is a great family dog and very sweet and even-tempered with children. Early socialization is advisable.

Left: Uncropped large, erect ears and a truly alert look.

Origins and History

The Chinese Crested is believed to have evolved from the African hairless dogs used for barter by merchants and sailors. In consequence, they made their way to many ancient ports throughout the world. The Chinese, favoring small dogs, selectively bred them to dogs of smaller size and by the 16th century the breed was found in ports throughout Central and South America as well as in Africa and Asia. Early in the 20th century the breed found an active following in the USA and an extensive stud book registry was retained from the 1930s. In the 1950s the famous Gypsy Rose Lee

Right and below: These two representatives of the Hairless variety, although similarly marked, show differences in their bodily substance.

A
B
C
D
E
F
G
H
I
J
K
L
M
N
O
P
Q
R
S
T
U
V
W
X
Y
Z

Below: *Loving and playful, with a gay personality.*

Opposite: *'I may be small in stature, but I feel like a king!'*

Above: *This lovely example of a Hairless, has hair only on head, ears, feet and tail.*

owned Cresteds and helped considerably to publicize the breed which was not registered with the AKC until 1991.

Health Issues

Problems to watch out for are luxating patellas and skin trouble, especially in the hairless variety. There is also a danger of early tooth loss. The hairless variety is sometimes sensitive to lanolin and wool.

Exercise and Grooming

This is not a particularly high

Johnson

A
B
C
D
E
F
G
H
I
J
K
L
M
N
O
P
Q
R
S
T
U
V
W
X
Y
Z

energy breed, so a sensible walk and some games or romps in the garden will suffice daily. When exercising outdoors in cold weather, the hairless variety should wear a coat or sweater. Hairless Chinese Cresteds need to be bathed frequently and sunscreen applied to help protect the skin, which will sweat if in the sunshine without proper care. The Powder Puff needs a little more time spent on grooming by way of brushing.

Left: Two Powder Puff friends.

Below: Pigment varies according to coat and body color.

Right: A lovely example of the Powder Puff variety.

Johnson

Chinese Shar-Pei

Average height: 18-20 inches
Average weight: 45-60 pounds

Appearance

This is an alert, compact dog of medium size and substance, his head seemingly rather large for his body. The hippopotamus muzzle shape gives him a highly unique appearance. His small, dark eyes are sunken, giving a scowling expression, and the small high-set, triangular ears point forward and may be rounded at the tip. The Chinese Shar-Pei's topline characteristically dips slightly behind the withers then rises slightly over a short, broad loin. The tail is high set. Loose skin and wrinkles covering the head, neck and body are particularly noticeable in puppies but less so in

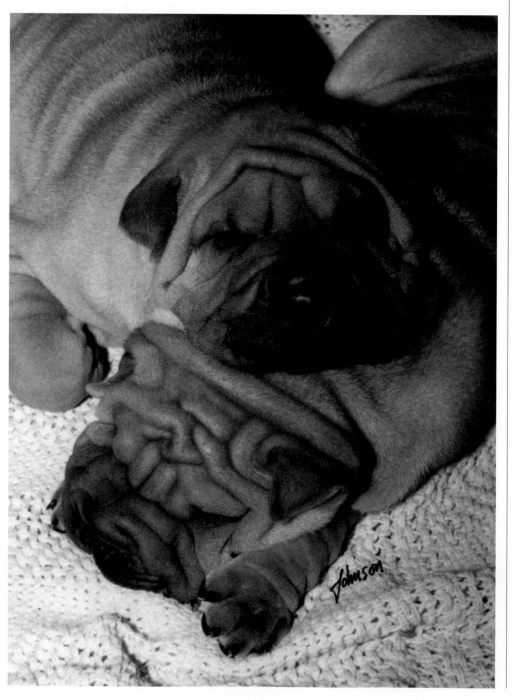

BREED NOTES

SIZE	GROOMING
✓✓	✓
EXERCISE	**LIFESPAN**
✓✓	✓✓

Left: Shar-Pei puppies are simply "munchy"!

Opposite: This puppy seems to love wearing his jewels, hand-made in the Himalaya.

adulthood. The noticeably harsh coat is absolutely straight and off-standing. There are two coat types; the extremely short "horse coat" ranging up to the "brush coat" that must not exceed one inch. In the USA solid colors and sable are acceptable, but the latter is not permitted in some other countries. Pigmentation can vary in accordance with coat color. Tongue, roof of mouth, gums and flews are a solid bluish-black, except in dilute colors, in which they are solid lavender.

Characteristics

This is an intelligent breed that will

A
B
C
D
E
F
G
H
I
J
K
L
M
N
O
P
Q
R
S
T
U
V
W
X
Y
Z

Above left: Characteristically the topline dips slightly behind the withers and then rises slightly lover the loin.

Above: The small, dark eyes are sunken, giving a scowling expression.

give its loyalty and affection to its owner or handler, provided that person has earned the dog's respect. The Chinese Shar-Pei will not blindly follow orders and can be dominant, but can get along with other household pets if introduced at an early age. He can be rather stubborn but this can be overcome with gentle, firm training. The breed is essentially independent and somewhat standoffish with strangers; he can even be described as snobbish.

Origins and History
The breedcan be traced back to China's Han Dynasty, particularly in the southern provinces where it was

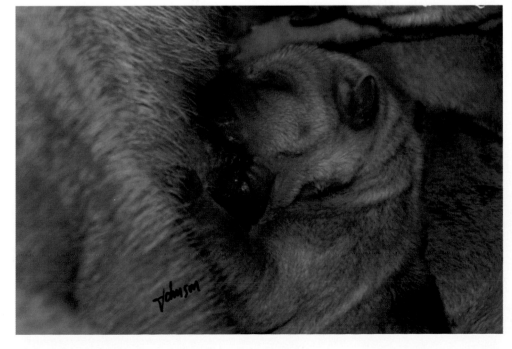

Above: This Champion carries himself with pride.

Left: Puppy suckling immediately after birth.

used for dog fighting, hunting, herding and guarding. Statues bearing a strong resemblance to this breed date back to 200 BC. During China's Communist era, the entire dog population was virtually eliminated, but a few Shar-Pei were bred in Hong Kong and in Taiwan. A few were imported to the USA   in

1966 and following a timely appeal for help to rescue the breed in the 1970s it has continued to grow in popularity, so that now there are over 70,000 in the USA alone.

Health Issues

Amongst the problems encountered are swollen hock syndrome, hypothyroidism, entropion and cherry eye. Some skin problems occur, but these should not be confused with a heavy moult which leaves the coat temporarily very patchy. Shar-Pei can sometimes suffer from allergies too.

Exercise and Grooming

The Chinese Shar-Pei's exercise needs are moderate, but a thirty minute walk each day is always welcome. Grooming is not overly time consuming, but special attention should always be paid to the folds of the skin, where irritation can arise. Brushing needs to be done thoroughly during the moulting season.

Above: Dam and her litter at just a few days old.

Opposite: This Champion has a brush coat.

Johnson

Chinook

Average height: dogs – 23-27 inches; bitches – 21-25 inches
Average weight: dogs – 70 pounds; bitches – 55 pounds

Appearance

The Chinook is distinguishable from other Northern breeds by his more rectangular shaped head and his close-fitting, tawny coat. He may also have dropped ears. He has a keen, intelligent expression and his proud carriage displays dignity. This

BREED NOTES

SIZE	GROOMING
✓	✓
✓	✓
✓	
EXERCISE	**LIFESPAN**
✓	✓
✓	✓
✓	

Left: This puppy and adult show a clear resemblance to one another.

is a large working dog, capable of pulling light to heavy loads and looks very much the athlete with his well-muscled body, deep chest, well-developed forelegs, strong back and powerful thighs. He has a double coat of medium-length hair, with a thick, soft undercoat that is downy in texture. The neck has a protective ruff and the sabre tail is well-furred. The breed is always tawny in color, ranging from light honey to reddish-gold.

Characteristics

One of the key characteristics of this breed is his gentle, affectionate disposition, with a calm and willing work ethic. Inquisitive by nature, he is gregarious with other dogs and shows patient tolerance with

children. Although a social dog, bred to work in teams, he is dependent upon his owner and is sensitive to harsh handling. He thrives as a family companion and should never be either timid or aggressive.

Origins and History
The Chinook was created in

Above: Thoroughly "at home" in the country..

Below: A charming family group.

A
B
C
D
E
F
G
H
I
J
K
L
M
N
O
P
Q
R
S
T
U
V
W
X
Y
Z

Left: Snow doesn't worry the Chinook at all.

Chinook declined in numbers from the mid 1960s to the early 1980s but it has since been revived and has been recorded in the AKC's Foundation Stock Service since 2001.

Health Issues

A generally healthy breed, seizures are known to cause problems in some Chinooks. They have different types of episodes, some of which appear to be classic seizures while others are different. Other problems found are hip dysplasia, cryptorchidism and allergic skin diseases.

Exercise and Grooming

This is a working dog and, as such, needs plenty of opportunity for hard exercise. Grooming is not difficult, but special attention should be paid to the coat during the moulting season

America by author and adventurer Arthur T Walden in the 1920s. The breed is named after Walden's dog, "Chinook" who was born in 1917, his dam a Greenland Husky (descended from Admiral Peary's lead dog, Polaris) and his sire a large St Bernard-type mixed breed. By breeding Chinook to several different types of working dogs to lighten the fame and maintain intelligence, Walden created a new breed of sled dog that had tremendous power, endurance, speed, and a friendly, gentle nature. In 1927 Chinooks were used to haul freight on Admiral Byrd's expedition to the South Pole. Interestingly 'Chinook' is the Inuit word for warm winter winds. The

Left: The Chinook is capable of pulling light to heavy loads.

Chow Chow

Average height: 17-20 inches
Average weight: 40-70 pounds

Appearance

With his lion-like appearance and regal manner the Chow Chow is surely one of the most recognisable and impressive dog breeds. He is powerful, sturdy, squarely built, with strong muscular development and heavy bone. The Chow Chow has very distinctive hind movement, short and stilted; viewed from the side, the hind legs have little angulation. His head is large in proportion to his size, with an unmistakable scowling expression and blue-black tongue. The small, thick, triangular ears have a slight forward tilt. There are two types of coat; rough and smooth, both are

BREED NOTES

SIZE	GROOMING	
	Rough	Smooth
✓		
✓	✓	✓
✓	✓	✓
	✓	
EXERCISE	**LIFESPAN**	
✓	✓	
✓	✓	

Left: The Chow Chow has an unmistakable scowling expression.

double. In the rough, the outercoat is abundant, dense, straight and offstanding, forming a ruff all around the neck to frame the head. The tail is well-feathered. The smooth coat is hard and dense with a definite undercoat, but without obvious ruff and no feathering on legs and tail. Colors are red (light golden to deep mahogany), black, blue, cinnamon (light fawn to deep cinnamon) and cream.

Characteristics

It is a Chow's nature to be reserved and discerning with strangers, causing him to be aloof and standoffish. With the human members of his family, he is extremely protective and loyal, although he does have a tendency to

A
B
C
D
E
F
G
H
I
J
K
L
M
N
O
P
Q
R
S
T
U
V
W
X
Y
Z

Left: The Chow moves rather differently from other dogs.

be a one-man dog. Because of the Chow's deep set eyes, he has limited peripheral vision so is best approached from the front.

Origins and History

The Chow Chow is at least 2,000 years old, probably older. The breed may have originated as a result of crossing the Tibetan Mastiff with the Samoyed of Siberia but others refute this on the strength of the breed's blue-black tongue. An alternative theory is that the Chow is the basic breed behind the ancestors of the Samoyed, Norwegian Elkhound, Keeshond and Pomeranian. The breed was certainly used as a hunting dog but has had other uses too. Thanks to its great scenting powers, staunchness on point and cleverness in hunting tactics, the Chow has been used frequently on Mongolian pheasant and on the francolin of Yunnan. Today a fashionable pet and guard dog, unfortunately he was often used as food in China, with the coat of the long-haired variety sometimes being used as clothing. The Chow was first exhibited in America in 1890 and was officially recognized by the AKC in 1903.

Health Issues

Breeders have worked hard to eliminate eye problems in Chow Chows, but entropion does still occur in some. Other problems include hip dysplasia and skin and hormonal troubles.

Left: The ruff around the neck frames the head.

Left: A black Chow Chow.

Exercise and Grooming

Not a high-energy breed, the Chow Chow will be content with a brisk daily walk and some free exercise in the yard. His thick coat requires considerable care, thorough grooming being necessary at least once each week. Almost daily attention is necessary during the transition period from puppy to adult.

Below: Only a youngster, but already highly successful in the showring.

A B C D E F G H I J K L M N O P Q R S T U V W X Y Z

A
B
C
D
E
F
G
H
I
J
K
L
M
N
O
P
Q
R
S
T
U
V
W
X
Y
Z

Above: *Note the solid blue-black tongue on this successful showdog.*

Below left: *Dam playing with her pup.*

Below: *A red Chow Chow displaying good black pigment.*

Cirneco Dell' Etna

Average height: dogs – 19-20 inches; bitches – 16.5-19 inches
Average weight: dogs – 22-26.5 pounds; bitches – 17.5-22 pounds

Appearance

The Cirneco is squarely proportioned, its depth of chest being slightly less that the height from ground to elbow. The muzzle is pointed with a straight bridge to the nose and is at least 80% the length of the skull. The skin is fine and taut, fitting well into the underlying tissue. Hair is smooth on head, ears and legs and longer, but close-lying, on body and tail. Color can be a self-colored tan, more or less intense, or diluted; or it may be tan with white. Self colored white, or white with tan patches is tolerated, but pigment should never show black patches, not should it be unpigmented. When moving, the Cirneco tends to move at a gallop, with intermittent trotting phases.

Characteristics

A hunting dog that has a strong temperament, this is not a breed that is particularly easy to train and needs to be introduced carefully to

Below: A lovely example of the breed, showing the fine, taught skin.

BREED NOTES

SIZE	GROOMING
✔✔	✔

EXERCISE	LIFESPAN
✔✔✔	✔✔

Johnson

A
B
C
D
E
F
G
H
I
J
K
L
M
N
O
P
Q
R
S
T
U
V
W
X
Y
Z

Above: The Cirneco is a self-colored tan.

other dogs and to children. But the Cirneco is a lively, friendly companion that is gentle and affectionate.

Origins and History

The Cirneco dell'Etna, also known as the Sicilian Greyhound is a small, primitive breed used in Sicily to hunt rabbits on and near the slopes of the Mount Etna volcano. It has almost identical roots to the Pharaoh Hound and is remarkably similar in appearance, although much smaller. The breed appears to have arrived in Sicily around 3,000 years ago, since when it has bred true to type due to its isolation.

There are claims, however, that the breed was in Sicily even earlier. Almost disappearing over the centuries, in the 1900s it was revived and is now fairly common in its homeland. The Cirneco is also capable of tracking and is also used for feathered game.

Exercise and Grooming

An agile and energetic breed the Cirneco dell'Etna should be ample opportunity for exercise in a safely enclosed area. A smooth coated dog, grooming is minimal, a thorough occasional brushing being needed to keep the coat in good order.

Right: The muzzle is pointed with a straight bridge to the nose.

Opposite: Always on the alert.

A
B
C
D
E
F
G
H
I
J
K
L
M
N
O
P
Q
R
S
T
U
V
W
X
Y
Z

Clumber Spaniel

Average height: dogs – 18-20 inches; bitches – 17-19 inches
Average weight: dogs – 70-85 pounds; bitches – 55-70 pounds

Appearance

Long, low and substantial, the Clumber Spaniel has a deep chest, massive bone and good feet, essential if he is to move though dense underbrush in pursuit of game. His white coat enables him to be seen by the hunter as he works within gun range. His head is

Below: The Clumber has a massive head with a heavy brow.

massive with a heavy brow, the muzzle broad and deep to facilitate retrieving many species of game. The flews of the upper jaw are strongly developed giving a square look when viewed from the side. The tail may be docked or left natural. Coat on the body is dense, straight and flat. It is soft to the touch, but weather-resistant. There is a good neck frill and slight feathering on ears,

BREED NOTES	
SIZE	GROOMING
✓	✓
✓	✓
✓	
EXERCISE	LIFESPAN
✓	✓
✓	✓

legs, belly and tail. The Clumber is primarily a white dog with lemon or orange markings

Characteristics

Gentle, loyal and affectionate, the Clumber Spaniel has an intrinsic desire to please. He is an intelligent and independent thinker, displaying determination and a strong sense of purpose while working. The Clumber is dignified and may initially seem aloof with people he does not know, but in time will display his playful, loving nature.

Origins and History

The Clumber is different from the other spaniels, causing is origin to be shrouded in doubt. It is generally believed that amongst his ancestors are Basset Hounds, early Alpine Spaniels and various

Above: *The Clumber can retrieve many types of game.*

Below: *Long, low and substantial.*

other breeds. Originating in France possibly as early as the 18th century, during the French Revolution the Duc de Noailles moved his kennel of spaniels to England for sanctuary, housing them in the Duke of Newcastle's kennels at Clumber Park in Nottinghamshire. Clumbers were first shown in England in 1859 but had arrived in Canada in 1844 with a member of the British army. There has always been controversy over the exposure of the haw (the skin that covers the eye) but eventually, the AKC standard settled that "some haw may show", definitively ending the debate.

A
B
C
D
E
F
G
H
I
J
K
L
M
N
O
P
Q
R
S
T
U
V
W
X
Y
Z

Above: This youngster is already very successful in the showring.

Caption: An intelligent and independent thinker.

Health Issues

Heath concerns include hip dysplasia, hypothyroidism, eye problems and possible ear problems due to the drooping ears.

Exercise and Grooming

The Clumber Spaniel needs a lot of exercise to keep fit and in good shape. Daily walks and free exercise are important, and too much weight gain should be avoided by controlling the diet. Do not over-exercise young puppies as this can cause joint problems. Although the breed sheds heavily, a thorough grooming once a week will usually suffice, with trimming as applicable about every two months.

Cocker Spaniel

Average height: dogs – 15 inches; bitches – 14 inches
Average weight: none specified

Appearance

The American version of the Cocker Spaniel is smaller than the English, with a shorter muzzle and more prominent eyes. Here it is simply known as the Cocker Spaniel, but in England and most other countries it is prefixed by "American". This is the smallest breed in the Sporting Group with a sturdy, compact body,

BREED NOTES	
SIZE	**GROOMING**
✓✓	✓✓✓
EXERCISE	**LIFESPAN**
✓✓✓	✓✓

Left: A quality junior, the coat not yet having reached full maturity.

long, elegant ears and a cleanly chiseled, refined head. The topline slopes slightly toward strong, moderately bent, muscular quarters. The tail is docked. Coat on the head is short and fine, on the body medium length with an undercoat. Ears, chest, abdomen and legs are well feathered. The coat is silky, flat or slightly wavy and of a texture that permits easy care. Color may be black (with or without tan points), parti-color or any solid color other than black, ranging from lightest cream to dark red and including brown, or brown with tan points.

Left: A stunning example of a highly successful Champion, presented to perfection.

A
B
C
D
E
F
G
H
I
J
K
L
M
N
O
P
Q
R
S
T
U
V
W
X
Y
Z

Above: Head coat is short and fine, with well feathered ears and chest.

Characteristics

The Cocker Spaniel has a cheerful, sweet personality and is a wonderful companion, making a great friend for children. Playful, intelligent, trusting and loyal, he gets along well with other animals.

He is a gentle and trusting dog, but socialization at a young age is advisable to avoid any possible timidity when older. He is well suited either to the life of a

258

Above: Enjoying a romp with a youngster.

companion dog, or a gundog.

Origins and History

The American version of the Cocker Spaniel developed from the English Cocker that was taken to the USA.

In 1949 the AKC recognised this as a new and distinct breed and it is now one of the most popular. The name is believed to derive from the woodcock and today the breed is still used as a hunting dog that finds, flushes and retrieves upland game birds. As a rule he takes readily to water.

Health Issues

The American Cocker Spaniel is susceptible to some health problem such as deafness, autoimmune thyroiditis, chronic hepatitis, hypothyroidism, skin problems and autoimmune haemolytic anemia (AIHA) in which the dog's own immune system attacks its blood cells.

Exercise and Grooming

This is an energetic breed with a healthy dose of stamina, so will need daily walks and exercise in the yard to keep it fit and to provide mental stimulation as this is a dog that was bred to work. Correct presentation of a Cocker Spaniel is quite an art, trimming being done to enhance the dog's true lines should appear as natural as possible. The coat also needs to be gently brushed regularly. Eye care is important.

Left: The topline slopes slightly toward strong, muscular quarters.

A
B
C
D
E
F
G
H
I
J
K
L
M
N
O
P
Q
R
S
T
U
V
W
X
Y
Z

Collie

Average height: dogs – 24-26 inches; bitches – 22-24 inches
Average weight: dogs – 60-75 pounds; bitches – 50-65 pounds

Appearance

The Collie is a lithe, strong, responsive and active dog, with two coat varieties, rough and smooth. The head has a bright, alert expression and is rather light in comparison with body size. It has a smooth, clean outline, tapering gradually from ears to nose. The well-rounded muzzle is blunt but not square. The eyes have a clear, bright appearance, expressing intelligent inquisitiveness, particularly when the ears are drawn up on the alert. They are dark for preference, but in blue

BREED NOTES

SIZE	GROOMING	
	Long Coat	Smooth Coat
✓		
✓	✓	✓
✓	✓	
✓		

EXERCISE	LIFESPAN
✓	✓
✓	✓
✓	

merles either or both eyes may be merle or china in color. The body is a trifle long in proportion to height and the tail moderately long and bushy on the rough variety. Both coat textures have four recognized colors, sable and white, tricolor, blue merle, and white(predominantly white, preferably with sable, tri-color or blue merle markings). The smooth variety has a short, hard, dense, flat coat of good texture, with an abundance of undercoat, but the coat of the rough is abundant except on head and legs, the outer coat straight and harsh, the undercoat soft, furry and very dense. The coat is very abundant on the mane and frill, and well feathered at the back of the pasterns

Johnson

Left: A stunning tri-color

Characteristics

The Collie is no longer in great demand as a herder but has become a devoted family dog that has a particular affinity with small children. For many years he has been among the top twenty of the favorite dogs registered by the AKC. He is loyal, affectionate and a self-appointed guardian of everything he can see or hear.

Right: A blue merle.

Below: A well-proportioned show dog.

A
B
C
D
E
F
G
H
I
J
K
L
M
N
O
P
Q
R
S
T
U
V
W
X
Y
Z

Origins and History

Sheep-herding is one of the world's oldest occupations and the Collie's ancestors date far back in the history of the herding dogs of Scotland and northern England, but early shepherds saw no need for pedigrees which were not kept until the 19th century. The smooth variety was mainly used as a drover's dog used for guiding cows and sheep to market, not for standing over and guarding them at pasture. A dog called "Old Cockie"

Left: Always attentive

Below: These Rough Collies get along well together.

Right: This Best in Show winner show all the attributes of the breed, including the abundant mane and frill.

was born in 1867 and is credited with stamping characteristic type on the rough Collie and being responsible for introducing the sable coat color. Over the years the Collie has become slightly larger and heavier on this side of the Atlantic but there is no fundamental difference from the ideal Collie of the late 19th century. In recent years the TV programme "Lassie" brought the breed to the attention of a wide dog loving public of children and adults alike.

Health Issues

Generally a healthy breed, problems to look out for are epilepsy, Collie eye anomaly and canine cyclic neutropenia (Gray Collie Syndrome) which is a blood disorder present at birth. Some Collies have an

Johnson

A B C D E F G H I J K L M N O P Q R S T U V W X Y Z

A
B
C
D
E
F
G
H
I
J
K
L
M
N
O
P
Q
R
S
T
U
V
W
X
Y
Z

intolerance to Invermectin and its sister drugs.

Exercise and Grooming
Collies need plenty of exercise and are usually very good off the leash, but they do have a tendency to round up people and other animals, so please bear this in mind! Grooming the smooth variety is not a demanding task, but dead hair does need to be removed. The rough variety needs though grooming and brushing once a week.

Right and opposite: The Smooth Collie comes in the same variety of colors.

Below: Smooth Collie, Bearded Collie, Border Collie and Rough Collie.

A
B
C
D
E
F
G
H
I
J
K
L
M
N
O
P
Q
R
S
T
U
V
W
X
Y
Z

Coton de Tulear

Average height: dogs – 10-12.5 inches; bitches – 8.5-11 inches
Average weight: dogs – 8.8-13.2 pounds; bitches – 7.7-11 pounds

Appearance

This is a small, sweet, long-haired dog, the coat soft and fluffy to the touch with the texture of cotton. It is dense and profuse and can be very slightly wavy. The ground color is always white, but there may be a few slight shadings of light grey or red roan on the ears. His eyes are rather rounded, dark, lively and wide apart, the eyelids well pigmented with black or brown in keeping with the color of the nose. His ears are pendulous and high-set.

Characteristics

The Coton thrives on love and companionship. He will never tire

Left: The soft, fluffy coat has a cotton-like texture.

Opposite: Although the ground color is always white, there may be a few shadings on the ears

of TLC! Lively and always ready to play, he seldom tires and likes to jump around to attract attention. Very much an indoor dog, he acts as a useful alarm. He is very protective of his house and family and because of his keen hearing is constantly alert to strange noises.

Origins and History

The Coton de Tulear originates from the island of Madagascar off the south east coast of Africa. Small white dogs arrived in Madagascar in the 15th century, on ships sailing to the West Indies. Sometimes ladies travelled on these ships and their

Johnson

little dogs accompanied them. They also took care of the mice and rat population on board and were excellent seafaring companions. There is a story that some little white dogs survived from a shipwreck near Tulear, a small seaport at the southern tip of the island. These eventually bred with local dogs creating the breed we know today. The breed soon became a favourite of nobles became known as the "Royal Dog of Madagascar". The Coton has only been recognized since 1971,

when a Frenchman took some back to Madagascar and established the breed in France.

Health Issues

The Coton is seldom ill and has an average life expectancy of 16 years. Health problems to look out for are neo-natal ataxia, Progressive Retinal Atrophy (PRA), patella luxation and hip and elbow dysplasia.

Exercise and Grooming

The Coton enjoys a walk on a

leash and doesn't mind playing in the rain or snow, but his coat must always be thoroughly dried off. The coat needs gently brushing with a pin brush (without balls on the end) three or four times each week. Particular attention should be paid to coat care when it is changing from puppy to adult coat at around nine to fourteen months of age. The frequency of bathing is a matter of personal preference, but the choice of a suitable shampoo is important.

Curly-Coated Retriever

Average height: dogs – 25-27 inches; bitches – 23-25 inches
Average weight:

Appearance

This is a multi-purpose hunting retriever and to work all day he must be balanced and sound, strong, robust, quick and agile. He is a little higher on the leg than other retriever breeds. When in motion everything blends into a smooth, powerful, harmonious symmetry. His head is a longer-than-wide wedge, the muzzle clean cut. His rather large, almond-

BREED NOTES

SIZE	GROOMING
✓	✓
✓	✓
✓	

EXERCISE	LIFESPAN
✓	✓
✓	✓
✓	

Left: The head is a longer-than-wide wedge.

shaped eyes are black or brown in black dogs or amber in liver dogs. His rather small ears lie close to the head and his tail is carried straight or fairly straight, never docked. The hallmark of the Curly is his coat, which is a dense mass of small, tight, distinct, crisp curls lying close to the skin. It is water resistant and sufficiently dense to provide protection against weather, water and punishing cover. On the forehead, face, front of forelegs and feet the coat is short.

Characteristics

A proud, intelligent and steadfast dog, the Curly-Coated Retriever is intelligent and a charming, gentle family companion, biddable, responsive, calm and affectionate.

He is also a determined and durable hunter. Sometimes he can appear aloof and self-willed but his independence and poise should not be confused with shyness, or a lack of willingness to please.

Origins and History

Believed to be descended from the 16th century English Water Spaniel, the St John's Newfoundland, the

Below: This breed has a dense mass of small, tight, crisp curls.

retrieving setter and later the Poodle, this is one of the oldest retriever breeds. First exhibited at a show in England in the mid-19th century, in 1889 some were exported to New Zealand where they have long been used to retrieve duck and quail. In Australia the breed is still used on duck in the swamps and lagoons of the Murray River and is admired as a steady and tender-mouthed retriever. The breed was introduced to the USA in 1907 and first registered with the AKC in 1924.

Health Issues

Heath issues to be aware of in this breed are skin disorders, hip dysplasia, epilepsy, cancer and eye problems. The Curly can also be prone to obesity.

Exercise and Grooming

The Curly-Coated Retriever loves exercise and at least an hour each day should be set aside for this. He

Johnson

A
B
C
D
E
F
G
H
I
J
K
L
M
N
O
P
Q
R
S
T
U
V
W
X
Y
Z

Above: *The eyes are amber in liver dogs, but black or dark brown in blacks.*

loves a long walk followed by a swim, for he has a natural affinity for water. Grooming is minimal and should be limited so as not to flatten the curls. Feathering may be trimmed from the ears, belly, backs of forelegs, thighs, pasterns, hocks, and feet. On the tail, feathering should be removed. Short trimming of the coat on the ear is permitted but shearing of the body coat is undesirable.

Left: *The Curly-Coat is charming and affectionate.*

Czechoslovakian Wolfdog

Average height: dogs – at least 25.5 inches; bitches – at least 23.5 inches
Average weight: dogs – at least 57 pounds; bitches – at least 44 pounds

BREED NOTES

SIZE	GROOMING
✔ ✔ ✔	✔ ✔

EXERCISE	LIFESPAN
✔ ✔ ✔	✔ ✔

Left: This breed closely resembles the wolf.

Appearance
Closely resembling the wolf in appearance, the Czechoslovakian Wolfdog is tall, but light and strong. Its straight, thick hair is from yellow-gray to silver-gray, with a characteristic pale mask. The light eyes are set obliquely and although he does not look directly at his master he always knows where he is and what he is doing. He has a complete set of 42 teeth; these are very strong and may be a scissors or level bite. His chest is large, but more flat than barrel shaped. The forelimbs are straight and narrow set, with the paws slightly turned out.

Characteristics
This breed can run 100 km in a day, at a speed of 12 km per hour. It has a great sense of direction, reacting with lightening speed. The Czechoslovakian Wolfdog develops a very strong social relationship, not only with its owner but with the whole family. He can learn to live alongside other domestic pets, but difficulties can occur when he meets other animals. It is vital his passion for hunting is subdued during puppyhood. This is a playful breed that learns easily, but behaviour is strictly purposeful, so it is necessary to find motivation for training.

Origins and History
In 1955 a biological experiment took place in what was then the CSSR. This was the crossing of a German Shepherd Dog with a Carpathian Wolf and established

A
B
C
D
E
F
G
H
I
J
K
L
M
N
O
P
Q
R
S
T
U
V
W
X
Y
Z

section of the Border Guard and in 1982 the Czechoslovakian Wolfdog was recognized as a national breed.

Health Issues

Hip dysplasia can be a problem and sensitivity to some anesthetics has also been noted.

Exercise and Grooming

This breed cannot be left tied to a tree or alone in a backyard for Czechoslovakian Wolfdogs love being with people and need plenty of supervised exercise. The breed is not really suitable as a guard dog, nor is it suitable for the novice owner. Coat care is not difficult, but combing and brushing will need to be done, particularly so during the moulting season.

Left: Still a baby, but already portraying breed character.

Below: A typical show specimen.

Opposite: Puppies of this breed need lots of socialisation and understanding.

that the resultant offspring could be reared. A very high proportion of the products of these matings possessed the genetic requirements for continuation of breeding. In 1965, after the experiment had ended, a plan for development of this new breed was worked out combining the usable qualities of the wolf with the favourable qualities of the dog. During the 1970s most hybrids were sent to kennels belonging to the Bratislava

Dachshund

Average height: varies according to weight
Average weight: there are two sizes, Miniatures – under 11 pounds; Standards – 16-32 pounds

Appearance

Whether a Miniature or Standard variety, the Dachshund is low to ground, long in body and short in leg, with robust muscular development. For effective underground work, his front is strong, deep, long and cleanly muscled; his hindquarters are also strong and the pads of his feet are thick. The elastic, pliable skin does not have excessive wrinkling. He has a bold and confident head carriage and intelligent, alert facial expression. The head tapers uniformly to the nose and the dark-rimmed, almond-shaped eyes have an energetic, piercing expression. Only dappled dogs may have wall eyes; otherwise they are very dark. There are three coat varieties, smooth, wirehaired and longhaired.

Smooth: The coat is short, smooth and shining, neither too long nor too thick. The tail, tapering to a point, is well covered but not too richly haired. One colored Dachshunds include red and cream, with our without shadings of dark

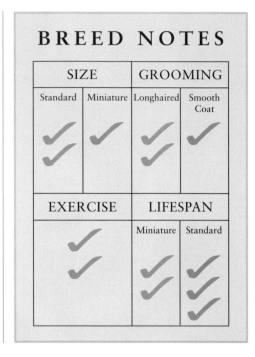

BREED NOTES

SIZE		GROOMING	
Standard	Miniature	Longhaired	Smooth Coat
✓✓	✓	✓✓	✓

EXERCISE	LIFESPAN	
	Miniature	Standard
✓	✓✓	✓✓

Above right and left: Wirehaireds in classic dachshund colors.

Left and right: Black and tan standard smooths with elegant carriage and heads held high.

hairs; two-colored include black, chocolate, wild boar, gray (blue) and fawn (Isabella), each with rich tan or cream markings. Dapple (merle) is a pattern expressed in the lighter areas, contrasting with the darker base color. Brindle is a pattern in which there are dark stripes over the entire body, though sometimes they are only visible on the tan points. Sable consists of a dark overlay on red dogs, the overlay hairs being double pigmented, the tip being much darker than the base color.

the legs, giving an elegant appearance. The tail is carried gracefully and here the hair attains its greatest length and forms a veritable flag. Hair color is as for the smooth variety.

Characteristics

This is a clever, lively, persistent and fearless dog with an outgoing personality. He can be courageous to the point of rashness! Full of fun, he is an affectionate family pet and wonderful companion. He has a fine hunting spirit, good nose, loud tongue and distinctive build, making him well-suited for below-ground work and for beating the bush. His keen nose

Below: A wirehaired standard with beard and eyebrows.

Above: This black and tan longhaired standard has a thick silky coat.

Wirehaired: The whole body is covered with a uniform, tight, short thick, rough, hard, outer coat but with a finer, somewhat softer undercoat. The distinctive facial furnishings include a beard and eyebrows. On the ears the hair is shorter than on the body, almost smooth. The robust tail is thickly haired, gradually tapering to a point. The most common colors are wild boar, black and tan, and various shades of red, but all colors and patterns listed for the smooth are admissible.

Longhaired: The sleek, glistening, often slightly wavy hair is longer under the neck, on forechest, underside of body, ears and behind

Above: This lightweight standard smooth puppy plays on the shore.

Below right: A chocolate and tan smooth dog puppy.

Below left: A litter of black and tan and chocolate and tan standard smooths.

makes him proficient at trailing.

Origins and History

The Dachshund, known as Teckels in many counties, are German in origin. As far back as the 15th to 17th centuries illustrations showed long-bodied, short-legged dogs with hound-type ears hunting badgers.

They had the tracking ability of hounds and the proportions and temperament of terriers. It was early in the 17th century that the name Dachshund, meaning "badger dog" in German, came to denote an actual type; and there were long and smooth coated varieties. Wirehaired Dachshunds followed much later, in

A B C **D** E F G H I J K L M N O P Q R S T U V W X Y Z

1890. Two sizes developed; dogs of 30-35 pounds were used on badger and wild boar, while the smaller ones, 16-22 pounds, proved effective against fox and hare. Dachshunds came to America in the 1880s and in 1935 they were added to AKC field trials to encourage hunting capacity and exemplary conformation and temperament.

Health Issues

The most common problems found are, diabetes mellitus, hip dysplasia, epilepsy, eye diseases, hypothyroidism, bloat and invertebral disc disease. Back problems occur because of the long length of back, so it is essential not to allow a Dcahshund to gain excess weight, nor to jump down from heights.

Above: A lustrous-coated longhaired miniature dachshund.

Below: A beautiful chocolate and tan standard smooth.

Above: A beautifully presented Minature Wirehaired Champion.

Right: A silky-coated miniature longhaired dog.

Exercise and Grooming

This is a game little dog of sturdy build and needs 20 to 40 minutes of exercise each day to keep him fit, including a good walk on a leash. Because of the breed's hunting instinct, the garden or yard must be well-fenced, always bearing in mind that this breed can dig! Coat care for the Smooth variety is limited; Longhaired Dachshunds must be thoroughly groomed at least once each week. Wires need their face furnishings combed at least once a week, plus occasional trimming and their coats need plucking two or three times a year. It is important to check ears regularly for all varieties.

A
B
C
D
E
F
G
H
I
J
K
L
M
N
O
P
Q
R
S
T
U
V
W
X
Y
Z

Dalmatian

Average height: 19-23 inches
Average weight: 50-55 pounds

Appearance

One of the most characteristic features of the Dalmatian is his spots, which should be round and well-defined, varying in size from a dime to a half-dollar. Spots are usually smaller on the head, legs and tail than on the body. He is poised, alert; strong, muscular and active, with an intelligent look about him. Not exaggerated in any way, nor coarse, he is capable of great endurance. His back is level and strong, the loin short, muscular and slightly arched and his tail, which is never docked, is not too low down and carried with a slight upward curve. The head is of fair length and without any loose skin, the eyes medium sized and rather rounded in appearance. The Doberman's rather high set ears are carried close to the head and should ideally have spots. The nose pigment corresponds with coat color, black on black spotted dogs and brown in liver-spotted; in both the base color of the short, dense coat is white. Feet are very important; they are round and compact with thick, elastic pads and well arched toes.

Below: Dalmatian bitch attentive to owner.

Characteristics

The Dalmatian has a stable,

BREED NOTES

SIZE	GROOMING
✓ ✓ ✓	✓

EXERCISE	LIFESPAN
✓ ✓ ✓	✓ ✓

Opposite: There are more black spotted dogs, but liver spotted ones occur too.

A
B
C
D
E
F
G
H
I
J
K
L
M
N
O
P
Q
R
S
T
U
V
W
X
Y
Z

Above: This puppy (left) already shows similarities to the older dog

outgoing temperament, and yet he is dignified. He should be carefully reared and disciplined during puppyhood to prevent hyperactivity; because of his determined nature he can easily acquire bad habits. This is an affectionate breed that enjoys company.

Origins and History
Despite the name, there is no firm evidence that the breed actually originated in Dalmatia. The

Left: This dog lives on a farm and constantly needs legs and feet washing!

Dalmatian is a very old breed, virtually unchanged through many centuries, spotted dogs having appeared in Europe, Asia, and Africa. Such dogs have been depicted on walls of tombs, running behind Egyptian chariots and have also been found on frescos dating back to the 14th century. Spotted dogs often accompanied Romanies, or gypsies, as they wandered from India throughout Europe and on to England. In England this was used as a coach dog, traveling many miles alongside the coach and even under its wheels. When brought to the USA he was used as a Fire House mascot and often helped to locate and rescue victims of the fire.

Left: The Dalmatian should have an intelligent look.

Below: Perhaps because of their coat color, these two are the best of friends!

A
B
C
D
E
F
G
H
I
J
K
L
M
N
O
P
Q
R
S
T
U
V
W
X
Y
Z

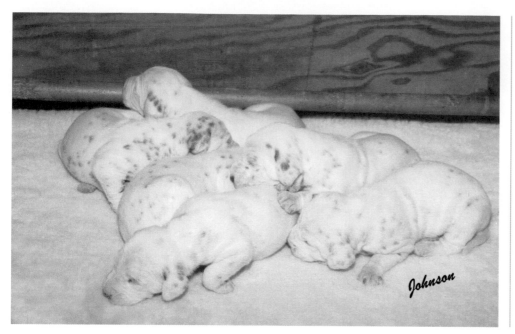

Health Issues

Dalmatians, like all other breeds, encounter health problems form time to time. Some of these are genetic, others viral. They include skin and coat disorders by way of allergy, epilepsy, deafness, hip dysplasia, hypothyroidism and

Left: Dalmatian puppies are born white and develop their spots later.

Below: A fine looking show dog.

Above: 'We always look forward to feeding time!'

Left: The Damlatian is not exaggerated in any way.

urolithiasis (crystals forming in the urine to create stones).

Exercise and Grooming

This high energy breed will enjoy two hours of exercise each day; should have sufficient running time and roadwork to build up and maintain his muscles. Puppies should not be over-exercised and owners should remember that Dalmatians can not only run, but also often jump and climb! Grooming once a week with a grooming mitt or curry comb is sufficient, finishing off with a soft cloth to give a nice shine.

Dandie Dinmont Terrier

Average height: 8-11 inches
Average weight: 18-24 pounds

Johnson

BREED NOTES

SIZE	GROOMING
✓ ✓	✓ ✓
EXERCISE	LIFESPAN
✓ ✓	✓ ✓

Left: Most dogs love toys and this
Dandie is no exception.

Opposite: Displaying all the characteristics of the breed.

Appearance

The Dandie Dinmont Terrier was
bred to go to ground, so is a long,
low-stationed dog with a curved
outline. His body is sturdy and
flexible, with ample bone and
muscle He has a very distinctive,
large head with a silky topknot and
his large, dark eyes have a soft, wise
expression. The Dandie's teeth are
very strong, especially the canines,
which are an extraordinary size for
a small dog, giving great holding
and punishing power. His ears are
set well back, low on the skull and
hang close to the cheek. The coat is
about two inches long, a
combination of hardish and soft
hair, giving a crisp texture, termed
"pily" or "pencilled". The head is
covered with very soft, silky hair,
framing the eyes. There is feathering
on some parts and the upper-side of
the scimitar-shaped tail is crisper
than on the body. Color is mustard
or pepper.

Characteristics

This is an independent breed,
determined, reserved and intelligent.
A game little dog, the Dandie
Dinmont combines an affectionate
and dignified nature with tenacity
and boldness when working. He is
devoted to his family and very
sociable, getting along well with
other pets provided they have been
introduced whilst young. He is fond
of children and an excellent guard,
but does have a will of his own.

Origins and History

First recorded as a distinct type of
breed around 1700, the Dandie
Dinmont Terrier was created from
selected specimens of the rough
native terrier of the border country
between England and Scotland. He
had been bred true to type long
before he was given a name and
was renowned for his hunting of the
otter and badger. Sir Walter Scott
made these dogs famous in his book
Guy Mannering, published in 1814.

His character Dandie Dinmont, a farmer: kept six called Auld Pepper, Auld Mustard, Young Pepper, Young Mustard, Little Pepper and Little Mustard. From this time on the breed has been known as the Dandie Dinmont Terrier.

Health Issues

Being a long, low dog, the Dandie Dinmont is susceptible to intervertebral disc problems so care should be taken to avoid stair-climbing and jumping on and off furniture. Other problems include hip dysplasia, kneecap luxation, torn ligaments, arthritis and glycoma.

Exercise and Grooming

The Dandie Dinmont will be content with about twenty minutes' exercise each day, but take care when he is off the lead as he is a hunter by nature and might just dash off after a squirrel! During puppyhood the coat will need to be combed daily to avoid matting. Adult Dandie Dinmonts require hand-stripping (ideally by an expert) two or three times each year. If the coat is neglected for a long period, it may be necessary to strip it down close to the skin; it can then take months for the coat to grow back in properly again. Feet need regular trimming.

Above: Moving beautifully in the show ring having won Best of Breed.

A
B
C
D
E
F
G
H
I
J
K
L
M
N
O
P
Q
R
S
T
U
V
W
X
Y
Z

Doberman Pinscher

Average height: dogs – 26-28 inches; bitches – 24-26 inches
Average weight:

Appearance

A compact, muscular, powerful dog, the Doberman has been built for great endurance and speed. His appearance is elegant with a proud carriage, reflecting great nobility; it is often said that he bears a likeness to a thoroughbred horse. He is Energetic, watchful, determined, alert, fearless, loyal and obedient. His head resembles a blunt wedge and the almond-shaped, moderately deep-set eyes have a vigorous, energetic expression. Ears are normally cropped and carried erect. The tail is usually docked at about the second joint and appears to be a continuation of the spine. This is a smooth-haired breed, the short, hard, thick coat lying close. Colors are black, red, blue and fawn (Isabella), with sharply defined rust markings above each eye and on the muzzle, throat, forechest, on all legs and feet, and below the tail.

Characteristics

The Doberman was bred as a guard dog and is energetic, watchful, determined, alert and fearless, but also loyal and obedient. Being an intelligent dog, he is easy to train, but he must be trained properly and taught clearly taught who is boss. A bored dog will develop behaviour problems. Socialized early with

BREED NOTES

SIZE	GROUMING
✔ ✔ ✔	✔
EXERCISE	**LIFESPAN**
✔ ✔ ✔	✔ ✔

Below: Energetic, watchful and determined.

Above: *A Doberman in training.*

Right: *Loyal and obedient*

other dogs, pets and children, the Doberman can make a lovely family pet. He can be very protective of his owners, so socialization with other dogs is important to prevent over protectiveness

Origins and History

The Doberman takes its name from Louis Dobermann of Apolda a tax collector who wanted a medium size dog as a guard, as well as a companion. Originating in Germany around 1900, the breeds that may have been involved in its formation are the old shorthaired shepherd, Rottweiler, Black and Tan Terrier and the German Pinscher. When

A
B
C
D
E
F
G
H
I
J
K
L
M
N
O
P
Q
R
S
T
U
V
W
X
Y
Z

properly bred and trained, Doberman has become well known as a friend and guardian. The breed's intelligence and ability to absorb and retain training have caused it to be used as a police and war dog. A life-sized bronze Doberman, called Always Faithful, is located in Guam at the war dog cemetery at the US naval base in Orote Point. The Doberman Pinscher Club of America was founded in 1921.

Health Issues

Generally a healthy breed, the Doberman does have some health problems including bloat, dilated cardiomyopathy (DCM), cancer, chronic hepatitis, von Willebrand's Disease, hypothyroidism, color

Above: Two baby puppies, tiny enough to hold in each hand.

Below: These dogs have natural ears, but in America they are often cropped.

Above: A successful show dog, displaying the attributes of the breed.

dilution alopecia and wobbler's syndrome (cervical vertebral instability).

Exercise and Grooming

A dynamic breed, the Doberman needs thorough exercise daily, for around two hours, and he should have a well fenced, spacious yard to run in. Exercise should limited until the age of twelve months. He is rather sensitive to the cold, so should not be left outside at night. Grooming is minimal; a good rub down with a rubber grooming mitt will remove any dead or loose hair.

Right: This splendid head clearly shows the rust markings.

A
B
C
D
E
F
G
H
I
J
K
L
M
N
O
P
Q
R
S
T
U
V
W
X
Y
Z

Dogue de Bordeaux

Average height: dogs – 23.5-27 inches; bitches – 23-26 inches
Average weight: dogs – at least 110 pounds; bitches – at least 99 pounds

Appearance

One of the most ancient French breeds, the Dogue de Bordeaux is a very powerful dog with a muscular body, yet retaining a harmonious outline. He is built rather close to the ground, the deepest point from chest to ground being slightly less than the depth of the chest. His massive head, furrowed with symmetrical wrinkles, is characteristic; it is large angular, broad and rather short. He has a frank expression. His rather high set ears are quite small in proportion to the size of the skull. The nose, with its well-opened nostrils, is self colored and the jaws are very powerful and broad with a pronounced chin. The Dogue de Bordeaux has an undershot bite with no contact between the upper and lower incisor teeth. The fine, short coat is soft to the touch, the skin thick and sufficiently loose fitting. The coat is self colored, in all shades of fawn, a rich color being desirable.

Characteristics

This breed is gifted for guarding with vigilance and great courage, but without aggressiveness. A very good companion, he is attached to and affectionate toward his master and bonds closely with his family. The breed is usually very good with children and will accept other household pets if introduced hen young. This is not a breed suited to being left alone for a long period of time as he will associate this as punishment. The Dogue de Bordeaux will protect his family and territory if threatened.

Origins and History

There are numerous different theories as to how and when the breed evolved; what is certain is that that the Dogue de Bordeaux shares the same common links as all modern molossers. The breed was used as a guardian, a hunter, and fighter, trained to bait bulls, bears, and

BREED NOTES

SIZE	GROOMING
✔ ✔ ✔	✔

EXERCISE	LIFESPAN
✔ ✔ ✔	✔ ✔

Johnson

Left: A powerful dog with muscular body.

A B C **D** E F G H I J K L M N O P Q R S T U V W X Y Z

jaguars, to hunt boars, herd cattle, and protect the homes, butcher shops, and vineyards of their masters. The Dogue was often found in wealthy French households, but many perished with their masters during the Revolution. Adolph Hitler was said to have demanded the

execution of all dogs of this breed because of their devout loyalty to their owners! During the 1960s a group of enthusiasts set about rebuilding the breed. It was known in the USA in the 1890s but the breed's modern history here really began in 1959 and the Dogue can now be found in small numbers across the country.

Health Issues

Health problems that have been encountered include hip and elbow dysplasia, demeodectic mange, bloat, heart problems, eye problems and hypothyroidism. Puppies can gain as much as four pounds a week in weight, so may experience eosinophilic panosteitis (Pano). This

Left: His massive head has a rather frank expression.

Above: The Dogue de Bordeaux has common links to all modern molossers.

is usually seen between five and twelve months and is caused by excessive bone production in the long bones; although dogs thus affected will grow out of it, it is painful.

Exercise and Grooming

A good hour a day is needed, ideally divided into several short walks, allowing short periods for free run and play. Too much exercise at a young age can easily lead to bone and joint related problems later in life. Grooming is relatively easy; a rubber grooming mitt used on the short coat once a week will remove any loose or dead hair. The skin folds on the face should be cleaned regularly to prevent skin infections.

English Cocker Spaniel

Average height: dogs – 16-17 inches; bitches – 15-16 inches
Average weight: dogs – 28-34 pounds; bitches – 26-32 pounds

Appearance

The English Cocker Spaniel is a solidly built dog, but not cloddy or coarse. He is compactly built with a powerful gait, capable of covering the ground effortlessly, penetrating dense cover to flush and retrieve game. He is alive with energy, an active, merry sporting dog, the incessant action of his tail while working conveying his enjoyment. His strong head is softly contoured, without any sharp angles, his expression soft and melting, whilst at the same time dignified, alert and intelligent. His medium sized eyes are wide set and slightly oval, enhancing his expression. The low set ears lie close to the head and are covered in silky, straight or slightly wavy hair. Nostrils are wide for proper development of scenting ability and the strong jaws are capable of carrying game. Coat on the head is short and fine, on the body it is of medium length, flat or slightly wavy, silky

BREED NOTES

SIZE	GROOMING
✓✓	✓✓
EXERCISE	**LIFESPAN**
✓✓	✓✓

Left: The wide set eyes are slightly oval, the expression soft and melting.

Opposite top: The English Cocker is compactly built.

Opposite: 'This bed is so snug!'

Opposite right: Low set ears are covered in silky hair.

A
B
C
D
E
F
G
H
I
J
K
L
M
N
O
P
Q
R
S
T
U
V
W
X
Y
Z

Left: A tri-colored puppy

Below and right: *Just two of many different coat colors in this breed.*

Opposite bottom *Inseparable!*

in texture and well feathered. There is wide variety of colors to choose from in this breed.

Characteristics
The English Cocker has a happy

A
B
C
D
E
F
G
H
I
J
K
L
M
N
O
P
Q
R
S
T
U
V
W
X
Y
Z

Above: A good game with a suitable toy

Below: Not all play-things are safe!

disposition and is an affectionate dog. He is playful, energetic and always eager to please. Although he is an active, sporting dog, he thoroughly enjoys family life.

Origins and History
The English Cocker Spaniel descended from the original spaniels of Spain. Not until the 17th century did spaniels begin to divide into separate breeds, depending on size, type and hunting ability. The English Cocker Spaniel Club of America was formed in 1935 but the AKC did not recognise the English and American Cocker Spaniels as two separate breeds until 1946.

Health Issues
This is generally a healthy breed, but problems encountered include Progressive Retinal Atrophy (PRA), hip dysplasia, chronic hepatitis and familial nephropathy

(FN), a hereditary, fatal kidney disease found in young Cockers.

Exercise and Grooming

An English Cocker Spaniel should have 40 to 60 minutes of exercise each day, with time allowed off the lead to run off energy. They love to swim, so take care that any water they are near is safe. Grooming styles vary according to the purpose of the dog; show dogs are generally hand stripped three or four times a year. Trimming is permitted to remove overabundant hair and to enhance the dog's true lines, but it should appear as natural as possible. Brushing should be done weekly and ears must be kept clean to avoid infection.

Right: Training to move correctly on the left.

Below: This is an active, sporting dog.

English Foxhound

Average height: 23-27 inches
Average weight: 55-75 pounds

Appearance

Symmetry of the Foxhound is of greatest importance. The head is of full size, but not heavy, the brow pronounced, but not high or sharp. Ears are set on low, and lie close to the cheeks. Most English hounds are "rounded", meaning that about 1? inches is taken off the end of the ear. The long, clean neck leads into long, well sloped shoulders, clothed in muscle, without being heavy. The chest should girth over 31 inches in a 24 inch hound, and the back ribs must be very deep. Although coat color is not considered very important, it should be a good hound color which is black, tan, and white, or any combination of these three, also compounds of white and the color of the hare and badger, or yellow, or tan. The coat is short, dense, hard, and glossy. Hindquarters must be very strong and the topline of the back absolutely level. Every Master of Foxhounds insists on legs that are

Below: Judging English Foxhounds at a Hound Show.

BREED NOTES	
SIZE	GROOMING
✓ ✓ ✓	✓
EXERCISE	LIFESPAN
✓ ✓ ✓	✓ ✓

as straight as a post, and as strong; the size of bone at the ankle being especially regarded as all important.

Characteristics

An active hunter, the English Foxhound is very responsive and obedient to his master. Foxhounds need people; they are fairly friendly to strangers, especially children, and are generally good with other dogs. With a similar personality to the American Foxhound, the English is sturdier and slower.

Origins and History

The English Foxhound's roots lie in Great Britain where he was developed by mixing various hounds, then subsequently introducing Greyhound, Bulldog, and Fox Terrier blood. It was from these three breeds that he inherited

sudden spurts of speed during the chase, force, authority and passion for the hunt. Careful breeding records have been kept by the Masters of the Hounds for centuries. The breed has always been used for foxhunting, following the English tradition of riding to hounds. The earliest entries in the English Foxhound Stud Book of

Above: A well trained hunting hound pack.

America date back to 1890, but there are records indicating that there were many earlier importations. The English Foxhound is a versatile breed that can be trained to hunt almost any ground game. With his stamina, good nose and determination, he is a prized companion in the field.

Health Issues

This is a very healthy breed, and is not known for developing any serious heath issues.

Exercise and Grooming

A happy English Foxhound has plenty of daily running as this is active breed. He can run for hours at a consistent speed and can become destructive if confined too much. He is also likely to take off after any interesting scent, so should only be let off the leash in a safe place. Grooming is easy with a firm bristle brush. A Foxhound should be shampooed only when necessary.

Left: English Foxhound exhibited in conformation classes.

A
B
C
D
E
F
G
H
I
J
K
L
M
N
O
P
Q
R
S
T
U
V
W
X
Y
Z

English Setter

Average height: dogs – 25 inches; bitches – 24 inches
Average weight: dogs – 65-80 pounds; bitches – 45-55 pounds

BREED NOTES

SIZE	GROOMING
✓ ✓ ✓	✓ ✓

EXERCISE	LIFESPAN
✓ ✓ ✓	✓ ✓

Left: A blend of strength, stamina, grace and style.

The muzzle is long and square when viewed from the side, of good depth with flews squared and fairly pendant. A close scissors bite preferred but an even bite is acceptable. Eyes are dark brown, the darker the better; they are bright and spaced to give a mild, intelligent expression. Ears are set well back and low, and when relaxed are carried close to the head. The coat is flat, without curl or wooliness. The feathering on ears, chest, abdomen, underside of thighs, back of all legs and tail is of good length but not so excessive as to hide true lines and movement or to affect the dog's appearance or function as a sporting dog. The ground color is white, with intermingling of darker hairs

Appearance

The English Setter is an elegant, substantial and symmetrical gun dog; the ideal blend of strength, stamina, grace, and style. Males look decidedly masculine, without coarseness, and females decidedly feminine without over-refinement.

Above: Blue belton

Right: A suitable dish for feeding a number of pups together.

energy and suitable for families who can give them plenty of attention and engage them in activities. The English Setter is also a good hunting dog.

Origins and History

The English Setter was a trained bird dog more than 400 years ago. The breed has originated from crosses between the Spanish Pointer, large Water Spaniel and Springer Spaniel, producing a superb bird dog with a high degree of proficiency in finding and pointing game in open country. Edward Laverack was instrumental in the development of the breed; over time he inbred successfully to produce beautiful English Setters. The first show at which the breed was exhibited was held at Newcastle-on-Tyne in 1859. A few years later English Setters were imported to North America.

resulting in belton markings. Colors are orange belton, blue belton (white with black markings), tricolor (blue belton with tan on muzzle, over the eyes and on the legs), lemon belton and, finally, liver belton.

Characteristics

Gentle, affectionate and friendly, the English Setter is a good natured breed. However, he can be strong willed and irresponsibly playful. This is a people oriented dog, full of

A
B
C
D
E
F
G
H
I
J
K
L
M
N
O
P
Q
R
S
T
U
V
W
X
Y
Z

Johnson

Health Issues

A relatively healthy breed, illnesses that have been found in the breed are hip dysplasia, elbow dysplasia and hypothyroidism

Exercise and Grooming

Plenty of exercise is important, with the opportunity for free running. Without a long, daily walk, the English Setter can become difficult to manage. The coat needs regular brushing and combing, with extra care needed when it is shedding. The hair on the bottom of the feet should be trimmed. Any burrs picked up by the coat must be checked for daily and removed immediately. A bath should only be given when necessary. English Setters that are exhibited in shows in US are trimmed.

Opposite: Puppy enjoying the Springtime

Above: Always doing something interesting!

Below: A substantial, symmetrical gundog.

English Springer Spaniel

Average height: dogs – 20 inches; bitches – 19 inches
Average weight: dogs – 50 pounds; bitches – 40 pounds

Appearance

This is a medium sized, compact, sturdy sporting dog with a docked tail, carried at a right angle to the backline in Terrier fashion. The moderately long coat has feathering on legs, ears, chest and brisket. The expression is soft and gentle, the ears pendulous. The beauty of the English Springer's head lies in a combination of strength and refinement. His expression is alert, kindly and trusting, and his eyes, more than any other feature, are the essence of the Springer's appeal. He has an outer coat of medium length, flat or wavy hair, and a short, soft, dense undercoat. This double coat offers protection against water and thorns. There is fringing on ears, chest, legs and belly, while on the head, front of forelegs and lower portion of the back legs, the hair is short and fine. The tail may be trimmed but above all, the appearance should be natural. Coat color may be black or liver with white markings or predominantly white with black or

Below: Waiting attentively.

Opposite: A quality head.

BREED NOTES

SIZE	GROOMING
✔ ✔	✔ ✔

EXERCISE	LIFESPAN
✔ ✔ ✔	✔ ✔

Johnson

A
B
C
D
E
F
G
H
I
J
K
L
M
N
O
P
Q
R
S
T
U
V
W
X
Y
Z

Left: '*Can we go over this gate yet?*'

liver markings; blue or liver roan; or tricolour.

Characteristics

The English Springer Spaniel is first and foremost a sporting dog of the Spaniel family. He must look, behave and move in character. Friendly and eager to please, he is quick to learn and willing to obey. Most English Springers are gentle, sociable, good natured and suitable for children. They like to be with people and have

Below: *The docked tail is carried at a right angle to the topline.*

Above: Moving with finesse.

Above: An attractive trio.

a tendency to get into trouble when they are left alone. With other animals he is usually amiable, but not with birds! There is quite a difference between the working and show Spaniels, but both need sensible training from the outset.

Origins and History

In the 1880's, Springers and Cockers were often born in the same litter, size alone being the distinguishing factor, but in 1880 the American Spaniel Club was founded, and anything over 28 pounds was classified as a Springer. In 1902, the English Kennel Club granted Springers and Cocker separate breed status. The English Springer Spaniel

A
B
C
D
E
F
G
H
I
J
K
L
M
N
O
P
Q
R
S
T
U
V
W
X
Y
Z

Left: Ever ready for play!

unmistakable.

Health Issues
The health issues to look out for are hip dysplasia and eye problems. Ear problems can usually be prevented by regular cleaning.

Exercise and Grooming
The English Springer Spaniel needs a lot of exercise so should be taken on good walks and also be allowed to run and play off the leash. The breed loves swimming and makes a good retriever. Some grooming is needed, especially on the feathering, and discrete trimming will be necessary around the head, feet and ears. It is important to remove all debris from the coat following exercise.

Field Trial Association was formed in 1924, becoming the parent club of the breed. In America a breed standard was drawn up in 1927 and revised five years later, fostering the natural ability of the Springer as a hunting dog. This is a great sporting dog whose purpose is to hunt and find game, but his inherent elegance and economy of movement is

Below: Alert, kindly expression.

Below: Out on a shoot.

Above: *The English Springer loves a country life.*

Below: *The moderately long coat has some feathering.*

Above: *A great sporting dog.*

A
B
C
D
E
F
G
H
I
J
K
L
M
N
O
P
Q
R
S
T
U
V
W
X
Y
Z

English Toy Spaniel

Average height: 10-11 inches
Average weight: 8-14 pounds

Appearance

The English Toy Spaniel is a compact, cobby little dog with a short nose and domed head. It is his head that is his most distinctive characteristic, large in comparison to his size and with a plush, chubby look about it, coupled with a sense of refinement. The large eyes are very dark brown or black, adding to the soft, appealing expression and indicating an intelligent nature. The long, low-set ears, fringed with heavy feathering, lie close to the head. He has a slightly undershot bite with a square, broad, deep, well

Below: A Prince Charles, tri-color

turned-up jaw, the lips meeting properly. This little Spaniel's tail is usually docked, but not always; some are born with a short, screw tail. The feathering on the tail gives it a longer appearance. The silken, profuse coat has flowing feathering. Good coats and long ear fringes are a desired and prized attribute.

There are four distinct color varieties. Blenheim is red and white (deep red or chestnut markings on a pearly ground), often carrying a prized "thumb mark" in the centre of the skull; Prince Charles is a tri-color (pearly white ground with black and tan markings; King

Charles, which is black and tan and finally Ruby is a self-colored rich mahogany red.

Characteristics

The English Toy Spaniel is a bright, interested little dog, affectionate and willing to please. He is soft and quiet, but sometimes rather mischievous and occasionally likes to act the clown! He tends to choose his loved ones and can be a little shy when confronted with unfamiliar situations or people. This little breed can easily become overwhelmed in a chaotic household where children are left unsupervised. Usually they get along well with other dogs if sensibly introduced.

Origins and History

It is likely that the English Toy

Opposite: Blenheim, red and white.

BREED NOTES

SIZE	GROOMING
✓	✓
	✓
EXERCISE	LIFESPAN
✓	✓
	✓

A
B
C
D
E
F
G
H
I
J
K
L
M
N
O
P
Q
R
S
T
U
V
W
X
Y
Z

Above: A short nose and domed head.

Above right and below: These are both black and tans.

Terrier's distant ancestors hailed from Japan and possibly China. The breed was undoubtedly in England at least a hundred years before King Charles I, although it was from this king that the black and tan variety took its name. The breed was also closely associated with King Charles II; indeed in Britain today, all the colors go under the name of King Charles Spaniel. Although primarily a companion dog, this little spaniel was also used for hunting woodcock and small game birds. The Duke of Marlborough was a great fancier of the breed and, living as he did at Blenheim Palace, the Blenheim variety took this name. The AKC recognised this breed as far back as 1886.
Health Issues

Right: A good coat and long ear fringes are prized attributes.

Health problems include slipping patella, cardiac problems, occasional disc problems and eye problems including glaucoma, cataracts and retinal dysplasia. Chronic obstructive pulmonary disease can occur in hot humid weather, especially in heavily polluted areas. Some have molera (soft spot in the skull) until the age of about one year, but this is a breed trait, not a health problem.

Exercise and Grooming

This is not an outdoor dog; short walks and free run in a small,

Caption: Wearing a snood helps to protect the ear fringes.

enclosed yard is sufficient. Although a fairly long-coated breed, the English Toy Spaniel's grooming needs are only minimal. Especial care should be taken to keep the coat free of matts behind the ears, elbows and at the back of the legs. Ears too need special attention.

A
B
C
D
E
F
G
H
I
J
K
L
M
N
O
P
Q
R
S
T
U
V
W
X
Y
Z

Entlebucher Mountain Dog

Average height: dogs – 17-20 inches; bitches – 16.5-19 inches
Average weight: dogs – ? pounds; bitches – ? pounds

Appearance

The Entlebucher Mountain Dog is of medium size and compactly built, slightly longer than tall. His skull is flat on top and his muzzle straight and strong. He has dark brown lively eyes and his medium-sized ears are set high, triangular in shape and slightly rounded at the tip. He has a level topline and his chest is deep and capacious with a pronounced forechest. He may have a naturally grown tail or it may be a congenital bobtail. This breed is double-coated, with a short, close fitting, harsh, shiny topcoat and a

BREED NOTES

SIZE	GROOMING
✓ ✓	✓
EXERCISE	LIFESPAN
✓ ✓	✓ ✓

Left: Black and tan with white markings.

dense undercoat. He is typically tricolored, black and tan with white markings, as symmetrical as possible.

Characteristics

The Entlebucher has hereditary qualities of a lively, tireless, driving dog. He is suitable as a utility dog as well as a companion. Today, still on a modest scale, he has found admirers and enjoys increased popularity as a family dog. He is quiet, easy going and friendly, and enjoys the company of people and other dogs too. Gentle with children, he is extremely devoted to his family.

Origins and History

The Entlebucher Mountain Dog is

the smallest of the four Swiss mountain dogs, all of which are descended from molosser-types taken to the country by the Romans over 2,000 years ago. The Entlebucher was used as a cattle herding dog, bringing the dairy cows in from mountain pastures. The breed originated in Entlebuch, a valley in the district of Lucerne and Berne. There is reference to the breed under the name, "Entlebucherhund" in 1889. Following that date it appears that no distinction was made between the Entlebucher and the Appenzeller (the other smaller Swiss breed. Four were exhibited at a dog show in 1913 but the Swiss Club of Entlebuch Cattle Dogs was not founded until 1926; a year later the first breed standard appeared. This breed has been recorded in the AKC's Foundation Stock Service since 2000.

Below: A compactly built breed, often with a natural bobtail.

Above: Showing great respect for her owner

Health Issues

This is a strong, healthy breed but sometimes problems do occur such as hip dysplasia, Progressive Retinal Atrophy (PRA) and cataracts.

Exercise and Grooming

This is an active, high-energy breed the needs daily physical activity. He likes to have a job to do and enjoys agility, obedience work, tracking and of course herding. Coat care is minimal; regular brushing and combing will keep it in good order.

A
B
C
D
E
F
G
H
I
J
K
L
M
N
O
P
Q
R
S
T
U
V
W
X
Y
Z

Estrela Mountain Dog

Average height: dogs – 25.5-28.5 inches; bitches – 24.5-27 inches
Average weight: dogs – 88-110 pounds; bitches – 66-88 pounds

Appearance

This is a large, powerful, athletic breed, strongly muscled and with substantial bone.

Estrela Mountain Dog's head is long and powerful in appearance, but proportionate to the size of the dog. His cheek muscles are developed, but his cheek bones are flat; the lips are large and tight, without flews. The eyes are oval, medium sized and preferably dark amber in color, giving a keen, calm expression. He has uncropped, small, triangular rose ears and his thick tail hangs down; when at rest it has a natural "hook" resembling a scimitar. There are two coat types, both similar to goat hair. The long coat has a thick, slightly coarse outer coat, flat or slightly waved; the undercoat is very dense and normally lighter in color. On the front sides of the legs and on the head, the hair is short and smooth. The smooth coated Estrela has a short, thick, slightly coarse outercoat, with a short, dense undercoat. Colors are fawn, wolf gray and yellow, with or without brindling, white markings, shadings of black throughout the coat, and preferably with a dark facial mask.

Characteristics

The Estrela Mountain Dog is a faithful watchdog and is a formidable opponent for any predator; he makes a wonderful guardian of property and home. He is intelligent but independent; loyal and affectionate to owners but indifferent to others. He is calm but fearless, and quick to react to danger. He can also be trained as a draft dog. The Estrela loves to please but hates to be bullied.

Origins and History

The breed takes its name from the Serra da Estrela, a remote

BREED NOTES

SIZE	GROOMING
✓	✓
✓	✓
✓	
EXERCISE	**LIFESPAN**
✓	✓
✓	✓

Johnson

Left: The long, powerful head is proportionate to the dog's size.

Above: *A lovely example of the breed, in full bloom.*

Below: *Waiting with great patience.*

A
B
C
D
E
F
G
H
I
J
K
L
M
N
O
P
Q
R
S
T
U
V
W
X
Y
Z

Johnson

Above: A cuddle young puppy.

Left: Cooling off on a hot day!

mountain range in mid Portugal, and is believed to be one of the oldest breeds of the Iberian Peninsula. During the summer, when shepherds moved their flocks to the high mountain pastures, the Estrela was their guard and in winter, the flocks having returned to the foot of the mountains, the dogs guarded the shepherd's households and occasionally served as draft animals. The first breed standard for the Estrela was drawn up in 1933 and the breed was introduced to Great Britain in 1974. The first Estrela to be recorded by the AKC arrived here in 1998, but some had been imported several years earlier. The breed still works as a guardian of flocks in Portugal, where it is also used as a police dog.

Health Issues

The Estrela Mountain dog is a fairly healthy breed but hip dysplasia and cancer are causes for concern.

Exercise and Grooming

The Estrela loves open spaces and although he does not require a great deal of exercise, he is always ready if given the opportunity. Because of the breed's agility, a well-fenced garden is a must. Exercise must be limited during the growth period, as too much can cause bone and joint problems later in life. Grooming is fairly easy, but must be done regularly. A good slicker brush and a rake should be used keep coat healthy and free from dirt.

Below: A powerful, athletic, strongly muscled breed.

Johnson

A
B
C
D
E
F
G
H
I
J
K
L
M
N
O
P
Q
R
S
T
U
V
W
X
Y
Z

Field Spaniel

Average height: dogs – 18 inches; bitches – 17 inches
Average weight: 35-50 pounds

Appearance

The Field Spaniel is a medium-sized, well balanced, substantial hunter-companion, built for activity and endurance in heavy cover and in water. His head conveys the impression of high breeding, character and nobility, and must be in proportion to the size of the dog. With his grave, gentle and intelligent expression, the Field Spaniel's eyes are dark hazel to dark brown and the lids tight, showing no haw. The well-feathered ears are moderately long and wide. This breed has a single coat, which is moderately long, flat or slightly wavy. It is silky, glossy, dense and water-repellent. There is moderate setter-like feathering on chest, underbody, backs of the legs, buttocks, and sometimes also on the second thigh and underside of tail. The color may be black, liver, golden liver or shades thereof, in any intensity, dark or light. It may be either self-colored or bi-colored, the latter roaned and/or ticked in white areas.

Below: A well balanced, substantial hunting companion.

Right: Built for activity and endurance.

BREED NOTES

SIZE	GROOMING
✓✓	✓✓
EXERCISE	**LIFESPAN**
✓✓✓	✓✓

Characteristics

This is an unusually docile bred, sensitive, fun-loving, independent and intelligent. The Field Spaniel loves human companionship but may be somewhat reserved in initial meetings. He is generally excellent with children and other animals. The breed can be rather vocal, so

should be taught when to stop. Socializing and training need to start at an early age.

Origins and History

The Field Spaniel has gone through many exaggerations in type in order to arrive at the breed we know today. In England, Phineas Bullock set about creating a spaniel with tremendous body length and lowness to the ground, together with phenomenal bone. This resulted in a rather grotesque caricature of a spaniel! The breed was subsequently improved but it was difficult to establish the modern Field Spaniel in the US because it was found necessary to introduce Springer and Cocker crosses in an endeavor to eliminate the exaggerations. Although the breed came to America in the 1880s, it did not become a distinct breed from Cockers until the 20th century. From then on, anything above 25 pounds qualified as a Field Spaniel.

Health Issues

The Field Spaniel has a tendency to have ear infections and hip dysplasia.

Exercise and Grooming

Primarily a working field dog, the Field Spaniel needs plenty of exercise and loves the chance to explore and run. Because of the breed's hunting instinct, a secure garden or yard is essential. A reasonable amount of grooming is necessary. Dead hairs can be removed by hand-plucking and hair on ears. Legs and neck will need to be thinned out.

Finnish Lapphund

Average height: dogs – 18-20.5 inches; bitches – 16-18.5 inches
Average weight: dogs – 20-21 pounds; bitches – 19-20 pounds

Appearance

This is a powerful, strong-boned breed for its size, with a head that is strong in outline and rather broad. The muzzle tapers evenly, but only slightly and the jaw is strong, with a scissors bite. The Lapphund's dark brown eyes harmonize with its coat color, giving a soft, friendly expression. Ears are carried erect or semi-erect. The tail is impressive, medium in length and covered with long, profuse hair; there may be a hook at the end. The outer coat is long, straight and harsh, and the males have an abundant mane. On the head and on the front side of the legs, the coat is shorter. The Finnish Lapphund's undercoat is soft and dense. All colors are permitted, but the base color must be dominant.

BREED NOTES

SIZE	GROOMING
✓	✓
✓	✓
	✓

EXERCISE	LIFESPAN
✓	✓
✓	✓

Left: 'What would you like me to do next?'

Opposite top: One of many attractive colors in this breed.

Opposite: 'That last game made me flake out!'

Characteristics

Throughout Finland this breed is very popular, mainly as a house and hobby dog. The Lapphund is keen, courageous, calm and willing to learn. It is also a friendly, faithful breed. He has a natural herding instinct and makes an excellent watchdog.

Origins and History

For hundreds of years the

A B C D E F G H I J K L M N O P Q R S T U V W X Y Z

A
B
C
D
E
F
G
H
I
J
K
L
M
N
O
P
Q
R
S
T
U
V
W
X
Y
Z

Laplanders have used dogs of similar type to today's Finnish Lapphund to herd reindeer and to act as a watchdog in Fennoscandia and in the northern parts of Russia. Over hundreds of years the Sami culture, based in Finland, Sweden and part of Russia, developed a fairly sedentary existence, revolving around the keeping of reindeer herds. A breed standard for the Lapponian Herder was established by the Finnish Kennel Club in 1945.

Right: *The muzzle tapers evenly, but only slightly.*

Below: *A successful show dog.*

Above: Training in the yard.

Right: Enjoying the snow.

In 1967, the name was changed to Lapphund and then again in 1993 to Finnish Lapphund. With the arrival of the snowmobile, the use of dogs became less necessary, and the breed is now rarely used for its original purpose. None-the-less, it still retains a strong herding instinct and the breed is occasionally used on sheep in America. It is likely that Finnish Lapphunds arrived in the USA as pets of Finnish immigrants.

Health Issues

This is known to be one of the healthiest breeds in Finland. However, a small percentage have Progressive Retinal Atrophy (PRA) and a few cases of hip dysplasia have been found.

A
B
C
D
E
F
G
H
I
J
K
L
M
N
O
P
Q
R
S
T
U
V
W
X
Y
Z

Opposite top: The dark brown eyes harmonize with the coat color.

Opposite: A good vantage point.

Above: What an obedient group!

Right: In a field of buttercups.

Exercise and Grooming

The Finnish Lapphund enjoys having a job to do and many participate successfully in dog sports. They need three or four miles of exercise daily, with the opportunity for running off the lead. Due to the breed's abundant coat, regular grooming is required.

Finnish Spitz

Average height: dogs – 17.5-20 inches; bitches – 15.5-18 inches
Average weight: dogs – 33-35 pounds; bitches – 31-33 pounds

Appearance

The Finnish Spitz is highly fox-like in appearance, with pointed muzzle, erect ears, dense coat and curled tail. His whole being displays liveliness, especially evident in the eyes, ears and tail. His dark eyes, the outer corners tilted upward show a keen, alert expression. Males are decidedly masculine without coarseness and bitches decidedly feminine, but without over-refinement. This breed has a square well-balanced body with no exaggerated features. He carries a glorious coat, ranging from golden-red to pale honey or deep auburn. It is short, with a soft, dense undercoat, the topcoat having harsh, straight guard hairs on the body; these hairs are one to two inches long. On head and legs the hair is short and close, but there is a dense plume on the back of the thighs and on the tail. Males carry more coat than females, with a more profuse ruff at the shoulder.

Below: This Finnish Spitz is fox-like in appearance.

BREED NOTES	
SIZE	GROOMING
✓ ✓	✓ ✓
EXERCISE	LIFESPAN
✓ ✓	✓ ✓

No trimming of the coat is allowed, except for on the feet. His tail forms a single curl, falling over the loin and pointing toward the thigh.

Characteristics

This is an active and friendly breed, lively, eager, faithful and brave, but cautious. He has the manners of a true gentleman and makes an ideal family companion. He is generally good with children and an excellent watchdog.

Origins and History

The Finnish Spitz is the national dog of Finland and has long been used to hunt small game and birds.

Below: Erect ears are forever alert to sound.

The history of the spitz family of dogs can be traced back thousands of years, different strains developing as tribes migrated to different parts of the globe. In the far northern regions the Finnish Spitz emerged as a pure breed, an invaluable asset to the hunter. But as methods of transportation advanced, these dogs were bred with others so that by 1880 the breed was almost extinct. Thankfully two sportsmen from Helsinki, realizing the many merits of the native breed, decided to make an effort to salvage it. The breed was recognised by the Finnish Kennel Club in 1892 but was not imported to the USA until 1959. In 1988 the Finnish Spitz became eligible to compete in the Non-Sporting Group.

Health Issues

Generally a very healthy breed, occasional problems that have been found in the Finnish Spitz include luxating patella, epilepsy, and hereditary cataract. Fortunately these conditions are something of a rarity.

Exercise and Grooming

To keep fit a Finnish Spitz needs a 40 minute walk each day, with a well-fenced yard to run about in. However, he will be happy to have more exercise than that given the opportunity. The Spitz has a self-cleaning coat but it should be checked over once a week with a brush and comb. More grooming is necessary during the moulting season.

Flat-Coated Retriever

Average height: dogs – 23-24.5 inches; bitches – 22-23.5 inches
Average weight: dogs – 55-77 pounds; bitches – 55-75 pounds

Appearance

The distinctive and most important features of the Flat-Coat are his silhouette, both on the move and when standing, his smooth effortless movement, head type, coat and character. He has been traditionally described as showing "power without lumber and raciness without weediness". The Flat-Coat is a working hunting retriever he should be in lean, hard condition, free of excess weight. His head is long and clean, well-moulded and

BREED NOTES

SIZE	GROOMING
✓	✓
✓	✓
✓	

EXERCISE	LIFESPAN
✓	✓
✓	✓
✓	

Left: Training to sit.

adequate in size and strength to easily retrieve a large pheasant, duck or hare. His skull and muzzle are said to be "cast in one piece" and his relatively small, thickly feathered ears lie close to the side of the head. A scissors bite is preferred, but level is accepted. The coat is moderately long and moderately dense, straight and flat-lying, but a slight waviness is permissible. It is essential that the coat provides protection from all types of weather, water and ground cover. Since the Flat-Coat is a hunting retriever, his feathering is not excessively long. Coat color must be solid black or solid liver.

Characteristics

This is a responsive, loving member of the family and a

Above: Puppies at play.

versatile working dog. He is multi-talented, sensible, bright and tractable. He loves to please and has a good-humored outlook on life, right into old age. In the field he is keen, and flushes within gun range. On both land and in water he is a determined, resourceful retriever, hunting with self-reliance and an uncanny ability to adapt to changing circumstances. The Flat-Coat is a good-natured, optimistic dog, basically inclined to be friendly to all and needing affectionate attention.

Origins and History

The Flat-Coated Retriever is a selectively-bred bird dog, developed in the 19th century to pick up shot game. The Newfoundland, setter, sheepdog, and spaniel-like water dogs lie in his background and from these the breed developed into a fine water and land retriever. In addition these dogs could flush game from cover and hunt in upland areas. Mr. J Hull began breeding them in 1864, following which they were commonly used on estates throughout Great Britain. In the 20th century numbers declined, falling drastically after the Second World War. The breed was re-established in the 1960s and Stanley O'Neil showed selfless devotion in putting the breed on a sound footing once again.

Health Issues

Health problems to which the Flat-Coated Retriever is susceptible include cancer, hip dysplasia, glaucoma and luxating patella.

Exercise and Grooming

This is a tireless worker and

Below: Pups will take any opportunity to suckle!

A
B
C
D
E
F
G
H
I
J
K
L
M
N
O
P
Q
R
S
T
U
V
W
X
Y
Z

ideally needs two hours of exercise each day, though he will be content with moderate exercise. The Flat-Coat is keen to join in with any activity. An excellent water dog and natural swimmer, he thoroughly enjoys this form of exercise. Exercise should be limited during the first year of life to help prevent bone and joint problems. He needs daily brushing, with particular attention paid to feathering. Tidying of ears, feet, underline and tip of tail is acceptable.

Opposite left: The coat protects against all kinds of weather.

Opposite: 'I plan to grow up to be something really special!'

Opposite bottom: Power without lumber, raciness without weediness.

Right and below: Beware, Flat Coats, like many other breeds, can climb!

A
B
C
D
E
F
G
H
I
J
K
L
M
N
O
P
Q
R
S
T
U
V
W
X
Y
Z

French Bulldog

Average height: 12-12.5 inches
Average weight: maximum 28 pounds

Appearance

This is a compactly built, intelligent, muscular dog with heavy bone. He has a large, square head and his are wide apart and set low in the skull. The French Bulldog has "bat ears", broad at the base, elongated and with a round top, set high on the head. The muzzle is broad and deep, the cheek muscles well-developed. He has a hollow groove between the eyes with heavy wrinkles and a soft roll over the extremely short nose. The underjaw is deep, square, broad, undershot and well turned up. The Frenchie has loose skin at the neck and a roach back. His body is short and well rounded, his chest broad and deep. The tail may be either straight or screwed (but not curly); it is short, hung low with a thick root and fine tip. The moderately fine coat is brilliant, short and smooth,

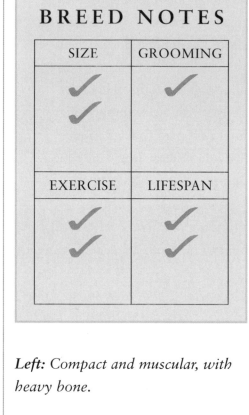

BREED NOTES

SIZE	GROOMING
✓✓	✓
EXERCISE	**LIFESPAN**
✓✓	✓✓

Left: Compact and muscular, with heavy bone.

the skin is soft and loose, especially at the head and shoulders, forming wrinkles. Colors are varied: all brindle, fawn, white, brindle and white, and any color except solid black, mouse, liver, black and tan, black and white, and white with black.

Characteristics

This is a well behaved, adaptable companion with an affectionate nature and even disposition. He is generally active, alert, and playful, but not unduly boisterous. He will usually tolerate well-behaved children, but if left alone for long periods can become destructive. The Frenchie can be relatively easy to train but this must be started at an early age before stubbornness sets in.

Johnson

Above: A broad, deep muzzle with well-developed cheek muscles.

Below: Bat ears and a short, well rounded body.

sensation and publicity surely helped the breed become "all the rage" in society.

Health Issues

If allowed to become overweight, the French Bulldog can encounter problems with his heart and his back. Intervertebral disc disease is not common but has been reported.

Exercise and Grooming

French Bulldogs do not need long walks; a few short walks each day will suffice. In warm or humid weather they should not be allowed to exercise too much as they can encounter difficulties in breathing. Grooming is easy with a rubber-grooming mitt to remove loose hair. Wrinkles on the face should be checked frequently and kept clean.

Origins and History

One of principle ancestors of the French Bulldog was the Bulldog, of which there were many of the Toy variety around in the latter half of the 19th century. Many of these Toy Bulldogs were sent from England to France where they were crossed with various other breeds. In France they were given the name, Bouledogue Français. Some of them had rose ears, other bat ears, the latter becoming one of features of today's breed. It was basically controversy over type that led to the French Bulldog Club of America being set up; the first organization in the world devoted to the breed. The American fanciers put on a specialty show in the ballroom of the Waldorf-Astoria; this proved a

German Hunt Terrier

Average height: 13-16 inches
Average weight: 16-22 pounds

Appearance

The German Hunt Terrier, also known as the Jagd Terrier is a functional hunting dog, neither too large to enter a varmint burrow nor too small to defend himself in a confrontation with his quarry. He has a rather square build, but not broad, his deep narrow chest allowing him to enter dens with relative ease. His tail is set fairly high, is straight and gaily carried; usually it is docked to about ? of its original length for it must be of sufficient length to serve as a handle for hunters to pull the terriers from the dens. The straight forelegs are well-muscled, their bone strong rather than fine. His head is wider between the ears than that of a Fox Terrier, tapering between the eyes. The powerful muzzle has pronounced cheeks and the strong lower jaw has a well-chiseled chin; the full compliment of teeth meet is a scissors bite. This terrier's dark, deep-set eyes have a determined expression and his V-shaped ears are set high and carried lightly against the side of the head; they are of adequate thickness to withstand work in briars and thickets. The coat may be smooth or harsh, or any texture in between, but it must be thick and abundant to withstand briars, dampness and cold. The main body color may be black, black and gray, or dark brown; with brown, red, yellow or lighter colored markings on the eyebrows, chest, legs and anus. Both light and dark colored masks are acceptable and a small amount of white on the chest and toes is permitted. The nose is usually black, except if the main coat color is brown, in which case the nose may be brown too.

Characteristics

This is a clever hunter, unrelenting, tough, robust and unafraid of the most formidable wild game, in the pursuit of which he is very intent. He is intelligent and affable with his master and other hunters, but although generally fairly people-friendly the German Hunt Terrier should not be kept solely as a pet as he has a strong prey drive. This can understandably make him

BREED NOTES		
SIZE	GROOMING	
	Long Coat	Smooth Coat
✓ ✓	✓ ✓	✓
EXERCISE	LIFESPAN	
✓ ✓ ✓	✓ ✓	

Left: This German Hunt Terrier has a harsh type of coat.

cantankerous with cats or other dogs. He has dash, gameness and pluck and has maintained the fearless characteristics of early den terriers. He is also called upon to run with the hounds.

Origins and History

It was during the 1940s that four German sportsmen decided to establish their own breed of all-purpose game terrier, to be used both for hunting and going to ground. They used dogs of the old broken-coated black and tan type from England crossed with German-bred Wire Fox Terriers. This crossing produced both wire-haired and smooth-coated dogs that could be used on wild boar, badger, fox and weasel; indeed any animal is fair game to the German Hunt Terrier. He is so aggressive that some label him as cruel to prey. He has been used for tracking as well as retrieving and working underground. Guarding of his master's home and property comes naturally to him. In Germany, these terriers must pass working tests prior to being granted club approval to reproduce, with the result that casual fanciers are discouraged and the breed is only rarely exhibited. In the USA and in Canada he has additionally been used by sportsmen as tree dogs, primarily for raccoon and squirrel.

Health Issues

Robust good health is a major point of the breeding program of the German Hunt Terrier.

Exercise and Grooming

Clearly the German Hunt Terrier needs to work and must absolutely not be kept confined totally as a house dog. His coat is easy to manage, the harsh coat taking just a little more work that the short.

Below: A smooth-coated bitch.

Cunliffe

German Pinscher

Average height: 17-20 inches
Average weight: None specified

A B C D E F **G** H I J K L M N O P Q R S T U V W X Y Z

Appearance

A medium sized, short coated dog, the German Pinscher is elegant in appearance with a strong square build. He is muscular and powerful for endurance and agility. His expression is sharp, alert and responsive, his eyes dark and oval in shape. Ears are high set and carried erect when cropped. If uncropped they are V-shaped with a folding pleat, or may be small standing ears. He has an elegant, strong neck and short, firm, level back. His tail

Below: The German Pinscher is strongly and squarely built, with an elegant appearance.

is customarily docked. His short, dense coat is smooth, shiny and close lying. Its color can be Isabella (fawn) to red, in various shades; stag red is red with an intermingling of black hairs. Bi-colored dogs are black with rich red or tan markings.

Characteristics

This breed is well-known for its loyalty, devotion and protective attitude towards its family. If threatened he will display fearless courage. Always alert and agile, he also has natural hunting abilities and is a good watchdog. He is alert, vigilant and very vivacious, but is not an excessive barker. He is strong

BREED NOTES

SIZE	GROOMING
✓ ✓	✓
EXERCISE	LIFESPAN
✓ ✓	✓ ✓

willed and determined, so can be rather stubborn and manipulative if he wants his own way.

Origins and History

The history of the German Pinscher dates back to the Middle Ages, when dogs of this type were bred to hunt beaver, badger and otter in southern Germany. A breed renowned for hunting vermin and as a protector of the home was the Rattler, which had evolved by the 15th century. There were two varieties of the Rattler, smooth and rough; it is believed that the German Pinscher is a direct descendent of the smooth variety. Anther breed with which the Pinscher is closely connected is the Standard Schnauzer, once referred to as the Wire Haired Pinscher. It was the German Pinscher that inspired the creation of the

Johnson

Doberman Pincher; this breed is certainly not a Doberman bred down in size, as many seem to believe! The German Pinscher was also involved in the development of the Miniature Pinscher and other Pinscher types.

Health Issues

Health problems relating to the German Pinscher include hip dysplasia, von Willebrand's Disease (vWD), hypothyroidism, heart disease and eye problems, including cataracts.

Exercise and Grooming

The German Pinscher is an active, high energy dog so requires plenty of daily exercise. He likes to have a job to do and enjoys obedience, tracking and agility. He also makes a good service dog. His short coat is easy to care for, but should be brushed and combed on a weekly basis to keep its healthy gloss.

Left: This is a bi-colored dog, black with rich tan markings.

Below: These natural, V-shaped ears have a folding pleat.

German Shepherd Dog

Average height: dogs – 24-26 inches; bitches – 22-24 inches
Average weight: 75-95 pounds

A B C D E F **G** H I J K L M N O P Q R S T U V W X Y Z

Johnson

BREED NOTES

SIZE	GROOMING
✓	✓
✓	✓
✓	
EXERCISE	LIFESPAN
✓	✓
✓	✓
✓	✓

Left: A direct, fearless expression.

Appearance

A good German Shepherd Dog is a strong, agile, well muscled animal, alert and full of life. Longer than he is tall, he is deep-bodied and presents an outline of smooth curves rather than angles. The breed displays muscular fitness and nimbleness, without any look of clumsiness or soft living. His noble head is cleanly chiselled. Eyes are as dark as possible and the ears, moderately pointed, open toward the front and are carried erect when at attention. The strong, muscular neck leads in to the dog's topline where the withers are higher than the back. The whole structure of the body gives an impression of depth and solidity without bulkiness and the thigh, viewed from the side, is broad, with both upper and lower

Above: Two puppies with a lot of growing still to do.

Right: It takes time for a pup's ears to become erect.

thighs well muscled. The bushy tail, when at rest, hangs in a slight curve, like a saber. The double coat is of medium length, the outer coat dense, straight and harsh. Most colors are permissible, but strong, rich colors are preferred.

Characteristics

The German Shepherd Dog has a very distinct personality, with a direct, fearless expression. He is self-confident and has a certain aloofness, being discriminating about the friendships he makes. He is, however, approachable and quietly stands his ground. The ideal German Shepherd is a working animal with an incorruptible

A
B
C
D
E
F
G
H
I
J
K
L
M
N
O
P
Q
R
S
T
U
V
W
X
Y
Z

A
B
C
D
E
F
G
H
I
J
K
L
M
N
O
P
Q
R
S
T
U
V
W
X
Y
Z

character, combined with a body and gait suitable for arduous work.

Origins and History

Captain Max von Stephanitz is recognised as the father of the German Shepherd Dog. He used various old German herding and farm dogs to develop this breed and in 1899 he and others formed the parent club for the breed. The club set down very strict guidelines and controlled which dogs could be allowed in breeding programmes. During the First

Left: A few German Shepherds are black.

Below: A top winning Champion show dog

World War the breed was used by both the German and French military. They helped with search and rescue, guarding and transporting ammunition, messages and first aid supplies between the trenches. Many soldiers were blinded in the war, and German Shepherds were often used as "seeing eye" dogs. In the 1920s, Strongheart and Rin Tin Tin hit the big screen, causing the breed to become popular outside its own country. Popularity declined during the Second World War but has risen again in recent decades so that now

Right: The noble head is cleanly chiselled.

Below: The breed has an incorruptible character.

the German Shepherd Dog is one of the most popular and recognizable breeds of the AKC.

Health Issues
The German Shepherd is susceptible to several health problems including heart disease, bloat, degenerative myelopathy (DM), von Willebrand's disease (vWD), hemangiosarcoma, epilepsy, eye problems and orthopaedic problems, which include hip and elbow dysplasia, OCD and others.

Exercise and Grooming
This a highly active breed so needs plenty of exercise, which should include walks on a leash and plenty of opportunity for play in a securely fenced yard. Daily brushing is needed to remove dead hair.

A
B
C
D
E
F
G
H
I
J
K
L
M
N
O
P
Q
R
S
T
U
V
W
X
Y
Z

German Shorthaired Pointer

Average height: dogs – 23-25 inches; bitches – 21-23 inches
Average weight: dogs – 55-70 pounds; bitches – 45-60 pounds

Appearance

A versatile gundog, capable of high performance in field and water, the German Shorthaired Pointer is an aristocratic, well-balanced, symmetrical dog with power, endurance, agility and a look of intelligence and animation. Symmetry and field quality are essential. He has a certain grace of outline with his clean-cut head, sloping shoulders, deep chest, powerful back, strong quarters, good bone, adequate muscle, well carried tail and taut coat. His hair is short and thick, and feels tough; on the ears and head it is softer, thinner and shorter. He may be solid liver in color, or a combination of liver and white such as liver and white ticked, liver patched and white ticked, or liver roan. The high-set tail is docked to about 40% of its length. It hangs down when the dog is quiet and is held horizontally when on the move.

Below: This show dog displays symmetry and field quality

BREED NOTES

SIZE	GROOMING
✔ ✔ ✔	✔
EXERCISE	**LIFESPAN**
✔ ✔ ✔	✔ ✔

Johnson

Characteristics

This is a friendly, intelligent dog that is willing to please. He is a very cheerful and sociable dog and loves his owner and family immensely. An ideal family dog, the German Shorthaired Pointer loves children. He has an abundance of energy and a stable temperament, but because he is a hunting dog can be quite reserved, especially towards strangers. Males tend to be more dominant than females.

Right: Happy in the fields.

Below: At work.

Below right: A look of intelligence and animation.

A
B
C
D
E
F
G
H
I
J
K
L
M
N
O
P
Q
R
S
T
U
V
W
X
Y
Z

A
B
C
D
E
F
G
H
I
J
K
L
M
N
O
P
Q
R
S
T
U
V
W
X
Y
Z

Origins and History

The versatile German Shorthaired Pointer was originally developed as an all-in-one hunting companion. The breed was created by crossing the descendants of the old Spanish Pointer, English Foxhound, and local German tracking hounds. He can work with pheasant, quail, grouse, waterfowl, coons, possum, and even deer. He can point, retrieve, track and can even be

Left: A pup has a lot to think about!

Below: 'Look, we've found the big boys' toys.'

Above: Friendly, intelligent and willing to please.

taught to toll. The German Shorthaired Pointer was first introduced to the USA during the 1920s, since when he has firmly established himself a sporting dog and family companion.

Health Issues

Although generally a healthy breed, the German Shorthaired Pointer can be prone to epilepsy, gastric torsion, hermaphrodism, lymphedema and pannus.

Exercise and Grooming

Being an active dog, this breed needs a good amount of exercise. Without this the German Shorthaired Pointer can become bored and destructive. He is an ideal companion for an athletic family. Grooming is easy, with a firm bristle brush used regularly and a piece of chamois leather to bring out the natural sheen.

German Spitz

Average height: Klein – 9-11.5 inches; Mittel 12-15 inches

A
B
C
D
E
F
G
H
I
J
K
L
M
N
O
P
Q
R
S
T
U
V
W
X
Y
Z

Appearance

This is a compact little dog that in most countries is divided into two varieties, Klein (small) and Mittel (Medium). One of the smallest members of the Spitz family, the breed is closely associated with the Pomeranian, by which name he was once actually called. The skull is quite broad, narrowing into a

Johnson

BREED NOTES

SIZE		GROOMING
Klein	Mittel	
✓	✓ ✓	✓ ✓ ✓
EXERCISE		**LIFESPAN**
✓		✓ ✓

Left: A wonderful coat, blowing in the wind.

wedge shape to the nose. The medium sized, dark eyes are oval in shape and the small, triangular ears are high set and held erect. The long, straight coat has a coarse feel to it and under this is a soft, woolly undercoat. Around the neck, the front legs and on the tail, which is curled over the back, the hair is profuse. The back legs have feathering on them but the hair on the face and ears is soft and short. All colours and markings are allowed.

Characteristics

A very intelligent dog, the German Spitz can be wilful so needs to be sensibly trained and rewarded for his good behaviour. Full of buoyancy, active and alert, this breed is particularly good at agility and some owners enter them into obedience competitions. The German Spitz is devoted to his owners making him a good family pet.

Origins and History

Spitz-type dogs go back to the hunter gatherers of the Stone Age, some 6,000 years ago. The immediate forebear of the German Spitz is the Turfspitz, found in the peat bogs of the Northern German plain that stretched from the Rhine, covering most of Denmark. Before 1871 Germany consisted of small kingdoms and dukedoms, with constantly changing boundaries, hence different dogs developed to suit different people's needs. All these dogs came under the general name of "Mistbeller", which means "dung-hill barker" – they stood on top of the dung hills and barked!

Above: A nicely balanced black and white.

Below: The German Spitz has a compact outline.

Below: Dancing for his owner's delight.

A
B
C
D
E
F
G
H
I
J
K
L
M
N
O
P
Q
R
S
T
U
V
W
X
Y
Z

Above: *Various colors of this delightful breed.*

Right: *Great companions; riding is a regular pastime!*

The breed became popular in England in the 18th century due to Germans marrying into royal and aristocratic families. These dogs were originally known as Pomeranians, even though they were much larger in size. Like other German breeds, the German Spitz fell out of favour during the First World War, but now holds its own in many countries around the world and is registered in the AKC's Foundation Stock Service.

Health Issues
The German Spitz, being a very natural breed, tends to be very healthy. Patella luxation can present

a problem and eye disorders have been known. It is best not to feed too high a protein food as he can become hyperactive.

Exercise and Grooming

This is a high energy breed that needs up to an hour's exercise each day. He thoroughly enjoys a run or a walk and will quite happily occupy himself in the garden all day. A thirty minute grooming session each week should ensure that the coat stays clean, healthy and free from matts. Hair should be brushed the "wrong way" and special attention paid to areas behind ears and elbows, where knots can easily form. Occasional trimming of the toes, hocks and anal area only may be necessary.

Above: Hoping for a reward for good behaviour.

Below: The skull is quite broad, the tail curled well over the back

A
B
C
D
E
F
G
H
I
J
K
L
M
N
O
P
Q
R
S
T
U
V
W
X
Y
Z

German Wirehaired Pointer

Average height: dogs – 24-26 inches; bitches – 22 inches minimum
Average weight: 60-70 pounds

Appearance

This is a well muscled, medium sized dog of distinctive appearance. The German Wirehaired Pointer is balanced in size and sturdily built. His most distinguishing feature is his weather resistant, wire-like coat and his facial furnishings. He has a moderately long head and brown, oval eyes, overhung with medium length eyebrows and a visible beard and whiskers. His rounded ears hang close to the head. His is a double coat, the undercoat dense enough to insulate against the cold in winter, but in summer so thin as to be almost invisible. The outercoat is straight, harsh, wiry and flat lying; from one to two inches in length. Over the shoulders and around the tail it is very heavy. The coat's color is liver and white, usually either liver and white spotted, liver roan, liver and white spotted with ticking and roaning or solid liver.

BREED NOTES	
SIZE	GROOMING
✔ ✔ ✔	✔ ✔
EXERCISE	LIFESPAN
✔ ✔ ✔	✔ ✔

Johnson

Characteristics

This is an intelligent, sharp, energetic and highly trainable breed. He is a determined hunter with the ability to retrieve well from water. Loyal and affectionate, the German Wirehaired Pointer makes a devoted companion, always eager to please. The breed gets along well with

Left: The rounded ears hang close to the head.

Right: A weather resistant, wire-like coat and facial furnishings.

A
B
C
D
E
F
G
H
I
J
K
L
M
N
O
P
Q
R
S
T
U
V
W
X
Y
Z

Above: Well muscled and sturdily built.

Below Posing for a studio portrait.

children when he has been raised with them. At times he can be aloof with strangers, but is not unfriendly toward them.

Origins and History

Sportsmen in Germany decided they wished to produce a dog with all the versatility of the German Shorthaired Pointer but with a coat that could protect him in rugged areas, and sufficiently robust to hunt larger game. As a result, about 120 years ago the breed was developed by crossing the Pudelpointer with various other hunting breeds, including the German Shorthaired Pointer and the Polish Water Dog. Today this is the most popular breed in Germany and is also a favourite in Scandinavian countries. The breed arrived in the USA in the 1920s and was officially recognized by the AKC in 1959.

Above: The head is moderately long.

Health Issues

Although generally a healthy breed, the German Wirehaired Pointer is susceptible to genetic eye diseases, skin cancers, ear infections and hip dysplasia.

Above An intelligent and highly trainable breed.

Left: A successful show dog.

Exercise and Grooming

This is an active dog that requires lots of exercise and is not a suitable breed for families that do not have sufficient time to devote to this. The German Wirehaired Pointer can become destructive if he becomes bored. He should be brushed twice weekly with a firm bristle brush. The coat should also be stripped occasionally to maintain a clean, but natural look. Bathing is only needed when necessary.

Giant Schnauzer

Average height: dogs – 25.5-27.5 inches; bitches – 23.5-25.5 inches
Average weight: 55-80 pounds

Appearance

The Giant Schnauzer resembles a larger and more powerful version of the Standard Schnauzer; he is a bold and valiant figure of a dog. Robust and strongly built, sturdy, active and well muscled, he is nearly square in proportion. His head is

Johnson

BREED NOTES

SIZE	GROOMING
✔ ✔ ✔	✔ ✔ ✔
EXERCISE	LIFESPAN
✔ ✔ ✔	✔ ✔

Left: This crop-eared male shows his strong, sturdy build.

rectangular and elongated, matching the sex and substance of the dog. The strong muzzle ends in a moderately blunt wedge. When cropped the ears are identical in shape and length with pointed tips, in balance with the head and not exaggerated in length. Uncropped ears are V-shaped "button ears" of medium length and thickness, set high and carried rather high and close to the head. The medium-sized, dark brown eyes are deep-set and have a keen expression. The Giant Schnauzer's moderately high-set tail is customarily docked so that is about 1.5 to 3 inches long in maturity. The breed's hard, wiry, very dense coat has a

soft undercoat and harsh outer coat which, when seen against the grain, stands slightly up off the back, lying neither smooth nor flat. The Schnauzer's hallmark is the coarse hair on top of his head, with harsh beard and eyebrows. Coat color may be solid black or pepper and salt.

Characteristics

The Giant Schnauzer is intelligent, easily trained, reliable, versatile and bold. He is a good-natured dog, deeply loyal to his family and when properly trained can be enjoy the company of the family's children and pets. He is an excellent guard and with his sound, reliable

Above: Both good specimens, square in proportion, one with cropped ears, the others natural (right)

temperament he is one of the most useful, powerful, and enduring working breeds.

Origins and History

One of the three distinct Schnauzer breeds, the Giant Schnauzer was developed in Germany, as were his cousins, the Miniature and Standard. The breed's origin is in Wurttenberg and Bavaria, both agricultural areas where the major occupation was raising sheep and livestock. The Schnauzer aided the shepherd in driving animals to market. Known as a great cattle and driving dog, for many years the breed was known as the Munchener. He was also used as a guard dog and from World War I onward his intelligence and trainability made him very suitable as a police dog.

Left: Strong and powerful.

Johnson

Above: The head is rectangular and elongated, the strong muzzle ending in a moderately blunt wedge.

Health Issues

The Giant Schnauzer is particularly susceptible to cancer, especially toe cancer. Other health problems to be aware of are bloat, epilepsy and hip dysplasia.

Exercise and Grooming

An active breed, the Giant Schnauzer needs a great deal of exercise. He loves to play around in open areas and if not given sufficient mental and physical stimulation can become destructive. Thorough brushing is needed weekly to prevent tangling and matting of the undercoat. The topcoat needs professional clipping at least four times a year, with special scissoring to head features.

Glen Of Imaal Terrier

Average height: 12.5-14 inches
Average weight: dogs – 35 pounds; bitches – somewhat less than 35 pounds

Appearance

This is a medium sized working terrier, longer than he is tall and sporting a double coat of medium length, The Glen of Imaal possesses great strength and conveys the impression of maximum substance for his size. He is still unrefined in his appearance. In his powerful, distinctive head are round, brown eyes and his small ears are rose or half-pricked when alert, thrown back in repose. His bowed forequarters with turned out feet, coupled with his unique outline and topline are hallmarks of the breed. The medium-length coat has a harsh texture, with a soft undercoat.

Although it may be tidied to present a neat outline characteristic of a rough-and-ready working terrier, it should not be over- trimmed. Coat color is wheaten, blue or brindle.

Characteristics

This is a game and spirited terrier with great courage when called upon, otherwise he is gentle and docile. He is generally less easily excited than other terriers, and yet always ready to give chase. When working he is active, agile, silent and dead game. Hardy and resilient to the point of stoicism, the Glen is very much a big dog on short legs, not only in his conformation, but in

BREED NOTES

SIZE	GROOMING
✓ ✓	✓ ✓
EXERCISE	**LIFESPAN**
✓ ✓	✓ ✓

Below: This breed has great strength and a unique outline.

A
B
C
D
E
F
G
H
I
J
K
L
M
N
O
P
Q
R
S
T
U
V
W
X
Y
Z

A
B
C
D
E
F
G
H
I
J
K
L
M
N
O
P
Q
R
S
T
U
V
W
X
Y
Z

Johnson

his approach to life. Most Glens can be trusted with children. He is a superb earth dog and loyal companion, completely unaltered by fashion.

Origins and History

An early 19th century reference to the Glen of Imaal Terrier lies in the following line, 'There is a glen, Imaal, in the Wicklow mountains that has always been, and still is, celebrated for its terriers.' Indeed the breed is named after a valley in Ireland's Wicklow mountains, in one of Ireland's least populated counties, Wicklow. It is because the valley was so difficult to reach that the breed developed along different lines from the other Irish breeds of terrier. The breed has evolved through generations of hard work,

into today's strong, sturdy dog. It hunted badgers and foxes and was used to keep the rat population down to a minimum. The Glen of Imaal and his ancestors were also used in dog fights and often obliged to spend long, hot hours on the treadmill, turning the roasting spits. The Irish Kennel Club recognised the breed in 1933 and it received full-breed status in England in 1980. Several Glens arrived in the USA during the 1930s, when families emigrated from Ireland with their dogs but the breed did not gain a true foothold here until the early 1980s.

Health Issues

The Glen of Imaal is generally a strong breed, but can be affected by skin allergies. Hip dysplasia and

Opposite: A powerful, distinctive head with round, brown eyes.

Above: A wheaten coat, which should not be over-trimmed

Progressive Retinal Atrophy (PRA) have also been found in the breed.

Exercise and Grooming

He needs at least 20 to 30 minutes' exercise each day to prevent him becoming overweight. A romp in the park or through the woods is always very welcome, but remember the Glen is a very proficient digger! Dead hair should be removed by stripping two or three times a year, for this is essentially a non-shedding coat. Meanwhile frequent brushing and occasional baths are needed to keep the coat fresh and clean.

A
B
C
D
E
F
G
H
I
J
K
L
M
N
O
P
Q
R
S
T
U
V
W
X
Y
Z

Golden Retriever

Average height: dogs – 23-24 inches; bitches – 21.5-22.5 inches
Average weight: dogs – 65-75 pounds; bitches – 55-65 pounds

Appearance

An active dog of medium build, the Golden Retriever is symmetrical, not clumsy, nor long in the leg. One of the breed's distinct characteristics is the dense, water-repellent coat that lies flat against the body and is either straight or wavy. There is an untrimmed natural ruff, with moderate feathering on back of

Johnson

BREED NOTES

SIZE	GROOMING
✔	✔
✔	✔
✔	
EXERCISE	**LIFESPAN**
✔	✔
✔	✔

Left: The breed has a dense, water-repellent coat.

forelegs and on underbody. There is heavier feathering on front of neck, back of thighs and underside of tail, this being well set on, thick and muscular at the base, carried with a merry action, but never over the back or between the legs. Coat color is a lustrous golden of various shades. This breed has a friendly, intelligent expression with medium-sized, dark eyes. His ears are rather short and fall close to the cheek.

Characteristics

Alert, eager and self-confident, the Golden Retriever has an outstanding character, generally being extremely friendly, reliable, trustworthy and devoted. This is a "people dog"; he thrives on human companionship and must be

Above: A lustrous coat of a deeper golden shade.

Left: A friendly, intelligent expression.

allowed to interact with people. He is devoted to his family, always happy, trusting and forgiving. He does not mature mentally until two or three years and many retain their playful personality well into their senior years.

Origins and History

During the 19th century hunting was both a sport and a practical way of obtaining food. Retrievers came into prominence because of the need for a medium-sized dog that could do well in wild-fowling, both with waterfowl and upland game. Lord Tweedmouth bought his

A
B
C
D
E
F
G
H
I
J
K
L
M
N
O
P
Q
R
S
T
U
V
W
X
Y
Z

suitability as a guide dog, assistance dog for the disabled and therapy dog, in addition to which the Golden frequently works in search and rescue, avalanche rescue and drug detection, as well as in several other fields.

Health Issues

Although generally a healthy breed, the following problems have been known to occur: hip and elbow dysplasia, von Willebrand's Disease, hypothyroidism, epilepsy, hereditary heart disease, cancer, arthritis, allergies and bloat. Various eye problems are also cause for concern, including Central Progressive Retinal Atrophy (CPRA), hereditary cataracts and retinal dysplasia.

Left: Mother and pups.

***Below:** A veteran*

first Yellow Retriever in the middle of that century and the location of his estate on the Tweed River had a direct bearing program undertaken to produce the characteristics he desired in his Yellow Retrievers. The local, light-colored Tweed Water Spaniel had tremendous influence on Tweedmouth's developing breed; later he additionally introduced the Irish Setter and Bloodhound to his breeding programme. The breed was first shown in England in 1908, under the name of Golden Flat Coats. They obtained separate status in 1913 and in the first Golden was registered with the AKC in 1925. Today it has become one of the most successful, recognizable, and popular breeds. The breed is well known for its

Above: After a good day's work in the field.

Above right: A remarkable obedience display.

Right: This is one of the most successful and popular breeds.

Exercise and Grooming

The Golden Retriever requires moderate, regular exercise to maintain his physical and mental health. Daily walks and free exercise are always enjoyable, but he also likes to swim ad to go on a good hike with his family. Grooming is not too demanding, but weekly brushing is needed; monthly trimming just to neaten stray hairs and to tidy the feet is usual.

A B C D E F **G** H I J K L M N O P Q R S T U V W X Y Z

A
B
C
D
E
F
G
H
I
J
K
L
M
N
O
P
Q
R
S
T
U
V
W
X
Y
Z

Gordon Setter

Average height: dogs – 24-27 inches; bitches – 23-26 inches
Average weight: dogs – 55-80 pounds; bitches – 45-70 pounds

Appearance

This is a good sized, sturdily built dog, well-muscled with plenty of bone and substance. He is active, upstanding and stylish, his soft, shiny black coat with tan markings, either of rich chestnut or mahogany, adding to his impressive good looks. The colors are clear and both straight and slightly waved coats are correct. Capable of doing a full day's work in the field, he has a strong, rather short back, with well sprung ribs. His tail does not reach below the hocks but is not docked; it is thick at the root and finishes in a fine point. The finely chiselled head is fairly heavy, his bearing intelligent, noble, and dignified, suggesting strength and stamina rather than extreme speed. His teeth usually meet in a scissors bite, but a level bite is not a fault.

Characteristics

The Gordon Setter is a devoted family companion, but is not generally considered over-friendly toward strangers. He usually gets along well with children, showing a strong protective instinct, both toward them and to his family. With his keen intellect and superb memory, he is renowned for his keen scenting ability and endurance, but is not so fast as other setters.

BREED NOTES

SIZE	GROOMING
✓ ✓ ✓	✓ ✓

EXERCISE	LIFESPAN
✓ ✓ ✓	✓ ✓

Below: A substantial black dog with tan markings.

Johnson

Above: Intelligent, noble and dignified.

He is fearless and willing, loyal and affectionate.

Origins and History

Hailing from Scotland, the Gordon Setter can trace his lineage back to the 17th century. The black-an-tan setter came to prominence in the fourth Duke of Gordon's kennels, early in the 19th century. The breed was notable for its beauty as well as its bird sense. George Blunt imported the breed to America in 1842 and here the breed's popularity rose. But as field trials became popular, the Gordon's popularity waned in favour of other gundog breeds, though he remained unrivalled as a one-man shooting dog. He did not need re-training at each season, thanks to his retentive memory. An added bonus was that his distinctive black and tan color was easily viewed in light fields and early snow.

Health Issues

Although generally a healthy breed, the Gordon Setter is known occasionally to suffer from bloat, hip dysplasia, hypothyroidism and Progressive Retinal Atrophy (PRA).

Exercise and Grooming

Plenty of daily exercise is needed for this breed to remain in the peak of mental and physical condition. Frequent on-leash walks are essential, but great care should be taken if allowed to roam freely, other than in a safely enclosed area. The coat of the Gordon Setter needs weekly brushing to keep it free from matts. The hair on the bottom of the feet and between the toes should also be trimmed.

Below: Active and stylish when moving.

Grand Basset Griffon Vendéen

Average height: 15.5-18 inches
Average weight: 39.5-44 pounds

A B C D E F **G** H I J K L M N O P Q R S T U V W X Y Z

Appearance

The Grand Basset Griffon Vendéen, is regularly called GBGV for the sake of simplicity. This is a medium sized, strong, scent hound, longer than he is tall. His coat is rough and harsh on top, with a thick undercoat making it weather-resistant. The color always has a white ground with lemon, orange, black, tricolour or grizzle. A prominent characteristic of the breed is the hair over the eyebrows, and a beard and moustache. The head is not too wide and the GBGV's muzzle and ears are longer than those of his close cousin, the Petit Basset Griffon Vendéen. His jaws are strong with a perfect scissor bite. The body is deep chested and the topline level. The high-set tail is carried proudly and covered with quite a lot of hair.

Characteristics.

A happy go lucky dog who loves to be kept active, the GBGV can be can be stubborn and independent, but is always willing to please. He is a bold kind of dog and quite vocal. He gets along well with other dogs, children and strangers too, but he is more suited to a country life than one in the town and needs a well fenced yard or garden, for he is likely to be off at the first scent of small game. This is not a naturally obedient breed and must be taught who is the top dog in the family. Constant training and socialization is important, especially through adolescence.

Origins and History

The GBGV developed in the west of France and can be traced back to the 16th century, the Griffon Vendéen being the breed's larger ancestor. The GBGV was bred slightly smaller to cope with the thick undergrowth in which it worked. Originally both the Grand and Petit Griffon Vendéen occurred in the same litters, but in the 1970's the cross breeding of these two varieties was forbidden. These dogs still work in the field, as individuals or in packs, to hunt wild boar, deer

BREED NOTES

SIZE	GROOMING
✓✓	✓✓
EXERCISE	**LIFESPAN**
✓✓✓	✓✓

Below: 'Will they ever finish chatting?'

Above left: This well-known Champion has a highly typical expression.

and to scent rabbit and hare. In Europe and the USA GBGVs been trained for mantrailing. The breed has been recorded in the AKC' Foundation Stock Service since 2004.

Health Issues

The Grand Basset Griffon Vendéen appears to be a hardy, healthy dog, relatively free from hereditary defects. However epilepsy does occur from time to time, but careful breeding has helped to reduce the incidence of this problem.

Right: The GBGV is longer than tall, and the high set tail is carried proudly.

Exercise and Grooming

This is an energetic hound so needs a couple of hours exercise each day. An area for free running is essential, but must be securely fenced. The

GBGV's coat should be groomed once each week to remove dead hair and dirt. Special attention should be paid to face furnishings to be sure they are kept clean.

Great Dane

Average height: dogs – 30 inches minimum, but preferably 32 inches or more;
bitches – 28 inches minimum, but preferably 30 inches or more
Average weight: dogs – 140-175 pounds; bitches – 110-140 pounds

Appearance

The Great Dane does not reach his full height until the age of 12 to 15 months of age, becoming fully mature at about three years. The male is more massive than the bitch with a larger frame and heavier bone. His regal appearance, dignity, strength and elegance are combined with great size and a powerful, well-formed, smoothly muscled body. The Great Dane's head is rectangular, long, distinguished, expressive and finely chiseled, especially below the eyes. He has a full, square jaw with a deep muzzle. His ears are high set and of medium size and thickness; when natural they are folded forward close to the cheek and if cropped are carried uniformly erect. The tail is broad at the base, tapering down to its tip; at rest it falls straight but may curve slightly when excited or running. The short, thick, smooth, glossy coat can be brindle, fawn, blue, black, harlequin or mantle, the latter black and white with a solid black blanket extending over the body (other black and white

BREED NOTES	
SIZE	GROOMING
✓ ✓ ✓	✓
EXERCISE	LIFESPAN
✓ ✓ ✓	✓

Left: A distinguished, finely chiseled, expressive head.

Opposite: Beginning to show signs of age.

markings as specified in the breed standard. The Great Dane moves with long easy strides, often compared to that of a thoroughbred horse.

Characteristics

The Great Dane is a lovely family dog, affectionate, loyal, devoted and a good guardian. He is very people-oriented and likes to play his full part in family life. Calm and well-balanced, he is known as "the Apollo of dogs". Although spirited and courageous, he is always friendly though his natural suspicion toward strangers makes him a good protector, and his very

A
B
C
D
E
F
G
H
I
J
K
L
M
N
O
P
Q
R
S
T
U
V
W
X
Y
Z

A
B
C
D
E
F
G
H
I
J
K
L
M
N
O
P
Q
R
S
T
U
V
W
X
Y
Z

dating back to 3,000 BC and from around 2,000 BC similar dogs have been found on Babylonian artefacts. Whatever his origins, today's Great Dane is considered a German breed, known in Germany as Deutsche Dogge. The breed has served as a Boar Hound in Germany for over 400 years, and the old-time boar was incredibly savage, swift and powerful. The Dane was also used as an estate guard dog and in 1870 became Germany's national dog. A breed standard was adopted for the Great Dane in Germany in 1891, but the German Mastiff or Great Dane Club of America was founded two years prior to that.

Health Issues
Unfortunately, being a giant breed,

Left: This puppy's legs show tremendous potential for growth.

Below: A excellent example of a Harlequin.

size is usually sufficient to ward off intruders! When raised with children the Great Dane is usually very gentle, but because of his size and weight careful supervision is important, especially in the case of toddlers.

Origins and History
Some believe the Great Dane to be descended from the Irish Wolfhound and Old English Mastiff, others believe that the Greyhound and Tibetan Mastiff were his progenitors. Certainly dogs resembling the breed have been found on Egyptian monuments

the Great Dane has a rather short life span, usually of 7 to 10 years. Amongst the health problems occasionally faced by this breed are bloat, cancer, heart disease and heart defects, hip dysplasia, hypothyroidism and cervical vertebral instability (CVI), known as wobbler's syndrome. In the Great Dane CVI usually appears between 3 and 18 months of age.

Exercise and Grooming

The Great Dane needs a long daily walk and plenty of opportunity for free exercise, but exercise must be limited during the growth stage. His coat is easy to groom with a firm bristle brush. As bathing a dog of this size can be quite difficult, dry shampooing is a useful alternative.

Above: A litter of pups intent on their food.

Below: This successful Champion displays dignity, strength and elegance.

A
B
C
D
E
F
G
H
I
J
K
L
M
N
O
P
Q
R
S
T
U
V
W
X
Y
Z

Great Pyrénées

Average height: dogs – 27-32 inches; bitches – 25-29 inches
Average weight: dogs – 100 pounds upwards; bitches – 85 pounds upwards

Appearance

The Great Pyrénées, known in most countries as the Pyrenean Mountain Dog, conveys elegance and unsurpassed beauty combined with great overall size and majesty. His head is not heavy and he has a kind, regal expression, somewhat contemplative. His eyes are a rich, dark brown, with close fitting black rims to match his lips and nose. His ears are reasonably small and carried low, flat and close to the head. A scissors bite is preferred, but level is acceptable. His hind feet have a structural tendency to toe out slightly; this breed characteristic is not to be confused with cow-hocks. The hind feet, like the forefeet, are rounded, close-cupped, well padded and with well arched toes; there must double dewclaws on each rear leg. The weather resistant double coat has a long,

Below: These puppies are not posing for the camera, simply relaxing.

Opposite: A moment of peace and tranquillity between games.

BREED NOTES

SIZE	GROOMING
✔	✔
✔	✔
✔	✔
EXERCISE	**LIFESPAN**
✔	✔
✔	

Johnson

Johnson

Above: *Highly typical bitch (left) and dog (right) relaxing in the shade.*

Below: *A top winning Champion clearly conveying elegance and beauty, coupled with great size and*

Opposite: *Being so large, it's a bit of a squeeze to travel with a friend in the car.*

flat, thick, outer coat of coarse hair, straight or slightly undulating, lying over a dense, fine, woolly undercoat. It is more profuse about the neck and shoulders where it forms a ruff, more pronounced in males. Longer hair on the tail forms a plume. The coat is white or white with markings of gray, badger, reddish brown, or varying shades of tan on ears, head, tail and as a few body spots.

Characteristics

The Great Pyrénées is confident, gentle, and affectionate. His is territorial and protective of his flock or family when necessary, but his general demeanor is one of quiet composure, displaying patience and tolerance. Although strong willed, independent and somewhat reserved, he is still attentive. This is a fearless dog, utterly loyal to his charges be they human or animal.

Below: *Having fun.*

A B C D E F **G** H I J K L M N O P Q R S T U V W X Y Z

A
B
C
D
E
F
G
H
I
J
K
L
M
N
O
P
Q
R
S
T
U
V
W
X
Y
Z

Origins and History

Descended from the molossian hounds taken to Spain by the Romans, the Great Pyrénées was originally used in the Middle Ages to protect sheep from predators and to guard fortresses. At this time packs of wild animals roamed the mountain slopes freely. The breed's physical and mental characteristics that have been so important in his work have hardly changed through the ages. With his ability to scent and his keen sight, the Great Pyrénées was an invaluable companion of the shepherd. The first pair was brought to the USA in 1824 and the breed was recognised by the AKC in 1933.

Health Issues

The Great Pyrénées is basically a healthy breed but needs to be checked regularly for ear infections and a fungal growth between the toes. Hip dysplasia is a health problem to watch out for. The breed

Left: Young puppies with their dam.

Below: This is a giant breed.

has a low metabolism and is sensitive to anesthesia.

Exercise and Grooming

It is the Great Pyrénées' natural instinct to patrol a large territory, so he needs regular exercise a large yard, garden or paddock. If allowed to become bored and lonely he can become destructive. A weekly grooming routine is essential, using a wire card brush to remove loose hairs. Despite its beauty, the coat sheds dirt easily so grooming is not a particularly onerous task. Occasional baths are needed.

Above: Coat can shed at certain times of the year

Below: Three very firm friends.

Greater Swiss Mountain Dog

Average height: dogs – 25.5-28.5 inches; bitches – 23.5-27 inches
Average weight: dogs – 105-140 pounds; bitches – 85-110 pounds

Left: An all-purpose draft and drover breed.

Appearance

The Greater Swiss Mountain Dog's structure is that of a draft and drover breed. He is a large, striking, powerful, confident dog of sturdy appearance; heavy boned, well muscled and agile enough to perform the all-purpose farm duties that were required of him in Switzerland's mountainous regions. He has an animated, gentle expression and his high-set, triangular ears are gently rounded at the tip; they hang close to the head in repose, but when alert are brought forward and raised at the base. His muzzle is large, blunt and straight, not pointed and most often with a slight rise before the end. The breed has a double coat, the topcoat measuring 1.25 to 2 inches in length; the thick undercoat sometimes shows. The topcoat is black and the markings are a rich rust and white, preferably symmetrical.

Characteristics

This is a bold, faithful, willing worker that is easygoing and obedient. He is alert, vigilant and always eager to work. The Greater Swiss Mountain Dog can be quite territorial, but will quickly warm up to newcomers provided they are accepted by his family. He loves children and makes an excellent watch dog.

Origins and History

The Greater Swiss Mountain Dog is the largest of Switzerland's four Swiss mountain dog breeds, and is considered the oldest. He is descended from the molossers that arrived in Switzerland with the Romans; in remote and isolated areas he then developed and was adapted to general farm use for herding, guarding and as a utilitarian draft dog. It is believed that this breed was instrumental in the early development of the Saint Bernard and the Rottweiler. By 1908 it had been assumed that the Greater Swiss Mountain Dog had already died out, its work having been replaced either by other dogs or by machines. However, dog expert, Dr. Albert Heim of Zurich, urged people to save the breed and two years later it was recognised by the Swiss Kennel Club. In 1968, the Greater Swiss Mountain Dog Club of America was formed and the breed's stud book was transferred to the AKC in 1993, with an initial 1,300 dogs as foundation stock. The breed gained full AKC recognition in 1995.

Health Issues

This is considered a healthy breed, but problems that have been encountered include hip and elbow dysplasia and some eye problems, including entropion and ectropion. Being a large breed, bloat is also a danger.

Exercise and Grooming

This breed requires regular moderate exercise, either by way of walks on a leash or a game in the yard; ideally both. He should not be over-exercised in hot weather for fear of heat stroke. Occasional vigorous activities such as hiking or cart pulling will help to keep the Greater Swiss Mountain Dog fit. The coat sheds twice annually and a little between time too, so regular brushing in necessary to keep skin and coat healthy.

BREED NOTES

SIZE	GROOMING
✓ ✓ ✓	✓ ✓

EXERCISE	LIFESPAN
✓ ✓ ✓	✓ ✓

A B C D E F G H I J K L M N O P Q R S T U V W X Y Z

Greyhound

Average height: 26-30 inches (Racing Greyhounds a little less)
Average weight: dogs – 65-70 pounds; bitches – 60-75 pounds (Racing Greyhounds a little less)

BREED NOTES

SIZE	GROOMING
✓ ✓ ✓	✓
EXERCISE	**LIFESPAN**
✓ ✓	✓ ✓

Appearance

The Greyhound is a strongly built sighthound; he has symmetrical formation and good muscle power, with a long head and neck and clean, well-laid shoulders. His chest is deep, his body capacious and loin well-arched, with good depth of muscle. His quarters are powerful, his legs and feet sound, and he has a suppleness of limb that emphasises the breed's distinctive type and quality. The Greyhound's teeth are strong and his dark, bright, intelligent eyes indicate spirit. Ears are small and fine in texture, thrown back and folded, except when excited, when they are semi-pricked. His tail is long and tapering, with a slight upward curve. The coat is smooth and firm

Left: The Greyhound's intelligent eyes show all the spirit of a sighthound.

A
B
C
D
E
F
G
H
I
J
K
L
M
N
O
P
Q
R
S
T
U
V
W
X
Y
Z

Left: These pups are bedded down on shredded white paper.

racing kennel to a loving home by the fireside following his retirement. Care should be exercised in his socialization with other family pets, and the neighbour's cat will hopefully not stray within his line of sight!

Origins and History

One of the most ancient dog breeds known to man, the Greyhound was the hunting companion of the Egyptians, Romans, Greeks and also of the Medieval European aristocracy. This is a sight hound, so hunts by sight rather than by scent. He was bred to hunt by way of out-running his prey, resulting in his athletic body, grace and agility. The Greyhound was used on practically all kinds of game

in texture and color is entirely immaterial.

Characteristics

When not racing, the Greyhound is a quiet, gentle breed that thrives on human companionship, of which he should never be deprived. He loves attention and is affectionate to those he knows, making him a wonderful family companion. He can be a little aloof with strangers, but is usually friendly when introduced. This is an intelligent and adaptable breed and, thanks to this, he is usually easily able to make the transition from

Below: The Greyhound is found in a wide array of colors.

from including deer, stags and foxes, but the hare is his natural quarry. Formal coursing events began over two centuries ago. In more modern times he has become well-known for his ability on the race track, but this is very recent in comparison to his hunting prowess. In America the Greyhound track racing industry began in about 1919 and today, as in Britain, racing Greyhounds are considerably more numerous than show dogs. The breed first arrived in America in the 16th century, having been brought here by Spanish explorers. During the American Revolution a Greyhound called Azor always accompanied George Washington. The breed was first exhibited in the USA as early as 1877 and appeared in the AKC's Stud Book in 1885.

Health Issues

This is a remarkably healthy breed, with few of the genetic problems that raise their heads in other breeds. However, being a deep-chested dog, bloat can be a problem. Like other sight hounds, the Greyhound is sensitive to a number of anesthetics, so it is important to discuss this with a vet prior to surgery.

Exercise and Grooming

Contrary to popular belief, the Greyhound does not require an enormous amount of exercise, but he does love to run and must be provided with that opportunity. However, his exercise area must be safely enclosed, for he is always ready to give chase and can run as

Above: The body is capacious and the loin well arched, with good depth of muscle.

speeds of up to 45 miles per hour! Grooming is simple, but regular brushing is important to keep skin and coat healthy, and a piece of velvet cloth will bring up a nice shine.

Below: A Greyhound moving well is pure symmetry.

Hamiltonstovare

Average height: dogs – 22.5 inches; bitches – 21 inches
Average weight: 50-60 pounds

Appearance

The Hamiltonstövare is a well proportioned, strongly-boned hound breed, giving the impression of great strength and stamina. He is never heavy, but the differences between males and females are clearly defined. He has a longish head, with a slightly arched, moderately broad skull. The muzzle is long, strong and almost rectangular, the bridge of the nose straight. The nose itself is always black, well developed and with

BREED NOTES

SIZE	GROOMING
✔ ✔ ✔	✔
EXERCISE	**LIFESPAN**
✔ ✔ ✔	✔ ✔

Left: A long, strong, almost rectangular muzzle.

large nostrils. His upper lips are rather thin, tight and nicely rounded, males having more pronounced lips than females. The Hamiltonstövare's eyes are dark brown, conveying a calm expression and the soft ears, set fairly high, should be raised only slightly when alert. His neck is long and powerful, the back level and the loin muscular and slightly arched. His chest is deep and long, reaching to the elbow. The tail is set in line with the back and may be straight or slightly curved in saber fashion; it should preferably not be carried above the level of the back when moving. His tri-colored coat is harsh, not too short and lies very close to the body. On head, ears and front of legs, the coat is very short and smooth, while

Johnson

Above: A superb specimen winning a high award at a prestigious Hound Show

under the tail and on the back of the thighs it is quite long, but not forming a fringe.

Characteristics

The Hamiltonstövare works alone and is used to find and flush game toward the guns, indicating his success by baying. He has an excellent nose and is hard to distract when on the trail, only returning when he is ready to do so. He is a typical, even tempered hound who is friendly and makes a fine house dog, provided his substantial exercise requirements are attended to.

Origins and History

A Swedish hound, the Hamiltonstövare is one of the country's best known hunting dogs and its most popular hound. Although hound breeds have been known in Sweden since the 16th century, until 1789 hunting with hounds was a privilege only enjoyed by gentry and royalty. At the end of the 18th century the ban that had previously prevented the peasantry from hunting the land was lifted and hounds consequently became more widespread. The Hamiltonstövare was developed in the late 19th century by Count Adolf Patrik Hamilton, a founder of the Swedish Kennel Club. His aim was to produce a superlative working hound. The origin is believed to be a mixture of scenthounds, Foxhounds and Harriers. Originally called the Swedish Hound, the breed was given its present name in 1921 as an honor to the man who had created the breed. In Sweden the breed is the subject of great affection and has even entered into folklore; a small elf, Tomten, is said to help Swedish housewives and this useful little chap is accompanied by none other than a Hamiltonstövare called Karo.

Exercise and Grooming

The Hamiltonstövare enjoys plenty of exercise, but is a breed that may not return to his owner when called. He must therefore be exercised in a safe, secure place, with careful consideration given to any livestock in the vicinity. His coat becomes quite thick during the winter months and a slicker brush is probably the most useful piece of grooming equipment for this breed. Boiled linseed oil, added to his feed, brings out a lovely gleam to his coat.

A
B
C
D
E
F
G
H
I
J
K
L
M
N
O
P
Q
R
S
T
U
V
W
X
Y
Z

Harrier

Average height: 19-21 inches
Average weight:

Appearance

The Harrier is sturdily built with large bone for his size, and all the attributes of a scenting pack hound. He is active, well-balanced and always appears to be able to work tirelessly for long periods, whatever the terrain. Basically a smaller version of the English Foxhound, his running gear and scenting ability are particularly important features. His expression is gentle when relaxed but sensible and alert when roused. His ears, set low and lying close to the cheeks, are rounded at the tips. His muzzle is substantial with good depth, and the lips complete the square look of the muzzle, without excess skin or flews. His nose must be wide, with well-opened nostrils. The bite may be scissors or level. His long tail is carried high and curled up (but not over the back), tapering to a point with a brush of hair. The short,

Below: Showing a substantial muzzle with good depth.

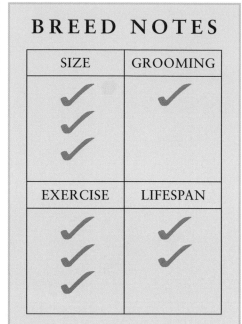

dense coat is hard and glossy, but finer on ears than on the body. He may be any color, including a unique blue mottle.

Characteristics

An outgoing and friendly hound, the Harrier is a working pack breed;

Below: At this age a puppy's ears look too big for his body!

as such he must be able to work in close contact with other hounds without showing aggression towards other dogs. Understandably, supervision is required if put together with non-canine pets unless they were raised together from puppy hood. The Harrier can be quite independent, willful and stubborn at times but displays great determination while tracking and cannot be easily swayed from his purpose. He makes a fine home companion, but is reputed to bond better with fellow canines than with humans.

Origins and History
The first pack of Harriers in England, the Penistone, was established by Sir Elias Midhope in 1260; these Harriers were held together for at least five centuries. An important reason for the breed's popularity was that a pack of Harriers could be followed on foot. There is a theory, albeit a cautious one, that the Harrier has origins dating back to the old Southern Hound, with an infusion of a little Greyhound blood.

Today it is accepted that essentially he is a smaller version of the English Foxhound, bred down in size by selection. With the exception of size, the Harrier is the external replica of the Foxhound. He has

Above: 'We are ready for out!'

Right: All the attributes of a scenting pack hound.

been known in the USA for as long as any of the scenthound breeds, and has been used for hunting since Colonial times. Used on fox, he is also particularly useful in drag hunts where speed is not a major consideration.

Health Issues
The Harrier is a very healthy breed with an average life expectancy of 12 to 15 years. He has few genetic problems, hip dysplasia being the most common problem found in this breed. Hypothyroidism and some eye diseases have also been known to occur.

Exercise and Grooming
Regular exercise is needed for the Harrier, who is prone to being rather destructive if confined. This is a great competitor in agility trials and in obedience and tracking competitions. Minimum coat care is needed; a harsh cloth should be used for a routine rubdown, followed by a massage to release dead hairs.

Below: A working Harrier pack.

A
B
C
D
E
F
G
H
I
J
K
L
M
N
O
P
Q
R
S
T
U
V
W
X
Y
Z

Havanese

Average height: 8.5-11.5 inches
Average weight:

Appearance

This is a small sturdy dog with immense charm. Slightly longer than tall, he has a mantle of untrimmed long, silky, wavy hair with a plumed tail carried loosely curled over his rump. This coat is remarkably soft and light in texture, profuse without being harsh or woolly, offering protection against the heat, the breed having spent centuries in the tropics. His head hair protects his eyes from the sun. He has a characteristic topline, rising slightly from withers to rump and resulting from moderate angulation both fore and aft, combined with a typically short upper arm. As a result of this, his gait is unique to the breed, flashy, rather than far reaching. His expression is soft and intelligent, mischievous rather than cute and his dark brown eyes are large, almond-shaped, and set rather widely apart. His medium length ears are set high on the skull and when the dog is alert they lift at the base. A scissors bite is ideal. Pigment is solid black for all colours except in chocolate colored dogs, in which case it is dark chocolate brown. In America the coat may be shown either brushed or corded. Corded coats will naturally separate into wavy sections in young dogs and will in time develop into cords; adult corded dogs are completely covered with a full coat of tassel-like cords.

BREED NOTES

SIZE	GROOMING
✓	✓
✓	✓
✓	✓

EXERCISE	LIFESPAN
✓	✓
✓	✓
✓	

Characteristics

Playful and alert, the Havanese is both trainable and intelligent with a

Above and opposite: A top winning show specimen, displaying the many attributes of this breed and correct head proportions from side and front.

sweet, non-quarrelsome disposition. He is the quintessential family pet of a people living on a small tropical island where he has been traditionally kept as companion, watchdog, child's playmate and herder of the family poultry flock. He will alert his owners to a stranger's presence, but will accept that person when he knows they have been welcomed. The breed gets along well with dogs and other pets, as well as with humans, becoming very attached to his family.

Origins and History

The Havanese is the National dog of Cuba and the country's only native breed. It appears that the breed arrived in Cuba with the trade ships sailing from the island of Tenerife in the 16th century. Cuban trade was highly restricted by the Spanish so these little dogs found their way into the homes of Cuban aristocracy and developed with little outside influence. The breed's tropical homeland seems to have influenced the development of the Havanese, especially its coat. In days gone by it has been called the Havana Silk Dog, or the Spanish Silk Poodle, its coat resembling raw silk floss. By the mid-18th century the breed had become well established in Europe and was often seen at shows. With the advent of the Cuban revolution, a handful of dogs found their way to the United States, and by the end of the 70s a gene pool was being rebuilt.

Health Issues

This is a generally healthy breed, but problems to watch out for include Progressive Retinal Atrophy (PRA), cataracts, luxating patella, Legg-Calve Perthes Disease, heart disease, deafness and chondrodysplasia (CD); this is a bone disorder which can manifest in various ways, the most recognisable sign being dwarfism.

Exercise and Grooming

The breed requires moderate exercise so a lead walk and a romp in the yard or garden should suffice. Most Havanese take naturally to water and love to swim. The soft coat needs regular attention to prevent matting (unless retained as a corded coat). He should never be so elaborately coifed as to preclude an impromptu romp in the leaves. This is a non-shedding breed and is hyper-allergenic.

A
B
C
D
E
F
G
H
I
J
K
L
M
N
O
P
Q
R
S
T
U
V
W
X
Y
Z

Ibizan Hound

Average height: dogs – 23.5-27.5 inches; bitches – 22.5-26 inches
Average weight: dogs – 50 pounds; bitches – 45 pounds

Appearance

The Ibizan Hound is slightly longer than he is tall, with clean-cut lines, fine bone and strong muscling, yet with no sign of heaviness. He has a hare foot with long, strong toes. A characteristic of the breed is that the elbow is positioned in front of the deepest part of the chest. His large, highly mobile, prick ears and light pigment give him a unique appearance. He is lithe and racy, with a deer-like elegance, combined with the power of a hunter, moving with a suspended trot that gives the appearance of skimming over the ground. His long, narrow head is in the form of a sharp cone, truncated at its base; it is finely chiselled and extremely dry fleshed. His small, oblique eyes range in color from clear amber to caramel and give an intelligent, alert, inquisitive look. Pigment is a rosy flesh color, never black or liver.

The Ibizan Hound has two different coat types, both of which are untrimmed. The short coat is shortest on head and ears; longest at back of the thighs and under the tail. The wire-haired Ibizan has hair from one to three inches in length and possibly a generous moustache. There is more hair on the back, back of thighs, and tail. Both types of coat are hard in texture and

BREED NOTES

SIZE	GROOMING
✔ ✔ ✔	✔
EXERCISE	**LIFESPAN**
✔ ✔ ✔	✔ ✔

Below: A wire-haired Ibizan (left) and a smooth (right).

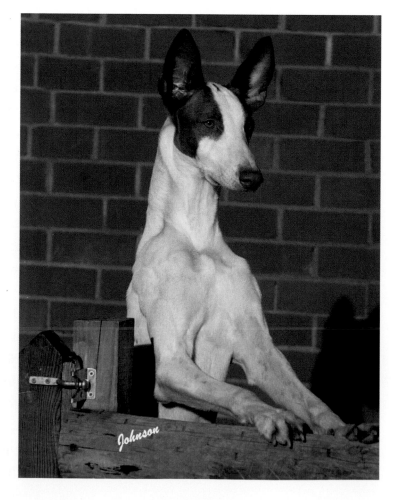

A
B
C
D
E
F
G
H
I
J
K
L
M
N
O
P
Q
R
S
T
U
V
W
X
Y
Z

neither coat is preferable to the other. Color is white or red, solid, or any combination of the two.

Characteristics

The Ibizan Hound is even-tempered, affectionate and loyal. He is clean, quiet, polite and playful. He is protective and therefore watchful of strangers. An extremely versatile and trainable breed, he makes an excellent family pet, but because he has historically hunted small game such as rabbits, great caution should be exercised with household pets to which he has not been carefully introduced. He is well suited to the breed ring, obedience, tracking and lure-coursing. His has a keen, natural hunting instinct with great determination and stamina in the field. Ther Pharaoh Hound is as fast as top coursing breeds and is without equal in agility, being able to spring to great heights from a standstill.

Origins and History

The Ibizan Hound's history can be traced back to around 3400 BC, to Ancient Egypt where this regal hound was owned by the pharaohs. Anubis, the Egyptian watchdog of the dead, is closely connected to the Ibizan Hound, showing many resemblances. The breed seems to have moved with the sea-trading Phoenicians to the island of Ibiza where the dogs helped them to provide necessary food. The Ibizan Hound reached America in 1956 when Colonel and Mrs Seoane brought the breed to Rhode Island. Today, American breeders pledge to

Caption: This high quality dog shows the correct positioning of elbow in relation to chest and ribbing

preserve the Ibizan Hound true to its original form.

Health Issues

Amongst the health problems found in the Ibizan Hound are eye problems, allergies, seizures, bloat and deafness, which may affect either or both ears

Exercise and Grooming

The Ibizan Hound needs plenty of opportunity for exercise, but bearing in mind that his original quarry was rabbits, he will chase small game and birds, so needs a large, secure, high-fenced area. Both coat types are simple to care for.

A
B
C
D
E
F
G
H
I
J
K
L
M
N
O
P
Q
R
S
T
U
V
W
X
Y
Z

Icelandic Sheepdog

Average height: dogs – 18 inches; bitches – 16.5 inches
Average weight: in proportion to height

Appearance

This is a Nordic herding spitz with the dense coat and curled tail that is so typical of Northern breeds. The quality coat is highly weather-resistant, thicker around the neck, forepart of the shoulders and chest, forming a ruff which is more profuse in the male. The rump and top of hind legs are also covered with thicker, longer hair forming characteristic breeches or trousers. This is a double coat with a short dense undercoat and longer guard hairs growing through it forming the outer coat. It may be straight or moderately wavy with a pronounced ruff around the neck, especially in longer coated males. This is a strong, compactly built breed with proportionate bone and muscle structure; he is slightly longer than he is tall. The Icelandic Sheepdog's expression is lively, keen, intelligent, friendly and alert; his medium–sized eyes are almond-shaped. Ears are strongly erect, triangular, with slightly rounded tips; they are very mobile, reacting sensitively to sound. The high-set tail curls over, touching the back, but varies from an arch to a double curl. Several colors are permitted, all with a single predominant color: shades of tan, ranging from cream to reddish brown, chocolate brown, gray or black. White markings should always accompany the predominant color.

BREED NOTES

SIZE	GROOMING
✓ ✓	✓ ✓

EXERCISE	LIFESPAN
✓ ✓	✓ ✓

Characteristics

The Icelandic Sheepdog is a hardy, agile herding dog that barks, making it extremely useful for herding or driving livestock in pastures or mountains or for finding lost sheep. He will also bark an enthusiastic welcome to announce the arrival of any visitor! His personality is outgoing, cheerful, intelligent, inquisitive, playful, yet gentle and unafraid. He is able to learn new tasks quickly and is eager to please. This is an affectionate companion, outgoing with both people and other dogs. His hunting instincts are not strong.

Origins and History

The Icelandic Sheepdog actually originated in Scandinavia, remains of very similar dogs having been found in graves in Denmark and Sweden, dating back to 8000 BC.

Above: These dogs show two of the many colors in this breed, always a double coat with trousers.

Iceland was colonized by the Vikings in 874 and they took with them their dogs. As time moved on, other breeds arrived in Iceland in small numbers but from the early part of the 20th century it was forbidden to take animals into the country so, in consequence, the breed changed little since the Vikings landed. Iceland has suffered hard times with epidemics, hunger periods and natural disasters, resulting in a breed that is tough and enduring. It appears the Icelandic Sheepdog has really been through some bad spells, for there is a written report from the 10th century saying that to remedy a serious famine on the island all old folks and cripples were to be killed as they ate, but did not work! This did not go down well with the chief, so it was decreed that instead dogs would be killed so that few or none remained, thus their food could be given to the people. Later, in 1855-56, an epidemic again reduced the number of dogs greatly. Now things are much brighter for the Icelandic Sheepdog, for between two and five dogs are found on each farm. He had survived only in very remote and isolated places on the island and other herding dogs were imported and introduced to the breed to improve herding instincts. From 1930 onward an Englishman, Mark Watson, opened people's eyes to the qualities of the original dog and in the 1950s collected some of the best specimens to establish the breed in California. The Icelandic Kennel Club was founded in 1969, its main aim being to watch over the Icelandic Sheepdog, which is now recognised as part of Iceland's cultural heritage.

Health Issues

This is a healthy, long-lived breed, but amongst the problems it is known to have encountered are hip dysplasia and distichiasis, thought to be a hereditary eye disorder.

Exercise and Grooming

The Icelandic Sheepdog needs a moderate amount of exercise. This is no problem at all as this breed tends not to wander off as he has no interest in hunting. He is a naturally clean dog and although it is quite a long coat it is easy to care for; a weekly brush should keep it in good order.

A
B
C
D
E
F
G
H
I
J
K
L
M
N
O
P
Q
R
S
T
U
V
W
X
Y
Z

Irish Red and White Setter

Average height: dogs – 24.5-26 inches; bitches – 22.5-24 inches
Average weight: 50-70 pounds

Appearance

The Irish Red and White Setter was bred as a working setter; he is aristocratic, keen and intelligent. His powerful, well-muscled hindquarters allow him to work all day in demanding countryside. The chest is deep, with well-rounded ribs to allow plenty of heart and lung room. His head is broad in proportion to his body, with a square muzzle, good stop and domed head. He has a moderate length of tail, strong at the root and tapering to a fine point. He is athletic rather than racy, and might be compared to a middle distance runner, rather than a sprinter. His is basically a white dog with red patches, always with a good bloom to the coat. It is short and fine on head and front of legs, and of moderate length on the rest of the body, with feathering on ears, back of legs, stomach, chest and throat.

Characteristics

This is a friendly, dependable breed that is easily trained as a gundog. A very versatile pointing breed, he can

BREED NOTES

SIZE	GROOMING
✔ ✔ ✔	✔ ✔

EXERCISE	LIFESPAN
✔ ✔ ✔	✔ ✔

Johnson

Above: Powerful, well-muscled hindquarters allow this breed to work all day.

Opposite: Who could resist these adorable puppies?

be trained to do just about anything. He has a good, kind nature, making him a thoroughly good companion both in the home and in the field.

Origins and History

The Irish Setter most probably came into its own at the end of the 17th century, when hawking went out of fashion. It is likely that the Irish Red and White Setter is the older of the two Irish Setters, selective breeding having created the solid red color. Actually many of the early setters were all white. Other people believe that the two colors of Irish Setter have always co-existed, the red being predominant in the north. Often the Red and White is referred to as "The Rossmore Setter", after Lord Rossmore of Monaghan. But by the end of the 19th century the Red and White became so rare that many thought them extinct. During the 1920s Reverend Noble Huston of County Down made efforts to revive the breed and pedigrees were compiled right back to 1790. In 1978 the breed was separately classified and given Championship status by the Irish Kennel Club, a specialist breed club having existed since 1944.

Health Issues

This is a healthy breed, living on average to between 12 and 15 years. Health problems encountered include cataracts, hip dysplasia, immune mediated hemolytic anemia

A
B
C
D
E
F
G
H
I
J
K
L
M
N
O
P
Q
R
S
T
U
V
W
X
Y
Z

Above: A patient mother and her pups.

Left: Pups enjoy a quick drink from their dam at any time!

(IMHA, formerly AIHA), hypothyroidism, von Willebrand's Disease and canine leucocyte adhesion deficiency (CLAD).

Exercise and Grooming
This breed needs plenty of exercise, both on a leash and free play, otherwise he becomes restless. The coat needs regular attention to keep it free from tangles and burrs, but bathing is only occasionally necessary unless being exhibited.

Irish Setter

Average height: dogs – 27 inches; bitches – 25 inches
Average weight: dogs – 70 pounds; bitches – 60 pounds

Appearance

This is a racy, athletic dog, longer in the leg than the English Setter. His long coat, without wave or curl is a blend of red, ranging from deep mahogany to rich chestnut. It has been likened to the color of a freshly broken horse chestnut. There is long, silky feathering and a long tail fringe. The head is long and lean, and square at the muzzle. His ribs are well-sprung, but not barrel-chested and his topline gradually slopes from shoulder to tail. The tail has a strong root, tapering to a fine point and it should not reach below the hock; neither should it be carried above the level of the back.

Characteristics

The Irish Setter is a great companion, both at home and in the field. He is fun-loving, playful and affectionate, bold and very

BREED NOTES

SIZE	GROOMING
✔ ✔ ✔	✔ ✔
EXERCISE	**LIFESPAN**
✔ ✔ ✔	✔ ✔

Left: The wonderful deep color can be liked to a freshly broken horse chestnut.

intelligent. It is said that once he is trained, he is trained for life. His calm and gentle disposition makes him an excellent candidate to work as a therapy dog, but he is of course successful at many dog sports too.

Origins and History

Perhaps the most familiar of all Irish dogs, the Irish Setter's history probably begins as the 17th century moved intjo the 18th. It is believed that setters are descended from land spaniels who helped in taking game with the net. In the 18th century they were trained to find game for the gun. Although there were red and white setters at that time, the Earl of Enneskillen certainly kept a kennel of all reds in 1796. Although still rare in

399

A
B
C
D
E
F
G
H
I
J
K
L
M
N
O
P
Q
R
S
T
U
V
W
X
Y
Z

the early part of the 19th century, popularity grew and in 1860 an Irish Red Setter took first prize at the famous Birmingham Dog Show. A breed club was formed in 1882 and by the end of the century Irish Red Setters were being exported in large numbers and bred outside Ireland. There was some concern that the color prevented it from being seen on a shoot, so some owners tied a piece of white cloth around its neck. Today it is a smaller, lighter boned Irish Setter that is used in the field, that seen in showring being larger and more heavily boned.

Above: A racy, athletic dog, the topline gradually sloping.

Left: This typical head is long and lean, with a square muzzle.

Health Issues

Health problems known to occur in this breed include Progressive Retinal Atrophy (PRA), hip dysplasia, canine leucocyte (CLAD), epilepsy, hypothyroidism and bloat. Also be on the alert for skin allergies.

Exercise and Grooming

This is a true sporting dog who likes to have lots of space in which to exercise. He needs long daily walks or will become restless. His coat does shed, though not excessively, so it needs brushing, with special attention paid to tangles and burrs following exercise. Bathing is only needed occasionally unless he is destined for the showring.

Opposite: This typical head is long and lean, with a square muzzle.

A
B
C
D
E
F
G
H
I
J
K
L
M
N
O
P
Q
R
S
T
U
V
W
X
Y
Z

A
B
C
D
E
F
G
H
I
J
K
L
M
N
O
P
Q
R
S
T
U
V
W
X
Y
Z

Irish Terrier

Average height: 18 inches
Average weight: dogs – 27 pounds; bitches – 25 pounds

Appearance

Sometimes this breed was referred to as the Irish Red Terrier to distinguish him from the other terrier breeds when all were thrown together in one classification. He is lighter in frame than the other Irish terrier breeds and his dense, wiry coat is always bright red, golden red, red wheaten, or wheaten red. At the base of the stiff outer coat there is an undercoat of finer and softer hair, lighter in color. Although built more along racing lines, he has plenty of bone and is no way '"whippety". The Irish Terrier is neither cobby nor cloddy, but built on lines of speed, with a graceful outline. His head is long, the skull flat and rather narrow between the ears, narrowing slightly toward the eyes. The jaws are muscular, of good punishing length. The hair on the upper and lower jaws is similar in quality and texture to that on the body, and of sufficient length to give additional strength and finish to the foreface.

Characteristics

Good tempered, spirited and game, the Irish Terrier has always been a family pet, guard dog and hunter. He shows fire and animation. He has a heedless, reckless, characteristic pluck about him, which has earned him the name, "Daredevil." He has a good temper, is affectionate, utterly loyal and devoted. He is ever on guard, and stands between his home and all that threatens it. He can be

difficult to housebreak because he likes to explore, dig, and chase things but is a thoroughly entertaining companion. Socialization should begin at an early age.

Origins and History

There are four Irish terrier breeds; the Irish Terrier is possibly the oldest of them all but due to scarcity of records this is difficult to prove.

Below: Hair on upper and lower jaws is of a similar quality to that on the body.

BREED NOTES

SIZE	GROOMING
✔ ✔	✔ ✔
EXERCISE	**LIFESPAN**
✔ ✔	✔ ✔

Johnson

Smallish terrier-like breeds were invaluable to Irish farmers and were always common in the countryside. Late in the 19th century, this was the first Irish terrier breed to be recognised by the English Kennel Club. Prior to the 1880s, the color of the Irish Terrier had not been settled, some were red, but others were black and tan or brindle. But efforts were made to breed out the other colors so that in the 20th century all Irish Terriers were red.

Below: Although built along racing lines, he has plenty of bone.

During the previous century some had docked ears, a sure sign that they were used for fighting. During the First World War they were used as messenger dogs, proving their intelligence and fearlessness. The first breed club was set up in Dublin in 1879 when the maximum weight for dogs was 24 pounds and bitches 22 pounds, but rules changed in 1929 allowing greater weight.

Health Issues
This is a very healthy breed and not particularly prone to any disease, said to have "nearly no genetic health problems".

Exercise and Grooming
The Irish Terrier is bred for active work, so needs a lot of exercise. He should be held firmly on a leash for he can be quarrelsome with other dogs and does not usually take kindly to other pets. The Irish Terrier should only be bathed when necessary. His coat is easy to groom and rarely sheds; dead hair should be removed with a fine-toothed comb and stiff bristle brush. For conformation competition, professional presentation is needed.

A B C D E F G H **I** J K L M N O P Q R S T U V W X Y Z

Johnson

A
B
C
D
E
F
G
H
I
J
K
L
M
N
O
P
Q
R
S
T
U
V
W
X
Y
Z

Irish Water Spaniel

Average height: dogs – 22-24 inches; bitches – 21-23 inches
Average weight: dogs – 55-65 pounds; bitches – 45-58 pounds

Appearance

The Irish Water Spaniel is a smart, upstanding, strongly built sporting dog. Perhaps his most distinguishing characteristics are his topknot of long, loose curls and the dense, crisply curled liver colored coat, contrasted by a smooth face and a "rat" tail. His head is cleanly chiselled, the skull rather high in the dome and his muzzle square and rather long, with a deep mouth. His large nose is liver in color and his eyes preferably dark hazel, the expression keenly alert, intelligent, direct and quizzical. The long, lobular, low-set ears reach to about to the end of the nose and are abundantly covered with long curls. Sound hindquarters are of great importance to provide swimming power and drive. A proper double coat is of vital importance to protect the dog while working.

Below: This Champion is a fine example of the breed.

Opposite: The large nose is liver and the eyes dark hazel.

BREED NOTES

SIZE	GROOMING
✓	✓
✓	✓
✓	✓

EXERCISE	LIFESPAN
✓	✓
✓	✓
✓	

Johnson

Johnson

A
B
C
D
E
F
G
H
I
J
K
L
M
N
O
P
Q
R
S
T
U
V
W
X
Y
Z

Most of the body and the legs are covered with tight, crisp ringlets; all curled areas clearly defined by curls of sufficient length to form a sharp contrast with the smooth coat on face, throat, tail, and rear legs below the hocks. The Irish Water Spaniel is always a solid liver color.

Characteristics

This breed is very alert and inquisitive, but can be reserved with strangers. Great intelligence is combined with rugged endurance and a bold, dashing eagerness. A stable temperament is essential in a hunting dog, but he also has an endearing sense of humor.

Origins and History

Evidence of dogs of Irish Water Spaniel-type goes back to the 7th and 8th centuries. Late in the 12th century, dogs found in southern Ireland, below the River Shannon, were called Shannon Spaniels or Irish Water Spaniels. There are records of "Water Spagnel" having been given to royalty; these were described as having long, rough, curled hair and their tail somewhat bare and naked. Boatswain, born in 1834 is the acknowledged ancestor of all modern Irish Water Spaniels and lived until almost 20 years old. At the first Westminster Kennel Club show in America in 1877, there was an entry of four Irish Water Spaniels.

Health Issues

Surveys conducted by the Irish Water Spaniel Club of America list the following areas of concern in this breed: hip dysplasia, hypothyroidism, entropion, seizures, cancer, irregular heat seasons, ear infections, skin and coat problems. The breed can also sometimes be sensitive to ivermectin, sulfa dugs and various forms of anesthesia.

Exercise and Grooming

The Irish Water Spaniel has tremendous stamina, being a hunting dog that enjoys retrieving and long hours of swimming. He is always ready for a lengthy walk The tight double coat does shed slightly, so should be thoroughly combed weekly or bi-weekly to keep it free of matts, and to keep the skin healthy. Scissoring is required every 6 to 8 weeks to shape the coat. Regular swimming helps to promote correct ringlets over the body.

Johnson

Left: Intelligence combined with rugged endurance.

Opposite top: Feeling at home by the water.

Opposite: Always happy to retrieve.

A
B
C
D
E
F
G
H
I
J
K
L
M
N
O
P
Q
R
S
T
U
V
W
X
Y
Z

Irish Wolfhound

Average height: dogs – 32-34 inches; bitches – 30 inches minimum
Average weight: dogs – 120 pounds minimum; bitches – 105 pounds minimum

Appearance

The Irish Wolfhound is a dog of great size and commanding appearance, combining power, swiftness and keen sight. He is the largest and tallest of the galloping hounds very muscular, strong but gracefully built. His skull is not too broad, long and moderately pointed, his ears small and Greyhound-like in carriage. He has a rather long, muscular neck and very deep chest with wide breast. The Wolfhound's back is rather long and the loins arched, while his tail is long and slightly curved. He has rough, hard hair on body, legs and head; it is especially wiry and long over eyes and under the jaw. The recognized colors are gray, brindle, red, black, pure white, fawn or any other color that appears in the Deerhound.

Characteristics

Despite his great size, the Irish Wolfhound is among the gentlest of breeds; when mature he has a very

Below: A fine example of a successful Champion.

BREED NOTES

SIZE	GROOMING
✔	✔ ✔
EXERCISE	**LIFESPAN**
✔ ✔ ✔	✔

Johnson

calm presence. He is a very social dog and should not be left alone for extended periods. Often known as the "Gentle Giant", he is wonderful with children and generally good with other dogs. Though alert he is not suspicious, and although courageous he is not aggressive. His nature and temperament make

Right: Often known as the "Gentle Giant".

Below: The Wolfhound has very keen sight.

A
B
C
D
E
F
G
H
I
J
K
L
M
N
O
P
Q
R
S
T
U
V
W
X
Y
Z

A
B
C
D
E
F
G
H
I
J
K
L
M
N
O
P
Q
R
S
T
U
V
W
X
Y
Z

him totally unsuitable as a guard dog. Combining power, swiftness and excellent sight, the Irish Wolfhound is good at lure coursing.

Origins and History

Early Irish literature makes many references to the dog we know today as the Irish Wolfhound, although over time he has been known by many different names. He was highly regarded for his hunting prowess, particularly in the pursuit of wolf and the Irish elk, which stood six feet at shoulder. These animals disappeared from Ireland and as a result the hound that had hunted them became virtually extinct.

Captain Graham began restoring the breed in 1862, gathering together the remaining specimens of the breed. After 23 years of his hard work, and that of others, the first breed standard was set down.

Health Issues

Various health problems can affect the Irish Wolfhound, amongst which are bloat, cancer, elbow dysplasia, fibrocartilaginous embolic myelopathy, heart disease, hip dysplasia, hypothyroidism, liver shunt, megaesophagus, osteochrondosis, Progressive Retinal Atrophy (PRA), seizures and von Willebrand's Disease.

Exercise and Grooming

Bearing in mind the breed's great size, power and exercise requirements, he is not a suitable choice for every family and serious consideration should be given as to whether a potential owner could actually cope. He needs a large, well-fenced area in which he can gallop freely. The Irish Wolfhound should not be over-exercised during puppyhood. To maintain a healthy condition, his coat should be brushed each or every other day.

Below: Despite his great size, this is one of the most gentle breeds.

Johnson

Above: Fun in the garden

Left: An Irish Guard and his mascot

Below: The skull is not too broad, long and moderately pointed.

A B C D E F G H **I** J K L M N O P Q R S T U V W X Y Z

A
B
C
D
E
F
G
H
I
J
K
L
M
N
O
P
Q
R
S
T
U
V
W
X
Y
Z

Italian Greyhound

Average height: 13-15 inches
Average weight: 6-10 pounds

Appearance

In many ways physically similar to a Greyhound, the Italian Greyhound is much smaller in all proportions. His head is narrow and long, tapering to the nose, the skull rather long and almost flat. His nose may be black or brown, in-keeping with his coat color, any color being acceptable except brindle and tan the markings normally found on black-and-tan dogs of other breeds. The dark eyes are bright and intelligent, the ears small and fine in texture, thrown back and folded except when alerted, when they are carried folded at right angles to the head. The long, slender, gracefully arched neck leads into long, sloping shoulders and a medium-length body with a curved back, drooping at the hindquarters. The chest is deep and narrow. Typical of the breed is its hare foot, with well-arched toes. The tail is slender and tapering to a curved end, the skin fine and supple, with the short hair glossy like satin, and soft to the touch. The movement of the Italian Greyhound is high-stepping and free.

Characteristics

The Italian Greyhound has a gentle nature but can be demanding in his need for attention. In fact, his

BREED NOTES

SIZE	GROOMING
✔	✔ ✔
EXERCISE	**LIFESPAN**
✔ ✔ ✔	✔

Below: Smaller in all proportions than the Greyhound.

arts of the Mediterranean countries dating back 2000 years. During the 16th century it was highly sought after by Italians and Southern Europeans, who gave the breed its name. The breed arrived in England in the 17th century where it steadily gained popularity. The first Italian Greyhound was registered with the AKC in 1886. Following the First World War the breed was in danger of extinction in Britain but fresh stock was imported from the USA, enabling its revival.

Health Issues

Some potential health problems that may be found in the Italian Greyhound include Progressive Retinal Atrophy (PRA), luxating patella, autoimmune thyroiditis, seizures, von Willebrand's Disease, cataracts, Legg-Perthes disease, and fractured limbs.

Left: A proud mother.

Below: The short, satin-like hair is soft to the touch.

temperament is quite different from his larger relatives, the Whippet and Greyhound. Although he appears fragile, he is actually a hardy little dog and very active. He has the sporting instincts of a sighthound. Because of his short coat, small size and low weight, this breed does not usually like to go outside in bad weather. When he does, protective clothing such as a sweater or rain jacket, as appropriate, is essential.

Origins and History

Dogs resembling the Italian Greyhound appeared on decorative

A
B
C
D
E
F
G
H
I
J
K
L
M
N
O
P
Q
R
S
T
U
V
W
X
Y
Z

Exercise and Grooming

Although small, the Italian Greyhound is essentially a sight hound and so enjoys exercise, including conformation, agility and obedience trails. He should also have regular walks on a leash. Grooming requirements are minimal for this short coated breed that sheds little. However, particular care is needed to keep the Italian Greyhound's teeth and nails in good

Opposite and right: There are various different colors in this breed.
Below: The head is narrow and long.

A
B
C
D
E
F
G
H
I
J
K
L
M
N
O
P
Q
R
S
T
U
V
W
X
Y
Z

Jack Russell Terrier

Average height: 10-12 inches
Average weight: 12.5-13.2 pounds

Appearance

The Jack Russell Terrier is a strong, active, lithe, working terrier, longer than he is tall. His skull is flat, of moderate width; the muzzle is wide. He has strong, deep jaws that are wide and powerful and his strong teeth close in a scissors bite. The Jack Russell's small, dark eyes have a keen expression and his button or dropped ears are very mobile. His chest is deep, rather than wide, with good clearance from the ground, his forelegs are straight and his back level. The tail may droop at rest but when moving is erect and, if docked, its tip should be on the same level as the ears. He has strong, muscular hindquarters and his feet are round, hard and padded, with moderately arched toes. His coat may be smooth, broken or rough, but it must be weatherproof

Below: This is a broken coated Jack Russell.

Johnson

BREED NOTES

SIZE	GROOMING
✓	✓
EXERCISE	**LIFESPAN**
✓✓	✓✓

and should not be stripped out in any way. The colour is predominantly white, with black and/or tan markings.

Characteristics

The Jack Russell is a vocal dog, for his work requires him to bark at his prey so that he can be located underground if necessary. He is very intelligent and has loads of stamina; this is a working dog who needs to problem-solve. He has become very popular as a pet but although he may enjoy sitting on a lap, he is not really a "lap dog", but is a breed that needs training and plenty of opportunity to keep both body and mind active. Most Jack Russells get along well with children, but they will not tolerate abuse, even though it may not be intentional. He is an outgoing little fellow and is usually friendly toward other dogs, but some do display same-sex aggression. The breed is utterly fearless, which can cause problems if he decides to take on an adversary that is considerably larger then himself! Jack Russells are often cat-aggressive and they cannot be trusted to tolerate the family hamster or guinea pig!

Origins and History

The Jack Russell Terrier originated in England in the 19th century, thanks to the valiant efforts of the Reverend John Russell. He needed a strain of Fox Terriers to suit his personal needs, namely to run with his foxhounds and to go to ground to bolt fox and other quarry from their dens. Effectively two different varieties evolved, the taller, more

Below: This smooth knows he is not supposed to have toys on the sofa!

squarely built dog now known as the Parson Russell Terrier and the shorter one, the Jack Russell. The names of these dogs did not actually come into being until after the Reverend's death. There has long been some controversy about the two, and whether they should be two distinct breeds or one of the same; most people strongly favour the latter, though kennel clubs do not always share that view. The red fox is the traditional quarry of the Jack Russell, and the fox can den in a wide variety of places from old badger sets to drain pipes, old rabbit holes and groundhog dens; so it is that the Jack Russell must be small enough to get to his quarry, his chest no larger than the animal he is pursuing. The Jack Russell Terrier Club of America is the largest Jack Russell registry in the world; this is

not a kennel club, but a breed-specific organisation.

Health Issues

Known for its good health and longevity, a Jack Russell can live for anything between 14 and 21 years. Having said that, there are some health concerns in the breed, including hereditary cataracts, primary lens luxation, congenital deafness, medial patella luxation, cerebellar ataxia, Legg-Calve Perthes disease, myasthenia gravis, atopy and von Willebrand's disease.

Exercise and Grooming

The Jack Russell is a veritable powerhouse of energy, so need plenty of opportunity for exercise. His coat is easy to manage, just requiring a thorough brush and comb on a weekly basis and the occasional bath, when necessary.

A B C D E F G H I J K L M N O P Q R S T U V W X Y Z

Japanese Chin

Average height: 8-11 inches
Average weight: 4-15 pounds, in proportion to height and body build

BREED NOTES

SIZE	GROOMING
✔	✔
	✔
EXERCISE	**LIFESPAN**
✔	✔
✔	✔
✔	

Appearance

With his distinctive oriental expression, the Japanese Chin is a small, well balanced, lively, aristocratic Toy dog. Looking bright, intelligent, alert and inquisitive, he has a large broad head, a short, broad muzzle and his large, wide-set, dark eyes have a touch of white in the inner corners, giving him a characteristic look of astonishment. His facial markings are evenly marked, and his ear featherings complete the picture. The dog's outline presents a square appearance. The jaw is wide and slightly undershot. The Chin's body is square, moderately wide in chest with rounded ribs and his high-set, profusely coated tail is carried arched up over the back and

Left top and left: Black and white adult and red and white puppy.

flowing to either side of the body. His hare-shaped feet have feathering on the ends of the toes. The coat is abundant, straight, single and silky, with a resilient texture making it stand out from the body, especially on neck, shoulders and chest areas. The rump area is heavily coated and forms culottes or pants. Coat color is either black and white, red and white or black and white with tan points. A clearly defined white muzzle and blaze are preferable to a solidly marked head.

Characteristics

The Japanese Chin is a sensitive and intelligent dog whose entire purpose in life appears to be to serve man as a companion. He is incredibly responsive and affectionate to those he knows, but is frequently reserved with people who are unfamiliar to him and in new situations. The breed's compact size and his charming personality make him an ideal companion.

Origins and History

It is believed that the breed now known as the Japanese Chin originated in China, centuries ago. It was eventually taken into Japan, having been presented as a gift to Japanese royalty. Because of this Chinese background, it is generally believed that the Chin shares its ancestry with the Pug and the Pekingese. In 1853, Commodore Perry took Chins from Japan to England and a pair of these dogs was given to Queen Victoria. In time, the breed arrived in America. As did so many other breeds, the Japanese Chin suffered during the First World War, and many losses were incurred when Japan suffered earthquakes. Dogs in Britain and Europe have helped to maintain a high quality and their bloodlines have been blended with American ones to establish the breed firmly here.

Health Issues

The Japanese Chin is a fairly healthy breed, and the majority of health problems that are sometimes encountered are common to many other Toy breeds. Those to watch out for in particular are luxating patellas, cataracts and early-onset heart murmurs.

Exercise and Grooming

Being so small, exercising the Japanese Chin is not a great issue, but he does enjoy a walk on a leash to explore fresh smells and to keep his senses alert. He loves to play in a safe, secure area. Being single coated, the hair does not matt, so is easily groomed. Weekly brushing will help to keep the coat healthy and shining.

Below: Moving with purpose.

Kai Ken

Average height: dogs – 18.5-22 inches; bitches – 17.5-20 inches
Average weight: 25-55 pounds

A
B
C
D
E
F
G
H
I
J
K
L
M
N
O
P
Q
R
S
T
U
V
W
X
Y
Z

BREED NOTES

SIZE	GROOMING
✓ ✓	✓ ✓

EXERCISE	LIFESPAN
✓ ✓ ✓	✓ ✓

Left: This sturdy dog is less independent than other Japanese breeds.

Appearance

This is a medium-sized Spitz-type dog of sturdy build and with exceptional courage and agility. He has a wedge-shaped head, strongly erect ears and a harsh, straight, double coat, the color of which is always brindle. This coat pattern has earned the Kai Ken the nickname "Tora", meaning "tiger". All brindle colors are acceptable, but the puppies are actually born with black, fuzzy coats and sometimes the brindle bars do not appear fully until the age of five years. Some white is allowed on the lower legs, forechest and belly, but this should never blend up into the body coat. The coat is longer than that of the Shiba Inu, but shorter than that of the Akita; it may lie flat or stand somewhat away from the body. Unlike other Japanese breeds, the Kai's tail does not form a double curl, but is carried over the back like a sickle. His teeth are of good size and a scissors bite is preferred, but level is acceptable. Generally the tongue is spotted, but it may be pink or blue-black. Pigment is always black.

Characteristics

The Kai Ken was once thought to be too primitive to fit in well as a family pet, but that myth has been dispelled, for in America the breed has proven to be a gentle and loyal family companion. He is highly intelligent and learns quickly. Compared with other Japanese breeds he is less independent and more willing to please his human companions. Highly regarded by the Japanese people, the Kai Ken is considered a trustworthy guardian and is extremely devoted to his owner, some saying he will even lay down his life to protect his master. He may be somewhat reserved with strangers, but is friendly with those he knows and not aggressive with other dogs. He is a great watch dog and is often found perched on a high object such as the back of the couch – just to keep an eye on things!

Origins and History

The Kai Ken is a native of Japan and was developed as a hunting dog on the island of Honshu, in the Kai province. Because of this isolated mountainous region, many believe this to be the purest of the Japanese breeds. The Kai was used for tracking deer and wild boar. Indeed traditional Japanese writings describe this breed as a natural hunter; it therefore comes as no real surprise to discover that some will swim and

Below: Coat pattern has led to the nickname "tiger".

even climb trees in pursuit of game. The breed was recognised in Japan in 1934 when it was designated a "National Treasure" but, even today, it is still quite rare. The Kai came to America in the 1950s with US service men. There is no trace of what happened to these dogs, but others arrived in the early1990s, creating a genetic pool for all the American-bred Kai Ken.

Originally there were two types and still differences emerge. The shishi-inu-gata type is thicker and stockier, with a more bear-like face, whilst the shika-inu-gata has a longer, thinner body and more fox-like face. Today no type is preferred over the other and in Japan the two types are no longer distinguished.

Health Issues

The Kai Ken seems not to be prone to most congenital and hereditary problems experienced by other breeds, but owners must still watch out for Progressive Retinal Atrophy (PRA) and hip dysplasia.

Exercise and Grooming

Unless very well trained, it is best to keep a Kai on a leash, or he will venture off to hunt. Of course he will also need a securely fenced area in which he can enjoy free exercise. The Kai is a naturally clean dog and his coat simply needs light brushing and the occasional bath.

A
B
C
D
E
F
G
H
I
J
K
L
M
N
O
P
Q
R
S
T
U
V
W
X
Y
Z

Karelian Bear Dog

Average height: dogs – 21.25-23.5 inches; bitches – 19.25-21.25 inches
Average weight: dogs – 55-61.5 pounds; bitches – 37.4-44 pounds

Appearance

This is a member of the Spitz family, with a strong, robust conformation and only slightly longer than he is high. His broad skull is slightly convex, his muzzle deep and tapering only slightly toward the nose. The jaws are very strong and close in a tight, scissors bite. His rather small eyes are never yellow, but different shades of brown and give an alert, fiery expression. He has a high set tail curved over the back; a natural bobtail is permitted but not favored. The Karelian Bear Dog is always black with distinct white markings on head, neck, chest, abdomen and legs. This is a double-coated breed, with a straight, stiff, thick outer coat and a dense undercoat providing insulation.

Characteristics

The Karelian Bear Dog has a stable temperament but he is reserved and very devoted to his master. He is very self-confident and may show aggression toward other dogs, especially on his own territory. The Karelian Bear Dog has a highly developed fighting spirit. He is fearless and his strong hunting instinct allows him to attack bear or large game without hesitation. This is a breed that is only suitable for an experienced owner who is well-able to control him. He is happiest with a hunter or outdoorsman.

Origins and History

This breed is native to Karelia, which was once part of Finland where, for centuries, this dog has

BREED NOTES

SIZE	GROOMING
✓	✓
✓	✓
EXERCISE	**LIFESPAN**
✓	✓
✓	✓
✓	

Left: Geared up for a day's work.

Below: On watch!

been used to hunt large game including moose, elk and bear. The breed has a keen sense of smell, which aided it greatly in its employ. But the breed almost died out in Finland until the Finnish Kennel Club undertook its restoration in the 1930s. The Karelian Bear Dog was registered in Finland in 1946 but went into decline during the 1960s. Thankfully today it is amongst the top ten most common breeds in the country.

The breed has become popular

Above and right: Strong, robust conformation and very strong jaws.

not only in Finland but throughout European Russia where it is called the Russo-European Bear Laika, or Karelian Bear Laika. The Russian strain (which is technically considered a separate breed) tends to be larger and more aggressive and is a more specialized elk and bear dog. It is, however, much the same in background, appearance and hunting style, but blood of a completely fearless sheepdog was introduced and the Russians embraced the breed as their own. It was especially used by the Russian aristocracy. Today in Russia the Laika is used on more diverse quarry including wolves, squirrel, fowl and mink. This breed usually hunts singly, due to its aggressive tendencies. Although the name "Laika" means "barker", this is a silent trailer, beginning to bark only when the prey is treed or cornered, attracting the hunter's

Below: The Karelian is alert, while her friend sleeps.

attention and bringing him into gun range.

Exercise and Grooming

This dog needs plenty of exercise but this should be in a restricted area, bearing in mind the breed's hunting temperament and his unsociability with other dogs. In Finland he competes in obedience trials, search and rescue and as a sled-dog competitor. Coat care is not particularly demanding, but brushing and combing is important fairly frequently to keep it in good condition.

A
B
C
D
E
F
G
H
I
J
K
L
M
N
O
P
Q
R
S
T
U
V
W
X
Y
Z

Keeshond

Average height: dogs – 17-19 inches; bitches – 16-18 inches
Average weight: 30-50 pounds

Appearance

The Keeshond is another member of the Spitz family, this breed having originated in Germany where he is known as the Wolfspitz. In Holland, he is known as the "Dutch Barge Dog". He has a foxy expression, typically erect ears and carries his tail over his back. The Keeshond has distinctive "spectacles" created by markings and shadings around the eye with a delicate line slanting from the corner of each, coupled with expressive eyebrows. The skull

BREED NOTES

SIZE	GROOMING
✓ ✓	✓ ✓ ✓
EXERCISE	**LIFESPAN**
✓ ✓	✓ ✓

Left: *A foxy expression.*

Opposite: *Showing very distinctive spectacles.*

is well-proportioned to the body size and is wedge shaped when viewed from above, the lips are black and closely fitting, not sagging; in fact the breed is often called the "smiling Dutchman" because of the toothy grin he sometimes displays. His ears are small, triangular and carried erect. The Keeshond's coat is a veritable abundance of long, straight, harsh hair, standing out from the downy undercoat. The appearance of a lion-like mane is created by the particularly thick hair around the neck, shoulders and chest. On the head, the hair is smooth, soft, short and velvety, and the muzzle dark in color. The plume of the tail is very

Johnson

Opposite top and bottom: The coat is a mixture of gray, black and cream, with black tipping.

Right: Expressing the friendly character of the breed.

light in color and the tail tip is black. The Keeshond's colour is a mixture of gray, black and cream, the outer coat's black-tipping producing characteristic shading.

Characteristics

This is an outgoing breed, friendly with both people and other dogs. He is loyal, protective and excellent with children, making an ideal companion for people of all ages. The Keeshond is full of fun, lively, alert and affectionate, temperament being considered of primary importance. He is always eager to please.

Origins and History

For many years this breed served on small boats called riinaken, on the Rhine River, although the Keeshond's distant ancestors come from the Arctic or possibly sub-Arctic regions. This is a breed that has changed little in the past two centuries. In the late 18th century he was the symbol of the Patriots, but when the Prince of Orange established his party as the dominant one, few wanted the Keeshond, for it stood for the opposition! Only the most loyal Keeshond enthusiasts retained the breed. It was at a very low ebb until 1920 when Baroness van Hardenbroek undertook an investigation to see how much of the old stock survived. Mercifully

the dog had still been kept in its original form by some captains of riverboats, farmers and truckmen. Within ten years the breed was on a much more solid footing and the Dutch Keeshond Club was established. The Keeshond found its way to England from Germany and from Holland and thence to America, where it was accepted for registration by the AKC in 1930.

Health Issues

Some of the health problems known in this breed are epilepsy, hypothyroidism, luxating patella, hip dysplasia, hyperparathyroidism, allergies, cancer, heart disorders and distichiasis, a hereditary disease in which there are two rows of eyelashes, one of which turns inward.

Exercise and Grooming

The Keeshond needs a good, hour-long run in an open field once a day, for this an active breed. A walk on a leash is also beneficial. Regular grooming is needed to maintain a healthy coat, free of matts. Owners should allow about an hour a week for brushing, but considerably more than that during the moulting season.

A
B
C
D
E
F
G
H
I
J
K
L
M
N
O
P
Q
R
S
T
U
V
W
X
Y
Z

Kerry Blue Terrier

Average height: dogs – 18-19.5 inches; bitches – 17.5-19 inches
Average weight: dogs – 33-40 pounds; bitches proportionately less

Appearance

The Kerry Blue Terrier has a well developed, muscular body with definite style and character. His head is long, but well-balanced, not exaggerated, and his dark eyes are small with a keen terrier expression.

The Kerry Blue's small, V-shaped ears are carried forward, close to the cheeks, with the top of the ear folded slightly. His strong, white teeth meet in either a level or scissors bite. His chest is deep and of moderate breadth, his loin short

BREED NOTES

SIZE	GROOMING
✓	✓
✓	✓
	✓

EXERCISE	LIFESPAN
✓	✓
✓	✓

left top and bottom: The coat becomes increasingly blue with maturity.

and powerful. The high-set tail is carried gaily erect, the straighter the better. The correct coat is soft, dense and wavy. In show trim it is well covered but tidy and, apart from the whiskers, the head, ears and cheeks are clear. Color is very important and differs from puppyhood to maturity. Born black, by the age of eighteen months the color will have cleared to a gray blue or blue gray; from deep slate to a light blue gray. The color is fairly uniform, but may appear distinctly darker or even black on muzzle, head, ears, tail and feet.

Characteristics

The Kerry Blue Terrier is a breed that is quick to learn; he thrives on activity and is happiest when kept busy. He enjoys human company and is both affectionate and loyal to his family, generally being good with children. However, in true terrier fashion, he may be aggressive with other dogs and is unlikely to get along well with family pets unless very carefully introduced when young.

Origins and History

A native of Ireland, the Kerry Blue Terrier was originally used as an all round working terrier, particularly in the region of County Kerry, hence his name. He played an important part in keeping farms free from pests, including rats, but also hunted small game and retrieved from land and, being a strong swimmer, also from water. In addition he was used to herd, to guard and even to operate the butter churn! At one time the Kerry had a very unkempt appearance, but today he is one of the best-tailored of the terrier breeds. The first important American show at which Kerry Blue Terriers were entered is thought to be Westminster Show in 1922 and the breed received championship rating from the AKC in 1924.

Health Issues

Although a healthy breed, the following problems have occurred in the Kerry Blue: cataracts, cerebellar and extrapyriamidal abiotraphy (PNA), haemolytic anemia, hypothyroidism, keratoconjunctivitis sicca (dry eye), von Willebrand's Disease and factor XI deficiency, which is a rare clotting disorder.

Exercise and Grooming

The Kerry Blue can adapt to life indoors but he requires plenty of daily exercise, both a walk on a leash and free exercise in a secure area, particularly bearing in mind that he can be aggressive with other dogs. The coat is non-shedding and needs very regular brushing to keep it in good order, and professional grooming is needed three or four times each year.

Below: A muscular body, long head and small, V-shaped ears carried forward.

Johnson

A
B
C
D
E
F
G
H
I
J
K
L
M
N
O
P
Q
R
S
T
U
V
W
X
Y
Z

Kishu Ken

Average height: dogs – 20.5 inches; bitches – 18 inches
Average weight: 44-55 pounds

Appearance

This is a medium-sized, well-balanced dog with well-developed muscle. He is just a little longer than he is tall. The Kishu's forehead is broad, the muzzle fairly thick, wedge shaped and tapering. His relatively small, dark eyes are nearly triangular in shape. The ears, too, are triangular; they are small, firmly pricked and incline slightly forward. The thick, muscular neck leads into a straight, short back and broad, muscular loins. His ribs are deep and the belly well tucked up. The Kishu's tail is set on high, is thick and carried vigorously curled, or curved like a sickle over the back. The official colors are white, red and sesame, which is red fawn hair with black tips. However, the color mostly seen these days is white. The Kishu has a double coat, the outer hair harsh and straight, with a soft, dense undercoat. The hair on his cheeks and tail is fairly long.

Characteristics

This is a dog of noteworthy endurance. He shows both nobility and dignity. The Kishu Ken is faithful, docile and very alert. Aggressive behaviour is not tolerated in this breed, nor is shyness.

Origins and History

The Kishu originated in Japan in ancient times, having developed from a common source of spitz-type hunting dogs that lived over 3,000 years ago. The word "ken" simply means "dog" in Japanese. This breed came from the medium-sized dogs that roamed the mountains in Japan centuries ago and were used to hunt boar and deer. They have also been used for fishing and for guarding livestock and property. The Wakayama and Mie regions are best known for the development of the Kishu. Originally there were different colors in the breed, but the white dogs showed superior qualities, so were used in breeding programmes; the hunters preferred white because it could be seen easily. Before 1934 some Kishus were spotted, but it was decided that the only acceptable colors were solids, so that by 1945 the spotted dogs had disappeared. Designated in its homeland as a "Natural Monument" in 1934, this is ne of the main reasons that the Kishu is rarely exported. To this day, the breed is still used for hunting in Japan.

Exercise and Grooming

The Kishu Ken requires plenty of exercise and therefore needs a considerable amount of space. To keep the coat in good order, regular brushing is necessary.

BREED NOTES

SIZE	GROOMING
✔ ✔	✔ ✔

EXERCISE	LIFESPAN
✔ ✔ ✔	✔ ✔

Johnson

Komondor

Average height: dogs – 27.5 inches minimum; bitches – 25.5 inches minimum
Average weight: dogs – 100 pounds minimum; bitches – 80 pounds minimum

Appearance

The Komondor has imposing strength, dignity and a courageous demeanor. Large and muscular with plenty of bone and substance, he is slightly longer than he is tall and has a strong, level back. His head is large, with a broad skull and well-developed arches over the eyes, which are surrounded by dark skin. The ears, shaped like an elongated triangle, hang down. The underjaw is well-developed and broad and this breed usually has a scissors bite, but a level bite is acceptable. The tail is long and slightly curved upwards, but even when moving or excited the greater part of the tail is raised no higher than the level of the back.

The Komondor's coat is very important, for in his homeland he spends the greater part of the year in the open; his coat helps him to

Below left: A large head and broad skull.

Below right: A splendid specimen exhibited in Hungary.

BREED NOTES

SIZE	GROOMING
✔	✔
✔	✔
✔	✔

EXERCISE	LIFESPAN
✔	✔

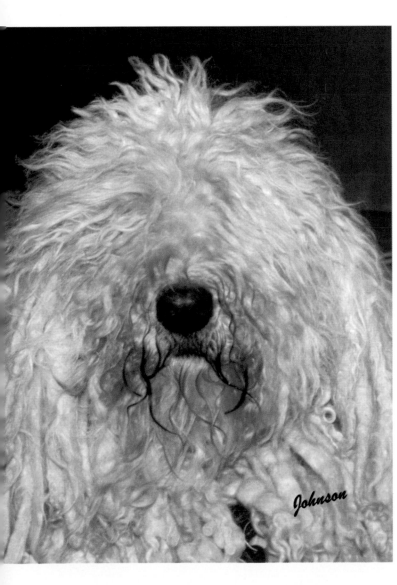

A
B
C
D
E
F
G
H
I
J
K
L
M
N
O
P
Q
R
S
T
U
V
W
X
Y
Z

Right: This puppy's coat has not yet developed its characteristic cords.

blend in with the flock and protects him against both the weather and predators. The puppy coat is relatively soft, but shows a tendency to fall into cord-like curls. The young adult coat consists of very short cords next to the skin, which may be obscured by the sometimes lumpy looking fluff on the outer ends of the cords. In maturity, the coat consists of a dense, soft, woolly undercoat, and a coarser outer coat that is wavy or curly. The coarser hairs of the outer coat trap the softer undercoat, forming permanent, strong cords that are felt-like to the touch. These tassel-like cords form naturally and a grown dog is entirely covered in them. The coat is white, but not always the pure white of a brushed coat. A small amount of cream or buff shading is sometimes seen in puppies, but this fades with maturity and is not acceptable in adults. The skin is ideally gray; pink skin, though not desirable, is acceptable.

Characteristics

Because of the nature of his work, the Komondor tends to stay close to his charges, whether they be sheep, cattle or humans! Typically, he does not wander far away. He is sensitive to the demands of his master, but will not tolerate heavy-handed training. He is reserved with strangers but demonstrative with those he knows and loves. This breed is selflessly devoted to the family and will protect them fiercely. All in all, he is an excellent guardian of herds or home, vigilant, courageous, and very faithful, but early socialization is very important.

Origins and History

In his native Hungary, the Komondor is known as the "King of the Working Dogs". In his homeland he works as a flock guardian, not a herder, and is believed to be related to the Russian Ovtcharka and to the Puli, which is another Hungarian breed. He was originally developed to guard large herds of animals on the open plains; he was left to guard the herds by himself, with no human assistance or commands. He is a vigilant guard with a fiercely protective nature and will fight a predator to the death. Apart from being used to guard sheep and cattle, the Komondor has also been used in police work. He was introduced to North America in the 1930s.

Health Issues

The Komondor has few hereditary problems but health issues to look out for include hip dysplasia, juvenile cataracts, entropion and bloat.

Exercise and Grooming

This breed needs plenty of outdoor exercise, both free run and lead work. The Komondor's remarkable coat requires regular maintenance and because it is not brushed, it must always be checked for parasites, with parasitic agents being used as appropriate. However owners should be aware that this breed's skin can be sensitive to some anti-tick and anti-flea remedies. Special attention must be paid to his ears and to his feet, the pads of which must be trimmed.

Kooikerhondje

Average height: 14-16 inches
Average weight: None specified

BREED NOTES

SIZE	GROOMING
✓	✓
EXERCISE	LIFESPAN
✓	✓

Appearance

The Kooikerhondje is a striking dog with his parti-colored coat of clear orange-red patches on white, ideally with a white blaze on the head. The length of his skull is about equal to his muzzle and he has a black nose and tight-fitting lips. His deep brown, almond shaped eyes give an alert expression. The Kooikerhondje's long feathered ears preferably have distinguishing dark tips; they are pendant and hang close to the cheeks. His white, plumed tail is carried level with his back or slightly above. The double coat can take two years to mature fully. It has a soft, silky texture and may be either straight or wavy.

Left: The Kooikerhondje needs gentle handling with strong leadership.

A
B
C
D
E
F
G
H
I
J
K
L
M
N
O
P
Q
R
S
T
U
V
W
X
Y
Z

Characteristics

This is a kind, attentive, playful dog that is alert and always willing to work. In addition he is very sensitive, intelligent and independent making him unsuitable for the novice dog owner because he can be very challenging. The Kooikerhondje needs gentle handling coupled with strong leadership. When properly trained he becomes a deeply loyal and devoted companion and if raised with children usually gets along well with them. The breed makes a good watch dog, being naturally suspicious of strangers and protective of his territory.

Opposite: Sensitive and intelligent.

Left and below: The coat has clear red patches on white, and ideally a white blaze on the head.

A
B
C
D
E
F
G
H
I
J
K
L
M
N
O
P
Q
R
S
T
U
V
W
X
Y
Z

Above: When properly trained the breed is deeply loyal.

Origins and History

The early origins of the Kooikerhondje, known also as the Dutch Decoy Dog, can be found as far back as the 16th century. It is believed that the decoy dog owned by William of Orange saved his life by warning him of the Spanish attack, and many of the Dutch Masters painted family portraits depicting a dog very similar to the Kooikerhondje we know today. It is believed that he originated from the spaniel. During the 17th century the breed was developed to work in the duck decoys, the hunter training his dog to lure the ducks into a trap using a weaving behaviour. His white bushy tail attracted the curiosity of the ducks, which would continue swimming deeper into the "pipe" and eventually the dog would lure the ducks all the way into the catching pen. By the 19th century, the duck decoy business had decreased significantly, but there are still a few working decoys found in Holland today, most of which are used for research and tagging of ducks. Although the breed was almost extinct by the 1930s, Baroness van Hardenbroek, located specimens to re-establish the breed. She began her breeding program in 1939 and the Dutch Kennel Club officially recognized the Kooikerhondje in 1966.

Health Issues

Despite its small gene pool, this is a very healthy breed, largely due to strict breeding rules and efforts to eliminate hereditary diseases though testing and selective breeding. Problems to be alert for are cataracts, epilepsy, patella luxation, von Willebrand's Disease and hereditary necrotizing myelopathy, a degenerative spinal disease.

Exercise and Grooming

This is an active dog with lots of stamina so requires plenty of exercise. He enjoys participating in agility, flyball, obedience, tracking and hunting. He is also a good swimmer and loves water. If allowed to become bored, the Kooikerhondje can become destructive. The breed's silky coat is worn naturally and needs no special grooming other than the occasional bath, a weekly brush and trimming of the hair on the pads of the feet. This is a naturally clean breed, described as having a "Teflon coat", to which dirt doesn't stick!

Kuvasz

Average height: dogs – 26-30 inches; bitches – 26-28 inches
Average weight: dogs – 100-115 pounds; bitches – 70-90 pounds

BREED NOTES

SIZE	GROOMING
✓✓✓	✓✓
EXERCISE	LIFESPAN
✓✓	✓✓

Left: Best of Breed winner at a major show.

Appearance

This is a sturdily built, large working dog; he is medium boned, well muscled and without the slightest hint of bulkiness or lethargy. His strength and activity is combined with light-footedness, allowing him to move freely on strong legs. His head is considered his most beautiful attribute. The almond-shaped eyes, the darker the better, are set well apart and are somewhat slanted. His ears are V-shaped with a slightly rounded tip. The underjaw is well developed and a scissors bite is preferred, but level is also acceptable. The nose and lips are black, and the inside of the mouth is preferably black too. The Kuvasz' chest is deep and long, the loin short, muscular and tight. His tail is carried low and ideally there should not be much difference in the carriage of tail, either when excited or repose. He has a double coat with guard hair and a fine undercoat. During hot weather it is natural for the Kuvasz to loose most of his long coat, which in some parts is 4 to 6 inches. Coat color is always white and the skin is heavily pigmented.

Characteristics

The Kuvasz is an intelligent dog and makes both a wonderful pet and working dog. Because of the nature of his work he is very independent and can be very strong willed, so is not always easy to obedience train except in the hands of a skilled dog person. Harsh training methods are absolutely not suitable for the Kuvasz, but early socialization and firm, consistent training is essential. As a sheepdog, the breed is highly protective, diligent, and against enemies such as wolves, he is fierce. As a pet, he is highly devoted, caring, gentle and patient although he must be carefully supervised when with children and family friends. Warm and humid weather conditions are not ideal for this thickly coated dog; plenty of water and shade are vital provisions.

Origins and History

It is believed that the Kuvasz may be descended from the Tibetan Mastiff and that he is possibly related to the Great Pyrenees and Maremma. The Turkish word

A
B
C
D
E
F
G
H
I
J
K
L
M
N
O
P
Q
R
S
T
U
V
W
X
Y
Z

"kawasz" means "armed guard of the nobility" and there is little doubt that the Kuvasz played a part in the history of the kingdoms and empires which flourished throughout Europe five to eight centuries ago. The Kuvasz was the constant companion of many rulers. In Hungary the breed developed into the breed as we know it today; he is still a big dog but not the giant of ancient times. King Mathias I, who reigned from 1458 to 1490 always had at least one Kuvasz with him and developed a large pack for hunting purposes. Puppies that were

Below: A fine example of a sturdily built working dog.

surplus to his requirements were presented only to noblemen and to visiting dignitaries. In time the breed also came into the hands of the commoners, and shepherds found the breed suitable to work sheep and cattle. During the Second World War the breed almost became extinct in Hungary, but dedicated breeders in Hungary and other parts of Europe helped to re-populate the breed in its homeland.

Health Issues
This is a generally healthy breed and although large, has a life expectancy of over ten years. It is, however, predisposed to some health problems including

osteochondritis disecans (OCD), hip dysplasia and bloat. He can sometimes suffer from skin conditions and allergies.

Exercise and Grooming
The Kuvasz needs plenty of vigorous outdoor exercise on a daily basis; a highly active lifestyle will avert his tendency to chew and to dig. His coat naturally sheds dirt so weekly brushing is usually sufficient. Frequent baths are not recommended as they will rid the coat of its natural oils that are responsible for the dirt-shedding function. A useful cleaning method is to apply corn starch to the coat and then brush it out.

Kyi Leo

Average height: 8-12 inches
Average weight: 9-14 pounds

Appearance

The Kyi Leo is not so small, nor so fragile as the Maltese, and his muzzle is longer than that of the Lhasa Apso. He may have a scissors or reverse scissors bite and his bright, alert eyes give a comprehensive and intelligent expression. Several colors are allowed, but the black and white dogs are really the trademark of the breed, black markings around the eyes and black ears being very desirable. Pigment is black. The coat is long and thick, of a silky texture; it may be straight or have a slight wave and tends to part naturally along the spine. It may take three or four years to reach its full length. The tail is well-feathered and curled over the back when alert, though may be dropped when the dog is relaxing, eating or unhappy. His feet are round and well covered with hair; the Kyi Leo has great control of his front feet in order to grasp, hold and play.

Characteristics

The Kyi Leo is very agile and rather cat-like in his quickness. He is playful and people-oriented, happy, outgoing, intelligent and ever willing to please. The breed can be reserved with strangers, and makes a good little alarm dog. Sometimes he can be a rather stubborn but owners consider this is just an expression of individual character.

Origins and History

This is a very new breed created in the early 1950s around the San Francisco Bay area of California where a handful of people experimented by crossing the Maltese with the Lhasa Apso, although their reason for doing this is really not known. This resulted in a small, adorable dog with a sparkling personality and several succumbed to his charms. Harriet Linn acquired her first Kyi Leo in 1965 and became the driving force behind the coalescing of this new breed. "Kyi" is the Tibetan word for dog and "Leo" is Latin for Lion. Although the breed is not yet recognised by the AKC, it is recognised by the

American Rare Breed Association and there is a specialist breed club. An interim breed standard has been adopted.

BREED NOTES

SIZE	GROOMING
✓✓	✓✓✓
EXERCISE	**LIFESPAN**
✓	✓✓

A B C D E F G H I J K L M N O P Q R S T U V W X Y Z

Labrador Retriever

Average height: dogs – 22.5-24.5 inches; bitches – 21.5-23.5 inches
Average weight: dogs – 65-80 pounds; bitches – 55-70 pounds

Appearance

A medium-sized, strongly built, well-balanced and athletic dog, the Labrador Retriever's conformation enables him to function as a retrieving gun dog. Above all he must be able to move in the show ring or in the field with little or no effort. As he is bred primarily as a working gun dog, structure and

BREED NOTES

SIZE	GROOMING
✓	✓
✓	✓
✓	
EXERCISE	**LIFESPAN**
✓	✓
✓	✓
✓	

Left: The eyes denote the breed's good temperament.

Opposite: *Waiting at the gate.*

soundness are of great importance. His skull is wide, well-developed but without exaggeration, the head clean cut and free from fleshy cheeks. His lips are not squared off or pendulous, but fall away in a curve toward the throat and his jaws are powerful and free from snippiness. A scissors bite is distinctly preferred. The Labradors eyes denote his good temperament, intelligence and alertness, all hallmarks of the breed. His underline is almost straight, with little or no tuck-up and his loins should be short, wide and strong, leading to powerful hindquarters. The thick "otter" tail is a distinguishing feature; it is very

A
B
C
D
E
F
G
H
I
J
K
L
M
N
O
P
Q
R
S
T
U
V
W
X
Y
Z

Above: Labradors make good Guide Dogs for the blind.

Below: A strongly built, athletic dog with a thick, "otter" tail.

thick at the base and gradually tapers toward the tip. His coat, which can be black, yellow or chocolate, is short, straight and very dense, feeling fairly hard to the touch. There is a soft, weather-resistant undercoat, providing protection from water and all types of ground cover.

Characteristics

This is a loyal, devoted, playful dog; he is people oriented and very hardworking. He has a kind, outgoing nature, non-aggressive towards man or animal, and always eager to please. The Labrador Retriever is gentle, intelligent and adaptable. His gentle ways, intelligence and adaptability make him an ideal dog for many people. This breed's many skills include hunting, tracking, retrieving, police work, illegal drugs detection, guide dog, helping disabled people, search and rescue, as well as agility and obedience.

Above: Training a puppy to stand. | *Below: All the fun of puppyhood.*

Origins and History

Despite his name, the Labrador Retriever came from Newfoundland, in Canada, not from Labrador. His distant ancestors had been taken to Newfoundland by explorers, fishermen and settlers from England and other parts of Europe. There were many small water dogs in the area, and when bred with Newfoundlands they produced the St Johns's Water Dog, which is the ancestor of today's Labrador Retriever. Dogs like these were taught to haul fishermen's nets into shore by jumping overboard into icy waters. In the early 19th century, the Earl of Malmesbury took a dog of this type to England where an eminent British Sportsman

A
B
C
D
E
F
G
H
I
J
K
L
M
N
O
P
Q
R
S
T
U
V
W
X
Y
Z

Opposite: Retrieving the game.

Opposite bottom: The Labrador also retrieves from water

Below: Patiently watching his owner judge a class.

described it thus, "the best for any kind of shooting... generally black and no bigger than a Pointer, very fine in legs, with short, smooth hair... is extremely quick running, swimming, and fighting... and their sense of smell is hardly to be credited". The name, Labrador, was introduced by the Duke of Malmesbury, for that was what he always called his own dogs. Over time this dog was bred with other sporting breeds, so the Labrador as we know it today is basically of

Johnson

A
B
C
D
E
F
G
H
I
J
K
L
M
N
O
P
Q
R
S
T
U
V
W
X
Y
Z

A
B
C
D
E
F
G
H
I
J
K
L
M
N
O
P
Q
R
S
T
U
V
W
X
Y
Z

English origin. The English KC recognised the breed in 1903 and in 1917 the AKC registered the first

Below: Chocolate and yellow Labradors

Labrador Retriever following which there was a great influx of imports to the USA from Britain, forming the backbone of the breed in this country where it is now the most popular breed.

Health Issues

The following are some of the health problems encountered in the Labrador Retriever: hip and elbow dysplasia and other joint problems, hereditary myopathy of Labrador

Above left: Structure and soundness is important.

Above: The head is clean cut, without fleshy cheeks.

Left: This youngster is already a loyal, devoted, playful dog.

Retrievers, bloat, exercise induced collapse in Labrador Retrievers, eye problems, tricuspid valve dysplasia, epilepsy, hypothyroidism, diabetes, chronic hepatitis, laryngeal paralysis and ear infections

Exercise and Grooming

The Labrador must be given plenty of opportunity for outdoor exercise, and he will enjoy a walk on a leash. If not provided with sufficient exercise he may become obese. Grooming-wise, the Labrador Retriever is low-maintenance, his short double coat just needs regular brushing using a firm bristle brush.

A B C D E F G H I J K L M N O P Q R S T U V W X Y Z

A B C D E F G H I J K **L** M N O P Q R S T U V W X Y Z

Lagotto Romagnolo

Average height: dogs – 17-19 inches; bitches – 16-18 inches
Average weight: dogs – 29-35 pounds; bitches – 24-31 pounds

Appearance

This is a medium-small sized dog of rustic appearance, squarely built, sturdy and robust. The Lagotto Romagnolo's head is moderately broad, the skull slightly convex and with well-developed eyebrow arches. The muzzle is strong, its depth almost equal to its length; the jaws are wide, large and powerful, usually with a scissors or pincer bite, but reverse scissors is permissible. The fairly large eyes, ranging from ochre to dark hazel and brown, give an attentive, intelligent expression. The triangular ears, slightly rounded at the tip, hang when at rest, but are slightly raised when alert. The Lagotto's feet are compact, with strong, curved nails; webbing between the toes is highly desirable. The tail hangs in a scimitar position when at rest but when working or excited may be carried over the back, although never curled. His woolly coat is rather rough on the surface, forming very thick, ring-shaped curls, with a visible, waterproof undercoat. The curls are evenly distributed all over the body, except on the head where they are less tight, forming eyebrows, whiskers and beard. Coat colors vary considerably; they may be solid off-white, white with brown or

BREED NOTES

SIZE	GROOMING
✔ ✔	✔ ✔
EXERCISE	**LIFESPAN**
✔ ✔ ✔	✔ ✔

Below and opposite: The coat forms thick, ring-shaped curls.

Johnson

orange markings, brown roan, solid brown or solid orange. A brown or dark mask is acceptable and pigmentation ranges from light to a very dark brown.

Characteristics

The Lagotto is an ancient Italian breed of waterfowler and truffle hunter, so this is an intelligent dog, lively and affectionate too. He makes an excellent watch dog, reputed for sleeping "with one ear open". He is rather noisy and lively as a puppy but grows up to be a sensible, happy fellow and a great family companion. The breed is quite territorial, so make take time before deciding to allow strangers into what he firmly considers to be "his space". The breed can live happily as a single dog in a family and loves human companionship. Being a non-shedding breed, he is a suitable choice for allergy sufferers.

Origins and History

The Lagotto Romagnolo is an ancient breed; similar dogs with extremely curly coats were portrayed in hunting and fishing scenes in the Etruscan necropolis of Spina and described in the 18th century as being widespread in the Mediterranean Sea area. Other dogs bearing a very close resemblance to the breed have been written about in poetry and in literature, as far back as the 16th century. We know from written evidence that this breed was found in the marshes of Romagna as early as 1600, and there are numerous references from the 19th century with early mention that the Lagotto was used as a truffle hunter. Between 1840 and

1890 the marshes were drained and reclaimed for farming, resulting in the Lagotto progressively losing its function as a water dog. From then onward the breed became more specialized as a truffle dog and between the two World Wars, the Lagotto was the breed used by almost all truffle hunters.

Health Issues

The breed has relatively few inherited diseases but cerebella anomaly has recently been discovered, although in most cases

puppies seem to grow out of the disorder. Other problems include cataracts, hypothyroidism and hip dysplasia.

Exercise and Grooming

The Lagotto needs a reasonable amount of free exercise and enjoys a walk on a leash. His coat is usually clipped short two or three times each year, but regular attention must be given to hair growing inside the ear canal to prevent problems occurring.

A
B
C
D
E
F
G
H
I
J
K
L
M
N
O
P
Q
R
S
T
U
V
W
X
Y
Z

Lakeland Terrier

Average height: dogs – 14-15 inches; bitches – generally one inch less
Average weight: dogs – 17 pounds; bitches – proportionaly less

Appearance

A small, workmanlike dog of sturdy build, the male Lakeland Terrier is more squarely built than the female. The body is deep and relatively narrow, allowing him to squeeze into rocky dens and yet he has sufficient length of leg under him to cover rough ground easily. He has a long neck and a high tail set; his movement is lithe and graceful. The head is rectangular, the jaws powerful and he has large teeth meeting in a scissors or level bite. His expression depends on his mood of the moment; although typically alert, it may be intense and determined, or gay and even impish. The ears are small, V-shaped, and fold just above the top of the skull. The double coat, known as two-ply in terrier circles, has a hard, wiry outer coat and soft undercoat, close to the skin. The coat on the skull, ears, forechest, shoulders and behind the tail is trimmed short and smooth, but that on the body is longer and may be slightly wavy or straight. On legs and foreface, the furnishings are crisp and plentiful, but tidy. He comes in a variety of colors, solid blue, black, liver, red or wheaten, or saddle marked, the saddle covering the back of the neck, back, sides and up the tail.

Characteristics

The Lakeland Terrier is lively spirited, gay and friendly, with a confident, cock-of-the-walk attitude. Typically he is bold, but not overly-aggressive or argumentative. He is very affectionate and loyal to his owners and can be a great companion, even with children. Unlike other terriers, he usually enjoys the company of other pets, but of course they should always be carefully introduced under supervision. He enjoys digging and is a feisty protector.

Origins and History

This is one of the oldest working terrier breeds still known today, having been bred, raised, and worked in the Cumberland lake district of England. Its name is a relatively recent acquisition, as formerly it was known as the Patterdale Terrier. Before packs of hounds were formed, this breed was kept by farmers in the mountain districts, who formed a hunt with a couple of hounds and these terriers. Their work was to hunt the foxes that raided the sheepfolds. The breed has always had great courage and would follow underground for tremendous distances. In 1871 there is a report of one crawling 23 feet under a rock to follow an otter – he was recovered after three days, none the worse for his experience! Indeed there are other reports of terriers that have been underground for as long as 12 days and have still come out alive; sadly all have not been so lucky. The Lakeland Terrier was accepted for registration in the AKC Stud Book in 1934.

Health Issues

The Lakeland Terrier is a hardy breed and is reputed to have no serious hereditary diseases.

Exercise and Grooming

The Lakeland is a high-spirited and energetic breed, so needs plenty of opportunity for exercise, both on and off the lead. His coat needs to be hand stripped two or three times a year, with professional attention essential if entered in conformation competition.

BREED NOTES

SIZE	GROOMING
✓ ✓	✓ ✓ ✓
EXERCISE	LIFESPAN
✓ ✓	✓ ✓

Lancashire Heeler

Average height: 10-12 inches
Average weight: 7-13 pounds

Appearance

The Lancashire Heeler is a small, sturdily built dog, slightly longer than he is tall. His skull is flat and wide between the ears, tapering toward the eye and continuing to the nose. His jaws are strong, with a scissors bite. His almond shaped eyes are dark, except in liver colored dogs when they may be lighter to match the coat color. The ears show an alert lift, or may be erect. The Lancashire Heeler's

Below: Sturdily built, he is slightly longer than tall, with a natural tail.

pasterns allow the front feet to turn slightly outward. His tail is set on high, left natural and carried in a slight curl over the back when alert, but not in a complete ring. The topcoat is short, thick, hard, flat and weather proof and is slightly longer on the neck; the undercoat should not show through the topcoat. Color may be black or liver, with rich tan markings.

Characteristics

The Lancashire Heeler is courageous, happy and affectionate with his owner. This is an intelligent

BREED NOTES

SIZE	GROOMING
✔	✔
EXERCISE	LIFESPAN
✔ ✔	✔ ✔

A
B
C
D
E
F
G
H
I
J
K
L
M
N
O
P
Q
R
S
T
U
V
W
X
Y
Z

Above: Puppy smelling the daffodils.

Above right: Black with rich tan markings.

dog with a stubborn streak, so training should be consistent and firm, as he will quite readily do his own thing if given the opportunity.

Origins and History

The exact origins of the Lancashire Heeler are uncertain, but he appears to have originated when the Welsh Corgi that was used to drive cattle from Wales to market in north west England was bred with the local Manchester Terrier. This resulted in a dog that worked cattle in the same way as the Corgi, by nipping at its heels, but also had the ratting instincts of the terrier. These qualities made it a useful dual purpose dog, an alert, tireless and energetic worker that became popular on farms in Lancashire. But there are other theories about his origin. Some say he has some Dachshund blood running though his veins and there are others who believe he was an ancestor of the Corgi, not the other way around. Certainly there are references to little dogs matching his description as far back as the early 16th century. In the 1960s there was a resurgence of interest in the breed. The Lancashire Heeler Club being formed in Britain in 1978 and granted full recognition by the English KC in 1982. The breed has been included in the AKC's Foundation Stock Service since 2001.

Health Issues

The breed appears to have few health problems other than Collie eye anomaly, lens luxation and luxating patella.

Exercise and Grooming

The Lancashire Heeler enjoys a good romp and a lead walk, exercise being important to him to keep him physically fit and his senses alert. His coat is undemanding, but regular brushing is important to keep both coat and skin in healthy condition.

Leonberger

Average height: dogs – 28-31.5 inches; bitches – 25.5-29.5inches
Average weight: dogs – 132 pounds and over; bitches – 105 pounds and over

Appearance

The Leonberger is large, muscular and strong, and yet very elegant. His head is generally deeper than it is broad, elongated rather than stocky, and the skin is close fitting without wrinkle. The teeth, with their scissors bite, are set in strong jaws. Ears are set on high and hang close to the head. The tail is very well furnished with hair and hangs straight down; when the dog is moving, the tail is slightly curved. The Leonberger's double coat is medium soft to coarse, fairly long, profuse and close fitting. It never has a parting. There is a mane on the neck, especially in males, distinct feathering on the front legs and ample breeches on the back ones. Color is lion yellow, red, reddish brown or sandy and all combinations in between, always with a black mask. Black hair tips are permitted but black must not determine the dog's basic colour.

Characteristics

BREED NOTES

SIZE	GROOMING
✔ ✔ ✔	✔ ✔
EXERCISE	**LIFESPAN**
✔ ✔ ✔	✔ ✔

Left: An excellent example of a showdog, displaying all the qualities of the breed.

The Leonberger is a very agreeable family dog who fits into most situations and is notable for his gentleness with children, usually getting along well with other pets also. He is confidently calm and yet has quite a lively temperament. Neither shy, nor aggressive, he is obedient and unafraid in all situations. He has a good learning capacity and remembers things well.

Origins and History

It was around the close of the 1830s that Heinrich Essig, Town Councillor of Leonberg near Stuttgart in Germany, crossed a black and white Newfoundland bitch with a St Bernard from the monastery hospice. He then added other giant breeds,

A
B
C
D
E
F
G
H
I
J
K
L
M
N
O
P
Q
R
S
T
U
V
W
X
Y
Z

Above: Waiting patiently.

including the Great Pyrenees. Essig's goal was to develop a powerful dog that could be used for draft work or as a flock guardian. He was also aiming for a lion-like appearance as the town crest of Leonberg has a lion rearing up on its legs. The first dogs that could really be called Leonbergers were born in 1846 and only a short time later many were sold as status symbols from Leonberg. By the end of the 19th century it was kept in Baden-Württemberg as the preferred farm dog. During both World wars, and in post war years, breeding stock was dramatically reduced but the breed kept going and is now an excellent family dog that suits all the demands of modern-day life.

Health Issues

Thanks to very strict breeding guidelines set down by Leonberger Clubs, this breed does not encounter many of the illnesses encountered in other giant breeds. However the following problems may be of concern: hip dysplasia, osteochondritis dissecans (OCD), panosteitis (Pano), Addison's disease, osteosarcoma, bloat and hypothyroidism.

Exercise and Grooming

An adult Leonberger needs 40 to 60 minutes of exercise each day, made up of long walks with opportunity to run and play. Puppies, however, should have their exercise restricted during the growth stage, gradually increasing this when the bones are developed. This breed has a great love of water and enjoys a good swim. The coat needs to be brushed and groomed at least once each week to remove any dead and loose hair.

Below: The breed always has a black mask.

Lhasa Apso

Average height: dogs – 10-12 inches; bitches – slightly smaller
Average weight: 13-18 pounds

Appearance

The attractive Lhasa Apso is rather longer than he is high and is distinguished by his long, straight coat that is hard in texture with an undercoat, the two combining to give him the protection needed to live in the harsh geographic climate of Tibet. His hair falls over his eyes, which are protected by long eyelashes preventing the hair falling into them, instead creating a curtain

BREED NOTES

SIZE	GROOMING
✓ ✓ ✓	✓ ✓ ✓

EXERCISE	LIFESPAN
✓ ✓ ✓	✓ ✓

Johnson

Left: Long eyelashes prevent the hair from falling into the eyes.

providing protection from the glare of the white snow and strong sunlight. The muzzle should not be too short, but is about one third the total length from nose to the back of the skull, making this a partial-brachycephalic breed. In America the accepted bite is slightly undershot or level, but in the majority of countries the only acceptable bite is a reverse scissors. The Lhasa Apso has good whiskers and a beard, and his pendant ears are heavily feathered. It is important that this breed is well ribbed up, allowing sufficient heart and lung room to survive at such high altitude. The high-set tail is well feathered and carried well over theback, and there may be a kink at the end; if present this is a highly

Above: Young puppy already trained to stand correctly.

Below: The Lhasa Apso has a long, straight coat.

typical feature. All colors are equally acceptable, with or without dark tips to ears and beard. However, because the breed standards require a black nose, liver and chocolate pigment is not an option in the western world, although it is perfectly acceptable in Tibet.

Characteristics

The Lhasa Apso's personality is gay and assertive, but with strangers he is chary or rather aloof. Visitors to the home must allow the resident Apso to make friends in his own time; he will probably sit at a distance for a while and then make

Above: Puppies love to play with soft, safe toys.

Below: 'Kitty' is thoroughly content with her litter of only two.

his own approach if and when he feels the time is right. He has a keen sense of hearing and an uncanny ability to distinguish friend from foe. Lhasa Apsos enjoy the company of their own kind, but can be rather dominant, and males do not always live in harmony with each other.

Origins and History

Historically, in Tibet the Lhasa Apso was kept inside the monasteries to give a warning bark if intruders managed to get past the Tibetan Mastiffs that were tethered outside. In fact in Tibet the breed is also called "Abso Seng Kyi", which means "bark sentinel lion dog". But the Lhasa Apso was also kept inside the homes of more prosperous people and used by traders to keep guard over their goods and chattels, often travelling on horseback. The Apso was never sold, but presented only as a gift, and was often used as

457

A
B
C
D
E
F
G
H
I
J
K
L
M
N
O
P
Q
R
S
T
U
V
W
X
Y
Z

Above: *'I know I'm a boy, but I love bluebells.'*

Below: *An elderly Apso, his coat clipped for ease.*

on an expedition to Tibet with Theodore Roosevelt. In 1930 Cutting went back to Tibet and met His Holiness the Dalai Lama who later sent four Apsos to Mr Cutting and his wife, who are famous for their Hamilton kennels.

Health Issues

Lhasa Apsos are generally very hardy, but Progressive Retinal Atrophy (PRA) has been found, so all breeding stock must be tested for this inherited disease in an endeavour to eliminate it. Kidney problems have also occasionally been known to occur. Other eye problems found, though less serious because they can be well managed, are dry eye and cherry eye, the latter a swelling of the nictitating membrane in the inner corner of the eye.

Opposite top: *A well-presented Champion with excellent coat texture.*

Opposite bottom: *'Millie', bred and owned by the author.*

a tributary gift for safe passage, especially to China. The Lhasa Apso is still considered by Tibetans to be the reincarnation of a monk that has erred in a previous life. The breed first arrived in Britain in the mid-19th century but the various small Tibetan breeds and their Sino-Tibetan cousin, the Shih Tzu, were not finally divided up as completely separate breeds until 1934. The Lhasa Apso was admitted to AKC registration in 1935, having been brought here initially by world traveller Suydam Cutting, who went

A
B
C
D
E
F
G
H
I
J
K
L
M
N
O
P
Q
R
S
T
U
V
W
X
Y
Z

Exercise and Grooming

Apsos enjoy a walk on the lead and a good romp, but if they have canine companions of the same breed, or at least of similar size, they are always happy to create their own exercise in play. But playing can play havoc with the coat so it essential to check for burrs, knots and tangles. The coat, which is not shedding and therefore knots easily, is very demanding. It must be carefully combed and brushed at least three times each week and ideally should be bathed every 7 to 10 days.

Left: 'Up here I almost feel as if I'm in Tibet.'

Opposite and below: Puppy and adult coats (l & r)

Above: 'Adam' didn't learn to climb until he was 11 yrs old!

Above: The author's very first Apso, 'Donnie'.

A
B
C
D
E
F
G
H
I
J
K
L
M
N
O
P
Q
R
S
T
U
V
W
X
Y
Z

A
B
C
D
E
F
G
H
I
J
K
L
M
N
O
P
Q
R
S
T
U
V
W
X
Y
Z

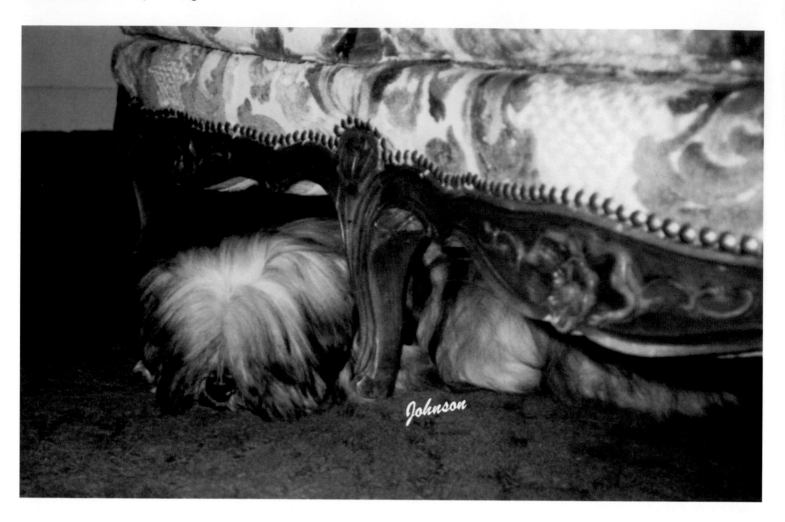

Above: *'I can keep an eye on things from here.'*

Below: *Living a life of luxury.*

Opposite: *A woodland walk can create havoc with the coat!*

Johnson

Löwchen

Average height: 12-14 inches
Average weight: 12-17 pounds

Appearance

In Pre-Renaissance Europe ladies of the court groomed this little dog in the likeness of a little lion, and that is just how the Löwchen is presented today. His head is a hallmark of the breed, the expression bright, alert and lively, the eyes large and round in shape; usually they are dark, but may be slightly lighter in brown and champagne colored dogs. The nose is dark and this breed should have complete pigmentation. The pendant ears are well fringed and set on slightly above the level of the eye. The muzzle is relatively broad and is equal in length to the back skull, or slightly shorter. The Löwchen has a scissors bite. Strong and sturdy in bone, but never coarse, his body is slightly off-square and there is a slight tuck-up to the underline. His tail is high-set and carried in a cup-handle fashion when moving. The untrimmed coat is long, rather dense and moderately soft in texture, with a slight to moderate wavy appearance. The breed is traditionally trimmed in "Lion Trim" clipped to about $\frac{1}{8}$ inch from the last rib back to and including the hindquarters, leaving a ruff or mane which just covers the last rib. Cuffs of hair are left on all four legs and a plume is left at the

BREED NOTES

SIZE	GROOMING
✓ ✓ ✓	✓
EXERCISE	**LIFESPAN**
✓	✓ ✓

Below: A youngster in the grass.

Right: In the likeness of a little lion.

end of the tail. The unclipped areas are completely natural and untrimmed. All colors and color combinations are acceptable.

Characteristics

This is an alert, intelligent and affectionate breed that makes a loving companion dog and indeed originated as just that, a companion. He usually gets along well with children as well as with other pets. His personality is lively, outgoing and inquisitive. The Löwchen undoubtedly has a positive outlook on life and when challenged will not hesitate to reveal his courageous tough spirit.

Origins and History

For many years the Löwchen was believed to have originated in the Mediterranean, but it now appears to have strong roots in Germany. Certainly it has been a distinct breed for several centuries for it was depicted in 14th century French tapestries, in German woodcuts and Belgian paintings. Clearly it was known in many parts of Europe. Dogs similar to the

Below: Worn out after a game.

A
B
C
D
E
F
G
H
I
J
K
L
M
N
O
P
Q
R
S
T
U
V
W
X
Y
Z

Opposite: Although small, the Löwchen has strong, sturdy bone.

Opposite bottom: The body is slightly off-square, with a slight tuck-up

Löwchen have existed for over 2000 years but other breeds used also to be trimmed in the way this breed is trimmed today, so this has caused some confusion amongst them. In the 19th century the breed virtually disappeared but the great efforts

Above: Typical movement.

Left: The head is a hallmark of the breed.

of a Belgian enthusiast assured its continued existence. The name translates from the German "little lion" and of course is related to the breed's traditional lion clip, with close-cut hindquarters and a full mane.

Health Issues
Generally a healthy, long-lived breed, patella luxation is something to watch out for.

Exercise and Grooming
Although he is a small breed, the Löwchen thoroughly enjoys a long walk and the opportunity to run about, but will generally fit in with whatever the lifestyle of his owner. The heavy coat needs regular grooming to keep it in tip-top condition and to prevent tangles from forming. Clipping the Löwchen takes a certain amount of expertise.

A B C D E F G H I J K **L** M N O P Q R S T U V W X Y Z

Lucas Terrier

Average height: dogs – 10-12 inches; bitches – 9-11 inches
Average weight: dogs – 14-20 pounds; bitches – 11-17 pounds

Appearance

The Lucas Terrier, a thoroughly amiable little chap, has the general appearance of a sturdy, symmetrically built working terrier like that of an old-fashioned Sealyham type. There should be a combination of substance, power, balance and hard muscular condition. It is important to remember that the Lucas terrier was developed to work in a pack environment to push game out of heavy cover to waiting guns, not as an earth dog. The head, in keeping with the breed's general conformation, is broad in skull and only slightly curved between the ears. The cheeks are muscular but not prominent, and the underjaw is strong, deep and well-developed with a scissors bite. Eyes are dark and the nose is black, whatever the color of the dog. The ears, which are preferably small are V-shaped and carried close to the head. The Lucas Terrier is slightly longer than he is tall and his tail is customarily docked, thick with a rounded tip and carried erect. When undocked it is of moderate length, thick at root and tapering toward the tip; ideally carried erect but not excessively over the back. The fairly harsh, medium length coat is weather resistant; its color either

BREED NOTES

SIZE	GROOMING
✔ ✔	✔ ✔

EXERCISE	LIFESPAN
✔ ✔	✔ ✔

Below and opposite: A sturdily built working terrier.

Johnson

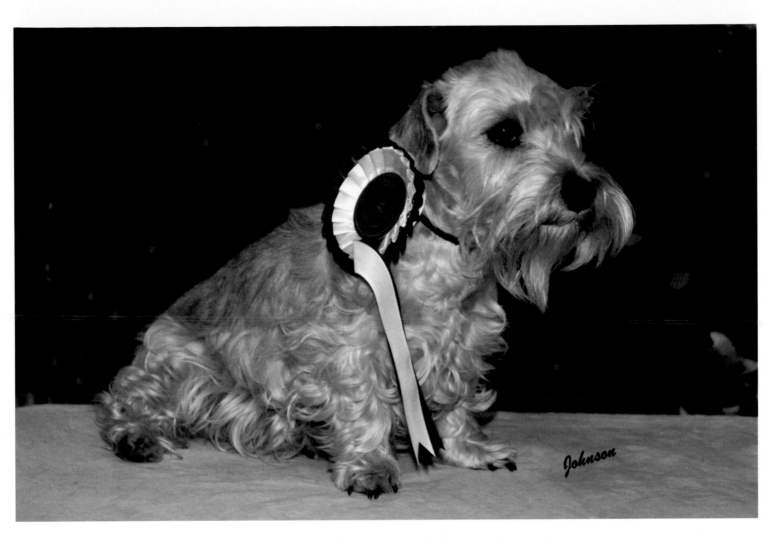

Johnson

predominantly tan, or predominantly white (black or bluish grey should not be he overall or predominant color).

Characteristics

This is a friendly breed with no aggressive tendencies, either towards people or other dogs. Having said that, the temperament should not be overly soft, neither should the Lucas be fearful or nervous. He is eager to please, smart and easy to train; indoors he is calm and content, loving and affectionate, and gets along well with children.

Origins and History

The Lucas Terrier was developed by Sir Jocelyn Lucas, born in 1889, the second son of the third Baron Lucas. He has had an interest in

dogs from a very young age, as a boy having hunted a trencher-fed pack of Smooth Fox Terriers. From his twenties, Sir Jocelyn bred Sealyhams, Labrador Retrievers and Spaniels, and kept a pack of Beagles. By the 1930s he was concentrating on Sealyhams, but all worked as a pack, pushing rabbits and old pheasants out of heavy cover to waiting guns. As time went on he became concerned that the Sealyham was becoming rather too large for the work he had in mind so introduced Norfolk Terrier blood; thus the Lucas Terrier was born. Sir Jocelyn and his kennel partner, The Hon Mrs Enid Plummer, worked hard to develop this new breed. He gave up his kennels in the 1950s but Enid Plummer continued breeding. She died in 1986 but happily others

were by now involved in the breed and Mrs Jane Irwin, Mrs Irwin's uncle, Mr Basil Wallwork and Miss Jumbo Frost joined forces to set up the Lucas Terrier Society in Britain. The breed has never sought KC recognition but thanks to its devotees continues to thrive. Its enthusiasts are all very special people, devoted to the breed in a very special way. The Lucas Terrier Club of America was founded in 2006.

Health Issues

No health problems have yet been reported in this breed.

Exercise and Grooming

The Lucas Terrier is a working breed and, as such, no extra exercise is needed. The long coat requires weekly brushing.

Lurcher

As lurchers vary so greatly in size, it not possible to indicate any particular height or weight. Most, however, tend to be of middle size and are never overly heavy in frame.

An Introduction

Although this Illustrated Directory of Dog Breeds covers primarily pure breeds, no general dog book would be complete without a word about lurchers and longdogs, as some of them are known. Lurchermen hunt different species of game, so they need slightly different dogs according to the quarry and the terrain on which they work.

Origins and History

The name "lurcher" is derived from

BREED NOTES

SIZE	GROOMING
✔ ✔	✔
EXERCISE	**LIFESPAN**
✔ ✔ ✔	✔ ✔

a Romany word meaning to rob or to plunder, but although these dogs were named by the Romanies or gypsies, they were also much favored by Ireland's tinkers. Even though they are effectively crossbreeds, usually about three quarters sighthound, most lurchermen breed selectively and carefully.

Dating back even as far as 1449, there is reference to people described as "masterful beggars" going about Scotland with their horses, hounds and other goods. It is believed that lurchers probably came into being because centuries ago Greyhound ownership was restricted to those of royal and noble blood; equally the Scottish Deerhound was rarely found in the

Left: Lurcher of strong Greyhound type.

hands of commoners. But common people also needed a good hunting dog, for this would be a valuable asset in helping to provide food for the family table. In 1668 the Dean of Ripon wrote an essay for the Royal Society and this is believed to be the first mention of the lurcher in print, 'Greater Beasts: Greyhounds. Lesser Beasts: Lurchers'. From this we can conclude that the lurcher was certainly known in the latter half of the 17th century, and that it was smaller than the Greyhound. Just two years later we find that gamekeepers were authorized to seize lurchers as well as Greyhounds and setting dogs.

As time went on, more and more references to lurchers crept into books and essays written about sporting dogs and field sports. Sometimes these dogs were referred

to as "mungril greyhounds". A highly descriptive image of early lurchers is to be found in Fairfax's Compleat Sportsman of 1760: 'Lurchers is a kind of hunting dog,

Above: This lurcher has made great friends with his rescued Greyhound companion.

Below: A Saluki cross.

A
B
C
D
E
F
G
H
I
J
K
L
M
N
O
P
Q
R
S
T
U
V
W
X
Y
Z

Above: Borzoi in the blood.

red color. The coat was rough and "wirey-haired", the ears were naturally erect but drooping a little at the tip. His remarkable skills, however, often brought him into the possession of "poachers of the most unprincipled and abandoned description".

Until relatively recently, about half the gypsies in Britain kept lurchers, but not all of them were breeders. Because a lurcher is unmistakable in looks, alarm bells were set ringing for gamekeepers and police, so

much like a mongrel greyhound, with prickt ears, a shagged coat, and generally of a yellowish-white colour; they are very swift runners so that if they get between the burrows and the conies they seldom miss; and this is their common practice in hunting; yet they use other subtleties, as the tumbler does, some of them bringing in their game and those are the best. It is also observable that a lurcher will run down a hare at a stretch.'

A tumbler, as referred to above, was a dog that somewhat resembled a small Greyhound, so called because of his ability to turn and tumble, winding his body about with ease. He hunted alone and took home his catch.

The authoritative writer, William Taplin, said in 1804 that the lurcher was originally produced by crossing the Greyhound and the shepherd's dog. Then, by breeding in and in with the Greyhound, little of the shepherd's dog was retained, except its docility and fidelity. He said lurchers were usually three-quarters the height of a Greyhound and that they were of a yellowish or sandy-

Below: Sighthound features often shine through.

Above left and right: Lurchers may be rough- or smooth-coated

some gypsies preferred to keep terriers or guard dogs instead. When the Romanies first arrived in Britain, it was a sparsely populated land with plenty of open heaths, forest and commons in which they could hide when necessity called. They carried out many trades to bring in a little cash, but what food they could not buy or barter, their dogs helped them to obtain. Hunting by scent takes time, but those that hunt by sight work quickly and, very importantly, silently, so the lurcher came into his own.

After the Second World War, buildings and roads encroached on the countryside, as did street-lighting which posed a bit of a problem for poachers! Many of them abandoned their horse-drawn carriages and moved into lorries and shiny new caravans and, in time, their dependence on lurchers dwindled. Still these dogs were used for poaching, but many turned to coursing, with large amounts of money exchanging hands.

What Breeds Are In a Lurcher's Blood?

Generally a lurcher is made up from one of the sighthound breeds, mixed with the blood either of a terrier breed or one of another group of mixed breeds. Different breeding combinations suit different purposes and lifestyles.

Amongst the most popular used in hare coursing are Deerhound-Greyhound, Saluki-Greyhound, a three-quarters cross and lurcher to lurcher. Other lurchers are all-round dogs, expected to hunt, jump, kill and carry the game back in the same manner that a retrieving breed would. These are made up rather differently such as Bedlington-Greyhound, Collie-Greyhound or Whippet-Greyhound.

Amongst lurchermen who hunt rabbits on land where there is plenty of cover, the Bedlington-Whippet is very popular, yet for those who hunt fox on the same terrain a Bedlington-Greyhound or

A B C D E F G H I J K L M N O P Q R S T U V W X Y Z

perhaps a Bull Terrier cross would be more suitable.

Breeds other than sighthounds used in lurcher breeding programmes are as follow:
Terriers: Bedlington, Staffordshire Bull Terrier, English Bull Terrier, Kerry Blue Terrier, Soft Coated Wheaten Terrier, Irish Terrier, Jack Russell or Airedale.
Other Breeds: Foxhound, Beagle, Golden Retriever, Setter, Spaniel, Labrador Retriever, Old English Sheepdog, Rottweiler, Doberman, Collie (Rough), Bearded Collie or Border Collie.

Over the last century, different people have broken down lurchers

Above: *Jack Russell Whippet cross*

Below left: *Irish Wolfhound cross*

Below right: *Bedlington Whippet cross*

This is generally a cross between either a Greyhound or a Deerhound and a collie or cattle dog, or indeed the offspring of such a cross. Another lurcher-type is the "Smithfield", an old type of breeding that was a cross between a Greyhound or Deerhound and a drover's dog. This produced a rather lanky, rough-coated dog used for sheep and cattle droving.

All the breeds involved in a lurcher's makeup will be found under their specific names throughout this book. It goes without saying, that all of them need plenty of exercise and when not hunting should be kept under strict control as their prey drive is strong. Coat care varies according to its length and texture, but guidance will be obtained from grooming information given for each individual breed.

Above and right: *Lurchers come in all colors.*

into different categories. Some have used the term "lurcher" to loosely describe any cross-bred Greyhound-type of dog. Some use the term "longdog" specifically to include hounds that are made up of two different types of coursing dog, usually Deerhound-Greyhound, Greyhound-Saluki and such like. This of course may be the result of many generations of cross breeding. (Technically, however, the term "longdog" can also be used to mean one of the specific sighthound breeds such as the Deerhound or Greyhound.)

A rather unusual lurcher is a dog known as the "Norfolk lurcher".

Maltese

Average height: up to 10 inches
Average weight: 4-6 pounds (no more than 7 pounds)

Appearance

The Maltese is well known as a Toy breed, covered from head to foot with a mantle of long, silky, white hair. His skull is slightly rounded, his muzzle medium in length, fine and tapered, but not snipy, with teeth meeting in an edge-to-edge or scissors bite. His nose is black and his eyes round and very dark, with

BREED NOTES

SIZE	GROOMING
✓	✓
	✓
	✓
EXERCISE	LIFESPAN
✓	✓
	✓

Opposite top: An ideal bed for a little Maltese.

Left and opposite: Covered from head to foot with long, white hair.

black rims. The drop ears are rather low set and hang close to the head. The head of the Maltese is carried high, his topline level and his ribs well sprung. The chest is fairly deep, the loins taught and strong and he is just slightly tucked up underneath. The tail is carried gracefully over the back, with a long-haired plume. The Maltese has a single coat (without undercoat), which hangs, long, flat and silky over the sides of the body. The long head hair is usually tied up in a topknot, or may be left hanging. Coat color is pure white; light tan or lemon on the ears is

Above: These cute little characters are kept as pets.

permissible but not desirable,. This little white dog moves with a jaunty, smooth, flowing gait, making a delightful picture.

Characteristics

This is a gentle-mannered, affectionate dog, his trust and responsiveness being very appealing. Despite his diminutive size he seems entirely without fear. He is eager and sprightly in action, lively and vigorous, making a delightful companion. The Maltese is smart, and can be trained with relative ease. He should not, however, be allowed to become over jealous so should not be over-protected, and he does not always take kindly to other pets. This little dog, although tiny and artistic in appearance, possesses a healthy and spirited temperament.

Origins and History

The Maltese is believed to be the oldest of the European Toy breeds, an aristocrat of the canine world, known for many centuries. This is the ancient dog of Malta,

Above right: *Maltese make a pretty picture on the lawn.*

Right: *Waiting at their baby gate.*

considered an object of great beauty and value. The Maltese has appeared on many Greek artefacts, innumerable paintings and literary accounts firmly establish the breed as holding a place of esteem and

A
B
C
D
E
F
G
H
I
J
K
L
M
N
O
P
Q
R
S
T
U
V
W
X
Y
Z

Johnson

Johnson

Johnson

Opposite and above: Well-groomed Maltese make a stunning sight.

privilege in royal households. The first Maltese exhibited in the USA was one listed as a "Maltese Lion Dog", this at Westminster Show in 1877. The AKC recognised the breed for registration in 1888

Health Issues

The Maltese does not do well in damp conditions and can be prone to chills. He can also get rather uncomfortable in overly hot weather, with a tendency to suffer from sunburn, especially along the hair parting. The breed can encounter respiratory, eye and tooth problems. Slipping stifles are also possible, as are digestive problems.

Exercise and Grooming

Being a playful breed, the Maltese enjoys regular walks and plenty of outdoor fun; he will enjoy a good game in his owner's yard or garden. The long, silky coat needs to be brushed and combed on a daily basis; eyes and beard cleaned regularly to prevent staining. Weekly shampooing is recommended and if destined for the showring many owners tie at least some of the hair in wraps to promote a long flowing coat without breakage to the ends.

Manchester Terrier

Average height: toy variety – 10-12 inches; standard variety – 15-16 inches
Average weight: toy variety – 12 pounds maximun; standard variety – 12-22 pounds

Appearance

The Manchester Terrier is a small, black, short-coated dog with distinctive rich mahogany markings a sleek, sturdy, yet elegant look, and a taper-style tail. He has a wedge-shaped, long, clean head with a keen, bright, alert expression and small nearly black, sparkling, almond-shaped eyes. The teeth are white and strongly developed, usually with a scissors bite, but level is acceptable. Although there are two size varieties in the USA and in Canada, there is no difference between them, other than their ears, the Toy just being a diminutive version of the Standard. The latter may have a naturally erect ear, cropped ear or button ear, whereas the only correct ear for the Toy is a naturally erect. The Manchester Terrier's body is compact and muscular, expressing great power and agility. The topline shows a slight arch over the robust loin falling slightly to the tail set. The smooth coat is short, dense, tight, and glossy, its color jet black and rich mahogany tan with clear, well defined lines of color. The tan markings are in very specific places such as over each eye and on each cheek. There is a distinct black "pencil mark" line running lengthwise on the top of each toe on all four feet, and the toenails must be black.

Characteristics

The Manchester Terrier is neither aggressive nor shy, but observant and discerning. Because he is not a sparring breed, he is generally friendly with other dogs. He is a loyal, devoted and affectionate companion and most of his kind enjoy a spending a comfortable day lounging around, just as much as they do in some active pursuit, making a good dog for any lifestyle.

Origins and History

The breed hails from Manchester in the north of England where rat killing and rabbit coursing were two well-known "poor man's sports". A dog fancier called John Hulme had the idea of producing a dog that could be used at both contests so mated a Whippet bitch with a celebrated rat-killing dog, a crossbred, dark brown terrier. The dogs proved useful and other fanciers took to breeding them and so, around 1860, the Manchester Terrier was created. Soon the breed spread all over Britain and came to the USA in considerable numbers, a

BREED NOTES	
SIZE	GROOMING
✓✓	✓
EXERCISE	LIFESPAN
✓✓	✓✓

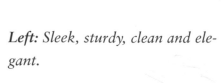

Left: Sleek, sturdy, clean and elegant.

Above: Characteristic, well-defined tan markings.

breed club being set up in America in 1923. Until 1959 the Manchester Terrier and the Toy Manchester Terrier were registered as two separate breeds, although interbreeding was permitted. Since then, here they have been registered as a single breed with two varieties, the Toy and the Standard.

Health Issues
Health issues of which to be aware in the Manchester Terrier include Legg-Calve Perthes disease, hypothyroidism, juvenile dilated cardiomyopathy, luxating patella and sensitivity to anesthetics.

Exercise and Grooming
The Manchester Terrier will enjoy daily walks and off-leash romps in a secure area. His coat needs minimal care but ears especially need to be kept clean and nails will need

A
B
C
D
E
F
G
H
I
J
K
L
M
N
O
P
Q
R
S
T
U
V
W
X
Y
Z

A
B
C
D
E
F
G
H
I
J
K
L
M
N
O
P
Q
R
S
T
U
V
W
X
Y
Z

Mastiff

Average height: dogs – 30 inches minimum; bitches – 27.5 inches minimum
Average weight: dogs – 175-230 pounds; bitches – 130-190 pounds

BREED NOTES

SIZE	GROOMING
✓ ✓ ✓	✓
EXERCISE	**LIFESPAN**
✓	✓

Left: The Mastiff's personality is a combination of grandeur, good nature, courage and docility.

powerful muscle structure, his chest wide, deep and rounded. His topline should be straight, level, and firm and there should be a reasonable, but not exaggerated, tuck-up. The tail, which is wide at the root and tapering to the end, hangs straight in repose forming a slight curve, but is never carried over the back in motion. The head is massive when viewed from any angle and the wide-set, medium-sized eyes are never too prominent. The Mastiff has an alert, kindly expression and his ears, small in proportion to the skull, are V-shaped, rounded at the tips and lie close to the cheeks in repose. The broad skull is somewhat flattened between the ears, with a furrow up the centre of

Appearance

A large, massive, symmetrical dog with a well-knit frame, the Mastiff conveys a distinct impression of grandeur and dignity. His length from forechest to rump is somewhat higher than from ground to withers, but the height should come from depth of body, not from length of leg. He is heavy-boned with a

problems with toddlers so sensible management is highly important. Early socialization with other dogs is also essential. He responds only to kind training, not to heavy-handed methods. Shyness or viciousness must never be tolerated. A Mastiff needs human companionship and should not be left along for long periods.

Origins and History

The Mastiff, perhaps more correctly known as the Old English Mastiff, has a longer history than most breeds. There is certainly evidence

Above and right: The chest is wide, deep and rounded, the head massive.

the forehead. The broad nose is always dark with spread, flat nostrils. The jaws are powerful; a scissors bite is preferred but a moderately undershot jaw is also accepted providing the teeth are not visible when the mouth is closed. The outer coat is straight, coarse, and moderately short, while the undercoat is dense, short, and close lying. Colors are fawn, apricot, or brindle, the latter having fawn or apricot as a background color, completely covered with very dark stripes. Muzzle, ears, and nose must be dark.

Characteristics

The Mastiff is a giant breed but his personality is a combination of grandeur and good nature, courage and docility. His demeanor is dignified and he makes a loyal pet that is protective of his home and his people. He is usually good with children, but his very size can cause

A
B
C
D
E
F
G
H
I
J
K
L
M
N
O
P
Q
R
S
T
U
V
W
X
Y
Z

of mastiff-like dogs dating back as far as 2500 BC in Asia, but it is generally accepted that the British developed the bred we know today simply as "Mastiff". In Britain the Mastiff was used to guard castles and estates and as war dogs when the Romans invaded Britain. They took dogs back with them to Italy where they guarded both property and prisoners, in addition to which they fought in the arena. In Britain during the time of Queen Elizabeth I the Mastiff also fought large game including bears and tigers, often these displays being put on especially for the entertainment of her majesty; whether or not she actually enjoyed this so called sport is another matter! By the late19th century Mastiffs had been imported to North America where they were used as plantation guards. Back in

Above: These cuddly puppies will become four giant sized dogs.

Below: Feeding time for the pups.

Opposite top: 'My legs are still a bit wobbly!'

Opposite left and right: A paved yard is ideal.

Britain again, the breed was used to pull munitions carts during the First World War, but by 1920 had almost become almost extinct there, primarily because of the amount of food it consumed; sometimes entire kennels of dogs were put to sleep. When the Second World War was over British fanciers imported stock from the USA and Canada in order to revive the breed, but even today the breed is numerically stronger in the USA than in Britain.

Health Issues

Although there are exceptions, the

A
B
C
D
E
F
G
H
I
J
K
L
M
N
O
P
Q
R
S
T
U
V
W
X
Y
Z

Johnson

Above: A fine example of a highly successful Champion.

Below and opposite: Mastiffs genuinely need human companionship.

Mastiff is generally not a long-lived breed, 6 to 10 years being the general rule. Health problems of concern within this breed include eye disorders, hip and elbow dysplasia, cancer, aortic stenosis and other heart diseases, epilepsy, hypothyroidism, von Willebrand's disease and bloat.

Exercise and Grooming

The Mastiff can be a little lazy and may need to be motivated to get the exercise he needs to remain active and healthy. Moderate daily walks will suffice, with the occasional game of fetch. His coat is easy to maintain, with minimal brushing and polishing with a towel cloth in order to keep it healthy and glossy. Baths can be given occasionally, or a dry shampoo.

Johnson

Miniature Bull Terrier

Average height: 10-14 inches
Average weight: in proportion to height

Appearance

Strongly built, symmetrical and active, the Miniature Bull Terrier's Kennel Club Breed Standard is exactly the same as that for the Bull Terrier, except for its size. Actually no weight is specified for this breed, but it is in proportion to a dog's height. His head is long strong and deep, right to the end of the muzzle, but it is not coarse. The head is oval in outline and filled up completely, giving the impression of fullness with a surface devoid of hollows or indentations; perhaps this is best described as "egg shaped". His well-sunken eyes have a piercing glint and are as dark as possible.

The lips are clean and tight and the small ears capable of being held stiffly erect. The top teeth should fit in front of and closely against the lower teeth, in a scissors bite. The Miniature Bull Terrier's neck is very muscular, long and arched, tapering from the shoulder to the head and his underline, from brisket to belly, forms a graceful, upward curve. The low-set tail is short, fine, and carried horizontally. The Miniature Bull Terrier, like his larger cousin, the Bull Terrier, has round, compact feet, with well arched toes like those of a cat. The short, flat, harsh coat has a fine gloss. On white dogs, markings on head and on skin

BREED NOTES

SIZE	GROOMING
✔ ✔	✔
EXERCISE	**LIFESPAN**
✔ ✔	✔ ✔

Below: This lady is a miniature version of her larger cousin, the Bull Terrier.

Johnson

pigment are acceptable; in colored dogs, any color may predominate. When moving the Miniature Bull Terrier has a jaunty air that suggests agility and power.

Characteristics

Like his larger relative, the Miniature Bull Terrier is courageous and full of fire, but is even and amenable to discipline. He has a delightful nature and likes to have

Above left and right: The head is oval in outline, with no indentations or hollows.

Below: Correct movement.

A
B
C
D
E
F
G
H
I
J
K
L
M
N
O
P
Q
R
S
T
U
V
W
X
Y
Z

Johnson

plenty of affection bestowed on him. He has a high activity level, is smart, creative and an independent thinker.

Origins and History

For over eighty years the Miniature Bull Terrier has been highly prized as a small dog notable for his tenacity and remarkable courage. His history takes us back to the early 19th century when the Bulldog and now extinct White English Terrier were bred together to produce the Bull Terrier, then known as the "Bull and Terrier". These early representatives of the breed came in a variety of sizes, some weighing as little as 4 to 7 pounds, some considered of medium size being about 15 or 16 pounds, whilst there were others as

substantial as the Bull Terrier we know so well today. The Toys, as they were known, were exhibited until the beginning of the First World War, but they did not really catch on with dog fanciers as their type was rather poor. Those of a more medium size fared better as they were better in eye and in foreface. It is these that have developed into the Miniature Bull Terrier we know today, identical in every way to the full-sized Bull Terrier. The breed became eligible to be shown in the AKCs Miscellaneous class in 1963 and was accepted as a breed in 1991.

Health Issues

The average life expectancy of this breed is 11 to 12 years and the few health problems of which owners

Above: The breed has a delightful nature.

should be aware include deafness, skin allergies and lameness. The latter is often caused by weight and a density of muscles as a puppy matures to adulthood, so he should be discouraged from jumping and from any exercise that could strain his muscles during the growth stage.

Exercise and Grooming

The Miniature Bull Terrier needs a good amount of exercise; he thoroughly enjoys playing and going for long walks on a leash. Coat care is minimal, just the occasional brush and comb, with more attention being paid to the removal of dead hair during the moulting season.

Miniature Pinscher

Average height: 10-12.5 inches
Average weight: 8-10 pounds

Appearance

This is a well balanced, sturdy, compact, short-coupled breed; in males the length equals the height at withers but bitches may be slightly longer. His skull appears flat and the head is narrow, tapering to a not too prominent foreface, which balances with his skull. The full eyes are slightly oval in shape, clear, bright and dark. The Miniature Pinscher's high set ears stand erect from base to tip; they may be cropped or uncropped. The back is level or slightly sloping to the rear, the loins short and strong. His tail is high set, held erect and docked in proportion to the dog. Shoulders have moderate angulation, permitting the characteristic hackney-like action of this breed. This is a high stepping, reaching, free and easy gait in which the front leg moves straight forward and in front of the body, the foot bending at the wrist. The smooth, hard, short coat is straight and lustrous, uniformly covering the body. Color can be solid clear red, stag red (red with an intermingling of black hairs), black with sharply defined rust-red markings as specified in the breed standard, or chocolate with rust-red markings.

BREED NOTES

SIZE	GROOMING
✓	✓
EXERCISE	LIFESPAN
✓	✓✓

Left: A chocolate with rust-red markings.

Characteristics

The Miniature Pincher, often known as the "Min Pin" for short, is rarely inactive; this is a lively, energetic breed that is always on the move. He is an adventurous, rather feisty dog, not always friendly toward strangers. He has an ability to learn

A B C D E F G H I J K L **M** N O P Q R S T U V W X Y Z

Above: *A very well-balanced show specimen.*

Below left: *A red 'Min Pin'.*

Below: *Black with rust-red markings.*

quickly and enjoys competitive obedience and agility. The Miniature Pinscher has fearless animation, complete self-possession and a spirited presence. This is not really a suitable breed for very cold climates and should live indoors, not in a kennel situation.

Origins and History

The Miniature Pinscher is not a scaled down version of another breed but, like the Doberman, is very possibly descended from the German Standard Pinscher. In historical documents this breed was often referred to as the Zwarg Pinscher, meaning "Dwarf Pincher"; it is certainly a German breed. Sometimes it was also mentioned as the Red Pinscher, but this term was only used for those of a stag-red color, the color that related to the small red deer that used to be found in German forests. Certain it is that the Miniature Pinscher originated several centuries ago and was used as an effective barnyard ratter. The breed's actual origins are still open for debate and factual records only date back some 200 years. Another two of the breed's ancestors are very possibly the Dachshund and the Italian Greyhound. Until the beginning of the 20th century the breed was principally only found in Germany and Scandinavia, the first was registered with the AKC in 1925, gaining great popularity since then. It was, however, originally classified as a Terrier but in 1930 was re-classified as a Toy. In 1972 the breed's name was changed from Pinscher (Toy) to Miniature Pinscher.

Health Issues

The Miniature Pinscher is a fairly healthy breed, but is susceptible to some health problems including patella luxation, cervical (dry) disc, Legg-Calve Perthes disease, epilepsy, thyroid disorders, heart defects and eye problems.

Exercise and Grooming

The Miniature Pincher will benefit from regular play sessions, although he can meet his own exercise needs when left to his own devices. He needs to exercise in a secure area as he likes dashing off to investigate things. His coat is not difficult to maintain; occasional brushing and shampooing is enough. When the coat sheds it should be wiped with a washcloth soaked in lukewarm water, which will take away loose hair strands.

Below: This breed enjoys obedience and agility trials.

Miniature Schnauzer

Average height: 12-14 inches
Average weight: 12-15 pounds

Appearance

The Miniature Schnauzer is characterized by its stocky build, wiry coat and abundant whiskers and leg furnishings. He is a robust, active dog of terrier type, resembling in appearance his larger cousin, the Standard Schnauzer. His head is strong and rectangular, with an unwrinkled forehead. The topskull is flat and fairly long. The muzzle is strong in proportion to the skull, ending in a moderately blunt manner, with thick whiskers accentuating the rectangular shape of the head. The small, dark brown, oval eyes give a keen expression and the ears may be cropped or uncropped; the latter are small and V-shaped, folding close to the skull. The teeth must close in a scissors bite. The erect, high-set tail is docked and only long enough to be clearly visible over the backline. The double coat has a hard, wiry, outer coat and close undercoat; head,

Below and opposite: Two lovely examples of this robust, active dog of terrier type.

BREED NOTES

SIZE	GROOMING
✓ ✓	✓ ✓ ✓
EXERCISE	**LIFESPAN**
✓ ✓	✓ ✓

Johnson

Johnson

A
B
C
D
E
F
G
H
I
J
K
L
M
N
O
P
Q
R
S
T
U
V
W
X
Y
Z

Above: White is a color now also sometimes seen.

Right: Salt and pepper coloring.

neck, ears, chest, tail, and body coat are hand stripped. Furnishings are fairly thick but not silky. Recognized colors are salt and pepper, black and silver and solid black. Salt and pepper, the most common color, is a combination of white and black banded hairs and solid black and white unbanded hairs, the banded ones predominating. (White is not allowed in the USA, but has recently been accepted in the UK.)

Characteristics

The Miniature Schnauzer is alert and spirited, and yet he is obedient to command. Friendly, intelligent and willing to please, he is usually very fond of children. This breed can cover a substantial amount of ground without tiring. As a rule he is not a fighter, but will stand up for himself when he considers it necessary.

Origins and History

Of German origin the Schnauzer is

Above: Friendly, intelligent and always willing to please.

Left: 'Poppy' enjoys regular romps in the Canadian snow.

recognisable in pictures dating back to the 15th century. The Miniature Schnauzer was developed as a small farm dog that could be used as a ratter, and is derived from the Standard Schnauzer. Apparently small Standards had Affenpincher and Poodle blood introduced and the Miniature Schnauzer was exhibited as a distinct breed in 1899. In the USA the breed falls into the Terrier Group, but in Britain it is classified in the Utility Group for the Schnauzer has a different origin from terriers and has a naturally happy temperament.

Health Issues

In general the Miniature Schauzer is a healthy breed, but problems to look out for include Cushings disease, hypothyroidism, pancreatitis, Progressive Retinal Atrophy (PRA), urinary tract infections and mycobacterium avium infection. The latter is a relatively new and very

A
B
C
D
E
F
G
H
I
J
K
L
M
N
O
P
Q
R
S
T
U
V
W
X
Y
Z

Above and below: Black (above) and black and silver (below)

Opposite: A typical head, with keen expression.

serious wasting disease belonging to the tuberculosis family.

Exercise and Grooming

The Miniature Schanuzer breed needs healthy walks on a daily basis, with an opportuinity to play off-leash. Regular grooming of this breed is very important. Hand stripping (essential for showring presentation) or clipping is needed every five to eight weeks and weekly brushing of beard and leg furnishings is also needed on a weekly basis. Because the breed is susceptible to periodontal disease, the teeth need to be cleaned regularly.

Johnson

A
B
C
D
E
F
G
H
I
J
K
L
M
N
O
P
Q
R
S
T
U
V
W
X
Y
Z

Mudi

Average height: dogs – 16-18.5 inches; bitches – 15-17.5 inches
Average weight: dogs – 24-29 pounds; bitches – 17.5-24 pounds

Johnson

BREED NOTES

SIZE	GROOMING
✓	✓
✓	✓
✓	✓
EXERCISE	**LIFESPAN**
✓	✓
✓	✓
✓	

Appearance

The Mudi is a medium-boned, compact dog with a wedge-shaped head tapering toward the nose and giving an alert, cheerful, intelligent appearance. The skull and forehead are slightly domed and the muzzle moderately strong, with a straight bridge The slightly oblique, dark eyes give the Mudi a "dare devil" expression. In blue-merle dogs, wall (white/blue) eyes are not a fault. The high-set, prick ears are abundantly covered with hair that reaches beyond the edges of the actual ear. The ears can turn independently of each other, like a radar screen! When alert the tail is carried in a sickle shape, higher than the topline. The tail is not normally docked, but if so, two or three vertebrae must be left visible. The hair on the head and front of

the limbs is short, straight and smooth. On other parts of the body it is very wavy or slightly curled, always dense and shiny and from 1 to 2.75 inches long; in some spots there are ridges, known as "cow licks". On the back of the forearms and upper thighs the coat is longest, forming pronounced feathering. Coat colors are fawn, black, blue-merle, ash, brown or white.

Characteristics

This rare breed has a pleasant disposition, is highly intelligent and learns quickly, even as quickly as a Border Collie, some say even faster! Afraid of nothing, he is extremely powerful and courageous and can quickly overpower a wild boar. He makes a good guard dog for he is always ready to defend his people and their property. The Mudi is

gentle and loving with his family and can get along with children and other pets provided he is introduced to them at a young age. He is obedient and playful, but can sometimes be rather noisy.

Origins and History

The origin of the Mudi goes back to somewhere between the 15th and 18th centuries, but the exact time is difficult to pinpoint because the naming of Hungarian herding dogs was not always clear. In the early 1930s Dr Dezsõ Fényes, a historian and cultural museum curator, often saw this local shepherd dog type in the countryside; it was then known as the "Driver Dog". Dr Fényes started to collect and breed the best specimens and found they bred true as a breed, possessing highly inheritable and stable characteristics. This is not a breed that was created by someone's dreams of an ideal herding dog but had come about due to need and performance selection. There were descriptions in the 17th and 18th centuries of dogs with pricked ears like those of the Mudi, and with coat like his too, but they were called "Pulis". It appears that the Puli is actually the oldest of Hungary's herding breeds and that the Mudi and Pumi were derived from that breed. The creation of the Mudi may have involved some crossing with spitz-type breeds. Well into the 20th century, Mudi-like puppies could be born into Puli litters and even today they can appear in Pumi litter; but not the other way around. The breed was recognised in Hungary in 1936. A new standard was written for the breed in 1966, since when it has changed several times. The Mudi has been used a flock guardian, sheep herder, cow herder, guard, hunter, vermin killer and as a companion; this breed is capable of handling a flock without assistance. In Finland the Mudi has been employed as a rescue dog.

Health Issues

Health problems that have occurred in the Mudi are cataracts and other eye diseases, elbow and patella problems, wheat allergy, skin problems and hip dysplasia. Albinism is very rare, but has occurred.

Exercise and Grooming

This is an active breed that needs to run and exercise to maintain good bodily condition and for mental stimulation. He loves to play flyball and frisbee. The Mudi's coat is easy to groom requiring occasional brushing and combing to remove dead hair.

Opposite and below: The Mudi is said to have "dare devil" expression.

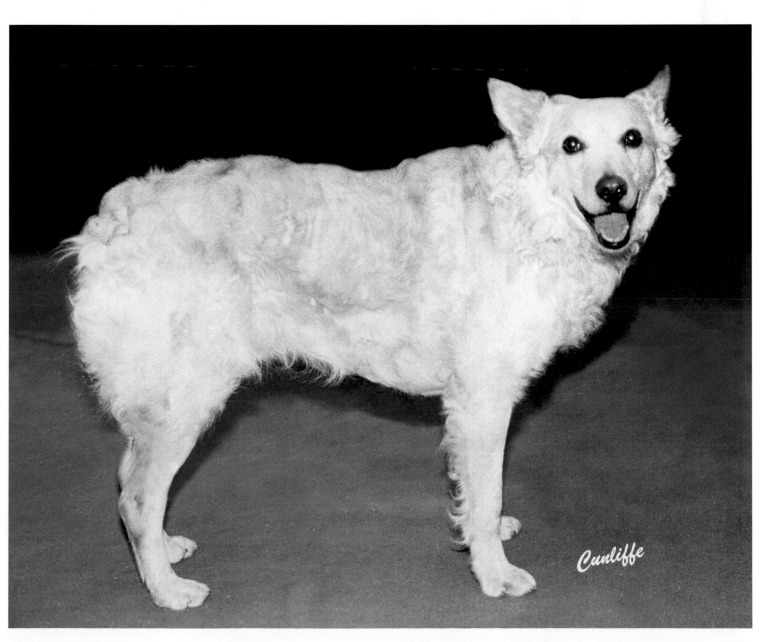

Cunliffe

Munsterlander (Large and small)

Average height: Large: dogs – 23.5-25.5 inches; bitches – 23-25 inches
Small: dogs – 20-22 inches; bitches – 19.5-22 inches
Average weight:

A
B
C
D
E
F
G
H
I
J
K
L
M
N
O
P
Q
R
S
T
U
V
W
X
Y
Z

Appearance

There are two sizes of Munsterlander, Large and Small, but it is the larger of the two that is better known. This is a well proportioned dog that carries himself with pride. He is well-balanced and has a free and easy, long striding movement with drive from the rear. His coat is flowing and dense with a good deal of feathering on legs and tail, which should be carried horizontally or slightly upwards. Docking of the

BREED NOTES

SIZE		GROOMING
Large	Small	✓
✓ ✓ ✓	✓ ✓	✓

EXERCISE	LIFESPAN
✓ ✓ ✓	✓ ✓

tail is optional. He is similar in appearance to the Small Munsterlander who is rather more setter-like, the only other difference being color. The Large Munsterlander's color is white or blue roan with black patches, flecked, ticked or in combination; the Small is liver and white with variable amounts of ticking.

Characteristics

Munsterlanders are multi-purpose gundogs with fantastic staying power, both on land and in water. He is a lovable and affectionate dog who bonds well with his family and generally has great patience with children. He will act as a watchdog when necessary and can be quite vocal. The Munsterlander is brave

Left: The Large Munsterlander is better known than the Small.

setter-types and in 1919 the Large Munsterlander was given separate recognition to differentiate it from the smaller version.

Health Issues

There appear to be very few hereditary problems in Munsterlanders and the fact that the breed is screened for cataracts suggests that this problem is under strict control. Hip dysplasia does occur from time to time.

Exercise and Grooming

This is an energetic breed so needs regular exercise, ideally a combination of free run and walks on a leash. Munsterlanders should be brushed and combed once each week. Feathering on ears, front, legs and tail needs tidying occasionally.

and eager to work, but has a gentle nature and is ever ready to please his owner. Both Large and Small Munsterlanders are bright, keen and relatively easy to train, but they can be rather dominant so need consistency in handling.

Origins and History

In the 19th century there were various shapes and sizes of bird dogs in Germany, and they were also very varied in color. As the century drew on there was growing interest in individual breeds and the different types became separated. The Long-Haired Pointer Club was established but, for whatever reason, it decided only to allow liver and white, resulting in puppies of other colors being given away to farmers and hunters from the Munster area. To them, color was of no importance; what mattered was their working skill. It is possible that they introduced other breeds, maybe the spaniel or other

Above and below: The better-known Large Munsterlander (above) and the Small Munsterlander (below).

Neapolitan Mastiff

Average height: dogs – 26-31 inches; bitches – 24-29 inches
Average weight: dogs – 150-200 pounds; bitches – 110-175 pounds

Appearance

The Neapolitan Mastiff is a stocky, heavy boned dog, massive in substance and rectangular in proportion; the length of body is 10% to 15% greater than the height. He is characterized by his loose skin, all over his body. His head is large and compared with other Mastiff breeds it has more wrinkling and pendulous lips, blending into his ample dewlap. The face is made up of heavy wrinkles and folds and his deep set eyes are almost hidden beneath his drooping upper eyelids; the lower lids droop to reveal haw. The Neapolitan Mastiff's expression is wistful when at rest, but intimidating when alert, with a penetrating stare. The muzzle is one third the length of the whole head and is as broad as it is long; it is also very deep and has a "squared" appearance. The heavy lips form an inverted V from below the nostrils and a scissors bite or pincer bite is standard, but slightly undershot is allowed. The ears are set well above the cheekbones and may be cropped or uncropped, in which case they are medium sized and triangular, held tight to the cheeks. His back is wide and strong, the highest part of shoulder blade barely rising above the strong, level topline of the back. The tail, which

BREED NOTES

SIZE	GROOMING
✔ ✔ ✔	✔
EXERCISE	**LIFESPAN**
✔ ✔	✔

Below: He is massive in substance and rectangular in proportion.

Johnson

solid white marking in certain areas only. Due to his massive structure, the Neapolitan Mastiff's characteristic movement is rolling and lumbering, not elegant or showy.

Characteristics

The Neapolitan Mastiff is a steady dog and very loyal to his owner who he is always ready to protect. His feelings of protection toward his property are just as strong and he does not relish intrusion by strangers into his personal space. Always watchful, his attitude is calm but wary. He can be wonderful with children if raised with them. This breed will not show aggression or bite without good reason.

Origins and History

The Neapolitan Mastiff is a direct descendent of the very ancient molosser war dog which existed some 5,000 years ago. This remarkable breed fought alongside the Romans when at war and was also left at home to protect family and property. In the Roman arenas he was pitted against lions, bears and gladiators. With the fall of the

is docked by one third, is set on slightly lower than the topline, wide and thick at the root and tapering gradually toward the tip. At rest it hangs straight or in slight "S" shape, but in action it is raised. The large, round feet have strong toes and a slight turn out of the feet is characteristic of the breed. The coat is short and dense, of uniform length and smoothness all over the body. Colors are gray (blue), black, mahogany and tawny. Some brindling is allowable in all colors, but this must be tan. There may be

Above and below: Some brindling in the coat is allowed.

Johnson

A
B
C
D
E
F
G
H
I
J
K
L
M
N
O
P
Q
R
S
T
U
V
W
X
Y
Z

A
B
C
D
E
F
G
H
I
J
K
L
M
N
O
P
Q
R
S
T
U
V
W
X
Y
Z

Opposite top: The puppies are already oozing with character.

Caption: caption to fill this space caption to fill this space caption to

Roman Empire the descendents of the Roman Molossian diverged into various different Mastiff breeds, but the Italian Molossian has stayed the same since Roman times, having survived in the countryside virtually unchanged in appearance and personality. Following World War II the breed was recognized as a treasure of Italy and has been refined over the last sixty years to its current

Above and below: The muzzle is as broad as it is long, and very deep.

A B C D E F G H I J K L M **N** O P Q R S T U V W X Y Z

Exercise and Grooming

A fully grown Neapolitan Mastiff needs a good walk twice a day, but during the growing stage exercise must be limited so as not to create problems with the development of muscles and bones. Plenty of shade must be provided in hot weather. His short coat requires minimal care, and it sheds only moderately; at such times dead hair should be removed with a rubber brush.

Left: The Neapolitan has remained virtually unchanged since Roman times.

Opposite: Already showing signs of quality and breed type.

Below: The heavy lips form an inverted V.

form. The first breed standard was written in 1948, then re-written for greater precision in 1971. He has long been used in the Neapolitan area of southern Italy as a guard for homes and estates. Many say that the Neapolitan Mastiff's unique type was developed purposely as an alarmingly ugly dog whose looks alone were enough to deter any intruder! (Beauty of course, is in the eye of the beholder.)

Health Issues

Although a sturdy, healthy breed, the following are some of the health problems that occur from time to time: hip dysplasia, cardiomyopathy, cleft palate, hare lip, hypothyroidism, cherry eye and bloat.

Johnson

A
B
C
D
E
F
G
H
I
J
K
L
M
N
O
P
Q
R
S
T
U
V
W
X
Y
Z

Newfoundland

Average height: dogs – 28 inches; bitches – 26 inches
Average weight: dogs – 130-150 pounds; bitches – 100-120 pounds

Appearance

This is a large, heavily coated, well-balanced dog, deep-bodied, heavy boned, muscular and strong. The Newfoundland is a dignified dog with a proud head carriage. He is slightly longer than he is tall with a massive head; his broad skull has a slightly arched crown and strong occipital bone. The relatively small ears are triangular with rounded tips and lie close to the head. The Newfoundland has a soft expression reflecting the character of the breed, benevolent, intelligent and dignified. The muzzle is broad throughout its length, and deep, the teeth meeting in a level or scissors bite. The strong neck leads into a strong, broad, muscular back and his chest is full and deep. His tail is broad at base and strong, covered with long, dense hair. The Newfoundland's feet are proportionate to his body size, cat like and webbed. He has a flat, water-resistant, double coat that falls back into place when rubbed against the nap; it is coarse, moderately long and full, either straight or with a wave. The soft undercoat is dense, but maybe less dense in warmer weather. On the face and muzzle the hair is short and fine. Colors for this breed are solid black, brown or gray (not accepted in the UK) and Landseer, which is a white base coat with black markings.

BREED NOTES	
SIZE	GROOMING
✓ ✓ ✓	✓ ✓
EXERCISE	LIFESPAN
✓ ✓ ✓	✓ ✓

Characteristics

A sweet-dispositioned dog that is neither dull nor ill-tempered, the Newfoundland is a multipurpose dog, equally at home on land and in water. He makes a highly devoted companion and, as is so well known, is capable of draft work and has lifesaving abilities when occasion demands. He is able and willing to work to command, but also has the intelligence to act on his own responsibility when demanded by rescue work. His wonderful temperament is a hallmark of the breed. Today the

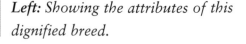

Left: Showing the attributes of this dignified breed.

Above: Note the thickness of the pads of the pup on the left.

Left: A Landseer is white with black markings.

Newfoundland is a talented participant in water trials, weight pulling, competitive obedience, guarding and carting.

Origins and History

Although it is certain that this breed originated in Newfoundland, there are differing opinions as to how this came about. The Canadians believe that his early origins stem from dogs indigenous to the island and big black bear dogs introduced by the Vikings in 1001AD. Some say his ancestor is the Great Pyrenees, taken to Newfoundland by Basque fishermen; others think he is

A
B
C
D
E
F
G
H
I
J
K
L
M
N
O
P
Q
R
S
T
U
V
W
X
Y
Z

Above: Brown Newfoundland moving well.

descended from a French hound, possibly the Boarhound. Looking at old prints, the Newfoundland shows similarities to a Husky, but still other traits point toward other breeds. Whatever his ancestry, the Newfoundland developed into a dog that had sufficient size and strength to perform the tasks required of him, with a heavy coat to protect him from icy waters and large, webbed feet. He was eventually taken to England and today most Newfoundlands descend from those bred in the UK. Over time there have been wonderful stories about

Newfoundlands rescuing people from watery graves, often as the result of shipwreck. This remarkable breed also did valuable work helping fishermen with their heavy nets. Indeed this is a superior water dog that is still used in Newfoundland and Labrador as a true working dog, not just working in water but also dragging carts and carrying burdens in the same manner as a pack horse.

Health Issues

It is important not to allow the Newfoundland to put on excess weight as he is susceptible to the inherited heart condition, sub-aortic stenosis. Hip dysplasia is another

problem that can be encountered in the breed.

Exercise and Grooming

Inside the home the Newfoundland is not particularly active but he does need regular exercise and of course loves to swim! When outside in hot weather, he must have access to shady areas and plenty of drinking water. His coat needs brushing several times each week and needs particular attention at shedding time, usually autumn and spring. Excess hair may be trimmed for neatness but whiskers need not be trimmed. A dry shampoo is considered by many to be more suitable for this breed than bathing.

Norbottenspets

Average height: dogs – 17.75 inches; bitches – 16.5 inches
Average weight: 26-33 pounds

Appearance

The Norbottenspets is short and squarely built, with a strong body. His head is powerful, well-built and wedge shaped, the muzzle moderately long and sharply tapering. The high set ears are stiffly erect and rather more than medium size. Like the head, the neck is dry, the back short, strong and elastic. The croup is broad and moderately long with well developed musculature. The coat is very short and dense, forming a protection for the soft undercoat. Every color is permitted, but the ideal has yellow or reddish-brown patches.

Characteristics

The Norbottenspets is an alert dog who is not only extremely active but also independent and has a mind of his own. He may like to wander, so beware! He is intelligent and cunning. He also likes to bark, but is friendly. Because of the breed's individual nature, training is not easy and takes a great deal of effort even to achieve the most basic level. Certainly this is not a breed for the novice owner, but he can indeed make a good family dog and is usually kind with children.

Origins and History

The appearance of the Norbottenspets suggests he is connected with the Norwegian Lundehund, so is probably descended from similar dogs with bloodlines going back to the early spitz-type dogs of the Vikings. This breed was once a fairly common dog in Sweden, employed as an all-round farm helper and hunter of small game. But by the middle of the 20th century the hunt had somewhat waned and various foreign breeds had been imported, and so he became almost extinct. In 1948 the Swedish Kennel Club actually removed this breed from their lists. Today his popularity has risen once again thanks to local breeders who took an interest in this indigenous breed. Although some Norbottenspets are used to hunt game birds and in bird-hunting trials, many now live as companion dogs. The Swedish Kennel Club reinstated the breed in 1967.

Exercise and Grooming

The Norbottenspets is extremely energetic so needs lots of exercise. A leash walk is good, but if you let your dog off the leash don't expect him to come back when you call as his hunting instincts are strong, probably stronger that the bond with his owner! He can happily run alongside his owner on a bicycle, but such exercise will have to be built up gradually. The short coat needs little grooming, just occasional brushing at shedding time is sufficient.

BREED NOTES

SIZE	GROOMING
✓ ✓ ✓	✓ ✓ ✓

EXERCISE	LIFESPAN
✓ ✓ ✓	✓ ✓

Norfolk Terrier

Average height: 9-10 inches (bitches tend to be smaller than dogs)
Average weight: 11-12 pounds

Appearance

The Norfolk Terrier, is a game and hardy little breed with expressive dropped ears. He is one of the smallest of the working terriers but is active and compact with good substance and bone. He is reputed to be a "perfect demon" in the field and in the showring honorable scars from wear and tear are perfectly acceptable! He has short, powerful legs, for this is a digging terrier. He is slightly longer than he is tall with a good width of chest and a level topline, his tail docked and set on high. The Norfolk's wide skull is slightly rounded, the muzzle strong and wedge shaped. The jaw is clean and strong, with tight lips and large teeth in a scissors bite. His dark, oval eyes are small and ears are neatly dropped with a break at the skull line. The natural, weather-resistant coat is hard wiry and straight, the hair about 1? to

Below: These well-bred youngsters show enormous promise.

BREED NOTES

SIZE	GROOMING
✔	✔ ✔
EXERCISE	**LIFESPAN**
✔ ✔	✔ ✔

Johnson

A B C D E F G H I J K L M N O P Q R S T U V W X Y Z

Johnson

A
B
C
D
E
F
G
H
I
J
K
L
M
N
O
P
Q
R
S
T
U
V
W
X
Y
Z

Above and left: An occasional rest is an opportunity to think what to do next!

2 inches long and lying close to the body, with a definite undercoat. The mane on neck and shoulders is longer, forming a ruff. On head and ears the coat is short and smooth, except for slight eyebrows and whiskers. Coat color can be all shades of red, wheaten, black and tan, or grizzle.

Characteristics

The Norfolk Terrier is alert, gregarious, fearless and loyal, a brave little fellow with a lively and friendly personality, never aggressive. This is an inquisitive

Above: Ears are neatly dropped with a break at the skull line.

breed and he loves playing with toys, as well as barking and digging when left outdoors for some time! Training can be done quite easily, providing it is consistent. He is normally well behaved with other pets, but can sometimes be jealous. He is smart and has an iron will; he can go to ground, bolt a fox and tackle or dispatch other small vermin, working alone or with a pack.

Origins and History
Around the turn of the 20th century, working terriers from stables in Cambridge, Market Harborough and Norwich in England were used by Frank "Roughrider" Jones to develop a breed that was recognized in 1932 by the English Kennel Club as the Norwich Terrier. At this time there was diversity in type, size, color, coat and ear carriage, and there was many an argument about coat color and ear carriage! When the

breed standard was drawn up the drop ear and the prick ear terriers remained one breed. In 1964 the English Kennel Club divided them into two separate breeds; the drop ear variety became the Norfolk and the prick ear the Norwich. Some people in the USA still refer to the breed as the "Jones Terrier", after the man from whom American sportsmen who travelled to Britain bought their first red terriers. In 1936 the breed was accepted by the AKC. Here it remained as one breed until 1979, when it was divided into two on account of ear carriage. Each breed has developed with success since separation and now there are distinct differences between the two. Owners should always remember that the Norfolk Terrier is essentially a sporting terrier, not a toy. His chief attributes are gameness, hardiness, loyalty to his master, and great charm.

Health Issues
The Norfolk Terrier seems to have no major health concerns, and is reputed to resist sickness.

Exercise and Grooming
This breed needs an active lifestyle for mental and physical good health. He likes to keep busy, even when indoors where he enjoys joining in with his family's activities. His coat is not difficult to keep in good condition, but needs regular grooming, with extra attention at shedding time. Some tidying is necessary to keep the dog neat, but shaping is heavily penalized in the showring. The Norfolk Terrier may be bathed or cleaned with a dry shampoo.

Below: This is a digging terrier, with short, powerful legs.

A B C D E F G H I J K L M **N** O P Q R S T U V W X Y Z

Norwegian Buhund

Average height: dogs – 17-18.5 inches; bitches – 16-17.5 inches
Average weight: dogs – 31-40 pounds; bitches – 26-35 pounds

Appearance

This is a herding dog, a typical northern breed, somewhat less than medium size and squarely built with a tight, curled tail, carried over the back. The wedge shaped head is not heavy, almost flat, and parallel with the bridge of the nose. The muzzle is about the same length as the skull and the lips are black and close tightly, with the teeth meeting in a scissors bite. The oval shaped eyes

BREED NOTES

SIZE	GROOMING
✓✓	✓✓
EXERCISE	LIFESPAN
✓✓	✓✓

Left: On head and front of legs the coat is comparatively short.

are as dark as possible, with black eye rims. Ears are pricked, of medium size and carried strongly erect, and yet are highly mobile. The Norwegian Buhund's outer coat is thick and rather smooth lying, while the undercoat is soft and dense; on head and front of legs the coat is comparatively short but on the neck, chest and back of thighs it is longer. Color may be wheaten, which is from pale cream to bright orange, with or without dark-tipped hairs, or black.

Characteristics

This is a self-confident breed, alert, lively, and very affectionate with people. He gets along well with children and is naturally

Above left and right: *The wedge-shaped head is not heavy.*

Left: *Squarely built, with a tight, curled tail.*

gentle with the very young and the elderly. The Norwegian Buhund is extremely intelligent and strong-willed by nature, so consistent training is needed from early puppyhood. He has a great deal of energy, strength and stamina. He is a self-appointed watch dog but is also content lying at his owner's feet at the end of the day. This is a naturally clean breed and is basically odorless, even when wet.

Origins and History

The Norwegian Buhund is a northern spitz dog and the earliest representative found relating to the Buhund was in the ancient Gokstad excavation in Norway, where a Viking grave from about the year 900 AD was opened; skeletons from six dogs of various sizes were found. When Vikings died their most cherished and necessary possessions were buried alongside their owners, to care for

Right: An inseparable pair.

Below: Blacks are rather unusual.

Above: A self-confident dog, intelligent and strong-willed.

them in their afterlife. In life, the Buhund protected farms and herded cattle and sheep, so he was expected to continue these duties in the afterlife. These dogs travelled with Vikings on their many journeys, both by sea and by land. The type with which we are familiar today was found in the rainy western coastlands of Norway where they herded sheep and guarded farms. The first Buhund show was held in Norway in the 1920s and a breed club formed in 1939. This breed used to hunt bear and wolf but today, apart from being a livestock working breed, he is trained to aid the handicapped and to assist in police work.

Health Issues

Cataracts have been known to occur in the Norwegian Buhund and hip dysplasia is known too.

Exercise and Grooming

This breed has a very high activity level; he needs regular outdoor exercise and welcomes the opportunity to work. He is easy to groom and just needs a regular brushing to remove dead hair.

A
B
C
D
E
F
G
H
I
J
K
L
M
N
O
P
Q
R
S
T
U
V
W
X
Y
Z

Norwegian Elkhound

Average height: dogs – 20.5 inches; bitches – 19.5 inches
Average weight: dogs – 55 pounds; bitches – 48 pounds

Appearance

The Norwegian Elkhound is a hardy hunting dog, a typical northern spitz breed of medium size and substance, square in profile, close coupled and balanced in proportions. His head is broad at the ears, wedge shaped, strong and dry (without loose skin), his expression keen and alert, indicating his great courage. His eyes are a

Left and below: A typical northern spitz breed, keen, alert and courageous.

BREED NOTES

SIZE	GROOMING
✓ ✓ ✓	✓ ✓
EXERCISE	**LIFESPAN**
✓ ✓ ✓	✓ ✓

very dark brown and his ears firm and erect. Teeth meet in a scissors bite. The high set tail, tightly curled and carried over the centreline of the back, is thickly and closely haired. The Norwegian Elkhound's coat is thick, hard, weather resistant and smooth lying, made up of a soft, dense, woolly undercoat and coarse, straight covering hairs. On head, ears and front of legs it is short and even; the coat is longest on the buttocks and underside of tail. The coat color is gray and variations in shade are determined by the length of the black tips and quantity of guard hairs.

Characteristics

The Norwegian Elkhound as a hunting dog has the courage, agility and stamina to hold moose and other big game at bay by barking and dodging attack; he has the endurance to track for hours in all weathers and over rough and varied terrain. An athletic member of the northern dog family, he is an ideal multipurpose dog at work or at play. His temperament is bold and energetic. The Norwegian Elkhound makes an effective guardian but is normally friendly and has great dignity and independence of character.

Origins and History

The Norwegian Elkhound was not only a comrade of the Vikings but also a guardian of lonely farms, a herder of flocks and offered protection from wolves and bear. This breed has always been a hunter with a history of more than

six millennia, during which time the breed's Nordic traits have been untainted. He was selected and bred for his ability to accomplish a definite purpose, achieved by natural methods. The breed's structure has evolved from the tests of performance, every physical characteristic being the expression of a need. Through his constant contact with man in the pursuit of game he has developed as an extremely versatile dog, ready to hunt day after day for many a long hour, employing stamina rather than extreme speed. The breed was first exhibited in 1877 when the Norwegian Hunters' Association held its first show.

Above: A "Breeder's Team" in competition at a world-famous show.

Health Issues

The most prevalent health problems encountered in the Norwegian Elkhound are hip dysplasia, renal disease, cysts and eye disorders.

Exercise and Grooming

This is a very energetic breed that needs 20 to 30 minutes of exercise twice each day. He is strong and vigorous so will enjoy long walks or accompanying his master on a bicycle ride in a safe area. Although this is a fairly easy coat to maintain, regular grooming is advisable, especially when the coat is shedding.

A
B
C
D
E
F
G
H
I
J
K
L
M
N
O
P
Q
R
S
T
U
V
W
X
Y
Z

Norwegian Lundehund

Average height: dogs – 14-15.2 inches; bitches – 12.8-14 inches
Average weight: dogs – 15.4 pounds; bitches – 13.2 pounds

Appearance

The Norwegian Lundehund is a small, spitz-type dog, highly supple and rather lightly made. His anatomical peculiarities relate to his work of puffin-hunting on the steep rocks around the fjords and along the shore of his homeland. He has a clean-cut, wedge shaped head and a wedge shaped muzzle with a slightly convex nasal bridge. The eyes are slightly sloping and not protruding; they have a yellowish brown iris and the pupil is encircled by a dark halo. A scissors bite is preferred but a pincer bite is permitted. The absence of premolars on each side of the jaw is permitted in this breed, for this facilitates his ability to carry eggs in his mouth. His triangular ears are another special feature of the breed. They are carried erect and are very mobile, the cartilage of the ear lobe allowing it to fold itself so that it flops either backwards or at a right angle; this closes the auditory passage and keeps sea spray out of the ear canal. This is

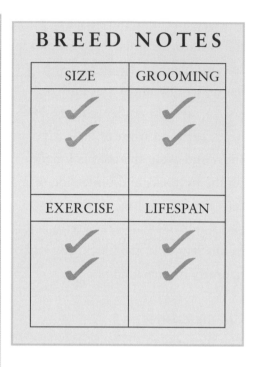

BREED NOTES

SIZE	GROOMING
✓ ✓	✓ ✓
EXERCISE	**LIFESPAN**
✓ ✓	✓ ✓

Left: The breed's anatomical peculiarities assist in puffin-hunting.

indeed a dog that is full of incredible feats; his well-furnished neck is quite strong and can bend back 180%! The front legs, too, are enormously flexible and the position of the hindquarters is somewhat close, but the thighs are strong and muscular. The body is basically rectangular, the back strong and straight and the high-set tail, which is well-covered with hair but without a flag, is either in a ring, slightly rolled over onto the back, or hanging.

The Norwegian Lundehund's feet are quite extraordinary too. The front feet are oval shaped and turn slightly outwards; there are eight pads on each foot and at least six toes, of which five must rest on the ground. The hind feet are also oval

Cunliffe

Above: The oval feet turn slightly outward.

Right: The front legs are exceptionally flexible.

in shape turning outwards slightly and have at least six toes, of which four must rest on the ground; here there are seven pads on each food, the middle one being attached to the inner pads of the two inner toes. The breed has a light, elastic movement which has a "rotary action" of the forelegs and the rather close action behind is characteristic of the breed, making this quite different from that of any other dog. The coat is dense and rough with a soft undercoat, short on head and front of the legs. Its color is always white with red to fawn, black, grey or dark markings. Adults usually have more marked

A
B
C
D
E
F
G
H
I
J
K
L
M
N
O
P
Q
R
S
T
U
V
W
X
Y
Z

Above: Clinging to the owner, as if he were a rock!

black tips in the coat than younger dogs.

Characteristics
No longer used in his original employ, today the Lundehund is a true companion, loyal, playful and virtually non-aggressive to people and other dogs, even when challenged. Alert, energetic and lively, he has a delightful personality and an even disposition, in addition to which his small size makes him an ideal, easy-to-live-with pet.

Origins and History
This has to be the most extraordinary of all dog breeds. The Norwegian Lundehund, also known as the Puffin Dog, is a rare and ancient breed with an intriguing history and uncommon physical characteristics. Its name is a combination of the Norwegian words "lunde," the Puffin bird, and "hund," meaning dog. Originally it was bred by Norwegian farmers of centuries past to hunt and retrieve the Puffin, both for meat and feather. These farmers lived along the fjords and on the islands off the west coast. There are written references to the breed dating back to the 15th century, but when the Puffin became a protected species in the 19th century these remarkable dogs were no longer of any particular use to the farmers, so their numbers began to dwindle. After the Second World War, thanks largely to two Norwegian enthusiasts, the breed was saved

Above: The neck can bend back 180 %.

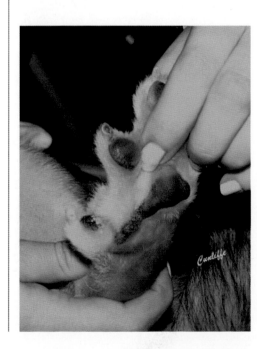

Below: The Lundehund has extraordinary pads

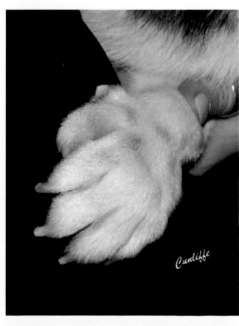

Below: Each foot has at least six toes.

(GI), which include protein-losing enteropathy (PLE), intestinal lymphangiectasia (IL), small intestinal bacterial overgrowth (SIBO) and intestinal bowel disease (IBD). The level of affliction is as varied as the diseases themselves. Some of the dogs will show signs of just one disease, others present with multiple problems, whilst others will remain asymptomatic for years. It is believed that all Lundehunds carry a gene that makes them prone to GI problems. Breed enthusiasts are keeping careful track of this inherited disorder in this wonderful breed; it has been found that a high protein, low fat diet can help control the problem.

Exercise and Grooming

The Norwegian Lundehund is a lively little dog and enjoys a fair amount of exercise. He loves a good romp and a game with his owner. Coat care is undemanding, but regular combing and brushing is important to keep skin and coat in a healthy condition.

from near extinction; but still there are less than a thousand Norwegian Lundehunds worldwide. The breed's unique structure allowed it to climb the steep, rocky cliffs and navigate the small burrows and crevices where the Puffins nest; these are truly primitive qualities that have been lost in other breeds as they have evolved.

Health Issues

The Lundehund is prone to various forms of gastrointestinal problems

A
B
C
D
E
F
G
H
I
J
K
L
M
N
O
P
Q
R
S
T
U
V
W
X
Y
Z

Norwich Terrier

Average height: no more than 10 inches
Average weight: 12 pounds

BREED NOTES

SIZE	GROOMING
✔	✔ ✔
EXERCISE	LIFESPAN
✔ ✔	✔ ✔

Left and opposite bottom: These little characters show all the spirit of the breed.

protective mane, whilst on head, ears and muzzle the hair is short, except for slight eyebrows and whiskers. The coat should always be as natural as possible. The color may be all shades of red, wheaten, black and tan or grizzle.

Appearance

One of the smallest of all terriers, the Norfolk has good bone and substance; a fit, working condition should always be a prime consideration. He is a sturdy little descendent of the ratting terrier. His head has a slightly foxy expression and his eyes are dark and oval shaped with black rims and a keen expression. His skull is broad and slightly rounded with good width

between the medium-sized, erect ears. The wedge-shaped muzzle is strong, the jaw strong and tight lipped, with a scissors bite. The Norfolk's body is moderately short, compact and deep with a good depth of chest, well-sprung rib and short loin. The erect tail must be of sufficient length to grasp. The hard, wiry coat is straight and close-lying, with a definite undercoat. On neck and shoulders the coat forms a

Characteristics

This is a spirited terrier, hardy, happy-go-lucky and ever ready to dispatch small vermin whether he is alone or in a pack. The Norwich is a fearless little dog with an endearing personality. He is always ready to announce the arrival of strangers, so makes a fine watchdog. Hardy, easy going and very active, his loyalty, devotion and affectionate behaviour make him an ideal companion, and he usually gets along well with children and other animals (except perhaps hamsters and gerbils!) provided introductions have been carefully supervised.

Origins and History

The roots of the Norwich, like those of the Norfolk Terrier are firmly planted in East Anglia, England. In the 19th century a small ratting terrier was something of a fad amongst the sporting undergraduates of Cambridge University and a popular strain developed from a mix of very small red and black-and-tan working crossbreeds from Yorkshire, and Irish den stock. These became known as Trumpington Terriers and one, named "Rags", moved to a stable near Norwich. It was "Rags" who was to become the progenitor of the breed we know today. From companions and barnyard ratters, there had gradually developed a line of excellent fox bolters, and one of these introduced the breed to America in 1914. The breed was recognised in England in 1932 and officially in America in 1936. In 1964 the drop ear variety was classified as a separate breed in England, but the AKC did not take this stance until 1979.

Above: The coat comes in various colors

Health Issues

Generally a healthy breed, the Norwich requires a proper diet and plenty of exercise to keep his body in good shape. Hip dysplasia and eye problems occur occasionally.

Exercise and Grooming

A good walk of 20 to 30 minutes each day will keep a Norwich fit, with additional opportunity to romp and play in the yard or garden. This breed enjoys earthdog tests, tracking and obedience classes, for he like to be exercised mentally, not just physically. Secure perimeter fencing is important as he has a strong hunting instinct and typical terrier curiosity. Weekly grooming of the coat is essential and this breed is usually stripped by hand twice a year. When in his senior years, some owners prefer to use a stripping tool than to hand strip. The coat is fairly dirt resistant, so bathing need not be frequent.

A
B
C
D
E
F
G
H
I
J
K
L
M
N
O
P
Q
R
S
T
U
V
W
X
Y
Z

Nova Scotia Duck Tolling Retriever

Average height: dogs – 18-21 inches; bitches – 17-20 inches
Average weight: dogs – 45-51 pounds; bitches – 37-43 pounds

Appearance

The Nova Scotia Duck Tolling Retriever, often called Toller for short, is the smallest of the retrievers, a medium sized, compact, balanced dog, just a little longer than he is tall. His clean-cut head is slightly wedge shaped and his skull only slightly rounded. His expression is generally alert, friendly and intelligent, but some Tollers have a slightly sad expression until they go to work, when it changes to intense concentration and desire. The color of the eye blends in with the coat or is darker; eye rims must be self-colored or black, to match the nose pigment. Jaws are sufficiently strong to carry a sizeable bird, softness in the mouth being essential; the bite is a tight scissors. The short-coated, drop ears are feathered only on the back of the fold. The neck is strongly muscled, the body deep, the back strong, short and straight. The Toller's tail is luxuriant and well-feathered; when alert it is held in a high curve. The strongly webbed feet are slightly oval and tight, with well-arched toes and thick pads. He was bred to retrieve from icy waters so has a water-repellent double coat of medium length and softness, with a soft, dense undercoat. It is basically straight but may have a slight wave on the back; some

Right: The body is deep, the back strong, short and straight.

winter coats may form a long, loose curl at the throat. Featherings are soft and moderate, whilst on the muzzle the hair is short and fine. The color is any shade of red, ranging from a golden red through dark coppery red, with lighter featherings on the underside of the tail, pantaloons and body. The Toller usually has one or more white markings on tip of tail, feet, chest and blaze, but not always.

Characteristics

This is a highly intelligent breed, alert, outgoing and always ready for action.

Affectionate and loving with family members, the Toller is good with children and displays patience with them. Some may display a rather reserved behavior in new situations, but this is not shyness. The breed of course has a strong retrieving desire and loves water. He is a very versatile breed and enjoys participating in many dog sports including conformation, obedience, field trials, tracking, flyball and agility.

Origins and History

The breed was developed in the early 19th century to toll, lure, and

BREED NOTES

SIZE	GROOMING
✓✓	✓✓
EXERCISE	LIFESPAN
✓✓	✓✓

retrieve waterfowl. The playful action of the Toller along the shoreline, its heavily feathered tail held high and in constant motion while working, was used to arouse the ducks, luring them in toward the shore within gunshot range. The dogs were then sent out to retrieve the dead and wounded birds. The word "Tolling" is actually an English word meaning to "lure or decoy game." Since the 17th century dogs have been used as hunting companions. Yarmouth County, Nova Scotia, Canada, is considered the place of origin of the Nova Scotia Duck Tolling Retriever. It is likely that that breed evolved from the red decoy dog that was taken to Nova Scotia with early European settlers, then crossed with other breeds, possibly spaniel and setter-types, retriever-types and farm collies. The breed was originally known as the Little River Duck Dog or as a Yarmouth Toller. It has bred true for generations and was granted official breed status by the Canadian Kennel Club in 1945. A few came to the USA in the 1960s, but it was not bred here seriously until the late 1970s and 1980s.

Health Issues

The Toller has few of the genetic problems associated with some of the more popular retrieving breeds. Breeders endeavour to keep hip dysplasia and eye problems to a minimum. Other health problems found in the breed include autoimmune deficiency, hypothyroidism and epilepsy.

Exercise and Grooming

As an active breed, the Toller needs to be kept busy and is not content to sit around all day. He is ideal as a companion for a family that does a lot of hiking, camping or fishing trips to the lake. Whilst regular grooming is important to keep the coat healthy, the Toller's coat should always appear natural, never barbered.

Below: The Nova Scotia is happy on land and in water.

A
B
C
D
E
F
G
H
I
J
K
L
M
N
O
P
Q
R
S
T
U
V
W
X
Y
Z

Old English Sheepdog

Average height: dogs – 22 inches and upward; bitches – 21 inches and upward
Average weight: dogs – 80-100 pounds; bitches – 60-85 pounds

Appearance

The Old English Sheepdog is a compact, well-balanced dog of square build. He is well muscled with plenty of bone. He stands lower at the withers than at his very stout, gently arched loin, but with no indication of softness or

BREED NOTES

SIZE	GROOMING
✔ ✔ ✔	✔ ✔ ✔
EXERCISE	LIFESPAN
✔ ✔ ✔	✔ ✔

Johnson

Left: 'We're both delighted about our wonderful win!'

weakness; this topline is characteristic of the breed. The body is rather short and very compact, broader at the rump than at the shoulders; the ribs well sprung and the brisket deep and capacious. The tail, when docked, is close to the body, otherwise it is naturally bobtailed. The head, which is rather square and covered with hair, gives a most intelligent expression and the eyes may be brown or blue, or one of each. If pearl, a china or wall-eye is considered typical. The medium sized ears are carried flat to the side of the head. The nose is black, large and capacious, the jaw strong, square and truncated and the bite either level or tight scissors. He is profusely, but not excessively coated. It is a good hard texture; not straight, but shaggy and free from curl; the undercoat is a waterproof pile when not removed by grooming. The coat may be any shade of gray, grizzle, blue or blue merle with or without white markings, or in reverse. When trotting, movement is free, powerful and seemingly effortless, at a gallop it is very elastic but at slower speeds

Right: Puppies feeding happily together.

Below: A fine example, showing the compactness of build.

A
B
C
D
E
F
G
H
I
J
K
L
M
N
O
P
Q
R
S
T
U
V
W
X
Y
Z

the Old English Sheepdog may amble or pace.

Characteristics

This is an adaptable, intelligent dog with an even disposition and no sign of aggression, shyness or nervousness. He is playful and agile, excellent with children and a dependable family protector. His bark is loud with a distinctive "pot-casse" ring in it. Full of affection and not too boisterous, the Old English Sheepdog makes a great family companion.

Right: '*He never did!*'

Below: It takes a lot of work to get the coat looking like this.

Health Issues
Health problems known to occur in the Old English Sheepdog include hip dysplasia, eye disorders, deafness and hypothyroidism.

Exercise and Grooming
The Old English Sheepdog likes to be taken on frequent walks and enjoys playing with his family members in a fenced yard; he needs lots of human attention and does not adapt to confinement. Although the coat's appearance can be a little off-putting, a thorough grooming once each week will keep it relatively matt-free, but regular attention is essential. For show purposes neither the natural outline nor the natural texture of the coat may be changed by any artificial means, except that the feet and rear may be trimmed for cleanliness.

Above and right: An adult (above) and puppy (right).

Origins and History
The Old English Sheepdog's origins can be traced back to the early 19th century. It appears that it was first developed in the west of England in the counties of Devon Somerset and Cornwall, though it is difficult to establish what breeds were involved in its makeup. Some believe the Scotch Bearded Collie was one of its progenitors, others feel the Russian Ovtcharka played a part. The Old English Sheepdog Club of America was stet up in 1904 and received official recognition by AKC the following year.

A
B
C
D
E
F
G
H
I
J
K
L
M
N
O
P
Q
R
S
T
U
V
W
X
Y
Z

Otterhound

Average height: dogs – 27 inches; bitches – 24 inches
Average weight: dogs – 115 pounds; bitches – 80 pounds

Appearance

The Otterhound is a large, rough-coated hound, slightly rectangular in body and with plenty of substance, well-boned legs and broad muscles, without being coarse. His strong body and long striding action make him fit for a long day's work. He has an imposing head that is large, fairly narrow, and well covered with hair; his expression is open and amiable. The eyes are deeply set and the haw shows only slightly. The ears are essential for this breed; they are long, pendulous and folded, giving a draped appearance. They hang close to the head and the leather reaches at least to the tip of the nose. The jaws are powerful and capable of a crushing grip. The neck is powerful too, and should be of sufficient length to allow the dog to follow a trail. The high set tail is long, thicker at the base and tapering to a point; it is feathered and carried saber fashion when

Below: This show dog is a winner of high honors.

BREED NOTES

SIZE	GROOMING
✓ ✓ ✓	✓ ✓

EXERCISE	LIFESPAN
✓ ✓ ✓	✓ ✓ ✓

Johnson

Johnson

Above: *The outercoat is rough, dense, coarse and crisp.*

the hound is moving or alert. Both front and rear feet are large and broad, compact when standing but capable of spreading thanks to the webbing between the toes, which are arched. The Otterhound's coat is an essential feature, its texture and quality being more important than length. The outer coat (2 to 4 inches long) is dense, rough, coarse and crisp, but softer hair on head and legs is natural. The water-resistant undercoat is short, wooly and slightly oily. Any color or combination of colors is acceptable but nose and eye rims should be dark and fully pigmented, black, liver, or slate, depending on the color of the hound. Characteristic movement for the Otterhound is a very loose, shambling walk, which springs immediately into a loose and very long striding trot with

natural extension of the head.

Characteristics

The Otterhound is an amiable, boisterous and even-tempered character, thoroughly devoted to his owner. He is generally good with other dogs and with other animals if raised with them or introduced carefully. Several are known to have lived happily with cats, parrots, horses and pigs; they seem quite willing to accept most two- and four-legged members of the household in their pack! He can be good with children but his size and boisterousness is unsuitable for a toddler or frail elderly person. The Otterhound is usually quite slow to mature, both physically and mentally. He has an extremely sensitive nose and is inquisitive and perseverant in investigating scents, in addition to which he loves water and is a strong swimmer.

Origins and History

Although there are allusions to Otterhounds in the time of King John, who reigned in England from 1199 to 1216, the most concrete descriptions of packs of these hounds really appear from early in the 14th century when they were described as a "rough sort of dog, between a hound and a terrier". Otter hunting, although now banned, long existed in Britain because the otters preyed on fish and the sport enjoyed a considerable vogue in the summer months, when this was the only form of hunting possible. This hound has an impressively deep voice and makes a good watchdog, but its friendly nature makes the breed unsuitable as a guard. Otterhounds first appeared in America around 1900 and were exhibited at a show in Claremont, Oklahoma in 1907.

A
B
C
D
E
F
G
H
I
J
K
L
M
N
O
P
Q
R
S
T
U
V
W
X
Y
Z

Left: Like other hounds, puppies tend to use their mouths in play.

Exercise and Grooming

The Otterhound needs a good amount of exercise, ideally in a very large, securely fenced area. He will also enjoy a walk on a leash or a brisk jog with his owner. The Otterhound is usually not ideally suited to walking off the leash! An Otterhound's coat needs a good brush once a week to keep it free from matts, paying especial attention to the head, legs and underneath the body. The Otterhound is shown in a natural coat, with no sculpturing or shaping of the coat.

Below: Already respectful of their owner.

Health Issues

Like many of the large breeds, the Otterhound is subject to hip dysplasia and bloat. Other problems that have been encountered include seizures and a potentially fatal bleeding disorder. The Otterhound Club of America's health surveys indicate that major health problems are uncommon until old age.

Papillon

Average height: 8-11 inches
Average weight: 5-9 pounds

Appearance

This small, elegant Toy breed is fine-boned, light and dainty, his body slightly longer than high.. He is distinguished from other Toy breeds by his butterfly-like ears, the word "Papillon" being the French word for butterfly. They are large with rounded tips and set on the sides, toward the back of the head. They may be erect or completely dropped, the latter type known as Phalene. The head is small and slightly rounded between the ears, the fine muzzle abruptly thinner than the head and tapering to the small, rounded, black nose. The eyes are dark and round, but not bulging, giving an alert expression. Teeth meet in a scissors bite. The backline is straight and the long tail, with its flowing plume, is set high and carried arched over the body. The feet are thin and elongated,

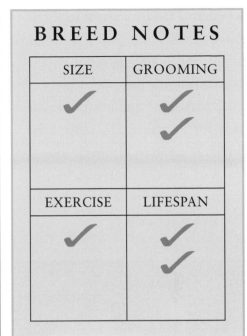

BREED NOTES	
SIZE	GROOMING
✓	✓ ✓
EXERCISE	LIFESPAN
✓	✓ ✓

Left: This breed was favorite of the ladies of the court.

pointing forward. The abundant, long, flowing coat is straight and silky, flat on the back and sides of the body with a profuse frill on the chest. The Papillon has no undercoat. On head and muzzle the hair is short, as it is on the front of the forelegs and the bottom of the hind legs. The backs of the forelegs are covered with feathers and the hind legs have abundant breeches, known as "culottes". The ears are beautifully fringed, the inside covered with silky hair of medium length. The Papillon is always parti-colored or white, with patches of any color. On the head a color other than white must cover both ears, extending over both eyes. A clear white blaze and noseband is preferable to a solid colored head

A
B
C
D
E
F
G
H
I
J
K
L
M
N
O
P
Q
R
S
T
U
V
W
X
Y
Z

and symmetry of markings is desirable.

Characteristics

The Papillon is a happy, alert and friendly little fellow and makes a wonderful family companion. Although he is protective of his family and home, he is not aggressive, nor is he shy. He is a good watchdog and always on the alert for strangers. He is also very useful as a ratter; although too small to kill a rat outright, he will worry it until it is exhausted, then dispatch it quickly.

Above and left: This is an active breed and enjoys mini-agility.

Origins and History

This breed was previously known as the "Dwarf Spaniel" and is believed to have originated in France, although it became highly popular in Italy and Spain and was a favourite of the ladies of the court from the 16th to 18th centuries. This breed was often depicted on paintings of that era. From the Bologna region of Italy many dogs were sold to the court of Louis XIV and it is known that dogs were transported through Spain on the backs of mules. Both drop-eared Papillons and those with erect-ears occur in the same litter and are judged together in AKC shows. The breed was first represented in the AKC in 1935.

Health Issues

This is a relatively healthy breed that generally remains active well into its teens. Amongst the problems it is known to encounter are patella luxation, open fontanels, bite and palate defects, and Progressive Retinal Atrophy (PRA). The breed can be sensitive to some anasthetics.

Exercise and Grooming

Although the Papillon does not require a great deal of exercise, he thoroughly enjoys being outdoors and fancies himself as a great hunter – anything small will do, a bird, squirrel, spider, or even a butterfly! The Papillon's silky coat is not prone to matting and the resilient coat texture sheds dirt and dry grass with the touch of a brush. The bottoms and sides of the feet can be trimmed to present a tidy appearance.

Above: Usually ears are up, like those of a butterfly.

Below: A lovely example of a Phalene, with dropped ears.

A
B
C
D
E
F
G
H
I
J
K
L
M
N
O
P
Q
R
S
T
U
V
W
X
Y
Z

Parson Russell Terrier

Average height: dogs – 14 inches; bitches – 13 inches
Average weight: dogs – 17 pounds

Appearance

Because the Parson Russell is a working terrier he must possess characteristics that allow him to perform his work both above and below ground. Although a little latitude in height is allowed, larger dogs must still be spannable around the chest, whilst smaller ones must have sufficient type and bone to allow them to work successfully. His small, flexible chest enables him to pursue his quarry underground and he has sufficient length of leg to follow the hounds. He has medium bone, neither coarse nor racy. His head is strong and his almond shaped, dark eyes give a keen expression, full of life and intelligence. He has small, V-shaped drop ears, their tip covering the orifice and pointing toward the eye. The jaws are of fair and punishing strength and teeth close in a perfect scissors bite. The Parson's tail is carried in the fashion of a squirrel tail. Feet are round and cat-like, very compact, the pads thick and tough. This breed has a smooth or broken coat, but whichever it is, it has a good sheen and is naturally harsh, close and dense, with no suggestion of a kink. The color is white, white with clear black or tan markings, or tri-color.

BREED NOTES

SIZE	GROOMING
✓ ✓	✓
EXERCISE	**LIFESPAN**
✓ ✓	✓ ✓

Below: A well-made show dog.

Johnson

Above: 'Come on, let's go for our walk!'

Characteristics

The Parson Russell Terrier is bold and friendly, athletic and clever. At home he is playful, exuberant and overwhelmingly affectionate, but when at work he is a game hunter, tenacious, courageous, and single minded. This is an independent and energetic terrier that appreciates attention. Typically he is not quarrelsome but has a tendency to explore, dig holes and chase after other animals whenever possible. He seems to have no capacity to feel fear, regardless of the odds or consequences!

Origins and History

A fox-hunting breed developed in southern England nearly 200 years ago, the Parson Russell is most probably a cross between the Old English White Terrier, which is now extinct, and a black-and-tan terrier similar in type to the early Manchester. His sound trotting gait and length of leg allow him to follow the hounds, and his compact flexible chest and length of body enable him to go to ground on fox, whilst with his strong head and muzzle and can hold the fox at bay. The breed was known in America in the 1930s, possibly even sooner.

Below: Looking for mischief.

A
B
C
D
E
F
G
H
I
J
K
L
M
N
O
P
Q
R
S
T
U
V
W
X
Y
Z

This terrier was named after the Reverend John Russell, whose terriers trailed hounds and bolted

Below: The Parson is playful and affectionate.

foxes from dens so the hunt could ride on. Old scars and injuries, the result of honorable work or accident, should not be allowed to prejudice a terrier's chance in the show ring.

Above: Tri-colors.

Opposite: 'We were having great fun, but now it's time for home.'

Health Issues
The Parson tends to be a generally healthy breed, but health concerns may include genetic eye diseases, deafness, slipping patella and hip dysplasia.

Exercise and Grooming
This breed has a high energy level, but given sufficient space he will create his own exercise, although he will of course enjoy leash walks and games with his owner. The short coat is not difficult to maintain and needs only regular brushing, occasional shampooing and hand stripping to clear out dead hair. When exhibited he is shown naturally, not excessively groomed.

Pekingese

Average height: 6-9 inches
Average weight: 14 pounds maximum

A
B
C
D
E
F
G
H
I
J
K
L
M
N
O
P
Q
R
S
T
U
V
W
X
Y
Z

BREED NOTES

SIZE	GROOMING
✓	✓
	✓
	✓
EXERCISE	LIFESPAN
✓	✓
	✓

Left top and bottom: These top quality show dogs are presented to perfection.

Appearance

The Pekingese has a heavy front and lighter hindquarters; his head is large in proportion to the body and he is slightly longer than he is tall. The topskull is massive, broad and flat which, combined with the large, lustrous, wide-set eyes, cheekbones and broad lower jaw, gives the desired rectangular, envelope-shaped appearance. In profile the face is flat, for this is a brachycephalic breed. The ears are heart-shaped and lie flat against the head; they have heavy feathering and long fringing, framing the sides of the face and increasing the appearance of width. The broad, short nose is black and it is important that the nostrils are wide, not pinched. The

Above: Pekingese puppies are just so sweet!

Pekingese has wrinkle on the face, effectively separating the upper and lower areas, but is never so prominent that it crowds the facial features. The lower jaw is undershot and the black lips meet neatly, neither teeth nor tongue showing when the mouth is closed. His body is best described as pear-shaped and the high-set tail is carried well over the back with long, profuse, straight fringing. The long, coarse-textured outer coat is straight and stand-off; the undercoat thick and soft. It is presented such that it accentuates the natural outline of the Pekingese. All coat colors and markings are of equal merit. Regardless of coat color the exposed skin of the muzzle, nose, lips and eye rims is black. The Pekingese moves in a rather special way; unhurried, dignified free and strong, with a slight roll over the shoulders.

Characteristics

The Pekingese portrays a combination of regal dignity, intelligence and self-importance, making for a good natured, opinionated and affectionate companion to those who have earned his respect. His temperament is direct, independent and highly individual. The breed's lion-like image implies courage, dignity, boldness and self-esteem rather than daintiness or delicacy.

Origins and History

Legend tells us that a lion fell in love with a marmoset; in order for him to wed his lady-love the lion begged the patron saint of the animals, Ah Chu, to reduce him to the size of a pigmy, but allowing him to retain his great lion heart and character. The offspring of this union are said to be the dog of Fu Lin, or the Lion Dog of China. This story is the very foundation of the history of the Pekingese and speaks

Below: Best in Show winner at a Peke specialty.

A
B
C
D
E
F
G
H
I
J
K
L
M
N
O
P
Q
R
S
T
U
V
W
X
Y
Z

Tsu Hsi is in large part responsible for the appearance of the Pekingese in the US as she gave many of the little dogs as gifts to influential Americans; because of this, at one time America could probably claim the largest population of authentic palace dogs. The AKC first registered the Pekingese in 1906.

Health Issues

Because the Pekingese is a brachycephalic (short-nosed) breed, he is sensitive to heat and his eyes are susceptible to injury. He can also encounter difficulties when anasthetics are administered. It is therefore essential to discuss this with the vet prior to surgery.

Exercise and Grooming

The Pekingese does not really need much exercise, but short walks should keep him healthy. He should not be over-exerted during hot weather conditions. The coat should be groomed weekly to prevent matting and wrinkles on the face should be inspected and cleaned daily.

Above: In profile the face is flat.

Right: All exposed skin on the head is black.

volumes. The Lion Dog can be traced to the Tang Dynasty of the 8th century but breeding reached its height between 1821 and 1851. The oldest strains were kept amazingly pure and Imperial dog books, illustrated with pictures, were used as the standards. The Pekingese, as we know him today, was highly prized with the utmost care lavished upon him. The Dowager Empress

Pembroke Welsh Corgi

Average height: 10-12 inches
Average weight: dogs – 30 pounds maximum; bitches – 28 pounds maximum

Appearance

This is a low-set, strong and sturdily built dog, showing substance and stamina. He is moderately long and low, not heavy, but not too racy either. His foxy-shaped head is fairly wide, the skull fairly flat and wide between the ears, the foreface nicely chiseled to give a somewhat tapered muzzle. The medium-sized, oval eyes give an intelligent, interested expression. Ears are erect and firm, tapering slightly to a rounded point; they are mobile and react sensitively to sounds. The preferred bite is scissors, but a level bite is acceptable. The Pembroke Welsh Corgi should have a firm, level topline, the ribcage is well-sprung, slightly egg-shaped and moderately long, whilst the chest is deep. The tail is usually docked as short as possible; sometimes it is naturally short, but should not be longer than two inches. The short forearms turn slightly inwards, so the front is not absolutely straight,

Below: Low set, strong and sturdily built.

BREED NOTES

SIZE	GROOMING
✓✓	✓
EXERCISE	LIFESPAN
✓✓	✓✓

Johnson

A
B
C
D
E
F
G
H
I
J
K
L
M
N
O
P
Q
R
S
T
U
V
W
X
Y
Z

Johnson

but the pasterns are firm and the feet should point forward. The medium-length coat has a short, thick and weather resistant undercoat and coarser, longer outer coat. Overall the length varies, with a slightly thicker ruff around the neck and fullness on the hindquarters. Colors are red, sable, fawn, or black and tan with or without white markings. White is acceptable on legs, chest, neck, underparts and as a blaze on the head.

Characteristics
The Pembroke Welsh Corgi has a bold outlook but is kindly and

young to relax his protective nature and tends to be more restless and excitable than his cousin, the Cardigan.

Origins and History

This is an old herding breed that is believed to date back to the 12th century, or even earlier. Although the Pembroke is believed to be younger than the Cardigan, its origin can be traced back to AD 1107 when the breed's direct ancestors were taken across the channel to Wales by Flemish weavers. Used to drive cattle, the method this dog used was to nip at their heels. In the 1920s both

Left: The foxy-shaped head is fairly wide.

Pembroke and Cardigan Welsh Corgis were recognised as pure-bred dogs by the English Kennel Club; in 1934 they were distinguished as two separate breeds, the Pembroke having a more stocky appearance with a shorter body; he is lighter in frame, straighter in leg and his ears are pointed (instead of rounded), in addition to which he has a short tail, while the Cardigan's is long.

Health Issues

Although generally a healthy breed, problems that have been known to occur are hip dysplasia, spinal disc problems, autoimmune diseases and cataracts.

Below: Posing for the family album!

makes an affectionate and charming household pet. He is intelligent and vigilant and excels at many activities including conformation, obedience, herding, and tracking. He needs proper socialization when

A
B
C
D
E
F
G
H
I
J
K
L
M
N
O
P
Q
R
S
T
U
V
W
X
Y
Z

Johnson

Exercise and Grooming

The Pembroke needs a moderate exercise regime, but he must also be mentally stimulated; indeed herding is still an ideal form of exercise for him if this fits in with his owner's lifestyle. But if this is not an option, there should be a good balance between training, play and walks of moderate distance. The coat sheds twice yearly and weekly combing and brushing is important to remove dead hair. The Corgi must be left in its natural condition without trimming, except for tidying of feet and, if desired, removal of whiskers. Baths should be given as needed.

Opposite: This youngster promises to be rather special.

Above and below: Two more high quality 'Pems'.

A
B
C
D
E
F
G
H
I
J
K
L
M
N
O
P
Q
R
S
T
U
V
W
X
Y
Z

Perro de Presa Canario

Average height: dogs – 23-26 inches; bitches – 22-25 inches
Average weight: dogs – 100 pounds; bitches – 85 pounds

Appearance

The Perro de Presa Canario is a moderately large, powerfully constructed dog, slightly longer than he is tall and giving the overall impression of an imposing, solid guard. His essential characteristics are those which enable him to drive and hold cattle and to guard its home and family. These tasks require a powerful, agile, courageous dog with a large head and powerful jaws. He has a broad, deep chest, but bitches may be slightly longer and have rather less spring of rib than males. The moderately high-set tail is very thick and the base, tapering to a point.

Tail carriage ranges from a pump handle tail when relaxed to a saber tail when alert. The head is massive and cuboid in shape, with the skull and muzzle roughly parallel to one another; when alert there are some symmetrical wrinkles on the furrow of the forehead, but not excessive. Cheek muscles are well-developed and the muzzle tapers just slightly to the nose. The top lip falls naturally over the lower one, forming an inverted "V" where they join. Whilst a scissors or reverse scissors bite is preferred, a level or slightly undershot bite is acceptable. The Pressa Canario's ears are of medium size and set wide apart,

BREED NOTES

SIZE	GROOMING
✓ ✓	✓
EXERCISE	**LIFESPAN**
✓ ✓	✓ ✓

Below and opposite: An imposing, solid guard.

Right: The massive skull is cuboid in shape, the skull and muzzle roughly parallel.

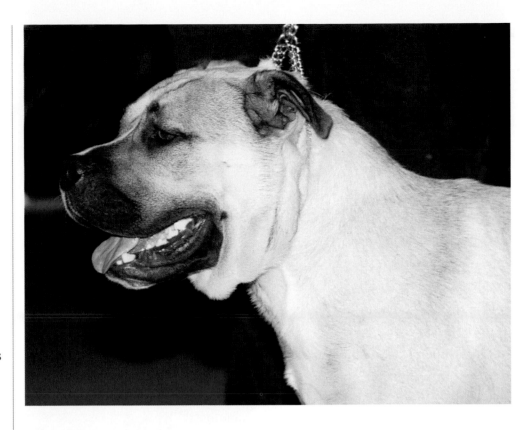

covered with short, fine hair; they may be cropped or natural, in which case they may be pendant or rose. Loose folds of skin at the throat form a slight dewlap and the neck is thick and well muscled. The short, flat, single coat that is harsh in texture and may be any shade of fawn, black or brindle, in any combination. The face must have a black or dark brown mask that does not extend over the eyes, with or without a white blaze or patch on the head.

Characteristics

The Presa is extremely affectionate, docile and well behaved with its owner and family, but this breed tends to be wary of strangers and aggressive with other dogs. He likes children and protects and tolerates them without protest, but of course careful introduction and supervision is needed. This breed needs sensible handling by an experienced owner. These days he is kept primarily as a guardian of property.

Origins and History

This breed's ancestors were probably taken by 15th century Spanish Conquistadors to Fuerteventura in the Canary Islands where they coexisted with indigenous cattle dogs. They served many purposes, guarding farms, helping to catch and hold cattle and exterminating wild or stray dogs. In the 1940s dog fighting was prohibited on the island and the breed began to decline in numbers, not helped by the introduction to the islands of the German shepherd, the Doberman Pinscher, and the Great Dane. However the breed survived in small numbers with farmers and herdsmen and was revived again in the 1970s. Now a renewed interest in the breed has extended through Europe and to the Americas.

Exercise and Grooming

This is a strong breed that needs sufficient exercise, always bearing in mind that he can show aggression towards other dogs. A large, securely fenced area is ideal. His short coat needs minimal attention.

Peruvian Inca Orchid

Average height: dogs – 18-22 inches; bitches – 17-21 inches
Average weight: 24-40 pounds, proportionate to height and bone structure

A
B
C
D
E
F
G
H
I
J
K
L
M
P
N
O
Q
R
S
T
U
V
W
X
Y
Z

Appearance

Classified as a sighthound, this is an elegant and graceful dog of moderate size, giving the appearance of speed, strength and balance, but without any indication of coarseness. The head is wide from the back, tapering to the nose and in profile the skull and muzzle are equal in length. The lips are tight and a distinctive lozenge placed high on the skull between the ears is desirable. Eyes, which are almond shaped, their rims self-colored or black, give an alert expression. A scissors bite is preferred, but level is acceptable. The long graceful neck has good muscle development and blends elegantly into the shoulders. Bones are light but strong, the substantial ribs well-sprung and the chest reaching almost to the elbow. The abdomen is well-muscled and clearly drawn up, whilst the rump is slightly rounded. The Peruvian Inca Orchid has a hare foot with webbing between the toes. The long tail tapers to a point and is carried saber-like when moving.

There are two coat varieties of Peruvian Inca Orchid, hairless and coated. In the hairless variety the ears are medium to large and pricked, though they may be folded when at rest, gaiting or coursing. Coated dogs have semi-prick ears, the tips of which fall forward, or outward to the side; these may be folded back when relaxed, gaiting

or coursing. Missing teeth are not penalised in the hairless variety, but coated dogs should have full dentition. The hairless dogs have smooth, supple skin with a narrow patch of hair from skull to stop; fuzz on the forehead is acceptable and there may be sparse hair on tail, lower hocks and feet. The coated variety has a short to medium-length single coat, its texture moderately coarse to soft, with feathering on ears and tail. In hairless Inca Orchids, seasonal changes may increase or decrease the depth of pigmentation. White/pink is preferred with any combination of rose, gold, tan, mahogany, chocolate, black, blue or gray. The coated variety comes is a variety of colors.

Characteristics

The Peruvian Inca Orchid is a quiet breed that is easy to live with. He is devoted to his owners but generally reserved with strangers until he has evaluate the situation, so socialization from a young age is very important. This is an intelligent breed that is rather independent, but seldom aggressive.

Origins and History

Although hairless and coated dogs of this breed can be found in the same litter, the Inca Indians preferred those without clothing. Indeed 2,000 year old Mochica pottery shows that they actually dressed these dogs in clothing, an indication of the high esteem in which they were held. Pre-Inca cultures kept the hairless variety of the Peruvian Inca Orchid in homes, serving as pets and bed warmers! They were not allowed to mix with the coated dogs to stop inter breeding.

Petit Basset Griffon Vendeen

Average height: 13-15 inches
Average weight: 31-40 pounds

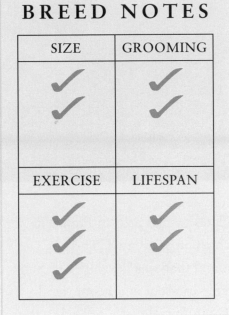

BREED NOTES

SIZE	GROOMING
✓ ✓	✓ ✓

EXERCISE	LIFESPAN
✓ ✓ ✓	✓ ✓

Above: Longer than tall, the PBGV is strong in bone.

Appearance

The Petit Basset Griffon Vendéen, frequently called PBGV for short, is a French scent hound that was developed primarily to hunt small game over the rough and difficult terrain of the Vendéen region; this work means that he must be endowed with certain features to function efficiently. He is somewhat longer than tall, strong in bone and with substance proportionate to the overall dog. His head, carried proudly, is also in balance with the overall dog and is longer than it is in width. The PBGV has an alert, friendly, intelligent expression with large dark eyes surmounted by long eyebrows. His low-set ears are supple, narrow and fine, covered with long hair and folding inward, oval at their ends. The strong underjaw is well-developed, the nose large with wide nostrils; the teeth ideally meet in a scissors bite, but level is acceptable. The back is level to the croup, with a barely perceptible rise over a strong loin. The chest is deep with a prominent sternum and the medium-length tail is set on high, well furnished with hair and carried proudly like a saber. The PBGV has strong, muscular hindquarters with a good bend of stifle. The rough coat is long and harsh to the touch, with a thicker, shorter undercoat. His lips are covered by long hair forming a beard and moustache and overall this charming breed has a casual, tousled appearance about him. He is white with any combination of lemon, orange, black, sable, tricolor or grizzle markings, providing easy visibility in the field.

Characteristics

He is bold and vivacious in character with an alert outlook on life. Confident, happy and extrovert, he is independent and sometimes a little stubborn, yet willing to please. This is a busy hunting hound but he requires human companionship and loves to be kept active. He gets along well with other dogs, children and strangers too. The PBGV has a good voice, freely and purposefully used.

Origins and History

This is one of many small varieties of French hound with an ancient origin. He can be traced to the 16th century and to his larger, more powerful ancestor, the Grand Griffon Vendéen. His name signifies his small size, the fact that he is low to the ground, that he has a rough or wire coat and of course Vendéen

A
B
C
D
E
F
G
H
I
J
K
L
M
N
O
P
Q
R
S
T
U
V
W
X
Y
Z

Left: This top show winner has a penchant for water; luckily the breed has a casual, tousled appearance.

epilepsy is now less frequent thanks to selective breeding.

Exercise and Grooming

This breed needs lots of outdoor activity, ideally a couple of hours each day. PBGV needs just a weekly groom to remove dead hair and dirt, but the areas around the mouth and rear quarters should be checked and kept clean on a regular basis. While some neatening is occasionally necessary, the PBGV should be shown naturally, his tousled appearance being vitally important.

Below: Just waiting for the next dip!

relates to that area of France in which he originated. This is a hound that was developed to hunt game by scent and his physical evolution is directly related to the environment and terrain on the western coast of France which has thick underbrush, rocks, thorns, and brambles. This is difficult terrain demanding a hound that is hardy, alert, bold, determined and intelligent, with both mental and physical stamina. His close relation, the Grand Basset Griffon Vendéen, was used for large game like roe deer and wolf, while the PBGV was used to trail and drive smaller quarry such as rabbit, hare and sometimes feathered game too. Originally the PBGV and GBGV were produced in the same litters; not until the 1950s was the PBGV given an official breed standard of its own and considered a separate breed. In 1975 the interbreeding of the Grand and Petit was disallowed. A breed club was established in America in 1984 and the PBGV was admitted to AKC registration in 1990.

Health Issues

This is known as a very healthy breed but, like all others has some health problems. These include Neck Pair Syndrome, hip dysplasia, patella luxation, heart murmurs and some eye diseases. Occurrence of

Pharaoh Hound

Average height: dogs – 23-25 inches; bitches – 21-24 inches
Average weight: 45-55 pounds

Appearance

A medium sized sight hound, the Pharaoh Hound has a noble bearing with clean-cut, graceful lines and giving the general appearance of grace, power and speed. His skull is long, lean and chiselled, the foreface slightly longer than the skull and his powerful jaws have strong teeth. The nose is flesh colored and blends with the coat, as do his amber-colored eyes which have an intelligent expression. His ears, which are broad at base, are carried erect when alert; they are very mobile, fine and large. His long, lean muscular neck has a slight arch to carry his head high. There is a slight slope from croup to tail, this well carried and curved when in action. The coat is short and glossy, ranging from fine and close to slightly harsh, with no feathering. Color ranges from tan through rich tan to chestnut with white in specific places only, a white tip on the tail being highly desirable.

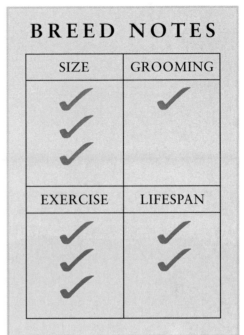

BREED NOTES

SIZE	GROOMING
✓ ✓ ✓	✓
EXERCISE	**LIFESPAN**
✓ ✓ ✓	✓ ✓

Characteristics

The Pharaoh Hound is intelligent, friendly, affectionate and playful. In the house he is generally calm and although well-behaved, he can be rather shy with strangers. He usually gets along well with children, but must be sensibly introduced. Socialization at an early age is advantageous. He is active and alert, very fast and a keen hunter, using both sight and scent; this means that pets such and cats and rabbits should be kept safely out of his way! It is also worth remembering that the Pharaoh Hound is a competent jumper.

Origins and History

One of the oldest domesticated dogs

Left: The amber eyes are intelligent.

561

A
B
C
D
E
F
G
H
I
J
K
L
M
N
O
P
Q
R
S
T
U
V
W
X
Y
Z

Left: A well matched Brace.

very healthy breed with no known deficiencies or inherited disorders. However, like all sighthounds, the breed can be extremely sensitive to anesthetics and can sometimes encounter difficulties with medications and insecticides.

Exercise and Grooming

This breed loves to stretch its legs with regular runs, but owners should always bear in mind that Pharaoh Hounds run at great speed and may well fly off after some animal or bird they have noticed. They should therefore be exercised in a large, enclosed paddock if possible. Long walks on a leash are also much appreciated. Grooming is minimal; a rubber brush may be used to remove dead hair and a chamois leather or similar will give a nice finish to the coat. The coat may be bathed or dry-shampooed as needed.

Below: Moving to perfection in the showring.

in recorded history, the Pharaoh Hound's lineage can be traced back to roughly 3000 BC. The history of Egyptian civilization was well documented and has been wonderfully preserved through paintings and hieroglyphs; from these we learn that dogs very similar to the Pharaoh Hound were treasured for their great hunting ability and that they also had a close affinity with humans. It appears likely that well before the birth of Christ this hound's ancestors were taken by Phoenician traders to the island of Malta where their purity was maintained. The breed first went to Britain in the early 1930s but the first one to be shown there arrived in 1963. The first Pharaoh Hound came to the USA in 1967 and the AKC admitted the breed to its Miscellaneous Class in 1979. The name "Kelb tal-

Fenek" is also used for the breed, the name "Pharaoh Hound" being allocated to the breed in Britain in the 1960s.

Health Issues

The Pharaoh Hound seems to be a

Plott

Average height: dogs – 22-25 inches; bitches – 20-23 inches
Average weight: dogs – 50-60 pounds; bitches – 40-55 pounds

Appearance

The Plott is a hunting hound of striking color, intelligent, alert and confident. Powerful, well-muscled yet streamline, he is noted for stamina, endurance, agility, determination and aggressiveness when hunting. Courage is combined with athletic ability. His head is carried well up and his skin is moderately tight. The Plott's prominent, brown or hazel eyes give him a confident, inquisitive, determined expression. Ears are soft textured, fairly broad and hang gracefully with the inside rolling forward. When attentive or inquisitive, some Plotts display semi-erectile ears. Flews give the muzzle a squarish appearance, pigment is black and the bite is scissors. He is slightly higher at the withers than hips, with deep ribs, strong, well-muscled back and a slightly arched loin. His long tail sometimes has a slight brush, and is carried like a saber. The coat is smooth, fine and glossy, but thick enough to provide protection from wind and water. Occasionally a Plott is double coated. He may be any shade of brindle, solid black, any shade of brindle with black saddle, or black with brindle trim. A rare buckskin (without brindling) sometimes appears. Some white on chest and feet is permissible, as is a graying effect around the jaws and muzzle.

Characteristics

Eager to please, loyal, intelligent and alert, his disposition is generally even but varies among strains, sometimes differing between those bred for big game and those bred as coonhounds. In all seasons he covers diverse types of terrain and water at speed and is a bold, aggressive, fearless hunter. Plott "music" is a loud, ringing chop on track and tree, but bawl or squall trailing mouths are also acceptable. He is a fine companion for a family and good with children.

Origins and History

In 1750, two young brothers left Germany for America with five Hanoverian Schweisshunds. Sadly one of the brothers died en route but 16 year old Johannes George Plott survived and settled in Bute County, North Carolina where he began a breeding program that continued in the family over 200 years. The Plotts remained mountain men, using their hounds to hunt bear and occasionally boar. The dogs became known by their family name, Plott, while hounds raised by other mountain families were called by their respective names.

Eventually Plott breeders realized an outcross was essential, choosing the tan, black-saddled, Blevin. Bred back to pure Plotts the breed was revitalised. Soon the breed became classified as a coonhound, but some still work with large game.

Health Issues

Although considered the hardiest of the coonhounds, the Plott has a tendency to eat large amounts of food quickly, which makes him susceptible to bloat.

Exercise and Grooming

This is a working hound and, as such, needs plenty of freedom and exercise but this should be in a large, safely enclosed area as he is always ready to wander off to hunt. Coat care for the Plott is minimal, needing the occasional brush and comb to remove dead hair.

BREED NOTES

SIZE	GROOMING
✔✔	✔

EXERCISE	LIFESPAN
✔✔✔	✔✔

Pointer

Average height: dogs – 25-28 inches; bitches – 23-26 inches
Average weight: dogs – 55-75 pounds; bitches – 45-65 pounds

Appearance

This is a breed that was bred primarily for field sports, so he should unmistakably look and act the part, giving the impression of compact power and agile grace. His noble head is carried proudly, the skull of medium width, roughly as wide as the length of the muzzle. The cheeks are cleanly chiseled and the nose is slightly higher at the tip than the muzzle at the point of stop. His jaws end squarely and level and he has an even or scissors bite. Ears hang naturally, close to the head, and they are set on at eye level. The Pointer's eyes are round and intense, the darker the better, and he portrays an intelligent alert expression. The long, dry neck is slightly arched and leads into long, thin, sloping shoulders. His chest is deep rather than wide and his back solid; his tail must not reach below the hock and is carried without curl. The coat is short, dense and smooth, with a sheen and its color

Below: A superb example of a Champion.

BREED NOTES

SIZE	GROOMING
✔ ✔ ✔	✔

EXERCISE	LIFESPAN
✔ ✔ ✔	✔ ✔

Above and right: The Pointer is alert, dignified and a hard-driving hunting dog.

can be liver, lemon, black, orange; either in combination with white or solid-colored. There is a saying that a good Pointer cannot be a bad color. All in all, the Pointer is a wide-awake, hard-driving hunting dog, possessing stamina and courage coupled with the desire to go.

Characteristics

The Pointer has an even temperament and makes a wonderful companion both at home and in the field. This breed should never show timidity, either toward man or dog. He is alert and dignified, loyal and devoted, and is gentle with children. In addition he is an excellent watchdog, always ready to protect his home and family.

Origins and History

It is likely that the Pointer originated in Spain where he was known as the Spanish Pointer, but

Opposite: Pointers make great companions, even from a young age.

Above and below: A Pointer is well suited to life on a farm.

was much heavier than the Pointers we know today. He also carries the blood of the Portuguese Pointer. He arrived in England in the latter half of the 17th century where he was crossed with the Italian Pointer. His arrival in England was some time

before wing-shooting with guns became popular so then he was frequently used to locate and point hares in conjunction with greyhound coursing. In the following century wing-shooting with the gun came into vogue so the

Pointer was used differently and became highly prized by sportsmen. During the 19th century some crosses were made with Setters, so the Pointer we see in the field and showrings today is somewhat removed from his predecessors.

Health Issues

Health concerns to look out for in the Pointer include hip dysplasia, entropion, cataract, and dwarfism. He can also encounter skin problems and tail injuries can occur.

Exercise and Grooming

The Pointer needs lots of exercise to be kept happy; without this he gets frustrated and can become destructive. Occasional brushing of the coat is needed to remove dead hair and if used in the field he must always be dried off upon return and his pads and feet

A
B
C
D
E
F
G
H
I
J
K
L
M
N
O
P
Q
R
S
T
U
V
W
X
Y
Z

Polish Lowland Sheepdog

Average height: dogs – 18-20 inches; bitches – 17-19 inches
Average weight: 30-35 pounds

Appearance

The silhouette of the Polish Lowland Sheepdog (whose other name is Polish Owczarek Nizinny, so he is known as "PON" for short) is rectangular rather than square. He is strong, cobby and muscular, with good muscle in neck, shoulders and hindquarters. His medium-sized head is in proportion to his body, but the profuse hair on forehead, cheeks and chin make it look bigger than it actually is. The oval eyes, which are brown or hazel, present a lively expression with a penetrating gaze. The dropped ears are heart-shaped and covered with long hair and the jaws are strong, meeting in a scissors bite. His tail is short and should be no more than two vertebrae; when puppies are born with long or partial tails, these tails are docked. This is a double-coated breed, the entire body covered with a long, dense, shaggy, thick coat that is reasonably straight, while the undercoat is soft and dense. All coat colors are acceptable, the most common being white with either black, gray or sandy patches and gray with white, or chocolate.

Characteristics

The PON is stable and self-confident but will tend to dominate his master, so needs to be taught who is boss and benefits from consistent training from a young age. He has an intense desire to please and has good herding and working abilities, known for being clever and perceptive, and for his excellent memory. When not used as a working dog he can be a great companion. He is extremely loyal, but somewhat aloof and suspicious of strangers.

Origins and History

Early in the history of Poland, the Puli was crossed with other blood, most probably the Huns' herding dog, creating a breed that was about 19 to 22 inches tall, with a

Below: Jaws are strong, meeting in a scissors bite.

Johnson

BREED NOTES

SIZE	GROOMING
✓	✓
✓	✓
✓	✓
EXERCISE	**LIFESPAN**
✓	✓
✓	✓
✓	

rather long coat, used for herding and guarding. There is evidence that the PON as we know him today has certainly been in existence since before the 16th century, appearing in both Poland and Pomerania. Around 1514, a Polish ship sailed from Gdansk to Scotland with cargo of grain to be exchanged for Scottish sheep. And on this ship were six PONs to help move the sheep. Two bitches and a dog were

Below: The entire body has a long, dense, shaggy coat.

exchanged for a fine horned ram and a ewe, and it is believed that these three dogs form part of the ancestry behind the Bearded Collie. The PON works well with both sheep and cattle and in recent years has also been kept as a pet dog. This hard working breed is obedient and fearless; when working with sheep he will attack any fox that threatens the flock.

Health Issues

The PON seems to be an

extremely healthy breed with no significant health concerns.

Exercise and Grooming

Physical and mental exercise is needed in abundance to keep the PON satisfied. This breed makes a great choice for the highly active owner. Walks on a leash are important too, but he also does well in agility classes, and of course herding! His coat needs to be brushed thoroughly two or three times a week to prevent matting. Trimming is not necessary.

A
B
C
D
E
F
G
H
I
J
K
L
M
N
O
P
Q
R
S
T
U
V
W
X
Y
Z

Pomeranian

Average height: 8-11 inches
Average weight: 3-7 pounds (Ideal weight 4-6 pounds)

Appearance

The Pomeranian is a compact, well-ribbed, short backed little dog, buoyant in deportment and inquisitive by nature. His head balances with his body, the muzzle being rather short, straight and fine, but never snipey. His alert expression is rather fox-like, the eyes dark, bright and almond-shaped. The top of the skull is slightly rounded, the erect ears mounted high and the teeth meet in a scissors bite. The plumed tail, which lies flat and straight on the back, is a characteristic of the breed and the buttocks are well behind the set of the tail. The breed is noted for its double coat, which has a soft dense undercoat and a long outer coat that glistens and is harsh in texture. The thickness of the undercoat holds up the guard hair, allowing it to stand off from the body. The coat is particularly abundant from the neck and front of shoulders and

Below: Small in stature, but with a "big dog" attitude.

BREED NOTES

SIZE	GROOMING
✔	✔ ✔ ✔
EXERCISE	**LIFESPAN**
✔	✔ ✔

Above left and right: Still very much a puppy, not yet carrying an adult's coat.

chest, forming a frill. On the head and legs, the coat is shorter. Trimming is permitted to present a clean outline. All colors and patterns (black and tan/brindle/parti-color) are allowed.

Characteristics
An extrovert little breed, the Pomeranian exhibits great intelligence and a vivacious spirit.

Right: There are various attractive colors in this breed.

A
B
C
D
E
F
G
H
I
J
K
L
M
N
O
P
Q
R
S
T
U
V
W
X
Y
Z

Opposite and above: These young pups are full of fun and mischief.

Right: The Pomeranian is a devoted family member.

Cocky, commanding and although small in stature, he has a "big dog" attitude. He has a docile temperament and is devoted to his family, making a wonderful companion. The Pomeranian is a competitive show dog and increasingly takes part in obedience trials. Pomeranians have also been successfully used as hearing dogs for the deaf, therapy dogs and even in search and rescue in situations where a small dog is needed.

Origins and History

The Pomeranian is the smallest member of the Spitz family of dogs and takes its name from the

A B C D E F G H I J K L M N O **P** Q R S T U V W X Y Z

A
B
C
D
E
F
G
H
I
J
K
L
M
N
O
P
Q
R
S
T
U
V
W
X
Y
Z

Opposite and above: Two lovely examples of their breed.

Right: Life is such fun for a "Pom"!

historical region of Pomerania, on the southern coast of the Baltic Sea (now present day Germany and Poland). It was in Pomerania that the breed was bred down in size, although it did not actually originate there. Before it became so tiny, this dog was an able sheep herder. It first came to notice in Britain in the middle of the 19th century, but at that time some weighed as much as 30 pounds, resembling the German Wolf Spitz in size, coat and color. The English Kennel Club recognised

A
B
C
D
E
F
G
H
I
J
K
L
M
N
O
P
Q
R
S
T
U
V
W
X
Y
Z

A
B
C
D
E
F
G
H
I
J
K
L
M
N
O
P
Q
R
S
T
U
V
W
X
Y
Z

Johnson

what was called a Spitz Dog in 1870, and in 1888 a Pomeranian named Marco was sent from Florence in Italy to Queen Victoria; this certainly helped to increase the breed's popularity, for she was a popular monarch and people liked to follow in her footsteps. In fact Queen Victoria helped greatly to promote the trend towards the smaller Pomeranian. The breed was shown in America in 1892, but it was in 1900 that the breed received regular classification from the AKC.

Health Issues

The Pomeranian is reputed to be a hardy, healthy, long-lived breed but they do encounter some health problems including luxating patella, collapsed trachea and hypothyroidism. Teeth need especial care as they can easily be lost at a relatively young age.

Exercise and Grooming

Although this is a highly energetic breed, it is easy to meet its exercise needs due to its small size. The Pomeranian enjoys long walks and simply loves to play in a safe area. Time must be devoted to the Pomeranian's coat care but, although profuse, it is quite easy to maintain. Combing is important twice weekly and more frequently during shedding time.

Opposite: This puppy's devoted owner has furniture especially made for all her Toy dogs!

Right top and bottom: Two more of the attractive colors found in this charming breed.

Poodle

Average height: Standard: Over 15 inches, but height is generally between 21 and 27 inches
Miniature: 15 inches or under, with a minimum height in excess of 10 inches
Toy: 10 inches or under
Average weight: Standard: 45-70 pounds
Miniature: 15-17 pounds
Toy: 6-9 pounds

Appearance

In America there are three varieties of Poodle, their differences only being in size; in all other respects their breed standards are identical. (In some countries there are four different size divisions.) Whatever his size, the Poodle is a very elegant

Johnson

BREED NOTES

SIZE			GROOMING
Min.	St.	Toy	
✔	✔	✔	✔
✔	✔		✔
	✔		✔
EXERCISE			**LIFESPAN**
✔			✔
✔			✔
			✔

Left: A beautifully presented white coat, blowing in the wind.

dog, squarely built and well-proportioned; he moves soundly and carries himself proudly, with a certain air of distinction and dignity about him. His eyes are very dark and oval in shape, his muzzle long, straight and fine, with slight chiseling under the eyes. The long, wide ears hang close to the head and are thickly feathered, but fringing should not be excessive in length. The chest is deep and moderately wide, the topline level and the loin broad and muscular, whilst the tail is straight, set on high and docked of sufficient length to give a balanced outline. (In some countries the Poodle's tail is un-

Above and right: *Poodles enjoy posing in front of the camera.*

docked.) His feet are rather small, oval in shape and with well-arched toes and thick, firm pads. The Poodle's coat is curly, of a naturally harsh texture and dense throughout. Alternatively it can be corded, hanging in tight, even cords of varying length; this is a distinct coat type, the cords starting to develop between the ages of 9 to 18 months. The color of the coat must be an even and solid color at the skin but in blues, grays, silvers, browns, cafe-au-laits, apricots and creams the coat may show varying shades of the same color. Clear colors are definitely preferred but such natural variation in the shading of the coat is not considered a fault. The color of nose pigment varies according to coat color. (Parti-colored Poodles are not allowed in the showring under AKC rules in America, but in some countries they are permitted.)

There are various different ways

A
B
C
D
E
F
G
H
I
J
K
L
M
N
O
P
Q
R
S
T
U
V
W
X
Y
Z

A
B
C
D
E
F
G
H
I
J
K
L
M
N
O
P
Q
R
S
T
U
V
W
X
Y
Z

Johnson

Above: A white Standard, just reaching maturity.

of presenting a Poodle's coat. Under 12 months he may be shown in what is known as a "puppy clip" in which the coat is long, but the face, throat, feet and base of tail are clipped. The entire shaven foot is visible and there is a pompon left on the end of the tail. Over the age of 12 months a Poodle must be shown in either "English Saddle" or "Continental" clip, whilst in certain classes only the "Sporting" clip is accepted. In all clips the topknot may be left free or held in place with elastic bands.

Characteristics

The Poodle is a calm, steady breed and should never appear shy or sharp. All sizes of Poodle generally get along well with children, but of course toddlers should not be allowed to tug at a Poodle's attractive coat! The Poodle is well known as a good-natured breed that is intelligent, amusing and eager to please, making a wonderful companion.

Origins and History

The Poodle is believed to have originated in Germany, although for many years has been regarded as the national dog of France where it was commonly used as a retriever and as a duck dog. The Standard, Poodle is the oldest of the three varieties, this being the variety that gained fame as a

Right: Sitting pretty!

Below: The UK's all-time Miniature record holder.

Johnson

A B C D E F G H I J K L M N O **P** Q R S T U V W X Y Z

A
B
C
D
E
F
G
H
I
J
K
L
M
N
O
P
Q
R
S
T
U
V
W
X
Y
Z

Above: Eyes are very dark and oval, the muzzle long.

water worker. The reason that portions of its coat were shorn was to facilitate its swimming abilities. Clipping then became fashionable, particularly in France. The Miniature and Toy Poodles developed very soon after the Standard and certainly the Toy was known in England in the 18th century. The breed came to North America at the end of the 19th century but failed to gain popularity until after the Second World War. By the mid-1950s it had become the most popular breed in America, holding this accolade for around twenty years.

Right: Brown Miniature puppy plays ball.

The wearing of a ribbon in the topknot is attributed to this being a means of identifying a dog in the water, and travelling gypsies and others who had performing Poodles added to the various styles of clipping and frequently

Above: A well-presented black.

dressed their dogs in little outfits, making them all the more appealing when it came to collecting money from their many admirers!

Above: *There are many different ways of clipping a Poodle.*

Below left: *"Lisa" enters into the spirit of Christmas!*

Below: *And her friend "Monica" joins in the fun.*

A
B
C
D
E
F
G
H
I
J
K
L
M
N
O
P
Q
R
S
T
U
V
W
X
Y
Z

Health Issues

Because there are many health controls carried out in the Poodle breeds, the list of health problems that have been discovered is lengthy and includes the following. Toys: epilepsy, hypothyroidism, Legg-Calves Perthes disease, patella luxation and Progressive Retinal Atrophy (PRA). Miniatures: epilepsy, hip dysplasia, hypothyroidism, Legg-Calves Perthes disease, patella luxation. Progressive Retinal Atrophy (PRA) and von Willebrand's Disease. Standards: Addison's disease, bloat, cancer, Cushings disease, epilepsy, hip dysplasia, hypothyroidism, Legg-Calves Perthes disease, patella luxation, Progressive Retinal Atrophy (PRA) and von Willebrand's Disease.

Exercise and Grooming

The amount of exercise a Poodle needs is largely determined by its size, but all like a good walk and

Above and left: An apricot head (above) and two browns (sitting).

an enjoyable game, whilst the larger ones enjoy a good work out and possibly a swim in a safe area. In order to keep the Poodle's coat free from matts, frequent brushing and regular bathing and clipping is essential. To keep a Poodle's coat in tip-top condition and suitably presented for competition in the showring, professional grooming expertise is a must. Regular attention must be paid to the ears to be certain they are clean at all times.

Porcelaine

Average height: dogs – 22-23 inches; bitches – 21-22 inches
Average weight: 55-62 pounds

Appearance

The Porcelaine has a solid white coat, the hairs of which are very fine and particularly short giving it a translucent appearance, from which its name is derived. The skin is pink with sparse, black mottling showing through the coat and, from a distance, giving the impression of pale blue glass. The white can be interrupted by orange spots on the body and on the thin, conical ears, which are notably large. This breed has a finely sculpted head and although moderate in build its appearance is quite delicate. The head is finely chiseled, the eyes dark and the nose black, with wide-open nostrils. The tails is heavy at the base, tapering to a point at the end.

Characteristics

An energetic, fierce hunter, the Porcelaine is easy to handle and gentle in the home. Generally he is friendly and good with other dogs and children. He is vigorous and tireless, with an excellent nose and musical voice. Generally he hunts in packs on various types of wild game. He does so with his comrades, without orders from his owner, so is very independent and brave. Given plenty of opportunity for exercise and stimulation, this hound can be suitable for a home environment.

Origins and History

Believed to be the oldest of the

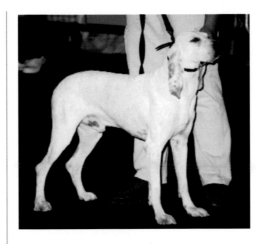

French scenthounds, in its ancestry is the now-extinct Montimboeuf and the smaller Laufhunds of Switzerland. The Porcelaine was decimated during the French Revolution, almost completely exterminated in the French countryside, but across the border in Switzerland local breeders endeavoured to maintain the breed, using some of their own Laufhund blood. The breed was reintroduced to France in the middle of the 19th century, following which more crosses were introduced by way of other French breeds. The Porcelaine in its revised form was exhibited at the Paris Show in 1889 but many people felt the original Porcelaine had effectively disappeared; certainly in the 18th century it had been a larger hound. Prior to this several dogs had travelled with their owners to America, where they had become firmly established, especially in the southern states. In 1861 there were no fewer than 250 Porcelaines working on the Rousseau estates in Louisiana. After

the American Civil War the great plantations of the south were broken up and the hounds were dispersed, following which they were randomly crossed with other dogs. Today in the France, Switzerland and Italy the breed is used in packs primarily for hare-hunting as well as on small deer and wild boar.

Health Issues

No hereditary problems have apparently yet been discovered.

Exercise and Grooming

The Porcelaine is an energetic hound that needs plenty of exercise and is certainly not suitable for apartment living. Grooming is minimal, just a medium to soft brush used once a day to remove loose hairs, and ears should always be thoroughly checked.

BREED NOTES

SIZE	GROOMING
✓	✓
	✓
	✓
EXERCISE	LIFESPAN
✓	✓
✓	✓
✓	

Portuguese Podengo

Average height: Average height: Grande (large): 21.6-27.5 inches
Medio (medium): 15.3-22 inches
Pequeno (small): 7.9-11.8 inches
Average weight: Grande (large): 66 pounds
Medio (medium): 35-44 pounds
Pequeno (small): 10-12.5 pounds

Appearance

There are three sizes of Podengo, small, medium and large, and each size has two hair types, wire and smooth. All three sizes are known for their erect ears, pyramidal head, elegant lines of body and agile movement. The largest, however, is virtually extinct and the medium size is the most popular variety. The Pequeno has also been on the verge of extinction, but has been making a comeback since the 1960s.

In appearance, the Grande is clearly of sighthound-type with well-proportioned head flat skull, pronounced stop and straight muzzle. His eyes are small and oblique, their color ranging from light honey to dark chestnut. The sizeable ears are pricked and triangular, the back level and the forelegs straight. The Medio is similarly proportioned to the Grande but the Pequeno, although a miniature sighthound-type, appears more sturdily built because it is so much lower in leg. The short-coated varieties have a hard coat that is actually longer than that of most sighthounds, whilst the wire coat is medium long, shaggy and coarse. Color for all three sizes can be yellow, fawn or black, with white markings.

Characteristics

This is a hardy, intelligent, lively

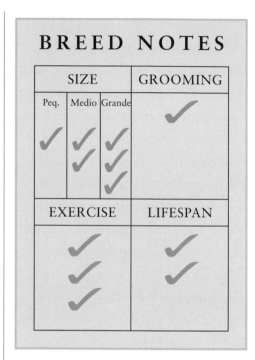

BREED NOTES

SIZE			GROOMING
Peq.	Medio	Grande	✔
✔	✔	✔	
	✔	✔	
		✔	
EXERCISE			**LIFESPAN**
✔			✔
✔			✔
✔			

breed that makes a fine companion. He is loyal and fearless, and makes a good watchdog. The Podengo possesses a keen sense of fun and is easy to train, excelling at agility and other sports.

Origins and History

This is the National Dog of Portugal, an ancient hound that went to the Iberian Peninsula with the Phoenicians who journeyed there from Asia Minor around 1,000 BC. In the 15th century the small Podengo traveled with Christopher

Left: The Medio is more usually found in the hunting field than in the showring.

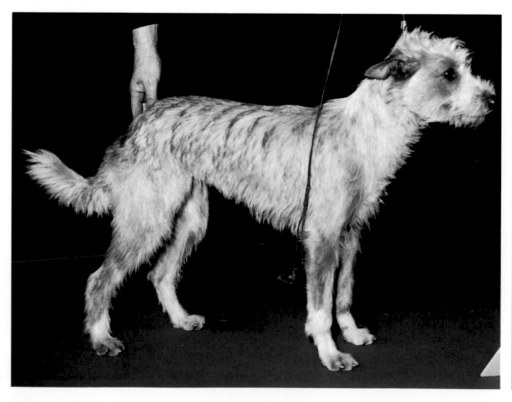

Columbus and Portuguese explorers, used aboard ship to keep down the vermin that brought disease.

The large Podengos hunt wild boar and the medium and small are fine rabbit hunters.

The first purebred Portuguese Podengos arrived in America in the 1990s and now over 200 reside in more than thirty different states. The breed has starred in several Hollywood films including Three Wishes, Soccer Dog, and Zeus and Roxanne.

Above and left: Both Pequeno, the wire coat (above) and smooth (below) are easy to care for.

Health Issues

The Portuguese Podengo is believed to be amongst the healthiest of breeds. This is a long-lived dog that can go on well into its teens. There have been a few cases of Legg-Calves Perthes disease, patella luxation, epilepsy, cancer and Cushings disease. There have also been some problems with teeth and with skin problems, most probably as a result of food allergies.

Exercise and Grooming

The amount of exercise needed depends to a large extent on size, but all three varieties are active hounds and so need a generous amount of freedom and leash work. Coat care for either variety of is undemanding, but both need a regular groom once each week to remove any dead hair, with more frequent care during the moulting season.

A
B
C
D
E
F
G
H
I
J
K
L
M
N
O
P
Q
R
S
T
U
V
W
X
Y
Z

Portuguese Pointer

Average height: 20-22 inches
Average weight: dogs – 44-59 pounds; bitches – 35-48 pounds

A
B
C
D
E
F
G
H
I
J
K
L
M
N
O
P
Q
R
S
T
U
V
W
X
Y
Z

Appearance

For at least a thousand years the Portuguese Pointer has always had the same square head, marked stop, triangular ears and compact look. His body is well-balanced with sufficient bone, presenting a quick and powerful appearance. The chest is deep, extending to the elbows. His skull is broad between the ears, the muzzle short and slightly convex, with a furrow to the brow. The ears, which hang down, are high set and the tail is traditionally docked to half or two thirds of its natural length. Usually this breed has a smooth, short coat but occasionally an older coat-type occurs; this is longer haired, with feathering on the ears, underside and tail. The color of the Portuguese Pointer is yellow or chestnut, sometimes solid, but usually showing small patches of white.

Characteristics

The Portuguese Pointer is outwardly affectionate, loyal to his master and energetic in the field.

Origins and History

The Portuguese Pointer has been bred down from ancient Iberian hunting dogs that are traceable in Portugal as far back as the 12th century. Originally this dog was bred in the royal kennels, used with hawks, but it developed as a very popular hunting dog and eventually found its way also into society's lower classes. In the 18th century many English families were in Portugal's Oporto region for wine production and several took this dog back to Britain, as a result of which the blood of Portuguese Pointer runs in the veins of the English Pointer. In the 19th century the breed's homeland experienced considerable social hardships causing the progressive decline of the Portuguese Pointer but in the 1920s efforts were made to salvage the breed. To do this some dogs were located in the inaccessible north of Portugal. This resulted in a pedigree book being established in Portugal in 1932 and the breed standard was written in 1938. The breed was accepted into the AKC's Foundation Stock Service in 2005. Today the breed's hunting abilities have been retained so the Portuguese Pointer is frequently used in Portugal for pointing and retrieving.

BREED NOTES

SIZE	GROOMING
✔ ✔	✔
EXERCISE	**LIFESPAN**
✔ ✔ ✔	✔ ✔

Exercise and Grooming

This is an energetic breed that needs a good amount of exercise, including free run. Coat care is minimal, but regular brushing is necessary to keep the coat clean and in healthy condition.

Portuguese Water Dog

Average height: dogs – 20-23 inches; bitches – 17-21 inches
Average weight: dogs – 42-60 pounds; bitches – 35-50 pounds

Appearance

This highly intelligent breed provides an indelible impression of strength, spirit, and soundness and is distinguished by two coat types, curly or wavy. He has an impressive head of considerable breadth and well proportioned mass. His medium sized eyes, set well apart and little obliquely give a steady, penetrating and attentive expression. Darker eyes are preferred, their rims fully pigmented with black edges in black, black and white, or white dogs; brown edges in brown dogs. Haws are dark and not apparent. The ears are heart shaped and thin and except for a small opening at the back, they are held nicely against the head. He is slightly longer than he is tall with a solidly built, muscular body to equip him for a full day's work both in and out of the water. The skull is slightly longer than the muzzle, which is substantial and wider at the base than at the nose. The forehead is prominent with a central furrow and the broad nose is black or brown, according to coat color. The canines are strongly developed and the bite can be either scissors or level. The strong neck is short and round, the topline level and firm, while the chest is broad and deep, reaching down to the elbow. Ribs are long and well-sprung to provide optimum lung capacity. The

Portuguese Water Dog's tail, which is not docked, is thick at the base and tapers; when attentive it is held in a ring. The tail is used as a rudder when swimming and diving. The Portuguese Water Dog's feet are round and rather flat, with webbing of soft skin between the toes; the central pad is very thick, whilst the others are normal. The coat is profuse, thickly planted and is strong, healthy hair that covers the whole body evenly, except where the forearm meets the brisket and in the groin area, where it is thinner. There is no undercoat, mane or ruff. There are two types of coat; when curly, the compact, cylindrical curls are somewhat lustreless and the hair on the ears is sometimes wavy; when wavy, the hair falls gently in waves and has a slight sheen. Color is black, white or various tones of brown; also combinations of black

BREED NOTES

SIZE	GROOMING
✔	✔
✔	✔
✔	✔

EXERCISE	LIFESPAN
✔	✔
✔	✔
✔	✔

A
B
C
D
E
F
G
H
I
J
K
L
M
N
O
P
Q
R
S
T
U
V
W
X
Y
Z

or brown with white. (In white coated dog the nose, mouth, and eyelids are black.)

The coat of the Portuguese Water Dog may be clipped in two styles: Lion clip: As soon as the coat grows long, the middle part and hindquarters, as well as the muzzle, are clipped. The hair at the end of the tail is left at full length.

Retriever clip: To give a natural appearance and a smooth unbroken line, the entire coat is scissored or clipped to follow the outline of the dog, leaving a short blanket of coat no longer than one inch in length. As in the lion clip, the hair at the end of the tail is left at full length.

Characteristics

The Portuguese Water Dog is spirited yet has an obedient nature; he is self-willed, brave and very resistant to fatigue. He has exceptional intelligence and makes a loyal companion, having long been highly prized by fishermen along Portugal's coast. He has exceptional diving and swimming abilities and is an alert guard. Although he is an excellent working dog he needs direction; being people-oriented, he does not suit a kennel environment and dislikes being left alone for long periods. He enjoys being part of a family and gets along well with children and other pets.

Origins and History

The Portuguese Water Dog was once popular all along Portugal's coast line where he was prized by fishermen both as a companion and guard. These dogs lived and worked on boats; they herded fish into nets, retrieved lost tackle or broken nets

and acted as couriers, carrying messages from boat to boat, or boat to shore. The large variation in size is explained by the fact that small dogs were more practical for small boats, while larger dogs worked on the larger vessels. Their work made them excellent swimmers with great diving capabilities. Sadly, modern technology meant they were no longer needed for these tasks and the breed almost became extinct. There are many theories about the origin of the breed, but it is thought to pre-date the Poodle and in pre-Christian times was seen as "almost sacred". The breed came to the United States in the late 1960s when it was extremely rare and was accepted for registration in AKC stud books in 1983.

Health Issues

This a reasonably long-lived breed that generally remains active into its

senior years, but the following health concerns are worthy of note: hip dysplasia, Progressive Retinal Atrophy (PRA), storage disease (GM-1), juvenile dilated cardiomyopathy (JDC), Addison's disease and follicular dysplasia.

Exercise and Grooming

This is a breed that loves to exercise, and given the opportunity to swim and enjoy a water retrieving game it is even happier! Plenty of time should be allowed for long walks and free runs. Regular grooming is essential both for curly and wavy coated varieties. To prevent matting the coat must be thoroughly combed or brushed on a weekly basis, for the coat does not shed. Frequent baths and regular clipping are also necessary.

Below: This handsome male is brown.

Pug

Average height: 10-11 inches
Average weight: 14-18 pounds

BREED NOTES

SIZE	GROOMING
✔	✔
EXERCISE	**LIFESPAN**
✔	✔✔

Left: The Pug is a real "character"!

Appearance

The Pug is of square proportions and decidedly cobby in appearance. His head is large, massive and round, his eyes dark, very large, bold and prominent, wonderfully described as "globular in shape" and with a soft, solicitous expression. When he is excited his eyes are full of fire. The Pug's ears are thin and small, soft, like black velvet; there are two kinds of ear, rose or button, the latter preferable. His wrinkles are large and deep and his muzzle short and square, but not upfaced. The bite should be very slightly undershot. The strong, thick neck has enough strength to carry the head proudly, the chest is wide and the forelegs straight and very strong. Hindquarters are also strong, the thighs and buttocks full and muscular. His tail is curled as tightly as possible over the hip, a double curl is perfection. The short, glossy coat is fine, smooth and soft and its color is silver, apricot-fawn or black. There are dark markings in specific places on the lighter colors; these include a black mask. To sum him up beautifully, the Pug is frequently described as multum in parvo – a lot in a little package!

A
B
C
D
E
F
G
H
I
J
K
L
M
N
O
P
Q
R
S
T
U
V
W
X
Y
Z

Characteristics

The Pug is an even-tempered breed showing stability, playfulness, great charm, dignity with an outgoing, loving disposition. This combination of attributes makes him an excellent companion and a fairly good watchdog who will alert his family to strangers. The Pug was really bred as a companion for humans and should not be left alone for long periods of time. He can be a little bit stubborn, but in reality he wants nothing more than to

Left and below: It's easy to see why this breed is described as multum in parvo.

please his family. On the down side, not everyone appreciates his snoring!

Origins and History

Maybe we shall never know exactly how the Pug came into existence, but it is now generally agreed that he hails from Asia, and has some basic similarities to the Pekingese. It is likely that he has bred fairly true to type since 400BC. The Pug was favored by Buddhist priests and is believed to have been kept in the monasteries as a companion. Most people consider him a Chinese breed for he was a prized possession of the Emperors of China and was afforded every luxury, sometimes even having

Left: The Pug was bred as a companion for humans.

Below: 'Who says I can't climb this cliff?'

A
B
C
D
E
F
G
H
I
J
K
L
M
N
O
P
Q
R
S
T
U
V
W
X
Y
Z

Health Issues

Problems to look out for in the Pug are Pug Dog Encephalitis (PDE), epilepsy, eye problems, hemi-vertebra, hip dysplasia, Legge-Calves Perthes disease and luxating patella. The Pug is also prone to obesity, so his diet and weight should be kept in check. The brachycephalic syndrome can also sometimes involve pinched nostrils and an elongation of the soft palate.

Left and opposite: When not sleeping, Pug puppies are usually eating or playing.

Below: You just wait, I'll soon get my legs sorted out!'

his own soldiers on guard! Later the breed was found in Japan and later still in Europe, where it was much admired in royal courts. The Pug became the official breed of the House of Orange, one of them giving alarm at the approach of the Spaniards at Hermingny in 1572. Later, when William II landed in England to be crowned King, his cortege included Pugs, so the breed became highly fashionable in England for generations after. In France, Napoleon's wife, Josephine sent a message secreted under the collar her Pug, "Fortune", when she was imprisoned. Moving on to 1860, British soldiers sacked the Imperial Palace in Peking and took Pugs and Pekinese dogs back to Britain; this was the first time dogs had been taken outside China in any great number. In 1885 the first Pug was accepted for AKC registration and the breed was exhibited in Britain for the first time in 1886.

A
B
C
D
E
F
G
H
I
J
K
L
M
N
O
P
Q
R
S
T
U
V
W
X
Y
Z

Exercise and Grooming

The Pug needs moderate exercise, but should not be over-exerted in the heat or when it is humid. At any sign of wheezing, he should be allowed to rest. Occasional brushing is needed to remove dead hair, and bathing can be done when necessary, always making sure he is thoroughly dried off afterwards. A Pug's wrinkles need daily attention to keep them perfectly clean.

Left and opposite: The chest is wide, the forelegs straight and strong.

Below: Waiting at the gate.

Johnson

Puli

Average height: dogs – 17 inches; bitches – 16 inches
Average weight: dogs – 22-33 pounds; bitches – 20-28.5 pounds

Appearance

The Puli is a medium boned, compact breed, his tightly knit body appearing square. His head is in proportion to his body, with almond-shaped eyes, deep set, rather large and dark brown in color, while his V-shaped, hanging ears are about half of his head length. The skull is slightly domed, the muzzle strong and straight, ending in a good-sized nose, which is always black. His comparatively large teeth meet in a scissors bite. The Puli's tail is carried over and blends into the backline. He has round, compact feet, with well-arched toes and thick cushioned pads. Surely the most striking feature of the breed is its characteristic coat that hangs in cords all over the body. His is a profuse, weather resistant coat, the outer coat wavy or curly, but never silky. The undercoat is wooly and dense. If allowed to develop naturally the coat clumps together

Below: The tightly knit body is covered in cords.

BREED NOTES	
SIZE	GROOMING
✓ ✓ ✓	✓ ✓ ✓
EXERCISE	LIFESPAN
✓ ✓ ✓	✓ ✓

typically lively, light, quick and agile, with an ability to change direction instantly. This agility, combined with soundness of mind and body, is of prime importance for the proper fulfilment of his work in the field.

Origins and History

The Puli, or Drover, has been an integral part of the life of the Hungarian shepherd for over 1,000 years, used to herd sheep and also horses. When the Magyars arrived in Hungary they took with them their sheepdogs; they had larger ones somewhat resembling the

Above and right: Young puppy (above) and youngster (right), their coats not yet corded.

in the adult, to form cords that vary in shape and thickness, either flat or round, depending on the balance of outer coat to undercoat. In America the Puli may be shown either corded or brushed, but in some other countries, such as in Britain, a brushed coat is undesirable. In maturity, the coat can reach the ground. Only solid colors of rusty black, black, all shades of gray, and white are acceptable; but there may be a white spot of not more than two inches on the chest. The fully pigmented skin has a bluish or gray cast, whatever the coat color.

Characteristics

By nature the Puli is an affectionate, intelligent and home-loving companion. He is sensibly suspicious and therefore an excellent watchdog. He is described as an "acrobatic dog" and is

A
B
C
D
E
F
G
H
I
J
K
L
M
N
O
P
Q
R
S
T
U
V
W
X
Y
Z

Johnson

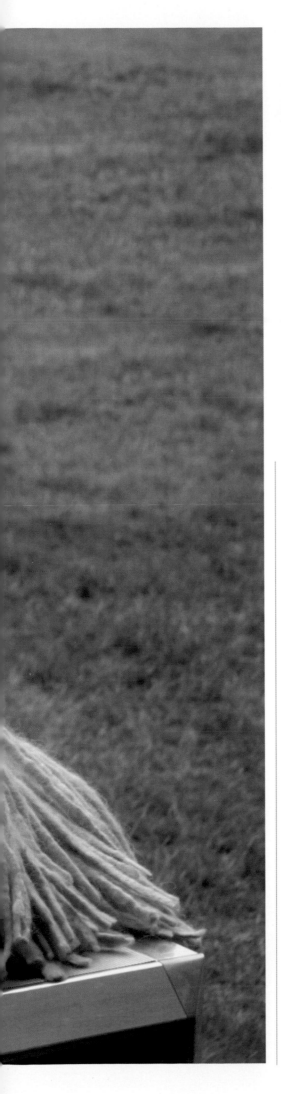

Johnson

Left and above: Colors are rusty black, black, all shades of gray, and white.

Komondor and Kuvasz and smaller ones, resembling the Puli. It is fairly certain that the ancestor of the Puli is the Tibetan Terrier which beneath the coat, is remarkably similar. The invasion of Hungary in the 16th century decimated the country, but in the following century it was repopulated by people from western Europe, who took with them their merino sheep and sheepdogs. Over time the Puli mingled with the sheepdogs of France and Germany, resulting in the "birth" of the Pumi and for many years even their names were interchanged, resulting in the decline of the Puli as we know it today. In 1912 a programme was begun to reconstitute the Puli, with two coat types noted, shaggy and curly. The first breed standard was written in 1915 and the breed was shown in Budapest in 1923. The standard was revised in 1934, dividing the Puli into three sizes, but the Hungarian Stud Book of the following year shows four size divisions, though the medium size seemed the most popular. In 1936 the breed was accepted for AKC registration.

Health Issues

The Puli appears to be a healthy breed, the prime concern being hip dysplasia.

Exercise and Grooming

Accustomed to herding, the Puli has a tendency to seek out work, so needs regular exercise and formal training to keep him motivated and therefore happy. He can be energetic both outdoors and inside the home. This is a non-shedding breed and management of the coat is done by hand if the coat is corded. After a bath, the coat takes two days or more to dry naturally.

A
B
C
D
E
F
G
H
I
J
K
L
M
N
O
P
Q
R
S
T
U
V
W
X
Y
Z

Pumi

Average height: dogs – 16-18.5 inches; bitches – 15-17.3 inches
Average weight: dogs – 22-33 pounds; bitches – 17.5-28.5 pounds

Appearance

The Pumi has a distinctly cheerful look about him. He is a medium sized herding dog of terrier type. His muzzle is elongated and the top of the head relatively broad and slightly domed. The cheeks are well muscled and the nose is blunt and always black, whatever the coat color. Once seen, the ears are never to be forgotten! They are upright and set on high, the upper third of the ear bending forward and showing an alert reaction to any sound. The Pumi's well-muscled neck leads into shoulders that have long blades but are a little steep; the back is straight and the chest, though not broad, is deep. The high set tail forms a wide circle above the croup. His medium-length coat is wavy or curly and forms tufts; it is never smooth or corded. The coat is elastic, shaggy and dense, consisting of a strong top coat and soft undercoat. On the ears the wiry protective hairs grow upward, while the hair on the foreface is shorter. The coat is only ever hand stripped; scissors are used only on head and legs. Coat color is various shades of gray, black, white or fawn, in which color a trace of black or grey and a distinct mask are desirable. The color must always be intense and solid, but a very small white mark on the chest and/or a white line on the toes are permissible.

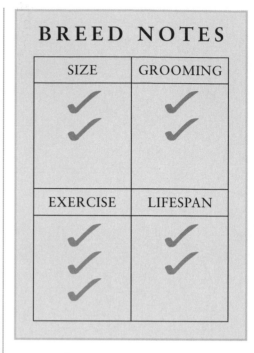

BREED NOTES

SIZE	GROOMING
✓ ✓	✓ ✓

EXERCISE	LIFESPAN
✓ ✓ ✓	✓ ✓

Characteristics

The Pumi is a lively herding dog with a rather restless temperament. He is extremely bold and a little suspicious of strangers, though never shy. He is an active dog, combining the biddability and intelligence of the herding dog with the activity and feistiness of a terrier. The Pumi is

Left: Once seen, the Pumi's ears are never forgotten!

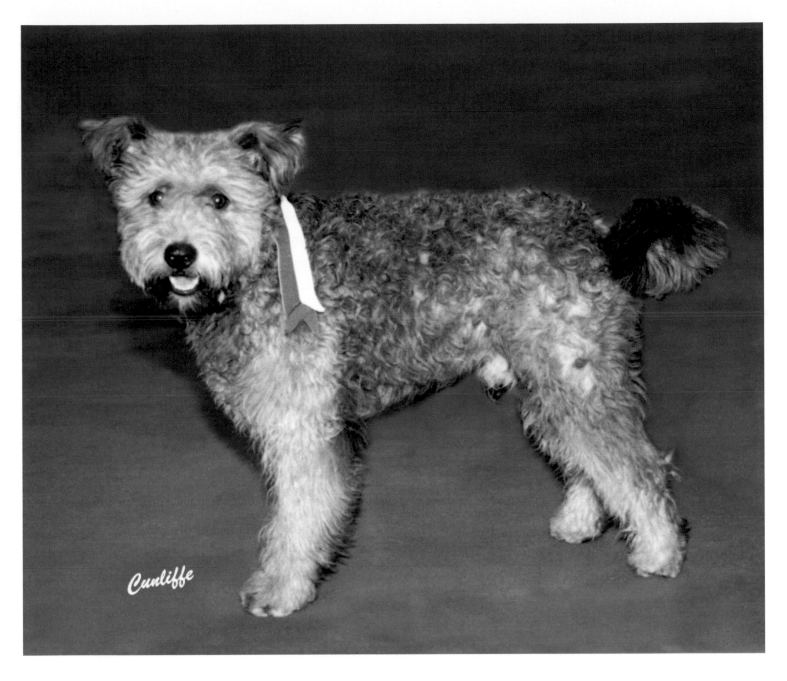

lively and expressive, always a crowd puller and always ready for duty. He is, however, rather noisy. He thoroughly enjoys life in a home environment, provided he has plenty of opportunity for work and exercise.

Origins and History

The Pumi's early history is the same as that of the Puli, this breed having been created by the introduction of crosses with the Pomeranian or Hutespitz dogs that were taken into Hungary during the 17th and 18th centuries by French and German traders. Dogs were frequently traded for sheep and other livestock. The Pumi was created particularly for cattle droving and to this day is still the Hungarians' favorite cattle dog. He also has a fine scenting ability and is ready and willing to combat wild animals and vermin. The Pumi was not defined by its own breed standard until 1935.

Health Issues

Because health checks have not been regularly carried out on this breed until recently, there is no proof of any health problems directly related to the breed.

Above: His medium length coat forms tufts and is hand-stripped.

However, hip dysplasia has occurred, albeit not with any regularity.

Exercise and Grooming

This is an active breed and needs daily work to do. This can be herding, obedience, flyball, jogging, or a strenuous ball game. His is non-shedding coat that needs careful combing once every two weeks, with thorough grooming roughly every three months.

A
B
C
D
E
F
G
H
I
J
K
L
M
N
O
P
Q
R
S
T
U
V
W
X
Y
Z

Pyrenean Shepherd

Average height: Rough-faced: dogs 15.5-18.5 inches; bitches 15-18 inches
Smooth-faced: dogs 15.5-21 inches; bitches 15.5-20.5 inches
Average weight: An absolute minimum of weight is required; just enough flesh to cover the bones, the ribs felt easily.

Appearance

The Pyrenean Shepherd is a sinewy, lively dog in which there are two varieties, Smooth-faced and Rough-faced, in both of which there are two coat types, semi-long and long. The Smooth-faced dogs appear more square than the Rough-faced ones. The head is generally triangular in shape, rather small in proportion to the size of the dog and well-filled-in under the eyes; the top skull is nearly flat. The almond-shaped eyes are open and very expressive with an alert, intelligent, cunning look, even a little mischievous. The eyes are dark brown in color, partially or completely blue eyes only being

Below: This energetic breed must be given the opportunity to do work of some kind.

Johnson

acceptable in merles. Eye rims are always black. The sides of the skull blend gently into the muzzle, giving the head a triangular wedge shape; in Smooth-faced dogs, the muzzle is slightly longer and more pointed than in the Rough-faced dog. A scissors bite is strongly preferred, but a level bite is admissible. Ears may be cropped or uncropped; when natural they are semi-pricked, with a third to a half of the leather falling either straight forward or to the side. The topline is firm and strong, the tops of the rather long shoulder blades clearly project above the line of the back, which is level, but the loin is slightly arched and slightly higher than the top of the shoulder blades. The tail may be docked, a natural bob, or naturally long, all being equally acceptable. Coat quality is more important than abundance; color is fawn (from tan to copper), with or without a mixture of black hairs; gray (from charcoal to silver to pearl grey); merle; brindle; black or black with white markings A little white is acceptable on the chest, head, and feet.

The Rough-faced dog's coat can be of long or semi-long hair, which is almost flat or slightly wavy; semi-longs have culottes on the rump, while the long-haired dogs are often more heavily furnished with woollier hair that may even cord,

especially on the elbows, croup and thighs. The harsh-textured coat is halfway between the hair of a goat and the wool of a sheep; undercoat is minimal. On the end of the muzzle and the chin the hair must be naturally short, lengthening as the muzzle widens toward the skull. Longer hair on the sides of the muzzle and cheeks is swept back giving a windblown look. Eyes are readily visible.

In the Smooth-faced variety the muzzle is covered with short, fine hairs, somewhat longer on the sides of the head, blending into a modest ruff. Body hair is fine and soft, attaining a maximum length of no more than 3 inches for the ruff and culottes, 2 inches along the back. The fronts of the legs are covered with short, fine hairs and there is

BREED NOTES

SIZE	GROOMING
✓✓	✓✓
EXERCISE	**LIFESPAN**
✓✓	✓✓

often some furnishing on the elbows and thighs.

Characteristics

The Pyrenean Shepherd is a versatile herder with the intelligence and initiative to adapt to all manner of changing circumstances and hence to meet the shepherd's every need. He has a powerful herding instinct from a very young age and is dominated by his love for his work. He tends to become passionately attached to his owner to the complete exclusion of all others, and is amazingly sensitive to his owner's moods. He makes a good companion and is affectionate with the members of his immediate family, but rather distrustful of strangers. When well-socialized from a young age he has a very lively, cheerful disposition.

Origins and History

Some say that the Pyrenean

Sheepdog was the original dog of the Cro-Magnon people who painted the cave at Lascaux. Certain it is that bones of small dogs abound in Neolithic sub-fossil deposits, and that sheep and goat herding were so well developed in the Pyrenees that by 6,000 BC the ecology of the region had been transformed by overgrazing. Herding has been the mainstay of the economy of the High Pyrenees and this ancient lifestyle persists even into the present century. While the Great Pyrenees guarded the flocks against predation by bears, wolves and lynxes, the Pyrenean Shepherd was used solely for herding and not for protection. These smaller dogs were quicker and more sure-footed on the windy crags, and they needed less food. Both varieties of the Pyrenean Shepherd were granted full recognition in France in 1926 and in the 19th century some came to

Above: An intelligent and versatile herder.

North America with flocks of sheep from the Pyrenees.

Health Issues

The Pyrenean Shepherd is a very healthy breed but a few health problems crop up occasionally including hip dysplasia, epilepsy and Progressive Retinal Atrophy (PRA).

Exercise and Grooming

This energetic breed needs the opportunity to carry out work of some form or another. He excels at herding, agility, flyball, tracking, protection, obedience and rescue work. Both coat types are surprisingly easy to manage with weekly brushing; this is particularly necessary for the long-haired dogs whose coat can cord if left unattended.

Rat Terrier

Average height: Miniature: 10-13 inches
Standard: over 13 inches to 19 inches
Average weight: 10-25 pounds

Appearance

The Rat Terrier comes in two sizes, but is always sturdy and compact. His head is fairly long with well-developed cheek muscles, the topskull slightly domed and the muzzle medium long, straight and tapered, but not snipy. His eyes are slightly prominent and portray a lively but soft, gentle expression. The strong jaws are of sufficient length to carry game easily and the evenly spaced teeth usually meet in a scissors bite, but level is acceptable. His V-shaped ears are prick, semi-prick or buttoned; there is no preference, but both ears should be the same! Forelegs are straight and the ribs fairly long, well

Below: Determined little workers!

sprung to allow for good expansion. He has long, powerful thighs and his tail is preferably docked, shorter than on the Fox or Jack Russell Terriers. The short, dense coat is soft to medium hard, with a sheen, and he comes in a wide variety of colors.

Characteristics

Because he is not a sparring breed, the Rat Terrier is generally friendly or just inquisitive with dogs he does not know. He is active, alert and always on the move, whether he is hunting or playing. This is a very vociferous breed that mumbles, growls and snarls. He is highly responsive to his owner and is loyal, affectionate and faithful; generally the Rat Terrier is friendly towards

BREED NOTES	
SIZE	GROOMING
✓	✓
EXERCISE	LIFESPAN
✓✓	✓

people, but he is protective and may be aloof or reserved toward strangers. Most Rat Terriers are good with children, especially if they are part of the family.

Left: A fine example with prick ears.

2,501 rats in a period of seven hours!

Health Issues

This is a hardy, long-lived breed with an average life expectancy of 12 to 18 years. Eye problems, hip and elbow dysplasia are rarely seen in the Rat Terrier, but he is susceptible to allergies and patella luxation has been reported. Demodectic mange has also been seen in the breed and is thought to be an inherited defect. Rat Terriers may also be sensitive to some anesthetics.

Origins and History

The Rat Terrier originated in America and was created by a mixture of crosses including old time Fox Terriers and other European Terriers that were common in the 19th century; these included the Old English White Terrier, Manchester Terrier and Bull Terrier. Later these were crossed with Beagles, more Smooth Fox Terriers, Toy Fox Terriers, Whippets, Italian Greyhounds and

Below: This young pup is already very alert.

other Feist breeds that may have been available. The Whippets and Italian Greyhounds increased speed and versatility to cope with the Kansas Jack Rabbits that were plaguing crops in the Midwest, while the Beagle brought out a stronger prey and pack drive for hunting. From 1910 to 1930 this was one of the most common farm dogs. Together, these early crosses gave the breed speed and nose, as well as the good disposition for which the Rat Terrier is known today. One Rat Terrier is reputed to have killed

Exercise and Grooming

This is a lively, energetic breed that needs a fair amount of exercise and enjoys many dog sports including agility and obedience. Coat care is minimal, but it should be brushed regularly to keep skin and coat in a healthy condition.

Below: The head has well-developed cheek muscles.

Redbone Coonhound

Average height: dogs – 22-27 inches; bitches – 21-26 inches
Average weight: 50-70 pounds

Appearance

The Redbone is a strong, robust, handsome Coonhound with a clean, well-modeled head, medium stop and pleading expression. His long, hanging ears extend to beyond the tip of his nose when following a scent, his saber-like tail with its slight brush is held upright. A scissors bite is preferred, but an even bite is acceptable. His feet are compact and cat-like, with thick, strong pads. The Redbone's withers are slightly higher than his hips, his chest deep and broad with well-sprung ribs to provide optimal lung capacity, denoting stamina. His short, smooth coat is coarse enough to provide protection and a solid red color is preferred. A dark muzzle and small amount of white on brisket and feet is permissible.

Characteristics

This is a happy, even-tempered hound who is usually very good with children. He can be very affectionate and seems to love being with his people. If raised in a household situation from puppyhood the Redbone Coonhound adapts well to family life and is always anxious to please. He is amenable to formal training. Although even-tempered at home, he is an aggressive hunter, hotter-nosed, better able to locate and faster to tree raccoons than many other Coonhounds. He is alert, quick and able to work over difficult terrain in all types of weather. He is said to have the thrusting grit of a terrier and the pumping stamina of a husky, a hunter's hot-tailed dream come true!

Origins and History

Red foxhounds were brought to America by immigrants in the late 1700s, and Red Irish Foxhounds were imported before the Civil War. Late the following century some hunters began to breed for hotter-nosed, faster dogs that were swifter at locating and faster at treeing raccoons. To do this they used the hot, swift Irish hounds in their breeding programs, leading to the development of the Redbone Coonhound. Firstly they concentrated on breeding mainly for color and once this eye-catching red color bred true they selected for performance. The Redbone Coonhound is widely used and prized for its speed and agility from lowlands to steep, rocky hills. He has a good cold nose and is an excellent swimmer with a sonorous voice, making a sensible choice for the hunter who wants an honest, versatile and capable trailer.

Health Issues

The Redbone Coonhound seems usually to be a healthy breed.

Exercise and Grooming

This breed requires a lot of physical exercise. Being a born, natural hunter, the Redbone Coonhound has a tendency to run off to hunt if not in a well fenced area when left to exercise without supervision. This breed is a light shedder and occasional brushing is sufficient to keep the coat in good order.

Below: The short, smooth coat is usually solid red.

BREED NOTES	
SIZE	GROOMING
✓ ✓ ✓	✓
EXERCISE	LIFESPAN
✓ ✓ ✓	✓ ✓

Rhodesian Ridgeback

Average height: dogs – 25-27 inches; bitches – 24-26 inches
Average weight: dogs – 85 pounds; bitches – 70 pounds

Appearance

A strong, muscular, active dog, the Rhodesian Ridgeback is handsome, upstanding and athletic, capable of great endurance with good speed. His head is fairly long, the skull flat and broad between the ears, free from wrinkles when in repose. The eyes are bright and sparkling, harmonizing with the coat colour, which is light wheaten to red wheaten. The medium-sized ears are set rather high, fairly wide at the base and carried close to the head. The Rhodesian Ridgeback's jaws are level and strong with well-developed

Johnson

BREED NOTES

SIZE	GROOMING
✓	✓
✓	
✓	

EXERCISE	LIFESPAN
✓	✓
✓	✓
✓	

Left: The short, dense coat is sleek and glossy.

teeth, especially the canines. A scissors bite is preferred. The chest is not too wide, but very deep and capacious and the tail is fairly long, curling slightly upward. The coat is short, dense, sleek and glossy in appearance and the hallmark of this breed is the ridge on the back. This is formed by the hair growing in the opposite direction to the rest of the coat; it is clearly defined, tapering and symmetrical, starting immediately behind the shoulders continuing to a point between the prominence of the hips and containing two identical crowns (whorls) opposite each other.

Characteristics

The Rhodesian Ridgeback is

A
B
C
D
E
F
G
H
I
J
K
L
M
N
O
P
Q
R
S
T
U
V
W
X
Y
Z

dignified and even tempered, but reserved with strangers. In the home he is calm, gentle and obedient, but some do not easily tolerate children as they do not like to be pestered and may not enjoy rough play. He is loyal to his family but has something of a mind of his own. He

Above: The Rhodesian is a dignified hound.

is a fine hunter and ferocious on the hunt. Obedience training is important, as is socialization with people and other dogs. He is intelligent and learns quickly, but can be a bit stubborn when it suits him.

Origins and History

The Rhodesian Ridgeback is sometimes referred to as the African Lion Hound. A native of South Africa, he was developed by the Boer farmers who had a specific need for a serviceable

Left: A healthy litter of pups.

Above: A fine example, showing the distinctive ridge.

Left: The eyes are bright and sparkling.

hunting dog in the wilds. In the 16th and 17th centuries, immigrants to South Africa took with them their Danes, Mastiffs, Greyhounds, Bloodhounds, Terriers and other breeds, but in 1701 European immigration was closed for a hundred years so native dogs played an important part in the development and ultimate character of the Ridgeback. The Hottentots had a hunting dog that was half-wild, with a ridge on his back formed by the hair growing forward. This dog was bred with the settlers' own dogs, establishing the foundation of the breed we know today as the Rhodesian Ridgeback. It was in 1877 that Rev. Helm introduced

A
B
C
D
E
F
G
H
I
J
K
L
M
N
O
P
Q
R
S
T
U
V
W
X
Y
Z

two of these dogs into Rhodesia where they excelled at hunting lions on horseback. They were highly appreciated for their exceptional hunting qualities and were bred and raised in the country, the ridge on the back

Opposite: Coat color ranges from light wheaten to red wheaten.

Below: Relaxing on a nice comfy blanket.

becoming a unique trademark. In 1922 a group of Rhodesian breeders set up a standard for the breed and this has changed little since then. The breed arrived in the USA in 1950 and was admitted to AKC registration in 1955.

Health Issues
Health problems that have been encountered in the Rhodesian Ridgeback include hip and elbow

dysplasia, thyroid problems, cataracts, dermoid sinus and cysts.

Exercise and Grooming
This breed has great stamina and therefore needs lots of exercise, but he will generally adapt to his owner's exercise regime. The short coat is easy to groom with a firm bristle brush. Baths should only be given when necessary.

Rottweiler

Average height: dogs – 24-27 inches; bitches – 22-25 inches
Average weight: 80-120 pounds

Appearance

The Rottweiler is a robust and powerful dog, his compact and substantial build denoting great strength, agility and endurance. Males are characteristically more massive throughout with larger frame and heavier bone than

Johnson

BREED NOTES

SIZE	GROOMING
✓ ✓ ✓	✓
EXERCISE	LIFESPAN
✓ ✓ ✓	✓ ✓

Left: The head is broad between the ears.

Opposite top: A puppy always seems ready for a game.

Opposite bottom: These pups show the breed's characteristic markings.

bitches, who are distinctly feminine, but without weakness. The head is broad between the ears with strong, broad upper and lower jaws and a scissors bite. Ears are pendant and triangular in shape, well set apart with the inner edge lying tightly against the head. The chest is roomy, broad and deep, reaching to the elbow, with a well pronounced forechest and well-sprung, oval ribs. His back is straight and strong, the loin short, deep and well muscled. The Rottweiler's

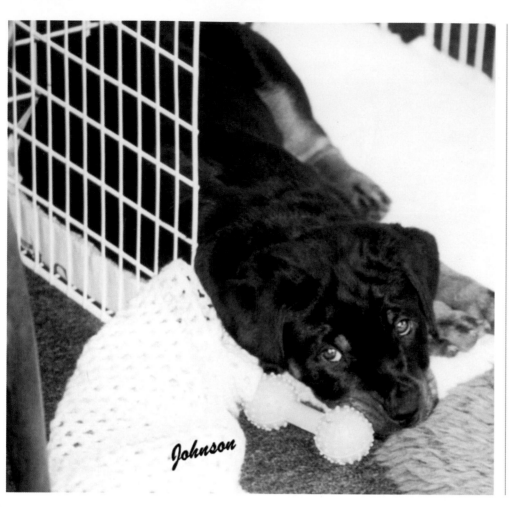

tail is docked short, close to the body, leaving one or two vertebrae. The outer coat is straight, coarse, dense, of medium length and lies flat, while the undercoat is present on neck and thighs, the amount influenced by climatic conditions. This breed is always black with rust to mahogany markings.

Characteristics

This is basically a calm, confident and courageous breed with a self-assured aloofness. He has a

Left: *Puppies usually consider the crate a "safe place".*

Below: *This pup is already trained for the show ring.*

Above: *A robust and powerful breed.*

Right: *Moving out in the showring.*

reliable temperament but is protective and will defend his family fiercely. His temperament does not lend itself to immediate and indiscriminate friendships. He is self-confident and responds quietly with a "wait-and-see" attitude to influences in his environment. He is intelligent and has a strong willingness to work, making him especially suited as a companion,

A
B
C
D
E
F
G
H
I
J
K
L
M
N
O
P
Q
R
S
T
U
V
W
X
Y
Z

guardian and general all-purpose dog. Early socialization and training is important and, if brought up sensibly with children, they can get along well. The same applies to other household pets, but it is important that the Rottweiler has had a positive experience with them while still young.

Origins and History
It is likely that the Rottweiler is

Opposite and above right: Calm, confident, and courageous, with self-assured aloofness.

Above and right: Socialization and training is important for the Rottweiler.

descended from one of the drover dogs indigenous to ancient Rome. This dog was very probably of Mastiff-type, a dependable, rugged, willing worker with great intelligence and a strong guarding instinct. Large armies were needed by the Romans when conquering Europe and meat for the soldiers had to accompany the troops "on the hoof"; dogs were needed for herding and these same dogs were put on guard at night. During the Middle Ages the Rotweiller was bred in the German town of Rotweil where he was used largely to drove cattle and also for carting. But in the middle of the 19th century cattle driving was outlawed and the donkey and railroad replaced the

dog cart so the "butcher's dog", as he was then usually called, fell on hard times. In the early years of the following century the breed was revived, due largely to some enthusiastic breeders in Stuttgart. He found favour as a police dog and several breed clubs were formed, since when the breed has never really looked back, despite the difficulties encountered during and in the aftermath of World War II. Today the Rottweiler is used for tracking, herding, guarding, police work, carting, competitive obedience and as a watchdog and schutzhund.

Health Issues
Health problems that can be encountered in this breed include hip and elbow dysplasia, von Willebrand's

Left: Training a puppy with the aid of a tid bit.

Below left and right: A youngster and a veteran.

disease, subaortic stenosis, hypothyroidism and eye problems.

Exercise and Grooming

The Rottweiler needs plenty of work and exercise, indeed it hardly possible to give him too much as he thrives on it. He loves a good run in the woods or in open country and generally has no desire to wander off. A firm bristle brush is needed for regular grooming, but this is undemanding. Baths need only be given occasionally.

Right: The chest is roomy, broad and deep.

Below: Displaying the many attributes of the breed.

A
B
C
D
E
F
G
H
I
J
K
L
M
N
O
P
Q
R
S
T
U
V
W
X
Y
Z

Saint Bernard

Average height: dogs – 27.5 inches; bitches – 25.5 inches
Average weight: dogs – 140-180 pounds; bitches – 120-140 pounds

Appearance
There are two coat types for the Saint Bernard, long and short; of these the longhaired is the more numerous, however in all other respects the dog is very same. This breed has a powerful, strong, muscular body, with a corresponding powerful and imposing head. The massive skull is wide with strongly developed, high cheek bones. Between the eyes is a

BREED NOTES

SIZE	GROOMING
✓	✓
✓	✓
✓	
EXERCISE	**LIFESPAN**
✓	✓
✓	

Left: 'I'm just thinking for a moment.'

deep furrow, which runs upward over the whole skull. The forehead forms noticeable wrinkles, converging toward the furrow. The short muzzle does not taper and its bridge is straight, not arched. The flews of the upper jaw are strongly developed, turning in a beautiful curve into the lower edge, and slightly overhanging; those of the lower jaw are not deeply pendant. A scissors bite is preferable, but it may be even, as long as the teeth are sound and strong. The Saint Bernard has a very substantial, broad nose with wide open nostrils; like the lips, it is always black. The medium-sized eyes are dark brown with an intelligent, friendly expression. The eyelids usually form an angular wrinkle towards the

Left: Puppies at play.

toward children. Some families, though, make not like the fact that he drools.

Origins and History

The true origin of the Saint Bernard is not well documented, but certainly in the 17th century this dog was bred at the Hospice du Grand St Bernard in Switzerland; the most commonly accepted estimated date of its origin is between 1660 and 1670. It is probable that he is descended from Asiatic mastiff-type dogs taken to the region by Roman armies during the first two centuries AD. Until around 1700 they were used by the monks as watchdogs and companions during their winter isolation, accompanying their masters in search of lost or trapped travelers during snowstorms. They had an uncanny way of detecting impending avalanches and learned

inner corner of the eye. Ears stand slightly away from the head at their base, then drop with a sharp bend to the side. The broad back is perfectly straight as far as the haunches, then slopes to the rump and merges imperceptibly into the root of the tail, which is long, very heavy and ends in a powerful tip. Feet are broad, with strong toes and rather high knuckles.

The shorthaired Saint Bernard has a very dense coat that lies smooth and is tough, without feeling rough to the touch. His thighs are slightly bushy and the tail has longer, denser hair at the root, becoming shorter toward the tip. The longhaired dog has medium length hair, plain to slightly wavy, but never rolled or curly, nor shaggy. Usually on the back it is more wavy. The tail is bushy with dense hair of moderate length, but face and ears are covered with short, soft hair. The color of both varieties is white with red, red with white, brindle with white patches, or red and brown-yellow. Specific white markings are

Right: Already an imposing head.

essential on chest, feet, tip of tail, noseband and collar (or spot on the nape).

Characteristics

The Saint Bernard has a steady, kindly temperament. He is intelligent, trustworthy and courageous. A wonderful family companion, he is good-natured, gentle and easy-going, and especially caring and understanding

A
B
C
D
E
F
G
H
I
J
K
L
M
N
O
P
Q
R
S
T
U
V
W
X
Y
Z

Above: *A splendid example of a Champion.*

Below: *A quality youngster.*

their rescue techniques from the monks. They were sent in twos or threes to locate travelers, one or two dogs remaining with the person to provide warmth, while another would go back to the hospice to alert the monks. People who could move were led to the hospice by the dogs. In 1830 the Saint Bernard, then still known as the Hospice Dog, Alpine Mastiff, Holy Dog or Saint Bernard Mastiff, was bred with the Newfoundland, because it was thought its longer hair would offer better protection against the elements. But this proved fruitless as ice formed on the long hair, creating great weight. Through selective breeding the Swiss breeders managed to return the breed to its original type, with longer and shorter coated varieties. In England the Hospice Dog had been imported from 1820 where it had been crossed with the English Mastiff, an English breed standard being written in 1887. But before then Saint Bernards had been exported to several countries from both Switzerland and England, with two very distinctly different types. Now, despite the building of railroad tunnels through the Alps, the Monks have continued to keep these remarkable dogs for

Above and left: Trustworthy, intelligent, courageous and kindly.

companionship and in honor of the Hospice tradition. Over time, Saint Bernards have saved the lives of well in excess of 2,000 people.

Health Issues
Amongst the health problems encountered by the Saint Bernard are hip and elbow dysplasia, entropion, epilepsy, heart defects and bloat.

Exercise and Grooming
Although exercise for puppies and youngsters should be restricted during the period of bone growth (until about two years), in adulthood the Saint Bernard enjoys long walks. The thick coat is actually very easy to clean and groom, brushing with a firm bristle brush. This breed should only be bathed when necessary, so as not to strip the coat of its natural oils. Eyes should be regularly cleaned with water.

Saluki

Average height: dogs – 23-28 inches; bitches may be considerably smaller
Average weight: 50-65 pounds

Appearance

The Saluki immediately gives the impression of grace, speed, endurance and symmetry. His long neck is supple and well-muscled, his chest deep and moderately narrow, his shoulders sloping and set well back, well-muscled, without being coarse. Forelegs are straight and long, the strong hipbones set well apart and the stifle moderately bent. The hocks are low to the ground for galloping and jumping power. The Saluki's back is fairly broad and the

BREED NOTES

SIZE	GROOMING
✓ ✓ ✓	✓ ✓

EXERCISE	LIFESPAN
✓ ✓ ✓	✓ ✓

Left: 'When I sit down I seem to be all legs!'

muscles slightly arched over the loin. His feet are of moderate length, the toes long and well arched. The head is long and narrow, but the skull is moderately wide between the ears; the nose may be black or liver, the eyes are dark to hazel, bright, large and oval, giving a gentle, deep and far-seeing expression. The long ears hang close to the skull and are covered with long, silky hair, while the long low-set tail, carried naturally in a curve, is feathered on the underside with long silky hair. The Saluki's coat is smooth, soft and silky, with slight feather on the legs, back of thighs and sometimes a slight woolly feather on thigh and shoulder. The smooth variety of Saluki is exactly the same as the coated one, except

Above: Tri-colored bitch (left) and dog (right).

Below: A perfect viewing point.

chase and to kill non-canine animals so if there are other pets in the household, careful supervision is an absolute must.

Origins and History

The Saluki, also known as the Gazelle Hound and Persian Greyhound, has a rich history and is believed by many to have been a distinct breed since 329 BC. By the Arabs it was called "ell hor", meaning "the Noble", and was bred just as carefully as the Arab horses, with both speed and endurance in mind. The Saluki has always been used for hunting and is believed also to have been a valued and honoured companion for the Egyptian nobility; indeed it was also mummified, in the same manner as the pharaohs. To the Arabs, the Saluki is unlike any other dog for through the centuries it has been held in high regard, despite Muslim traditions of that region. This breed was allowed to enter into the tents of the nomads and the courtyards of those who had settled homes,

that it has no feathering. Colors within this breed are white, cream, fawn, golden, red, grizzle and tan, tricolor (white, black and tan) and black and tan.

Characteristics

Although originally a hunting dog, the Saluki has a gentle, even-tempered nature. However he rarely shows affection indiscriminately and tends to be loyal only to one person. He needs moderate obedience training in order to balance his hunting instinct with today's lifestyle; his instinct is to

A
B
C
D
E
F
G
H
I
J
K
L
M
N
O
P
Q
R
S
T
U
V
W
X
Y
Z

whereas other dog were considered unclean. Today the Saluki is still highly prized in the Arab world and is used for hunting in many Middle Eastern countries. With the nomads, the Saluki covered a wide region from the Caspian Sea to the Sahara, resulting in a variance both in size and coat. The Saluki was first taken to England in 1840 but really came to the attention of the public in 1895 when the Hon Mrs Florence Amhurst imported one from the kennels of Prince Abdulla in Transjordania. Although in Arabia this hound has been used primarily to kill gazelle both on deep sand and in rocky mountains, in England the breed was used on hare, hunting largely by sight, although he also

Above left and right: Elegant in any pose.

Below: A beautiful example of movement.

has a fair nose. The breed was officially recognised by the AKC in 1927.

Health Issues

Like all members of the sighthound family, the Saluki is sensitive to various anesthetics, so this must be discussed with a vet prior to surgery. The other problem that can particularly affect the breed is bloat.

Exercise and Grooming

A natural athlete, the Saluki adores a good run and a roam around expansive areas. He has such exceptional strength and endurance that he can easily outrun human, so needs supervision as he can so easily get lost or come to harm. The coat is very easy to care for, but the feathering needs regular brushing.

Above: This is only a yawn, but look at those jaws!

Below: A successful winning show dog.

A
B
C
D
E
F
G
H
I
J
K
L
M
N
O
P
Q
R
S
T
U
V
W
X
Y
Z

Samoyed

Average height: dogs – 21-23.5 inches; bitches – 19-21 inches
Average weight: dogs – 45-64 pounds; bitches – 35-50 pounds

BREED NOTES

SIZE	GROOMING
✓	✓
✓	✓
✓	✓

EXERCISE	LIFESPAN
✓	✓
✓	✓
✓	

Left: Combining all the attributes of the breed.

Appearance

The Samoyed is essentially a working dog but combines beauty, alertness and strength with agility, dignity and grace. His body is neither long, nor short but is muscular with a deep chest, well-sprung ribs, straight front, strong neck and he is particularly strong in loin. Males are masculine in their appearance, but without aggressiveness, while bitches are feminine, without and weakness or softness in temperament. Bitches may be slightly longer in back than males. Bone is heavier than might be expected in a dog of this size, but not so massive that it would prevent the speed and agility required of

him. His feet are large and long, slightly spread, but not splayed out, their pads thick and tough with a protective growth of hair between the toes. The tail is profusely covered with long hair is carried over the back or side when alert. The Samoyed's skull is wedge-shaped, the muzzle of medium length and width with some depth to it. The lips are black for preference and slightly curved up at the corners, giving that distinctive "Samoyed smile". The deep set eyes, which are dark for preference, are almond shaped with a slant to the lower lid. The strong, thick ears are held erect and are slightly rounded at the tip. Because of his work in cold climates the coat

is highly weather resistant. The double coat is pure sparkling white, white and biscuit, cream, or all biscuit. The undercoat is soft, short and thick, while the outercoat stands straight out from the body. Framing the head, round the neck and shoulders is a ruff, more evident on males than females.

Characteristics

Quick-witted, inquisitive and mischievous, the Samoyed is an intelligent dog with a gentle and companionable character. His nature makes him well suited as a therapy dog but he is still used as a sled dog, for herding and as a watch dog. Although he can be independent, he is very loyal and is devoted to his family members.

Origins and History

A member of the Spitz family, the Samoyed was bred by the nomadic Samoyede tribes in north-east Siberia; for generations these nomads were dependent on their reindeer herds, also depending on their dogs which were used as reindeer herders, sled dogs and household companions. The Samoyed bred true through the centuries and is believed to be most nearly akin to the primitive dog. Constant companionship with man has given him an almost uncanny human understanding, but his long association with humans has not created a pampered pet. The breed has a wonderful record of achievement in Arctic and Antarctic expeditions, indeed the first dog to set foot on the South Pole was a Samoyed; this was the lead dog of Roald Amundsen's team in 1911. England's Queen Alexandra was a fancier of the breed and descendents of her dogs are found in many English and American kennels today.

Health Issues

This is generally a healthy breed but can encounter problems with hip dysplasia, hypothyroidism, von Willebrand's Disease and glaucoma.

Exercise and Grooming

The Samoyed needs a reasonable amount of exercise and will enjoy a good long leash walk and plenty of free run. It is generally wiser not to over exercise Samoyeds during hot weather as their thick undercoat limits the necessary loss of body heat. The coat requires extensive grooming using a metal comb to penetrate deeply, thereby removing dead hair. A mild shampoo should be used for bathing so as not strip the coat of its natural oils.

Below left and right: The "Samoyed smile".

A B C D E F G H I J K L M N O P Q R S T U V W X Y Z

A
B
C
D
E
F
G
H
I
J
K
L
M
N
O
P
Q
R
S
T
U
V
W
X
Y
Z

Schapendoes

Average height: dogs – 17-20 inches; bitches – 15.5-18.5 inches
Average weight: 33 pounds

Appearance

The Schapendoes has a distinctive, shaggy appearance, often with a wave to the coat. The undercoat is soft and all colors are acceptable, those between blue-gray and black being ideal. The strong head has a moderate furrow, the parting of the hair on the topskull enhancing this. The broad, strong muzzle carries a substantial beard and mustache. The chest is deep but not broad, and the back is long, strong and straight. The high-set tail is very thick, used as a rudder when jumping. Because he is fairly lightly built he is correspondingly light-footed and has a springy action.

Characteristics

High-spirited and friendly, this breed is intelligent and alert. The Schapendoes tends to gallop rather than trot and can jump and turn quickly, with little effort. He develops great affection and loyalty to people with whom he is familiar.

Origins and History

Known also as the Dutch Sheepdog, he has been valued in the Netherlands for centuries. He bears a resemblance to other European herding dogs such as the Bearded Collie, Polish Lowland Sheepdog, Briard and Bergamasco to which he is thought to be related. Primarily a herding breed,

numbers declined in the first half of the 20th century when many Dutch farmers sold off their lands. The popularity of the Border Collie also had a negative aspect on the number of Schapendoes that were retained and through the war years the breed was threatened with extinction. A specialist club for the breed was founded in Holland in 1947, the breed standard being established and Stud Book started in 1954. The breed was officially recognised in 1971 and has become increasingly popular in Europe, but in America this is still a rare breed.

Health Issues

Schapendoes breeders are recommended, and in some countries obliged, to check for hereditary eye defects including Progressive Retinal Atrophy (PRA) and cataracts.

BREED NOTES

SIZE	GROOMING
✓ ✓	✓ ✓ ✓
EXERCISE	**LIFESPAN**
✓ ✓ ✓	✓ ✓

Exercise and Grooming

The Schapendoes needs reasonable exercise and enjoys many different sports and activities, including herding, for which he was bred. The long coat needs obvious care, but it is essential that the Schapendoes is not overgroomed; this is first and foremost a natural breed.

Johnson

Schipperke

Average height: dogs – 11-13 inches; bitches – 10-12 inches
Average weight: dogs – 15-18 pounds; bitches – 11-15 pounds

Appearance

The Schipperke is a small, thick-set, cobby little dog with a fox-like face. Square in profile, he has a slightly arched neck which, in balance with the rest of the dog, gives the correct silhouette, appearing to slope from shoulders to croup. The chest is broad and deep, reaching to the elbows, while the loin is short and muscular, moderately drawn up. The hindquarters appear slightly lighter than the forequarters, but are well muscled, the croup broad and well-rounded and the tail docked so short that no tail is discernable. His expression is questioning, mischievous, impudent and alert. The upper jaw is moderately filled in under the eyes so, when viewed from above, the head forms a wedge that tapers smoothly from the back of the skull to the tip of the nose. The muzzle is slightly shorter than the length of the skull. The small, triangular ears are placed high on the head and when at attention are very erect. It is essential that the Schipperke's bite

Below: Small, thick-set and cobby, with fox-like face.

A
B
C
D
E
F
G
H
I
J
K
L
M
N
O
P
Q
R
S
T
U
V
W
X
Y
Z

Above: An excellent and faithful little watchdog.

is scissors or level. The coat of the adult Schipperke is highly characteristic, made up of several lengths, growing naturally. On face, ears, front of the forelegs and hocks it is short, of medium length on the body and longer on ruff, cape, jabot and culottes. There is a soft under coat, while the outercoat is straight and slightly harsh to the touch. In America the only permissible coat color is black, but abroad other whole colors are also allowed.

Characteristics

The Schipperke is curious fellow, interested in everything around him and always in search of adventure. He makes an excellent and faithful little watchdog. With strangers he is rather reserved and is always ready to protect his family and property if he deems it necessary. He has a confident and independent personality, which reflects his original purpose as a watchdog and hunter of vermin. The Schipperke is generally good with children and loves to learn, enjoying activities such as obedience, agility, flyball, tracking and herding.

Origins and History

Although visually the Schipperke may appear to be derived from one of the Spitz breeds, he has actually descended from a black sheepdog known as the Leauvenaar. This dog weighed around 40 pounds and used to follow wagons along the old highways of Belgium. By the middle of the 19th century, some of these dogs were still herding sheep in the area of Louvain, and it is from him that both the Belgian Sheepdog (Groenendale) and Schipperke have developed. A specialty club was formed for the Schipperke in 1888, until which time he had been known as "Spitz" or "Spitzke". His modern name is Flemish for "little captain" but although he has a reputation as a canal-boat dog, he was also popular with shoemakers and other workmen. Legend has it that the custom of cutting off the Schipperke's tail dates back to 1609 when a shoemaker cut off the tail to show its improved appearance; this was copied by others and the practise has continued until today. Some Schipperkes are actually born tailless, but there is little evidence that this was common centuries ago. The breed first arrived in America in 1888 but although a club was formed in 1905, it died out during the First World War. It was, however, revived several years afterward and the present Schipperke Club of America was founded in 1929.

Health Issues

This is a healthy breed that is generally long-lived, but the following health problems can occasionally be encountered: epilepsy, Legg-Calves Perthes disease and thyroid troubles.

Exercise and Grooming

This is an energetic breed that is seemingly tireless. Apart from leash walks, he loves to run around his own yard or, better still, a park or open field. The Schipperke is a natural breed and the only trimming that may be done is on the whiskers and between the pads of the feet. Although he seems to take care of his own coat very well, he should be brushed two or three times each week. A good time to bath him is when his coat is "blowing"; this is roughly a ten day period when he loses all his undercoat.

Scottish Deerhound

Average height: dogs – 30-32 inches; bitches – 28 inches upwards
Average weight: dogs – 85-110 pounds; bitches – 75-95 pounds

Appearance

The Scottish Deerhound is one of the largest of the Hound breeds, somewhat resembling a rough-coated Greyhound, but larger both in size and bone structure, and yet he is not so heavy as the Irish Wolfhound. His head is broadest at the ears, narrowing slightly to the eyes, the muzzle tapering more decidedly to the nose. The head is long, the skull flat rather than round with a very slight rise over the eyes. The nose is black (or blue in some blue-fawns) and is slightly aquiline. He carries a good mustache and a beard. His ears are set on high and in repose they are folded back. They are soft, dark and glossy, like a mouse's coat to the touch and the smaller the better. The neck, which has a mane, is strong enough to hold a stag and though long, it is not excessively so, as this would create weakness. The nape is very prominent where the head is set on and the shoulders are

Below: "Lilly" at 14 weeks with her dam, "Lottie".

BREED NOTES

SIZE	GROOMING
✓✓✓	✓✓

EXERCISE	LIFESPAN
✓✓✓	✓✓

Johnson

A
B
C
D
E
F
G
H
I
J
K
L
M
N
O
P
Q
R
S
T
U
V
W
X
Y
Z

well-sloped, the blades well back without too much width between them. The Deerhound's eyes should be dark, they are moderately full with a soft look in repose but a far seeing look when he is roused. The chest is deep rather than broad, a good girth of chest being indicative of great lung power. The loin is well-arched and droops to the tail, which tapers and reaches to within 1? inches of the ground. It is well covered with hair and held down or curved when still, but raised, though never out of line with the back, when in motion. The Deerhound's legs are broad and flat, the forelegs as straight as possible

and at the rear the stifles are well bent, with great length from hip to hock. The hindquarters are drooping and should be as broad and powerful as possible, the hips being set wide apart. The coat on body, neck and quarters is harsh and wiry, about 3 to 4 inches long; on head, breast and belly it is much softer. The ideal coat is thick, close-lying and ragged, harsh or crisp to the touch. In America a dark blue-grey coat is preferred, but this is really a matter of fancy. The coat may indeed be various shades of gray, brindle, sandy red or red fawn, but the latter are rarely seen in modern times. Although a little

Above: Deerhounds at the grave of Sir Walter Scott's "Maida".

white is permissible on chest, toes and as a tip at the stern, this is a self-colored hound, so the less white the better!

Characteristics
The Scottish Deerhound is a remarkable breed, for he has so much strength and power and yet is so docile and gentle. He is an obedient, quiet-mannered easy-going hound, and a thoroughly faithful companion. He is both affectionate and friendly and is excellent with children, although

636

Above: Enjoying the chase.

understandably supervision is necessary with toddlers, merely because of the disparity in size. The Deerhound carries himself with quiet dignity, is keen and alert, and although not aggressive, has great persistence and indomitable courage.

Origins and History

In history the Scottish Deerhound was called by many names including Scotch Greyhound, Rough Greyhound and Highland Deerhound. Certainly the breed has been clearly identifiable since the 16th and 17th centuries and, as his name implies, was best suited to the pursuit of deer. Not only did he course deer in open country, but could also overtake a wounded stag and hold it at bay; for this he needed both strength and speed. The breed has always been held in high esteem and at one time no-one lower than the rank of Earl was allowed to own one; indeed at times the desire for exclusive ownership has endangered the continuance of the breed. In Britain, the Highlands of Scotland was the last territory where the wild stag remained

numerically strong, and Scotland therefore became the last stronghold of this wonderful breed. By the late 18th century the breed had fallen seriously into decline but in about 1825 was successfully restored to its former glory. Today the Deerhound is one of a very few breeds that closely resembles his early ancestors in type, size and character.

Health Issues

Like all sighthound breeds, the Deerhound is sensitive to some anesthetics so it is essential to discuss this with the veterinarian prior to surgery. Health problems that can affect the breed include osteosarcoma (bone cancer), cardiomyopathy (heart disease), liver shunt and bloat.

Exercise and Grooming

Despite his large size, the Deerhound is usually very obedient when walking on a leash, but of course he also enjoys a really good run in a safe area. Many Deerhounds participate successfully in coursing or lure coursing. The harsh, wiry coat sheds very little, so needs fairly regular attention to prevent matts from forming. A rubber brush is useful to remove dead hair and also for massaging the skin, and a wide-toothed metal comb can be used to put the finishing touches. Bathing is not really necessary if the coat is kept clean and in good order, but some owners of Deerhounds do like to bath them occasionally.

Below: "Lottie" at home in the countryside.

Scottish Terrier

Average height: 10 inches
Average weight: dogs – 19-22 pounds; bitches – 18-21 pounds

Appearance

The Scottish Terrier is a small, compact, short-legged dog, sturdily built and with good bone and substance. His head is long in proportion to his overall length and size, the skull slightly domed and covered with short, hard hair, but in profile the skull appears flat. His eyes are set in under his brow, contributing to his characteristic keen, piercing, varminty expression. The cheeks are flat and clean, the muzzle approximately equal to the length of the skull, with only a slight taper toward the nose. It is said that a correct Scottish Terrier muzzle should fill an average man's hand. Regardless of coat color, the nose should be black and of good size, slightly projecting over the mouth. Teeth are large and evenly spaced, meeting in a scissors or level bite. His small, prick ears, set well up on the skull and covered with short velvety hair are never cut. The fairly short, strong, thick, muscular neck blends smoothly into the well-laid shoulders, while the body is moderately short with the ribs extending well back into a short, strong loin and very muscular hindquarters. His chest is broad, very deep and well let down between the forelegs which are very heavy in bone, straight or slightly bent. The tail is about seven inches long and always natural; it is set on high and carried erectly, either vertical or with a slight curve

BREED NOTES

SIZE	GROOMING
✔ ✔	✔ ✔ ✔
EXERCISE	LIFESPAN
✔ ✔	✔ ✔

forward. The Scottish Terrier has a weather-resistant, broken coat that comprises a hard, wiry outer coat with a soft, dense undercoat; it should be trimmed and blended into the furnishings to give a distinct Scottish Terrier outline. The longer coat on the beard, legs and lower body may be slightly softer than the main body coat. His color is black, wheaten or brindle of any color, and many black and brindle dogs have a sprinkling of white or silver hairs in their coat; otherwise only a very little white is allowed on chest and chin.

Characteristics

This is a determined and thoughtful dog whose "heads up, tails up" attitude conveys both fire and control. He is alert and spirited but also stable and steady-going. With people he is loving and gentle, but

can be aggressive with other dogs. The Scottish Terrier exudes ruggedness and power, living up to his nickname, the "Diehard."

Origins and History

The Scottish Terrier is believed to have originated sometime during the 16th and 17th centuries, so is one of the oldest and most recognisable

of the Terrier breeds. The breed was first classified at a show in Birmingham, England, in 1860 but, strange as it may seem today, it was not Scottish Terriers that were shown, but Skye Terriers, Dandie Dinmonts, and Yorkshire Terriers! But the Scotsmen who saw these other dogs winning were indignant and long discussions waxed furious in the Live Stock Journal. As a result, by 1880 a breed standard had been drawn up and this was accepted by all parties. Since that time there have been only minor changes to the standard. The first

Scottish Terriers known to have been imported to the USA came in 1883 and the first one was registered the following year.

Health Issues

Generally a healthy breed, there are a few health problems encountered in the breed; these include Scottie Cramp, von Willebrand's Disease, Cushing's disease, hypothyroidism, epilepsy and craniomandibular osteopathy (CMO).

Exercise and Grooming

The Scottish Terrier is a playful companion and enjoys accompanying his owner on long walks and taking part in a good ball game. He should have a small, enclosed yard in which to engage in his own exercise too. His wiry coat needs brushing at least a couple of times each week, more frequently at shedding time. He will need professional grooming about twice a year, in order to keep his characteristic shape.

Below: The Scottie is loving and gentle with people, but also alert and spirited.

Sealyham Terrier

Average height: 10.5 inches
Average weight: dogs – 23-24 pounds; bitches slightly less

Appearance

The Sealyham Terrier embodies power and determination; he has extraordinary substance and yet is free from clumsiness. His head is long, broad and powerful, its length being roughly ? of the dog's height at withers, and roughly an inch longer than his neck. The skull is very slightly domed with a shallow indentation between the brow, while the cheeks are smooth and flat. The Sealyham's teeth are sound and strong, set in powerful jaws and meeting in a scissors or level bite. His very dark, deep-set eyes present a keen Terrier expression and his ears, folded level with the top of the head, have their forward edge hanging close to the cheek. The shoulders are sufficiently wide to permit freedom of action and the forelegs strong with good bone, and as straight as the well-let-down chest will allow. The hind legs are longer and not so heavily boned. The topline is level, leading to powerful hindquarters that protrude well behind the set on of the tail, which is docked and carried upright. His weather-resistant coat is made up of a soft, dense undercoat and hard, wiry top coat, its color all white, or with lemon, tan or badger markings on head and ears.

Characteristics

This is an outgoing and friendly dog who is devoted and loyal to his family. He has a "big dog" bark so makes a good watchdog as he is keen, alert and determined, bearing all the characteristics of a true Terrier. Generally he has a calm and relaxed disposition and is reputed to be very good with children because of his playful attitude and outgoing

BREED NOTES	
SIZE	GROOMING
✓ ✓	✓ ✓ ✓
EXERCISE	LIFESPAN
✓ ✓	✓ ✓

Johnson

personality. Thanks to having been bred to work originally in a pack, he usually gets along well with other dogs, particularly those of similar size.

Origins and History

The Sealyham was developed by Captain John Edwardes between 1850 and 1891, the breed's name deriving from this gentleman's estate in Haverfordwest in south Wales. His aim was to develop a strain of dogs that would be notable for its prowess in quarrying badger, otter and fox, so he set out to create a Terrier that had extreme gameness and endurance, with as much substance as possible in a dog that was both small and fast enough to do battle underground. This sturdy little workman attracted public interest and eventually also found itself on the show bench. The breed's first appearance at a show was in Haverfordwest in 1903 and five years later a group of Welsh fanciers set up a breed club and drew up a standard for the breed; by 1911 the Sealyham had been granted championship status. The breed had arrived in America slightly before then, taking part in working trials and showring exhibition. Remarkably this fearless little breed, that set out as a cross between the Dandie Dinmont, Pembroke Welsh Corgi, Cheshire Terrier, Wirehaired Fox Terrier and West Highland White Terrier, has achieved the accolade of taking the title of Best in Show at Westminster on no fewer than four occasions!

Health Issues

Amongst the health problems to which the Sealyham is prone are Scottie Cramp and von Willebrand's Disease. The breed also seems to be susceptible to skin infections and flea allergies.

Exercise and Grooming

The Sealyham needs moderate exercise, which should be a combination of leash work and free run, always keeping in mind the breed's propensity to disappear down a hole! The coat needs to be brushed two or three times a week and professionally stripped from time to time to maintain the breed's characteristic shape.

Below: Showing all the qualities of this breed.

Shetland Sheepdog

Average height: 13-16 inches
Average weight: 12-18 pounds

Appearance

The Shetland Sheepdog is a small, alert, rough-coated, longhaired working dog; he is sound, agile and sturdy and gives the overall appearance of being moderately long but with no part of him appearing out of proportion. Dogs are visibly masculine, while bitches are decidedly feminine. His head is refined and from the side is a long, blunt wedge, tapering slightly from

BREED NOTES

SIZE	GROOMING
✔ ✔	✔ ✔ ✔

EXERCISE	LIFESPAN
✔ ✔	✔ ✔

Left: Sheltie head, capturing the character of the breed

ears to nose. The chiselling of the head, shape, set and use of ears, together with placement and color of eyes combine to produce the characteristic expression which is alert, gentle, intelligent and questioning. The eyes are dark, but if the dog has a blue merle coat, blue or merle eyes are also permissible. The small ears are flexible and placed high, the majority of the ear being erect with just the tips breaking forward. He has a muscular neck, arched and of sufficient length to carry the head proudly; his back is level and strongly muscled with the abdomen moderately tucked up. There is a slight arch at the loins and the croup slopes gradually to the rear. The tail is long enough to reach the

Right: Blue merle (left) and sable.

hock joint. The Shetland Sheepdog's coat is double, with an outer coat of long, straight, harsh hair and a short, furry undercoat, so dense as to give the entire coat its "standoff" quality. On the face, tips of ears and feet the hair is smooth, while mane, frill and tail are abundantly coated. Colors are black, blue merle and sable (ranging from golden through to mahogany); they are marked with varying amounts of white and/or tan.

Characteristics

This breed is intensely loyal, affectionate and responsive to his owner and family members, but may be reserved toward strangers. The Shetland Sheepdog has a strong desire to please, making him a wonderful companion. In general he gets along with children and other animals. Highly intelligent, he excels at obedience competition, agility, herding and tracking.

Origins and History

The Shetland Sheepdog is a Collie in miniature. He originated in the Shetland Isles off the north-east coast of Scotland where he was bred as a working dog, used primarily to herd and protect the livestock. He was once called the "Toonie", from the word "tun", this being the Norwegian word for farm. From

Below: The three colors of the breed.

A
B
C
D
E
F
G
H
I
J
K
L
M
N
O
P
Q
R
S
T
U
V
W
X
Y
Z

Above and Opposite: These puppies are full of charm and character.

the Border Collie, it is believed that the larger Collie developed on Scotland's mainland, with this smaller version developing on the islands, having been downsized to meet the needs of the Shetlands. The breed was recognised by the English Kennel Club in 1909 when it was called a Shetland Collie. In 1914, following pressure from the Collie breeders, he became known as the Shetland Sheepdog. The first of the breed registered in America was "Lord Scott" in 1911 and the first specialty show was held in 1933. The breed has the instinct to guard property or places and to give watchdog warning, making him

Left: This is a loyal, affectionate breed.

Opposite: The Sheltie has an alert, gentle, intelligent and questioning expression.

A
B
C
D
E
F
G
H
I
J
K
L
M
N
O
P
Q
R
S
T
U
V
W
X
Y
Z

invaluable for work as a farm helper and as protector for the home. He has the constant vigilance required to protect the crofters' cottages, flocks and herds from all kinds of invaders.

Health Issues

Health problems that can be encountered by the Shetland Sheepdog include Progressive Retinal Atrophy (PRA), Central PRA, Collie eye anomaly (also called Sheltie Eye Syndrome), corneal dystrophy, hip dysplasia, luxating patella, thyroid problems and von Willebrand's disease.

Exercise and Grooming

The Shetland Sheepdog has plenty of energy so enjoys a leash walk and the opportunity to get plenty of free exercise. He can adapt to small spaces, but is fairly active indoors too. His coat needs regular brushing and a mild shampoo should be used when bathing.

Opposite: *A moment for quiet contemplation.*

Above and below left: *A black with white and tan*

Below: *Waiting for a game.*

Shiba Inu

Average height: dogs – 14.5-16.5 inches; bitches – 13.5-15.5 inches
Average weight: dogs – 23 pounds; bitches – 17 pounds

Appearance

The Shiba Inu is the smallest of Japan's native dog breeds and was originally developed for hunting by sight and scent in the dense undergrowth of the country's mountainous areas. He has a compact frame with well-developed muscles. His dark brown eyes are somewhat triangular in shape, deep set and upward slanting, with black rims. The triangular ears are firmly pricked and small, well set apart and tilt directly forward. The Shiba's forehead is broad and flat, with a slight furrow, the bridge of the muzzle straight. Lips are tight and black, like the nose, and the full

BREED NOTES

SIZE	GROOMING
✔✔	✔✔
EXERCISE	**LIFESPAN**
✔✔	✔✔

Left: The triangular ears are firmly pricked.

Opposite: The Shiba Inu was bred to hunt by sight and scent.

Johnson

complement of strong teeth meet in a scissors bite. The topline is straight and level to the base of the tail, which is high-set, thick and powerful, carried over the back in a sickle or curled position. This is a double coated breed, the outer coat stiff and straight, the undercoat soft and thick. On face, ears and legs the coat is short. On the tail the hair is slightly longer and stands open in a brush. Three colors are allowed, all are clear and intense. The actual markings on the Shiba are carefully specified, but basically they are bright orange red with urajiro (a cream to white ventral color), black with tan points and urajiro, and

sesame, which is black-tipped hairs on a rich red background, with urajiro.

Characteristics

The Shiba Inu is alert and agile, with keen senses and a spirited boldness. He has a good nature and an unaffected forthrightness. By nature he is independent and can be reserved toward strangers, but is loyal and affectionate to those he

Left: These puppies' heads will soon change shape.

A
B
C
D
E
F
G
H
I
J
K
L
M
N
O
P
Q
R
S
T
U
V
W
X
Y
Z

respects. The Shiba can be aggressive toward other dogs and should always be kept under control when meeting other animals. He makes an excellent watchdog and companion.

Origins and History

The Shiba Inu, the smallest and oldest of Japan's dogs, has been with the Japanese people for centuries. They make excellent watchdogs and have established themselves as the number-one companion dog in Japan. Over time there have been various theories about how the breed came about, some think the name came about because of the way in which he

Left: A sesame coat.

Below: Bounding about!

Johnson

for breeding, the first litter being whelped in 1979. But it took until 1992 for the breed to be admitted to the AKC Stud Book.

Health Issues

Although a sturdy, healthy breed, the Shiba is susceptible to some health problems including patella luxation, hip dysplasia and eye problems, including cataracts. This breed also commonly suffers from allergies related to fleas, foods and inhalants.

Exercise and Grooming

This is an active breed, so needs a good amount of exercise to burn off his excess energy. The Shiba Inu is almost cat-like in his personal cleanliness, so does a lot to keep his coat in good condition himself; naturally, owners also need to groom the coat at least once each week, but this is not overly-demanding.

went freely through the brushwood; indeed sometimes he is referred to as the "Little Brushwood Dog". Others say that "Shiba" relates to the smallness of the breed. Something that is certain is that the name "Shiba" was given to this breed around the 1920s; in 1936 the breed received official recognition and was designated as a precious natural product of the Japanese nation. During the Second World War, it virtually reached extinction but some dogs survived from three different bloodlines and from these the Shiba Inu has evolved into the breed we know today. The first Shiba known in the USA was here in 1954 and in the late 1970s the Shiba was imported

Above: The dark brown eyes are rather triangular in shape.

Below: Bright orange red with tail carried over the back.

Johnson

Shih Tzu

Average height: 8-11 inches (ideally 9-10.5 inches)
Average weight: 9-16 pounds

Appearance

The Shih Tzu is a sturdy, long coated breed, rather longer than he is high and in America is classified in the Toy Group, whereas in some other countries he falls into the Utility category. There is more size variation here than in the UK, but even the smaller specimens should be solid and compact, with good weight for body size. This is a lively, alert dog with a long flowing

BREED NOTES

SIZE	GROOMING
✔	✔
	✔
	✔
EXERCISE	**LIFESPAN**
✔	✔
✔	✔

Johnson

Left: Showing a beautifully characteristic expression.

double coat and a distinctively arrogant head carriage; his heavily plumed tail is carried in a curve well over his back. His head is round and broad, with a warm, sweet, wide-eyed expression that is friendly and trusting. The muzzle is square and short with good cushioning, but unwrinkled and set no lower than the bottom eye rim. The length from tip of nose to stop is ideally not longer than one inch and the front of the muzzle is flat, the nostrils broad, wide and open. The jaw is broad with an undershot bite. The large ears are set slightly below the crown of the skull and are heavily coated. The Shih Tzu's topline is level and he is slightly longer than he is tall, with a broad, deep chest and good spring of rib.

The luxurious double coat, which may be any color, is dense, long and flowing, the hair on top of the head tied in a top-knot. The Shih Tzu moves effortlessly and smoothly, having aptly been described as being like a ship in full sail.

Characteristics

The Shih Tzu's temperament is happy, outgoing, affectionate, friendly and trusting towards all, as befits a breed whose purpose in life is a companion and house pet. He thrives on human companionship and needs the attention of his family, to whom he is utterly devoted.

Above: *Puppies enjoying their food.*

Below: *A high quality black and white youngster.*

A B C D E F G H I J K L M N O P Q R **S** T U V W X Y Z

Origins and History

Some consider the Shih Tzu a Tibetan breed, others think the breed is Chinese. There is an element of truth in both. There are various theories about his origin, but certain it is that he had roots in Tibet for the Lhasa Apso was frequently taken into China, used as a tribute gift for safe passage along the way. These dogs ended up in the royal courts and palaces and inevitably mingled and bred with the Pekingese. The Shar Pei is believed to have been kept as a house pet during the Ming Dynasty (1344-1644) and was highly favored within royal family circles. Later the Shih Tzu became a great favorite of the Dowager Empress Tzu Hsi, who also kept Pekingese and Pugs. She took great care and

Above: In pet trim.

Left: Record breaking Champion.

trouble over their breeding and welfare and there are wonderful records of the remarkable diets the Shih Tzu were fed, including sharks' fins, curlews' livers and antelope milk. After the Empress's death her dogs were dispersed and breeding virtually ceased, and when the Communist Revolution happened the Shih Tzu became almost extinct. Thankfully a few arrived in England and it is to these dogs that all today's Shih Tzu can be traced. A breed club was formed in England in 1935 and the Shih Tzu was admitted to the AKC Stud Book in 1969.

Health Issues

This is generally a healthy long-lived

Above: Champion in full coat.

breed but the following problems can sometimes appear: von Willebrand's Disease, thyroid disorders, renal dysplasia, umbilical hernia, autoimmune haemolytic anemia, Progressive Retinal Atrophy (PRA) and juvenile cataracts.

Exercise and Grooming

The Shih Tzu is a fairly energetic little breed, but he is happy to create his own games, though he will like his family to join in with these games too. He also enjoys a walk on a leash, but all debris must be removed from his coat upon returning home so that knots do not form. His coat is understandably demanding and at least a couple of hours should be put aside each week for grooming, probably three hours if he is also due for a bath.

Below: Gold sable and white puppy.

A
B
C
D
E
F
G
H
I
J
K
L
M
N
O
P
Q
R
S
T
U
V
W
X
Y
Z

Siberian Husky

Average height: dogs – 21-23.5 inches; bitches – 20-22 inches
Average weight: dogs – 45-60 pounds; bitches – 35-50 pounds

Appearance

The Siberian Husky is a medium-sized, moderately compact, working dog; he is quick and light on his feet, free and graceful in action. He does not carry excess weight and is capable of carrying a light load at a moderate speed over great distances. He has a keen, but friendly expression, his almond shaped eyes set a trifle obliquely. They may be brown or blue, or one of each color, or even parti-colored, all being acceptable. The medium-sized skull is slightly rounded on top and tapers from the widest point to the eyes. The bridge of the nose is straight and the muzzle tapers gradually to the nose which is black in gray, tan or black dogs, liver in copper dogs and may be flesh-colored in pure white dogs. A pink-streaked "snow nose" is acceptable. The teeth meet in a scissors bite. The Siberian Husky's ears are triangular in shape, close fitting and set high on the head. The arched neck is carried proudly erect when dog is standing and when he is moving at a trot is extended, so that the head is carried slightly forward. His chest is deep and strong, but not too broad, the ribs flattened on the sides to allow for freedom of

Below: Well-constructed show dog.

Opposite: Geared out in a harness.

BREED NOTES

SIZE	GROOMING
✔	✔
✔	✔
✔	
EXERCISE	**LIFESPAN**
✔	✔
✔	✔
✔	

A
B
C
D
E
F
G
H
I
J
K
L
M
N
O
P
Q
R
S
T
U
V
W
X
Y
Z

Characteristics

The Siberian Husky is generally friendly and gentle, but he is also alert and outgoing. He is not particularly suspicious of strangers, nor is he aggressive with other dogs. He does, though, display a certain measure of reserve and dignity. His intelligence, tractability and eager disposition make the Siberian Husky an agreeable companion and willing worker, although he does likes to see a reason for carrying out commands that are given.

Origins and History

The Siberian Husky was developed in north-eastern Asia by the Chukchi people who needed an endurance sled dog. Changing conditions forced these semi-nomads to enlarge their hunting grounds, so to do this they developed this unique sled dog

Above and right: Litter mates showing contrasting color patterns.

action, while the back is straight, strong and level. His well-furred tail is usually carried over the back in a graceful sickle curve when the dog is at attention, but it is normal for the tail to trail in repose. The double coat is of medium length, presenting a well-furred appearance. The undercoat is soft and dense and the guard hairs of the outer coat are straight and somewhat smooth lying, never harsh nor standing straight off from the body. All colors from black to pure white are allowed and indeed a variety of markings on the head is common, including many striking patterns not found in other breeds.

capable of traveling great distances at moderate speed, while carrying a light load in low temperatures without expending enormous energy. It appears that these dogs remained pure throughout the 19th century and that they are the direct ancestors of the Siberian Husky we know in America today. The first Siberian Husky team appeared in the All Alaska Sweepstakes Race of 1909 and the following year

Siberian Huskies won a grueling 400-mile race. Since then the breed's excellence in this field has become well known and AKC recognition was granted in 1930.

Health Issues

Generally a very healthy breed, the Siberian Husky is sometimes known to suffer from hip dysplasia and eye problems, including juvenile cataracts, corneal dystrophy and

Above left and right: The Siberian Husky displays a certain measure of reserve and dignity.

Progressive Retinal Atrophy (PRA). He can also be susceptible to zinc responsive dermatitis.

Exercise and Grooming

The Siberian Husky needs a fair amount of exercise and should ideally have a large yard with high

A
B
C
D
E
F
G
H
I
J
K
L
M
N
O
P
Q
R
S
T
U
V
W
X
Y
Z

A
B
C
D
E
F
G
H
I
J
K
L
M
N
O
P
Q
R
S
T
U
V
W
X
Y
Z

Above and below: This breed loves to race. These Siberians are all securely tethered and waiting with their own teams, anticipating their turn on the trail.

fencing, which must be very secure at its base. During hot weather, exercise should be moderated. His coat requires minimal grooming, but must be combed regularly

during the shedding season. Trimming of whiskers and hair between the toes and around the feet is permissible.

Silky Terrier

Average height: 9-10 inches
Average weight: lightly built

BREED NOTES

SIZE	GROOMING
✔	✔
	✔
EXERCISE	**LIFESPAN**
✔	✔
	✔

Left: This lovely Silky Terrier has an un-docked tail.

Appearance

The Silky Terrier, known is many countries as the Australian Silky Terrier, is a true "toy terrier". Longer than he is tall, he is moderately low set with refined bone structure. However, he has sufficient substance to hunt and kill domestic rodents. He has a strong, wedge shaped head that is moderately long, small, dark almond-shaped eyes with dark rims and a keen, piercing expression. His nose is black and teeth strong, meeting in a scissors bite, while his small ears are V-shaped, set high and erect. His neck, which is slightly crested, fits gracefully into his sloping shoulders; the chest is deep enough to extend down to the elbows and the topline is level. Although fairly low in stature, the Silky's forelegs are strong and straight. His tail is docked, set high and carried at the "two o'clock" position. His single, glossy coat is silky in texture, parted from the stop between the eyes to the tail to present a well groomed but not sculptured appearance. The coat should not approach floor length, but in maturity falls below the body line and is about 5 to 6 inches long. The bottoms of the legs and the feet have short hair. Color is blue and tan, the latter always a rich tan, but the blue may be pigeon blue or slate blue. The topknot is silver or fawn, which is lighter than the tan points.

Characteristics

The Silky has the keen, alert air if the terrier and has a quick, friendly, responsive manner. But he is not so active as other terriers and yet does not have the gentle lap-dog temperament of many of the toy breeds. His inquisitive nature and joy of life make him an ideal companion who generally enjoys the company of children. He often expresses his curiosity by digging and has a tendency to become a

barker. The Silky enjoys participating in various dog sports and activities.

Origins and History

This breed was developed in Australia around the turn of the 20th century from crossings of native Australian Terriers and imported Yorkshire Terriers, which had been taken to Victoria and New South Wales at the end of the 1800s. As a result, the Silky Terrier encompasses many of the best qualities of both these breeds. The breed was formed when a number of Yorkshire Terriers from England were brought into the Australian states of Victoria and New South Wales at the end of the 1800s. In 1906 a breed standard was fixed, but in 1909 a separate standard was drawn up in Victoria and there were discrepancies between the two. A revised standard came about in 1926 and in an effort prevent further crossings between the breeds the Kennel Control Council of Victoria introduced canine legislation in 1932. Originally the breed was called the Sydney Silky Terrier, but in 1955 in Australia it officially became the Australian Silky Terrier. In the USA the Sydney Silky Terrier Club of America was formed in 1955, but only three months after the club's first meeting members voted to change the name to the Silky Terrier Club of America.

Above: The coat is long, but is not floor length.

Health Issues

The health problems that sometimes occur in this breed include patella luxation, elbow dysplasia, intervertebral disc disease and Legg-Calves Perthes Disease

Exercise and Grooming

The Silky loves to run around and play, but can easily adjust to his owner's living conditions provided he is taken on regular leash walks to stimulate his senses. This is a breed that is usually active around the home. Regular combing and brushing is essential to avoid matts and tangles from forming.

Skye Terrier

Average height: dogs – 10 inches; bitches – 9.5 inches
Average weight: 23-26 pounds

Appearance

The Skye Terrier has style, elegance and dignity. He is agile and strong, with sturdy bone and hard muscle. This is a breed that is long, low and level; in fact he is twice as long as he is high. His head is long and powerful, his dark brown eyes of medium size, close-set and alight with life and intelligence. The gracefully feathered ears may be carried either prick or dropped; if pricked they are placed high on the

Below: A stunning example of this strong, elegant breed.

skull, while drop ears are somewhat larger and hang flat against the skull. The dark muzzle is moderately full as opposed to snippy, the nose is always black and the powerful jaws are absolutely true, meeting in either a scissors or level bite. His chest is deep, with oval-shaped ribs, the forearm curving slightly around the chest. The long tail is well-feathered, following the line of the rump. The Skye Terrier has a double coat, the undercoat short, soft, close and woolly, the outer coat hard, straight and flat. The body coat hangs

BREED NOTES	
SIZE	GROOMING
✔ ✔	✔ ✔
EXERCISE	LIFESPAN
✔ ✔	✔ ✔

Johnson

A
B
C
D
E
F
G
H
I
J
K
L
M
N
O
P
Q
R
S
T
U
V
W
X
Y
Z

and going to ground. He displays stamina, courage, strength and agility. He is reserved and cautious with strangers but is typically friendly and good natured with people he knows. He is fearless, good-tempered, loyal and canny, but should not be left alone with small animals because he loves to chase and can become aggressive with them.

Origins and History

Unlike most of the terrier breeds, the Skye Terrier of nearly four centuries ago was very like the specimens we know today. He takes his name from the Isle of Skye, the principal island off Scotland's north-western coast. In the middle of the 19th century this was the most widely known of all the terriers helped, no doubt, by Queen

Left and opposite top: There is always something rather cutely comical about Skye puppies!

Below: Long and low with a hard, straight, flat coat.

straight down each side, parting from head to tail. Head hair may be shorter with a veil over the eyes and forming a moderate beard and apron. The coat must be of one over-all color at the skin, although it may be of varying shades of the same color in the full coat. This can be black, blue, dark or light grey, silver platinum, fawn or cream. Puppy coat may be very different color from that of the adult coat.

Characteristics

The Skye is a typical working terrier, capable of overtaking game

The Skye Terrier can suffer a severe reaction to Ivermectin, which in this breed can cause paralysis and death. He is also susceptible to the premature closure of the distal radius.

Exercise and Grooming

The Skye Terrier enjoys creating his own exercise and loves to run around and play. His long coat is demanding and ideally needs combing and brushing on a daily basis to prevent matting.

Below: Ears are usually pricked, but may be dropped.

Victoria's early interest and Sir Edwin Landseer's paintings, featuring the breed. The breed is not now a numerically strong but still has many admirers, though gone are the days when "a duchess would almost be ashamed to be seen in the park unaccompanied by her long-coated Skye". From a practical point of view, the Skye's services were called upon wherever there were rocks, dens, burrow, cairns, or coverts to explore, or waters to take to. His flowing coat protected him from the attack of vicious animals that might otherwise have crippled him with a single bite. The Skye Terrier was registered with the AKC in 1887 and remained one of the most important breeds at shows until the century turned. As time has gone on the breed has been surpassed in popularity by other terriers but dedicated breeders are understandably reluctant to change him in any manner.

Health Issues

Sloughi

Average height: dogs – 26-28.25 inches; bitches – 924-26.75 inches
Average weight: 45-60 pounds

Appearance

The Sloughi is a typical oriental sighthound, elegant and racy, yet strong without coarseness. This is a dignified hound with fine skin and muscular leanness, capable of sustained effort over long distances. His long, refined head is an elongated wedge, showing strength without being excessively angular; it has a slightly marked frontal bone and pronounced occiput. His large, dark eyes are set slightly obliquely, giving a gentle expression that is rather sad and wistful. In light-coated hounds, lighter eyes are permissible. Jaws are strong, the teeth meeting in a complete scissors bite. The Sloughi's ears are not too large, triangular in shape and with rounded tips; generally they are folded down, close to the head, but may be carried away from the skull, or even thrown backwards. He has a strong, elegant neck, with slightly loose skin making fine pleats under the throat. The bone in the forelegs is flat and well-muscled, the chest not too broad, with a prominent sternum. The topline is almost level, with a slightly arched, broad, muscular loin. The Sloughi has a lean, elongated hare foot and his fine tail has a strong curve at its end. The coat is fine and short, and an undercoat may grow during the winter period. Color ranges from light sand to red sand, with or without black mask, black mantle, black brindling or black overlay.

BREED NOTES

SIZE	GROOMING
✓ ✓ ✓	✓

EXERCISE	LIFESPAN
✓ ✓ ✓	✓ ✓

Excessive white, however, is undesirable.

Characteristics

Provided he is well socialized, the Sloughi is affectionate, gentle and playful, and extremely devoted to his family. He is intelligent, sensitive, curious and independent, requiring regular exercise to keep him physically fit and to stimulate his senses. He is cautious with strangers, so makes an alert watchdog. Because of the Sloughi's prey drive, early socialization with other family pets is essential, but generally, if sensibly introduced and supervised, he can get along well with other pets and with children too.

Origins and History

The Sloughi is the sighthound of the Berber people of Africa and was

century by General Daumas who was stationed in Algeria. The breed was imported to France and the Netherlands around the close of that century and the first breed standard was drawn up in 1925 by the French Sighthound Association. The French occupation of Algeria, with its political upheavals, disrupted many Sloughi breeding programmes for a law was introduced preventing hunting with sighthounds. This resulted in the shooting of these dogs on sight, as well as epidemic rabies, causing the Sloughi population to be decimated. Even today, the breed is not common in any country and breeders have an important responsibility to conserve this ancient breed. The Sloughi was first imported to the USA in 1973, three years following Algeria's independence.

Health Issues

The only inherited genetic disorder that has been found in the Sloughi is Progressive Retinal Atrophy (PRA). Bloat can also be a problem for Sloughis and, like many sighthounds, the breed can be sensitive to certain anesthetics.

Exercise and Grooming

An energetic running breed, the Sloughi clearly needs plenty of free exercise in a safely enclosed area; this is in addition to walks on a leash. The Sloughi's smooth coat is undemanding, but still it needs regular attention to keep skin and coat healthy. Any dead hair can be removed with a rubber brush, otherwise a soft bristle brush and a chamois leather will leave it looking in tip-top condition.

Opposite and above: An elegant, racy sighthound, strong, without coarseness.

used to hunt gazelle, rabbits, foxes, jackals and wild boar. The breed's exact origins remain speculative but certainly African sighthound-like dogs date back to the 8th-7th millennium BC. It is likely that the lop-eared, smooth Egyptian sighthound originated in Asia but was also closely connected with the Pharaohs of Nubia, south of Egypt. This ancient hound closely resembled the Sloughi, Azawakh and smooth Saluki. In its countries of origin, Morocco, Algeria, Tunisia and Libya, the Sloughi, as a sighthound, was treated as a family member and allowed inside the tent, unlike common dogs. The Sloughi is bred with the same care as an Arab horse and it is said that its owner would go without his own blanket to provide his Sloughi with warmth in the cold desert nights. To aid a nursing mother, Sloughi puppies were often breast fed by Bedouin and Berber women. Often they were decorated with jewelry and amulets and their loss was mourned. Sometimes the Sloughi's legs were ritually branded and ears cropped to prevent their being torn when hunting. The first detailed descriptions of the breed were brought to us in the mid-19th

Smooth Fox Terrier

Average height: dogs – 15.5 inches maximum; bitches proportionately lower
Average weight: dogs – 17-19 pounds; bitches – 16-18 pounds

Appearance

The Smooth Fox Terrier has the appearance of a gay, lively, active dog; he has bone and strength in small compass but is in no way cloddy or coarse. He stands like a cleverly made hunter, covering a lot of ground, and yet having a short back. His flat skull is moderately narrow, gradually decreasing in width to the eyes, which are rather deep set, dark and full of fire, life and intelligence. His ears are V-shaped, small and moderately thick, dropping forward, close to the cheek, the topline of the fold being well above the level of the skull. The Fox Terrier's upper and lower jaws are strong, muscular and of fair punishing strength with the teeth as nearly as possible together. His clean, muscular neck leads into long, sloping shoulders that are fine at the points and clearly cut. His back is short, level and strong, the chest deep but not broad, while his loin is very powerful and slightly arched. His strong tail, which is docked to about ? of its original length, is set rather high and carried gaily, but not over the back. Hindquarters are strong and muscular, the thighs long and powerful. His coat is smooth and flat, but hard, dense and abundant. White is the predominant color.

Characteristics

The Smooth Fox Terrier is very affectionate to his family, but can be jealous, which he is capable of showing in no uncertain manner! He is energetic and playful, but supervision is sensible when playing with children. Highly territorial in nature, he will protect objects, places and food – even from his master. With other dogs he can be competitive and may well pick a fight, so when exercising around other dogs he should be kept on a leash. Introduction to other family pets should be made from a young age. He also loves to hunt, so this should be bone in mind when out exercising. The Smooth Fox Terrier often likes to dig and is also a "bit of a barker". This is an intelligent breed and is generally very loyal.

Origins and History

For many years in the USA, the Smooth and Wire Fox Terriers were

Below: Splendid example of a top winning Champion.

Johnson

considered one breed with two different coat varieties, but it is now believed that the two Fox Terriers probably derived from very different sources. The most important ancestors of the Smooth are believed to be the smooth coated Black and Tan Terrier, the Bull Terrier, the Greyhound and also the Beagle. One of the first records of this distinct breed came in 1790 when Colonel Thornton's "Pitch" was immortalised in print and in paintings. It seems the Smooth preceded the Wire by 15 to 20 years but early breeders crossed the two to give the Wire the predominantly white color, a cleaner-cut head and a more classical outline. This is a breed with a keen nose,

remarkable eyesight and great stamina used in driving foxes and other small animals from their holes. The original breed standard was drawn up in Great Britain in 1876 and the American Fox Terrier Club adopted this standard when it was founded in 1885. In 1984 the AKC approved separate standards for the Smooth Fox Terrier and the Wire Fox Terrier; a ruling that became effective in June, 1985.

Health Issues

Generally an extremely healthy breed, the Smooth Fox Terrier has been known to suffer from post nasal drip, lens luxation, distichiasis, cataracts, Legg-Calves Perthes Disease and

shoulder dislocation. Because his is predominantly white, deafness has also been known to occur.

Exercise and Grooming

This is a high energy dog that enjoys participating in many activities, including agility and flyball. He loves to run free, so needs a safe place in which to exercise off the leash. If not allowed sufficient opportunity he can become destructive and temperamental. His coat requires minimal grooming, but a firm bristle brush should be used to remove hair that is shedding.

Below: The breed has bone and strength.

A
B
C
D
E
F
G
H
I
J
K
L
M
N
O
P
Q
R
S
T
U
V
W
X
Y
Z

Soft Coated Wheaten Terrier

Average height: dogs – 18-19 inches; bitches – 17-18 inches
Average weight: dogs – 35-40 pounds; bitches – 30-45 pounds

BREED NOTES

SIZE	GROOMING
✓ ✓	✓ ✓ ✓
EXERCISE	LIFESPAN
✓ ✓	✓ ✓

Above: A fine example of this well-balanced, sporting terrier.

Appearance

The Soft Coated Wheaten Terrier is a hardy, well balanced sporting terrier that is square in outline, graceful, strong and well-co-ordinated. He is distinguished by his soft, silky, gently waving coat of warm wheaten color. His head is rectangular and moderately long; powerful, but with no suggestion of coarseness. His eyes are a dark reddish-brown or brown, slightly almond shaped and set fairly wide apart. Eye rims and lips are black, as is his nose, which is large for the size of the dog. His teeth are large, clean and white, meeting in a scissors or level bite. His ears break level with the skull, dropping slightly forward and his neck is carried proudly, gradually widening and blending into the body with its strong, level back. The tail is docked and well set on; it is carried gaily, but never over the back. The Soft Coated Wheaten Terrier's coat sets him apart form all other terriers for his is an abundant single coat that covers the entire body, legs and head. The head coat falls forward, shading the eyes. Its texture is soft and silky, with a gentle wave, but in puppies and adolescents the waves are not usually evident. For the showring he is presented in a terrier outline, but the coat must be of sufficient length to flow when he is in motion. The ears are relieved of their fringe, but not taken right down to the leather. Coat color may be any shade of wheaten, although puppies under a year may carry deeper coloring, with occasional black tipping.

Characteristics

The Soft Coated Wheaten is a steady, happy terrier, with an air of self-confidence. He shows less aggression than most other terriers. Always alert, he shows interest in his surroundings and enjoys activity, being ready and willing to learn. This is a lively breed and generally maintains a puppy-like attitude for most of his life. He is very affectionate and thrives on human companionship, showing devotion to his entire family, not just one individual. He has a patient, tolerant nature and is excellent with children.

Origins and History

This breed has been known in Ireland for more than 200 years and has so long been associated with the day-to-day work of the farming

English KC in 1943 and the Soft Coated Wheaten Terrier Club of America was founded, appropriately, on St Patrick's Day in 1962, the breed being admitted to the AKC Stud Book in 1973.

Health Issues

Although generally a healthy breed, the following problems have been known to occur: hip dysplasia, eye problems, protein losing nephropathy (PLN), protein losing enteropathy (PLE) and renal dysplasia. These last three disorders can affect kidney and bowel function, so routine tests are recommended.

Exercise and Grooming

This is an athletic breed that enjoys exercise and is a fun companion for outdoor recreation. He also benefits from moderately long walks on his leash. His thick, long coat needs regular attention, and should be trimmed and bathed roughly every 6 to 8 weeks. Trimming must be done with scissors, not with clippers, nor must it be plucked.

Above and below: Both adults and puppies enjoy the comforts of home.

community that he has rather been taken for granted. The four distinctly separate Irish breeds used to be lumped together under one name, the "Irish Terrier", largely because they were never taken up by wealthy enthusiasts. The current name was adopted in 1937, although then the breed was not officially recognised by the Irish Kennel Club. The Wheaten may be the oldest of the four breeds and is likely to be an important ancestor of the Kerry Blue and Irish Terriers. The Wheaten, like the other Irish terriers, was bred for his working qualities; only the brave, strong and proficient survived and reproduced, so nature really set the standard for the original stock of this breed. He chased otters, badgers, rats and other vermin, besides herding livestock and acting as a guard. At one time he had to qualify in field trials before attaining championship status on the show bench. The breed was registered with the

A
B
C
D
E
F
G
H
I
J
K
L
M
N
O
P
Q
R
S
T
U
V
W
X
Y
Z

South African Boerbel

Average height: dogs – 25-28 inches; bitches – 23-25.5 inches
Average weight: 154-200 pounds

Appearance

The South African Boerboel is a big, strong, intelligent working dog, well balanced with good muscle and buoyant movement. Impressive and imposing, males appear masculine and bitches feminine. The head represents the breed's total character; it is short, broad, deep, square and muscular with well filled cheeks, the top-skull is broad and flat with prominent muscle. The deep, broad muzzle tapers slightly, the loose, fleshy upper lip just covering the lower lip. The strong jaws are deep and broad, the teeth well-developed and the bite scissors. His V-shaped ears are set fairly high and wide. The strong, muscular neck has loose skin under the throat, but taut between the front legs. The broad, straight back has prominent muscles and a short loin; the rump is broad and strong, as is the chest. The tail is straight and short and the large feet well-padded, with dark curved toe-nails. His skin is thick, loose and well pigmented, with moderate wrinkles on the forehead when alert. The coat is short, dense and sleek, its color cream white, pale tawny, reddish brown, brown and all shades of brindle.

Characteristics

The Boerboel is a reliable breed, obedient and intelligent with strong guarding instincts. Self-assured and fearless, with his owners he is playful and affectionate and usually very gentle with children he knows. However, the Boerbel is a protector and can be very aggressive toward other people for he is always fully prepared to guard his family, friends and property. Visitors to the home must be properly introduced in order to gain his acceptance. Generally he gets along well with other dogs, cats and other non-canine pets. This breed requires firm, sensible training so that he knows exactly who is boss.

Origins and History

In 1652 Jan van Riebeeck went to the Cape of South Africa, taking along his own dog to protect him and his family in what was then a wild and unknown country. The dog was known as a "Bullenbitjer", a large, heavy Mastiff-type dog. Similar dogs arrived from many countries and survival being of utmost importance, the hardiness of today's Boerboel was bred into the dog. There were no veterinary services or medicines, so only healthy dogs could survive. During the Great Trek (1834-1840) the Boerboel was very similar to the breed today and is recognizable from old drawings. Following the Trek, the Boerboel was further interbred and only the largest, strongest dogs survived. This highly versatile dog acted as family friend, worker and protector. He was basically an all purpose utilitarian farm dog thriving in a wild an untamed land.

Health Issues

Due to natural selection, the South African Boerboel is reputed to be a very healthy breed.

BREED NOTES

SIZE	GROOMING
✓ ✓ ✓	✓
EXERCISE	LIFESPAN
✓ ✓ ✓	✓ ✓

Exercise and Grooming

He needs a good amount of exercise so needs a large yard in which to run and play, also enjoying a good leash walk and a game of ball. His coat is relatively easy to groom, requiring an occasional thorough brushing and a monthly bath or dip.

Spanish Water Dog

Average height: dogs – 17-20 inches; bitches – 16-18 inches
Average weight: dogs – 40-49 pounds; bitches – 30-40 pounds

Appearance

This is a rustic, well-proportioned medium sized dog with a strong head, carried elegantly. His skull is flat with only a slightly marked occipital crest. His expressive eyes are hazel to chestnut color, harmonizing with the color of the coat, as does his nose, which is the same color or slightly darker than the darkest color of his coat. The short, well-muscled neck is set well into the shoulders and his body is robust, with a straight topline. The withers are hardly marked and the back straight and powerful. His chest is broad and deep, the ribs well-arched, indicating considerable respiratory capacity. The tail is usually docked at the 2nd to 4th vertebra, but occasionally the breed has a congenitally shortened tail. The Spanish Water Dog's skin is supple and fine and may or may not be pigmented, according to the coat color, which may be white, black or chestnut. He may also be white and black or white and brown. Even puppies are born with curly hair. In maturity the curly coat has a woolly texture and when long can form cords.

Characteristics

An extremely intelligent, well-balanced, versatile dog, the Spanish

BREED NOTES	
SIZE	GROOMING
✓✓	✓✓
EXERCISE	LIFESPAN
✓✓	✓✓

Below: 'They must be joking!'

Johnson

A
B
C
D
E
F
G
H
I
J
K
L
M
N
O
P
Q
R
S
T
U
V
W
X
Y
Z

Water Dog has strong herding, hunting and guarding instincts. He makes a wonderful companion and is devoted to his family. With his attentive and happy personality, he shows both strength and stamina, combined with unusual agility. Easily trained, he can perform those tasks asked of him with competence and dignity. Although rather reserved with strangers, he should not exhibit any shyness. Socialization with people and other animals is advisable from a young age as he can be protective and territorial.

Origins and History
Although the Spanish Water Dog is known to be an ancient breed, his exact origin is not known. One theory suggests that Turkish merchants took him to the South Iberian Peninsula along with the flocks they were moving through the Mediterranean, while another theory suggests North African origin. Whatever the breed's very early history, there is evidence of a wooly-coated Water Dog on the Iberian Peninsula in 1110 AD. These dogs appear to have been the ancestors of the Water Dogs and it is relevant to mention that the Spanish Water Dog we know today has been known by numerous different names including, Perro de Agua, Perro Turco, Laneto, Perro de Lanas, Perro Patero, Perro Rizado, Churro, Barbeta, Turcos Andalucia and, most recently, Perro de Agua Espanol. During the 18th century, Water Dogs were used for herding livestock from the south of Spain to the north and back again in their search for fertile grazing areas. During the Industrial Revolution, although the north of Spain and Madrid were affected, the Water Dogs remained active in Andalusia, especially in the hills and mountains of Cadiz and Malaga, primarily due to their ability to work in this terrain. At the same time, in the ports of Seville, Algecieras and Malaga, Water Dogs were used to tow

Below: The strong head is carried elegantly.

Johnson

Above: This high quality puppy is destined to do well.

Above: The breed has an attentive, happy personality.

boats to shore and later they assisted the fisherman with their nets and hunted waterfowl and upland game. The breed's modern history really began as recently as 1981 when the breed was exhibited at a show near Malaga, Spain. A standard was accepted in 1983 and the breed is now familiar in many countries of the world, albeit in relatively mall numbers. But apart from the Spanish Water Dog's current use in Search and Rescue, drug and bomb sniffing, agility and water work, he can still be found herding cattle, pigs, goats and sheep in Andalusia, just as he has done for around the last 1,000 years.

Health Issues

Generally a healthy breed, amongst the problems that have been found in this breed are hip dysplasia and Progressive Retinal Atrophy (PRA).

Right: Always at home near water.

He may also be susceptible to ear infections because of the hair growing in the ear canal.

Exercise and Grooming

The Spanish Water Dog needs plenty of exercise for he is energetic, lively and must be given mental stimulation. He loves to romp and play and of course thoroughly enjoys a good swim! The coat is generally clipped down about twice a year, but this is not just for the sake of appearance. The recommended maximum hair length is about 5 inches (roughly 6 inches if the curl is extended); it should be no shorter than 1.25 inches in order to see the quality of the curl.

A
B
C
D
E
F
G
H
I
J
K
L
M
N
O
P
Q
R
S
T
U
V
W
X
Y
Z

Spinone Italiano

Average height: dogs – 23-27 inches; bitches – 22-25 inches
Average weight: 60-85 pounds

Appearance

The build of the Spinone Italiano tends to fit into a square; he is a solidly built dog, robust and muscular, with powerful bone. That he is a hard-working gundog is clearly evident from his appearance. His head is long and his expression denotes intelligence and gentleness. The skull is oval in shape, its sides gently sloping with a well developed occiput and pronounced furrow running up the front of the skull. From the front the muzzle is square and from the side its bridge is preferably slightly "Roman", though it may be straight. The eyes have a soft, sweet expression, their color varying according to coat color. They are large, well opened and almost round, the lids closely fitting to protect the eye from gathering debris while the dog is hunting. The nose is bulbous and spongy, with large, well-opened nostrils. The teeth, meeting in a scissors or level bite, are set into powerful jaws. The Spinone's ears are carried low and are practically triangular in shape, their length measuring to the end of the nose, but no more than one inch beyond. The neck is strong, thick and muscular, the chest broad, deep, well muscled and well rounded. His back slopes slightly downward in a nearly straight line from the withers to approximately 6 inches behind them, then rises gradually and continues into a solid and well-arched loin. The underline is solid,

with minimal tuck up. The tail, which has no fringing, is thick at its base and docked to between 5? to 8 inches; it is carried horizontally or down. His skin is very thick on the body, but finer on the head throat, groin, under the legs and in the folds of the elbows. Pigmentation depends on the color or markings of the coat, but must not be black. The ideal length of coat is 1? to 2? inches on the body, with shorter hair elsewhere except for a rough brush on the backsides of the legs and stiff hair forming eyebrows, mustache and tufted beard, which protect his foreface from laceration by briar and bush. The coat is dense, stiff and flat or slightly crimped, without undercoat and must be left in its natural state. Colors are solid white, white and orange, orange roan with or without orange markings, white with brown markings, or brown roan with or without brown markings.

Characteristics

The Spinone Italiano is naturally sociable, docile and patient. He is resistant to fatigue and an experienced hunter on any terrain, his wiry, dense coat and thick skin enabling him to negotiate underbrush and endure cold water that would severely punish any dog not so naturally armoured. The Spinone is an excellent retriever by nature and although serious when working, he enjoys having a good

BREED NOTES

SIZE	GROOMING
✓	✓
✓	✓
✓	
EXERCISE	**LIFESPAN**
✓	✓
✓	✓
✓	

time and can be quite clownish and entertaining. He is sociable, brave and loyal, with good learning capacity and a genuine desire to please. He gets along well with other animals and shows a great love for children.

Origins and History

The Spinone Italiano is also known as the Italian Pointer, or Italian Griffon. He is Italy's all-purpose hunting dog, developed in the Piedmont district of north-west

Below: The Spinone is solidly built with an intelligent, gentle expression.

Italy. This ancient Italian breed has excelled as both a pointer and retriever for centuries and is still a popular hunting dog in many countries. He is a rather slow-footed dog, similar to those used before the era of wing shooting. This is indeed an all-purpose gundog, said to outrank all other Italian gun dogs as a highly efficient worker.

Health Issues

Some of the health disorders than can affect this breed include hip

dysplasia, cerebellar ataxia, eye problems and bloat.

Exercise and Grooming

The Spinone Italiano is a fairly energetic breed so likes daily walks and frequent play. Some say their Spinones make good jogging companions. Although the coat requires brushing on a weekly basis, it must never be over-groomed as this is a breed that is presented naturally. Baths may be given as necessary, but not so frequently as to soften the coat.

Johnson

A
B
C
D
E
F
G
H
I
J
K
L
M
N
O
P
Q
R
S
T
U
V
W
X
Y
Z

Stabyhoun

Average height: 19-21 inches
Average weight: 33-44 pounds

Appearance

A well-balanced, sturdily built dog, the Stabyhoun has a broad, slightly rounded skull with a well defined stop. The muzzle tapers gradually toward the nose, without becoming pointed and his strong teeth meet in a scissors bite. His ears are set high, fringed at their base, but smooth-haired at the tip, a distinctive breed feature. Appearing rectangular in shape, his back is long, chest deep and hindquarters well-muscled. He has a moderately long, sleek coat without curl, although a little wave over the croup is acceptable. On tail and breeches the feathering is so thick as to appear bushy. His color is black, chocolate or orange, with white markings, in which there may be ticking and roaning. Pigment is black or brown according to the coat color.

Characteristics

With his sound temperament, the Stabyhoun is often described as the

Below: Feathering on tail and breeches is thick and bushy.

BREED NOTES

SIZE	GROOMING
✓✓	✓✓
EXERCISE	LIFESPAN
✓✓✓	✓✓

dog who wears his heart on his sleeve. He is calm and even in disposition and well known for being soft and gentle with children, even those he does not know. When retrieving he has a soft mouth and when searching for game he is an excellent pointer. The Stabyhoun makes a great companion around the family home.

Origins and History

The Stabyhoun originated in the Dutch province of Friesland, where he has been known since the 17th century. As the Spanish occupied the Netherlands until the middle of the 16th century, it is believed that they took with them setting and couching dogs from other parts of Europe. These dogs developed into Holland's native spaniels and setters, the Drentse Patrijshond, the Kooikerhondje and the Stabyhoun; they were also the foundation of

Below: The Stabyhoun is virtually unchanged since the 18th century.

several German breeds. From descriptions given by Frisian writers of the 18th century, we certainly know that the breed has remained virtually unchanged since that time. He has been exhibited in the showring since the 1940s, following which the breed was granted official recognition by both Dutch and international dog organizations. In his homeland he is affectionately called the "Bijke"; he is a quality pointing and retrieving dog who

Above: A pointing and retrieving breed, also a guard.

also doubles as a mole and polecat catcher and guard. Also used in duck and pigeon hunting, he calmly stays down, unobserved, until called upon to retrieve. Although a dog used as a mole catcher needed to be of sufficiently small size to be carried in a basket on the back of a bicycle, larger specimens have been used as draft dogs.

Health Issues

To maintain the breed's sound qualities, the Dutch breed club has very strict breeding policies and before dogs can be bred they must have hips tested for hip dysplasia, and have received an excellent or very good rating.

Exercise and Grooming

This gundog breed should be allowed plenty of opportunity for free exercise. His coat is fairly easy to manage, but should be groomed thoroughly on a regular basis to keep it in good condition.

A
B
C
D
E
F
G
H
I
J
K
L
M
N
O
P
Q
R
S
T
U
V
W
X
Y
Z

Staffordshire Bull Terrier

Average height: 14-16 inches
Average weight: dogs – 28-38 pounds; bitches – 24-34 pounds

Appearance

The Staffordshire Bull Terrier has great strength for its size and is muscular, active and agile. The short skull is deep and broad, the cheek muscles pronounced and the foreface short, with a distinct stop. His eyes are preferably dark, round and looking straight ahead, while his teeth meet in a scissors bite and his lips are clean and tight. Pigment is black, but if white surrounds the eye, the eye rim may be pink. The Stafford's ears, which are not large, are rose or half pricked. The muscular, rather short neck has a clean outline, gradually widening toward the shoulders. His front is wide, the brisket deep and the topline level. This breed is rather light in the loins. His medium length tail is undocked, low set and tapering to a point. It should not curl too much, and may be likened to an old-fashioned pump handle. Forelegs are straight, well boned and set rather far apart and the strong, well padded feet turn out just a little. Hindquarters are well muscled and the stifles well bent. The Stafford's smooth, short coat may be red, fawn, white, black or blue, or any of these colors with white. Alternatively it may be any shade of brindle, with or without white.

BREED NOTES

SIZE	GROOMING
✓✓	✓
EXERCISE	**LIFESPAN**
✓✓✓	✓✓

Johnson

Left: The dark eyes look straight ahead, depicting a courageous spirit.

Characteristics

The active, agile Staffordshire Bull Terrier is courageous, tenacious, curious, intelligent and protective, with a strong prey drive. However, with his family he is very affectionate and is highly devoted to his family members. With children

he is usually tolerant and affectionate. When "off-duty", he is quiet with a trustworthy stability, making him a good all-purpose dog.

Origins and History

The Staffordshire Bull Terrier's origins lie in England where the Bulldog and Mastiff were closely linked. During the Elizabethan era large bull breeds were used for bull- and bear-baiting, but later a more agile breed of up to 90 pounds

Left: This breed is highly devoted to its family.

Below: A splendid example of a top winning Champion.

A
B
C
D
E
F
G
H
I
J
K
L
M
N
O
P
Q
R
S
T
U
V
W
X
Y
Z

A
B
C
D
E
F
G
H
I
J
K
L
M
N
O
P
Q
R
S
T
U
V
W
X
Y
Z

Terrier was admitted to AKC registration in 1974.

Health Issues

Problems that may be encountered by the Stafford include hip dysplasia, cataracts, flatulence and over heating.

Exercise and Grooming

Although he is capable of adapting to many life styles, the Staffordshire Bull Terrier is an active breed, so requires vigorous daily exercise. His high energy level makes him especially suited to dog sports including competitive obedience, agility and flyball. The breed's short hair requires minimal grooming, but a firm bristle brush, used every day, will keep skin and coat in tip-top condition.

came into being. By the beginning of the 19th century dog-fighting had become popular and a smaller, faster dog was developed. This dog was called by several names, including the "Bulldog Terrier" and "Bull and Terrier", but still these dogs were larger than the Staffords we know today for they weighed around 60 pounds. This dog was crossed with a small terrier, producing a dog that weighed something between 30 and 45 pounds; this was the Staffordshire Bull Terrier we know so well today. The breed was recognized by the English Kennel Club in 1935. In America the breed has been known since the mid-1880s, but here it developed along different lines; dogs were taller and heavier and have become the American Staffordshire Terrier. The actual Staffordshire Bull

Above: Pups with a veritable monster of a toy!

Below: On the alert.

Standard Schnauzer

Average height: dogs – 18.5-19.5 inches; bitches – 17.5-18.5 inches
Average weight: 30-45 pounds

Appearance

This is a robust, heavy-set dog who is sturdily built with good muscle and plenty of bone. The Standard Schnauzer is squarely built, his body compact, strong, short-coupled and substantial, permitting great flexibility and agility. His head is strong, rectangular and elongated, narrowing slightly from ears to eyes, and again to the tip of his large, black nose. His dark brown eyes are oval in shape with an arched, wiry brow giving an alert, highly intelligent, spirited expression. The skull is flat and the cheeks have well developed chewing muscles. Teeth are strong and meet in a scissors bite. His ears are set high and carried erect when cropped; if left uncropped they are V-shaped and mobile, breaking at skull level and carried forward. Typically the Standard Schnauzer should not have an absolutely horizontal back; instead it has a slightly descending slope from withers to croup and set-

Below: A good example showing a strong, compact, short-coupled body.

BREED NOTES

SIZE	GROOMING
✔ ✔	✔ ✔ ✔

EXERCISE	LIFESPAN
✔ ✔	✔ ✔

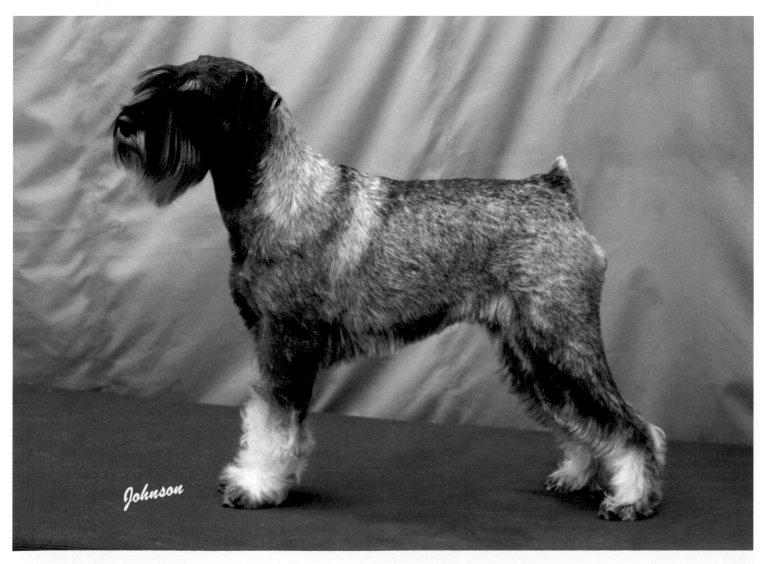

Johnson

A
B
C
D
E
F
G
H
I
J
K
L
M
N
O
P
Q
R
S
T
U
V
W
X
Y
Z

Johnson

Above: Another fine example, showing the strong, rectangular, elongated head.

on of tail. The tail is carried erect and docked to between one and two inches. The coat is tight, hard, wiry and as thick as possible, with a soft, close undercoat and a harsh outer coat. When seen against the grain, the outer coat stands up off the back, lying neither smooth nor flat; it is hand-stripped to accent the body outline. On the muzzle and over the eyes, the coat lengthens to form beard and eyebrows, and the hair on the legs is longer than on the body. He may be either pepper and salt (a combination of black and white hairs, and white hairs banded with black), or black.

Characteristics

The Standard Schnauzer is known as "the dog with the human brain". He has highly developed senses, and is noted for his bravery and devotion. He is intelligent, easy to train and seems resistant to both weather and illness. His nature combines high-spirited temperament with extreme reliability, making a good family companion.

Origins and History

The Standard is the oldest of the three Schnauzers; the other two being the Miniature and Giant. Each of these is bred and registered as a distinct breed. In the 15th and 16th centuries this German breed was highly favored as a household

Wolf Spitz. The Schnauzer was principally a rat catcher, yard dog and guard. In Germany, prior to World War I most of the dogs used to guard the carts of farm produce in the marketplaces were of strong Schnauzer blood. The breed was used by the army during the war as a dispatch carrier and Red Cross aide, and has also been used for police work. A highly versatile breed, he is still used as a guard dog today, and also for Search and Rescue. A standard was drawn up for the breed in 1880.

Health Issues

Known to be a very healthy breed, the Schnauzer sometimes suffers from hip dysplasia and eye problems.

Exercise and Grooming

The Standard Schnauzer needs lots of exercise; a minimum of an hour a day of hard play, which might include swimming, running, hiking or playing fetch. The coat is fairly demanding as it needs to be brushed regularly, with especial attention paid to combing beard and leg hair. In addition, the coat must be hand-stripped (or clipped if not being shown) roughly every four to six months.

Below: These ears are natural, but they may be cropped. The coat is tight, hard and wiry, the tail docked.

companion, his portrait appearing in many paintings of the period. Albrecht Durer owned one for at least twelve years, for the same dog is depicted in various paintings of his between 1492 and 1504. Another notable artwork is in the marketplace of Mechlinburg, Germany; this is a statue of a 14th century hunter, with a Schnauzer-type dog crouching at his feet. The most likely ancestors of the Schnauzer are the wire-haired Pinscher, black German Poodle and

A
B
C
D
E
F
G
H
I
J
K
L
M
N
O
P
Q
R
S
T
U
V
W
X
Y
Z

A
B
C
D
E
F
G
H
I
J
K
L
M
N
O
P
Q
R
S
T
U
V
W
X
Y
Z

Sussex Spaniel

Average height: 13-15 inches
Average weight: 35-45 pounds

Above: This substantial breed is rather massive in appearance.

BREED NOTES

SIZE	GROOMING
✓ ✓	✓ ✓

EXERCISE	LIFESPAN
✓ ✓ ✓	✓ ✓

somewhat pendulous and a scissors bite is preferred. His fairly large, thick ears are lobe shaped and set moderately low. All in all, he has a somber, serious expression, his fairly heavy brows causing a frown. The tail of the Sussex Spaniel is set low and docked to between 5 and 7 inches and, when he is moving, it is not carried above the back. The

Appearance

The Sussex Spaniel has a rectangular outline as he is longer in body than he is tall. A substantial breed, he is muscular and rather massive in general appearance. His skull is moderately long and wide, with a full stop and fairly heavy brows, giving an appearance of heaviness without dullness. The muzzle is about three inches long, broad, and square in profile, ending in a liver colored nose. His lips are

Below: Joining "Mom" on the sofa.

Left and bottom left: These puppies have found a Cavalier King Charles

and wide chest of the Sussex Spaniel, coupled with his short legs and long body, produce a rolling gait.

Characteristics

Despite his somber, serious expression, the Sussex Spaniel is friendly and makes a sweet and devoted pet with a cheerful disposition. He is steady, calm, and generally gets along with other dogs, but socialization is strongly advised at an early age. He is usually polite to strangers of the human kind. He tends to have a mind of his own, so consistent training is necessary, but when trained he is well adapted to hunting and retrieving things. He bays when working or having a game, but has a tendency to howl when left alone.

Origins and History

The Sussex Spaniel originated in the county of Sussex, England, as his name implies. There he was used as a field dog as far back as the 18th century. By the late 19th century, he

Right: When trained, he is well adapted to hunting and retrieving.

abundant body coat is flat or slightly waved, the legs well feathered but clean below the hocks. On the ears the hair is soft and wavy and the neck has a well marked frill. The thickly covered tail has moderately long feathering and the feather between the toes must be of sufficient length to cover the nails. Rich golden liver is the only acceptable color. The round, deep

A B C D E F G H I J K L M N O P Q R **S** T U V W X Y Z

Left: 'I'm showing off my puppy for the camera.'

there was an abundance of game and hunting was done on foot. This was amongst the first ten breeds to be recognized by the AKC when it was formed in 1884.

Health Issues

Health problems that may occur in this breed are hypothyroidism, prostate disease, hip dysplasia, eye problems and those relating to the heart.

Exercise and Grooming

The Sussex Spaniel needs regular exercise, particularly since this breed is prone to putting on excess weight. He generally enjoys retrieving, swimming and other outdoor activities. His coat requires regular brushing and cleaning, with special attention paid to the ears.

had gained a fine reputation as a hunting companion, his short legs, massive build, long body, and habit of giving tongue when on scent made the breed ideally suited to penetrating the dense undergrowth and flushing game within range of the gun. Although not a numerically strong breed, the Sussex today is essentially unchanged in character and general appearance from his 19th century ancestors. During the early years in England, the Sussex was used for rough shooting where

Below: Early training is important.

Swedish Vallhund

Average height: dogs – 12.5-13.5 inches; bitches – 11.5-12.5 inches
Average weight: 25-35 pounds

Appearance

The Swedish Vallhund is an old Spitz-type breed that has been known since the time of the Vikings. He is small, powerful, fearless and sturdily built, longer than he is high, with a correct height to body length ration of 2:3. Although small, he is thoroughly sound with a long, strongly muscled neck, good depth of chest and level topline. His tail may be long, stub, or bob, all types being equally acceptable, so it may be shown natural or docked. When viewed from the front, his forearms are slightly curved to give free action against the lower part of the chest, but from the side the forearms are straight. His feet point straight forward. The head is rather long and lean, forming an even wedge from skull to tip of nose. His expression conveys intelligence, alertness and energy; the oval eyes are dark brown with black eye rims. His strong, well-developed teeth must meet in a scissors bite. The medium sized ears are pointed and prick, smooth haired and mobile.

BREED NOTES

SIZE	GROOMING
✓ ✓	✓

EXERCISE	LIFESPAN
✓ ✓	✓ ✓

His coat is of medium length, harsh hair with a close, tight topcoat. The undercoat is soft and dense. On head and front of legs the hair is short, but slightly longer on neck, chest and back parts of the hind legs. This breed is always in an untrimmed, natural state. The coat is a sable pattern, found in colors of grey through red, and may be combinations of these colors in various shades. White is permitted as a narrow blaze, neck spot, slight necklace and white markings on legs and chest, but must never amount to more than one third of the total color. On the shoulder he has "harness markings", an essential feature of the breed.

Characteristics

The Swedish Vallhund is watchful, energetic, fearless, alert, intelligent, friendly and eager to please. He is active, and steady with a sound temperament, making a good herding and companion dog. He is always alert and watchful and although he will stand his ground, is not aggressive. The Vallhund is known for his friendly attitude, health and hardiness.

Origins and History

It is believed that this breed is indigenous to Sweden and dates

Johnson

back over 1,000 years to the days of the Vikings when he was known as the "Vikingarnas Hund", meaning the "Viking Dog". In the 8th or 9th century, either the Swedish Vallhund was taken to Wales, or the Corgi was taken to Sweden, which accounts for the similarity between the two breeds, though this breed is longer in leg, shorter in body and less stocky than the Corgi. The probability is that the Vallhund is

Left and above: Small, powerful and fearless, the breed is longer than high.

the older of the two. He is bred to work on farms and ranches as a cattle and sheep herder, working low to the ground by rounding up and nipping at the hocks. By 1942 the breed was almost extinct but enthusiasts finding a few of the old Swedish Vallhunds began a breeding program and in 1948 the Swedish Kennel Club recognized the breed as the Swedish Vallhund, "Vallhund," meaning "herding dog". The breed is sometimes also referred to as "Spitz of the West Goths". The Vallhund arrived in England in 1978 and the first two arrived in America in 1985.

Health Issues

The breed has relatively few genetic disorders, but problems that can affect the Swedish Vallhund include hip dysplasia, patella luxation and eye diseases.

Exercise and Grooming

This is a versatile breed and with proper training can compete in companion events such as obedience, tracking and agility. His coat is reasonably easy to care for but needs regular brushing and combing to keep it healthy and clean.

A
B
C
D
E
F
G
H
I
J
K
L
M
N
O
P
Q
R
S
T
U
V
W
X
Y
Z

A
B
C
D
E
F
G
H
I
J
K
L
M
N
O
P
Q
R
S
T
U
V
W
X
Y
Z

Thai Ridgeback

Average height: dogs – 24-26 inches; bitches – 22-24 inches
Average weight: dogs – 50-60 pounds; bitches – 45-55 pounds

Appearance

The Thai Ridgeback is a strong, muscular dog of medium build. His shoulders are strong and muscular, his back strong and firm. The head is carried high on a firm, clean cut neck, the muzzle is wedge shaped and appears powerful. The top of the skull is flat, sloping gently to the stop and the almond-shaped, dark brown eyes convey an alert expression. Interestingly this is one of the few breeds with a tongue that is blue, or bluish gray; nose pigment is black. The Thai Ridgeback's large, triangular ears are high set, pricked and inclined forward. His tail is thicker at the base and tapers to the tip. His skin is rather loose and there are two varieties of coat in this breed; one is regular short hair, the other extremely short and dense, giving a velvety appearance. An important characteristic of the breed is its ridge, formed by hair growing in the opposite direction. However, unlike the Rhodesian Ridgeback, his ridge grows in a variety of shapes and sizes, forming whorls and circles. The largest ridge is known as the "Bai Pho" and this covers most of the back and part of

BREED NOTES

SIZE	GROOMING
✓ ✓ ✓	✓
EXERCISE	**LIFESPAN**
✓ ✓ ✓	✓ ✓

the hips. Color ranges through a whole variety of solid colors including shades of fawn, black, blue and chestnut red.

Characteristics

Powerful and fearless, the Thai Ridgeback is good hunter and a natural watchdog, making him an excellent family protector. He is a very loyal and loving companion but can be rather aloof with strangers. A great jumper, he is very active and alert, but can be rather difficult to train, and a poorly trained Thai Ridgeback can show aggression. He therefore needs an owner who can understand the breed and who is not a novice.

Origins and History

This is a very ancient breed that was depicted in Cambodian and Thai cave paintings dating back some 3,000 years. It is believed that the Thai Ridgeback developed in eastern Thailand, where hunters used him to track down rabbits, deer and other quarry. Working in packs' they also hunted and cornered wild boar. Traditionally this breed was not taught to hunt, the young dogs simply learned from the older ones. He was also used to escort people's carts and as a watchdog and guard. Because of poor communications with this isolated part of the country, the breed had little chance to cross with other breeds and so remained true to type; he is probably one of the purest breeds in the world. Until fairly recently the Thai Ridgeback was little seen outside his homeland and is still quite rare, but it is recognised as the National Dog of its country and has officially received the title, "Royal Dog of Thailand".

Health Issues

There appear to be few hereditary health problems in this breed. Dermoid sinus is the main concern and this can usually be determined at birth.

Exercise and Grooming

This is a highly active breed and is perfectly capable of jumping 6 feet, so this should be borne in mind when planning his exercise area! The Thai Ridgeback can also be a proficient climber. He needs plenty of exercise and enjoys hunting, obedience and agility. His coat is very easy to manage; it hardly sheds and the breed has very little odour. However, as this is a tropical dog, he does not tolerate cold weather easily.

Opposite and left: There is a whole variety of colors, through fawn, black, blue and chestnut red.

Tibetan Mastiff

Average height: dogs – 26 inches minimum; bitches – 24 inches minimum
Average weight: dogs – 100-160 pounds or more; bitches – 75-120 pounds or more

BREED NOTES

SIZE	GROOMING
✔	✔
✔	✔
✔	

EXERCISE	LIFESPAN
✔	✔
✔	✔

Left: A Tibetan nomad, proud of her Tibetan Mastiff puppy.

Appearance

The Tibetan Mastiff is noble and impressive, a powerful, well built dog with plenty of bone and substance. He stands well up on his pasterns and has fairly large, strong, tight, cat feet with feathering between the toes and, although not mentioned in the breed standard, he needs good thick pads to equip him for him life on Tibet's desolate plateaux. He may have single or double dewclaws on the hind feet, although they may be removed. In balance he is slightly longer than he is tall and has a broad, heavy, strong head, with some wrinkling in maturity. He has very expressive eyes conveying his watchful aloofness. His broad skull has a strongly defined occiput, while his

Left: A successful Tibetan Mastiff male in the UK

lighter color; it is found on specific areas, the Tibetans prizing greatly tan spots above the eyes, which they call "four eyes", believing this allows the Tibetan Mastiff to "see" evil three days in advance. There may be a small white star on the breast and although white markings on the feet are accepted, these must be minimal. This breed's movement is powerful, steady and balanced, whilst also light footed; observers of the Tibetan Mastiff's movement should always keep in mind the terrain and narrow paths on which this dog is obliged to traverse in its homeland. Sound, powerful movement is more important than speed.

Characteristics

A highly intelligent breed, the

Below: Gold is less frequently found, but this a high quality male.

muzzle is square, viewed from all sides. His nose is broad and his thick lips well developed, with moderate flews and slightly pendulous lower lips. His teeth meet in a complete scissors bite, but level is acceptable. The Tibetan Mastiff's medium sized ears are V-shaped, pendant and set on high; they drop forward and hang close to the head, but are raised slightly when alert. The well muscled neck is moderately arched and is shrouded in a thick, upstanding mane. He is well muscled throughout, with his brisket reaching to below the elbow. The topline is level, without slope or angle to the croup and the underline has a pronounced, but not exaggerated tuck-up. His tail is well feathered and set on high; when alert or moving it is curled over the back or to one side. The Tibetan Mastiff has moderate angulation in both fore and hindquarters. The double coat has fairly long, thick, coarse guard hair, with a heavy soft, rather wooly undercoat, the latter becoming sparse in warm weather. Although the Tibetan Mastiff's hair is fine, it is hard, straight and stand-off. Hair on ears and legs is short but hind legs are well feathered on their upper parts. Color may be black, brown or blue/gray, all with or without tan markings, or various shades of gold. The tan ranges from a very rich shade to a paler or

Right: Tibetan Mastiff puppies are quite adorable.

Tibetan Mastiff is independent, strong-willed and rather reserved. He is highly protective of his charges, be they humans or animals, and is always willing to protect his property. It is therefore understandable that he is aloof with strangers. In his homeland he is an outstanding sheepdog and is ferocious with leopards and other intruders that attempt to approach his flock. He is very determined, but always willing to please his owners, showing great devotion to his family and love toward children. He can get along well with other animals provided he is sensibly introduced. With plenty of socialization and training, the Tibetan Mastiff can be a wonderful family companion. Males do not reach full maturity until 4 or 5 years of age, females a little earlier,

and they only come into season once each year.

Origins and History

The Tibetan Mastiff is the large guardian dog of Tibet, considered by many to be the basic stock from

which most of the world's large working breeds have developed; this includes both mastiffs and mountain dogs. Around 1100 BC in Asia there was certainly a large dog, and skulls of similar dogs date back to the Stone and Bronze Ages. For many years the breed remained in isolation on the high Tibetan plateaux, developing into the magnificent animal who is so prized by Tibetans and has captured Western interest today. Traditionally, in the daytime these dogs are kept tied up outside large homes and monasteries, or tied to stakes around nomad camps, but if circumstances permit they are let loose at night to keep away predators and intruders. When flocks are moved to higher pastures, the Tibetan Mastiffs are left behind to guard the family's children and possessions. There have been many accounts of this remarkable breed in recent centuries, Marco Polo having described them as being as large as donkeys. Lord Hardinge, Viceroy of India, sent the Tibetan

Above: A young blue/gray puppy.

Above right: A quality black with tan markings.

Below: Feeling at home on the mountain-top

A
B
C
D
E
F
G
H
I
J
K
L
M
N
O
P
Q
R
S
T
U
V
W
X
Y
Z

Mastiff, Siring, to Queen Victoria in 1847, following which there were several more imports to Britain. In the late 1950s two were sent from Tibet to President Eisenhower but the breed did not really begin to take a foothold in America until 1969 and first National Specialty Show was held here in 1983.

Health Issues

This is generally a hardy breed which, despite its size, usually lives for 10 years or more. Health problems that have been encountered include autoimmune hypothyroidism, hip dysplasia, epilepsy and canine inherited demyelinative neuropathy (CIDN), the latter an unusual, fatal condition that appears between 7 and 10 weeks of age.

Exercise and Grooming

During the stage of puppyhood a Tibetan Mastiff should not be over exercised. As he matures he will require daily exercise, but this should be at a relatively moderate pace, a leash walk or a ramble though the woods perhaps. This is a naturally clean breed, with little doggy odor and the coat can be maintained with regular weekly brushing. More frequent grooming is needed when he is shedding his undercoat.

Below: Tibetan Mastiffs living in a monastery in Nepal.

Above: the author speaking on Tibetan Mastiffs at the Nepal Kennel Club

Tibetan Spaniel

Average height: 10 inches
Average weight: 9-15 pounds

Appearance

The Tibetan Spaniel is small, active and alert, slightly longer in body than height at withers. His proudly carried head is small in proportion to his body and the skull is slightly domed. His medium-length muzzle is blunt with cushioning, free from wrinkle, and his chin shows some depth and width. The mouth is ideally slightly undershot, but a level bite is acceptable, provided the blunt appearance of the muzzle is preserved. His eyes are dark and expressive; they are set fairly well apart, but look forward, giving an ape-like impression to his features. The medium ears are pendant, well feathered and set fairly high. They may have a slight lift from the skull, but should not fly. The Tibetan Spaniel has a moderately short neck, level back and good depth of rib, the high set tail being richly plumed and carried in a gay curl over the back when moving. The bones of the forelegs are slightly bowed, the hindquarters well made and strong. He has a small, neat hare foot with feathering between toes, often extending beyond the feet. The double coat, which may be of any color or mixture of colors, has a silky texture; it is smooth on the face and front of legs and of moderate length on the body, but lying rather

BREED NOTES

SIZE	GROOMING
✓	✓
	✓
EXERCISE	LIFESPAN
✓	✓
✓	✓

Below: The muzzle is blunt with cushioning.

A
B
C
D
E
F
G
H
I
J
K
L
M
N
O
P
Q
R
S
T
U
V
W
X
Y
Z

flat. The ears and back of forelegs are nicely feathered, with longer hair on tail and buttocks. The neck is covered with a mane or "shawl", which is more pronounced in dogs than bitches.

Characteristics

This breed is gay and perky, with a happy temperament. He is very intelligent and can be rather aloof with strangers, but is very loyal to his family. Generally he gets along well with other pets and with children, but supervision is of course necessary from the outset. He does not bark excessively, but will give his owners notice of intruders and strange happenings.

Above and below: Tibetan Spaniels love to investigate.

Above: *This trio makes a perfect picture.*

Below: *Puppies out playing with their dam.*

Origins and History

The Tibetan Spaniel used to be kept primarily in the monasteries of Tibet, serving the monks as companions and bed warmers. Despite its name, this is not a spaniel, but the breed's origin has really been lost in the mists of time. It is likely that the Tibetan Spaniel is an ancestor of other breeds including the Japanese Spaniel and Pekingese; certainly old photographs of the Pekingese closely resemble today's Tibetan Spaniel. It has been rumoured that the Tibetan Spaniel turned prayer wheels in the monasteries, but this could be just a figment of the imagination. Undoubtedly they served as mobile "alarm bells" for the monks and, even today, Tibetan Spaniels like to position themselves high up, perhaps on a windowsill, so that they can keep watch.

In the Himalaya the Tibetan Spaniel comes in several different sizes, doubtless one of the reasons why there is so much variation in type in the breed today. The breed first arrived in Britain during the 1880s

A
B
C
D
E
F
G
H
I
J
K
L
M
N
O
P
Q
R
S
T
U
V
W
X
Y
Z

A
B
C
D
E
F
G
H
I
J
K
L
M
N
O
P
Q
R
S
T
U
V
W
X
Y
Z

but the first authenticated records of the Tibetan Spaniel in America refer to two imports in 1965. The breed became eligible for AKC registration in 1984.

Health Issues

This is a long-lived breed but the following health problems can sometimes arise: Progressive Retinal Atrophy (PRA), cherry eye and weeping eyes. The Tibetan Spaniel may also be susceptible to allergies, and it is worth bearing in mind that many dogs of Tibetan origin have an allergy to dairy products if fed in any quantity.

Exercise and Grooming

The Tibetan Spaniel is a fairly active little dog who enjoys a good walk and a romp in the yard. If he has

other canine friends of similar size, he will create much of his own exercise in play. His coat is fairly easy to manage, but requires regular combing and brushing, and the occasional bath.

Above: The plumed tail is curled over the back.

Below: He can be rather aloof with strangers.

Tibetan Terrier

Average height: dogs – 15-16 inches; bitches slightly smaller
Average weight: 20-24 pounds (but may be 18-30 pounds)

Appearance

A profusely coated dog of powerful build and with a square outline, the Tibetan Terrier evolved over many centuries and his make up is suited to life in Tibet's extreme climate and difficult terrain. His flat skull is neither broad nor coarse, the length from tip of nose to eye being equal to that from eye to occiput, the skull narrowing slightly from ear to eye. The jaws have a distinctive curve between the canine teeth which should meet in a tight scissors or level bite, but a slightly undershot bite is acceptable. The Tibetan Terrier's eyes are set fairly wide apart and are dark, as are the eye rims, while the nose is black. The entire head is well furnished

BREED NOTES

SIZE	GROOMING
✔	✔
✔	✔
	✔
EXERCISE	LIFESPAN
✔	✔
✔	✔

Left: A highly successful Champion.

with long hair, falling forward over the eyes and foreface, while the heavily feathered V-shaped ears are pendant, but not falling too close to the head. There is a small beard on the lower jaw. The Tibetan Terrier's compact body is square and strong, being capable of both speed and endurance, the chest extending down to the top of the elbow and the ribcage not too wide, allowing the forelegs to work free at the sides. His back is level and his loin slightly arched. The heavily furnished tail is set on fairly high and falls over the back; it may curl to either side. The feet of the Tibetan Terrier are unique; they are large, flat and round, producing a snowshoe effect. The dog should stand well down on its pads, which are thick and strong. They are

A
B
C
D
E
F
G
H
I
J
K
L
M
N
O
P
Q
R
S
T
U
V
W
X
Y
Z

Above: English and American Champion having won Best in Show at Crufts Dog Show, England.

Below: Proud of their Tibetan roots.

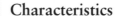

heavily furnished with hair between the toes and pads. This breed has a double coat, essential for the high altitude climate in Tibet. The undercoat is soft and wooly, the outer coat profuse and fine, but never silky, nor indeed wooly. It may be wavy or straight and although long, it should never hang to the ground. Any color or combination of colors, including white, are found in this lovely breed.

Characteristics

Highly intelligent, sensitive and loyal, The Tibetan Terrier makes a devoted and affectionate canine friend who can get along well with all family members. He has tremendous endurance and agility, and thoroughly enjoys competitive obedience or agility trials. He may, however, be rather reserved toward strangers.

Origins and History

Tibetan Terriers have long been prized companions of the Tibetan people and have often been said to bring luck to those who own them. He is a true herding dog, not a terrier at all. He assisted the Tibetan shepherd, and in remote area some still do so today, the author having witnessed them herding their flocks. They have also served as alarm dogs in villages, giving notice of any strangers or intruders who may have found their way past the Tibetan Mastiffs while tied up during the hours of daylight. The breed was brought to Europe by the Magyars and is believed to have contributed in no small way to the development of the Puli and other European herding breeds. The breed was introduced to Britain in the 1920s by Dr Grieg, her first Tibetan Terrier having been given to her by a patient when she was serving in India. In America the breed has been shown in the Non-Sporting Group since 1973.

Health Issues

Tibetan Terrier enthusiasts have gone to great pains to investigate health problems in their breed and issues of which owners should be aware are Progressive Retinal Atrophy (PRA), lens luxation and hip dysplasia. Eye testing is particularly important and, through this and well-considered breeding practises, the incidence of PRA has been very greatly reduced.

Exercise and Grooming

The Tibetan Terrier has lots of stamina and enjoys a good leash walk, as well as free run. Regular grooming is essential to keep the Tibetan Terrier's coat in good order and bathing is needed, at least from time to time, more regularly for the showring. However, the Tibetan Terrier is shown as naturally as possible and should not be trimmed, except for tidying of the feet.

Below: The compact body is square and strong.

A
B
C
D
E
F
G
H
I
J
K
L
M
N
O
P
Q
R
S
T
U
V
W
X
Y
Z

Tosa

Average height: dogs – 23.5 inches minimum; bitches – 21.75 inches minimum
Average weight: dogs – 140 pounds or more; bitches – 130 pounds

Appearance

The Tosa is a large-boned, athletic dog, his muscles well defined and massive. He has a broad, deep, powerful chest, a level back and broad, muscular loins. His tail is thick at the root, tapering to the tip and reaching the hocks, while his neck is thick and muscular, with dewlap. His skull is broad, with moderate wrinkle. His jaws are punishing and powerful. The Tosa's coat is short, hard and dense, the preferred color being a deep, solid red. Other colors are fawn, apricot, black and brindle; there may be slight white markings on his chest and feet, which are tightly closed, with thick, elastic pads.

Characteristics

The Tosa is a dog that puts his family first and foremost and will go to any lengths to protect them. He is usually good with children but should always be very carefully supervised when in their company. He treats strangers with caution. The Tosa is patient, calm, composed and utterly courageous. He can be very aggressive with other dogs, giving no ground and attacking head on. He is agile and athletic, so requires an owner who is capable of giving discipline and is also physically and mentally strong enough to handle this powerful breed. A Tosa is definitely not the breed for a novice owner.

Origins and History

The Tosa, often known Tosa Inu or Tosa Token (the latter meaning "fighting style dog"), is the most feared and yet revered of all Japan's dog breeds. He hails from Tosa Bay, Kochi prefecture. Although dog fighting has been a passion in Japan for centuries, when European and Western traders arrived there they introduced many of their own mastiff-type fighting dogs, which competed with those of Japan. Because the Japanese dogs were smaller, they were unable to compete on equal terms but in 1848 someone in Tosa bred a Bulldog to a pedigree Tosa dog and after repeated breed improvements, stronger, bigger and more capable fighting dogs were created. In the fighting arenas of Japan, the Tosa has no equal; this is the Sumo Wrestler counterpart in the dog world. In the Second World War dog fighting, as well as feeding 150 pound dogs, became illegal and the Tosa was reduced to near extinction. But dedicated enthusiasts smuggled a few to the island of Hokkaido in Northern Japan, where they were hidden until the end of the war. Following the war they returned to Tosa Bay, continued breeding and legal dogfight tournaments were resumed. Fights were ceremonial occasions, with the dogs paraded into the ring, controlled by thick, white ropes and held by strong men,

BREED NOTES

SIZE	GROOMING
✓ ✓ ✓	✓

EXERCISE	LIFESPAN
✓ ✓	✓ ✓

Below: The Tosa will go to any length to protect his family.

Johnson

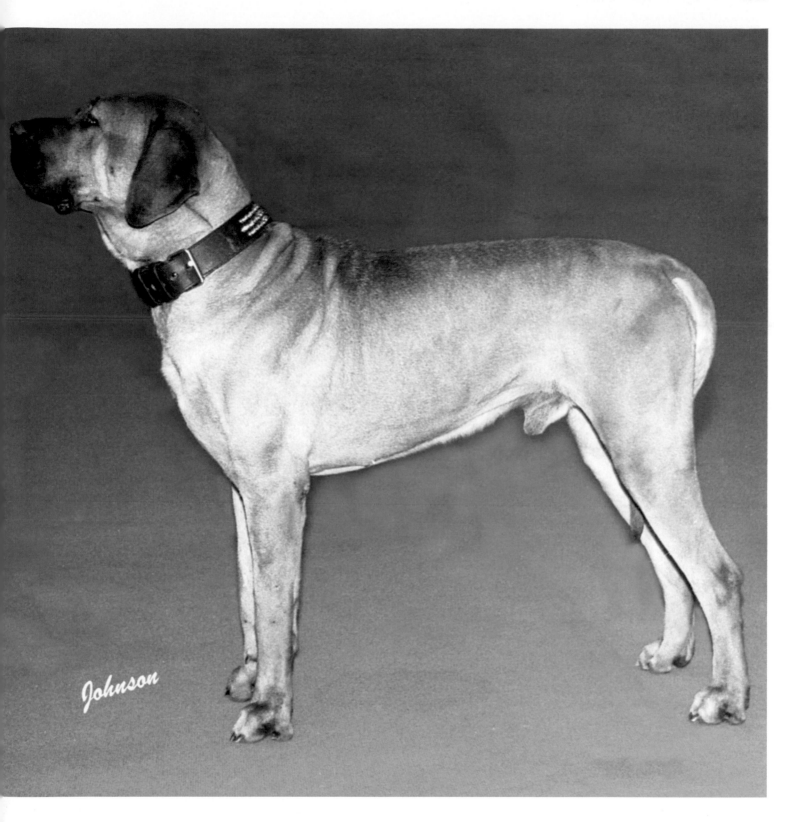

Johnson

bracing their legs. Generally fights were stopped if one of the dogs gave ground. Winners received ceremonial aprons, valued at as much as $31,000. Although the breed is now found in small numbers in a few other countries, including America, outside Japan the Tosa is used only as a companion and guard.

Health Issues
Prospective owners of a Tosa should be sure only to purchase from a reputable breeder, ensuring that both sire and dam have all necessary health clearances.

Exercise and Grooming
The Tosa needs a large, well fenced area of land where he will be able to look after his own exercise

Above: The most feared and yet revered of all Japanese breeds.

demands. He will enjoy an excursion out with his owner but must be kept under strict control at all times. If a Tosa picks a fight with another dog, he will win! Coat care is minimal, but regular brushing is needed to keep it healthy.

A
B
C
D
E
F
G
H
I
J
K
L
M
N
O
P
Q
R
S
T
U
V
W
X
Y
Z

Toy Fox Terrier

Average height: 9-11 inches preferred but 8.5-11.5 inches acceptable
Average weight: 3.5-7 pounds

Appearance

The well-balanced, athletic Toy Fox Terrier displays grace and agility in equal measure. He has a lithe muscular body, strength and stamina. His smooth elegant outline conveys the impression of effortless movement and endless endurance. His elegant head is balanced and expressive, his clear, bright, dark eyes conveying intelligence, eagerness and interest, coupled with a rather soft look. His slightly rounded skull is softly wedge-shaped, widening gradually from nose to base of ears. His cheeks are flat and muscular. The strong teeth meet preferably in a scissors bite. Ears are erect, pointed, set high and close together, without touching. He is square in proportion, bitches sometimes a little longer than males. Bone is strong, but not excessive. His neck is gracefully curved, blending smoothly into the shoulders, while the topline is level and the chest deep and muscular, with well-sprung ribs. The high set tail is traditionally docked, and is held erect. The Toy Fox Terrier's coat is shiny, satiny, fine in texture and smooth to the touch, slightly longer in the ruff. It may be tri-color; white, chocolate and tan; white and tan or white and black. Pigment is black, but self-colored in chocolate dogs.

Characteristics

Intelligent, alert and friendly, the Toy Fox Terrier is loyal to his owners and learns new tasks quickly. Always eager to please, he is adaptable. Like other terriers, he is self-possessed, spirited, determined and not easily intimidated, but is also a highly animated toy dog, comical, entertaining and playful. He generally gets along well with children, who will enjoy joining in his many energetic games.

Origins and History

To create this Toy Fox Terrier, some small Smooth Fox Terriers were crossed with various toy breeds including Miniature Pinschers, Italian Greyhounds, Chihuahuas and Manchester Terriers, resulting in gameness from the terriers, and a milder disposition from the other breeds used. This is an American creation and considered a big dog in a small package. Known frequently as AmerToy (American Toy Fox Terrier), he has become a cherished companion and excellent show dog, but given the opportunity many still delight in hunting and will readily go to ground, diligently pursuing the quarry of the back yard or barnyard.

BREED NOTES

SIZE	GROOMING
✓	✓

EXERCISE	LIFESPAN
✓	✓
✓	✓

Health Issues

This is generally a healthy breed, but problems include demodectic mange, patella luxation, Legg-Calve Perthes Disease, von Willebrand's Disease and congenital hypothyroidism with goiter (CHG). (The latter is evident from just a few days old, and by three weeks most affected pups will have died or have been euthanized.)

Exercise and Grooming

An active little dog, the Toy Fox Terrier will love to accompany his owner on a long walk, with some free run thrown in for good measure. He will also get plenty of exercise around his owner's back yard and enjoys obedience and agility trials. His short coat is easy to groom, and regular brushing will maintain its shiny texture.

Treeing Tennessee Brindle

Average height: 16-24 inches
Average weight: 40-50 pounds

Appearance

The Treeing Tennessee Brindle has a solid, muscular, square body. He is more 'houndy' than the Mountain Cur, which is his close relative. He has a flat-domed head, small, drooped ears and a medium length tail. The feet are tight and cat-like. He has an ample nose for trailing game. His coat is brindle in various shades, or may be black with brindle trim, and there may be a small amount of white on breast or feet. The coat is short, dense and smooth to the touch.

Characteristics

This breed is fearless and courageous when hunting, but friendly, relaxed and affectionate with his human owners. Small and fast moving, the Treeing Tennessee Brindle is a companionable and useful breed. This breed is particularly sensitive to neglect or abuse and during training care must be taken not to destroy his heart, "You can take it out, but you can never put it back!" He is an open trailer with a coarse chop mouth and fine treeing ability.

Origins and History

The original breeding stock for the Treeing Tennessee Brindle came from outstanding brindle tree dogs from many parts of the USA. It is one of America's mountain cur breeds, made up from various treeing coon dogs. A good number came from the Appalachian Mountains, the Ozark Mountains and various places in between. Instrumental in formation the Treeing Tennessee Brindle Breeders Association was Rev. Earl Phillips who had written a column for a national hunting dog magazine in the early 1960s. He had gathered a wealth of information about brindle colored Cur dogs, and entered into conversation with many people who owned them, commending these dogs on their hunting and treeing abilities. They praised them as open trailers with good scenting power and said they were very intelligent and courageous, and a very companionable dog. Many people were trying to promote Cur dogs, but none were specializing in brindles and so it was that in 1967 an Association was formed and recognized as a legal organization by the State of Illinois. The aim was to breed a dog of brindle color, smaller in size and with a shorter ear and different in conformation from the Plott. Dew claws and white feet and breast were allowed. This breed's quarry is generally coon, squirrel and opossum but it will also tree bears and large cats, such as bobcats and pumas.

Health Issues

The Treeing Tennessee Brindle is reputed to be a very healthy dog.

Exercise and Grooming

Clearly this is a working dog so needs plenty of opportunity for exercise, ideally carrying out the work for which he was bred. His coat is easy to maintain with regular brushing to keep skin and coat in good condition.

BREED NOTES	
SIZE	GROOMING
✓✓	✓
EXERCISE	LIFESPAN
✓✓✓	✓✓

A B C D E F G H I J K L M N O P Q R S **T** U V W X Y Z

A
B
C
D
E
F
G
H
I
J
K
L
M
N
O
P
Q
R
S
T
U
V
W
X
Y
Z

Treeing Walker Coonhound

Average height: dogs – 22-27 inches; bitches – 20-25 inches
Average weight: 50-75 pounds

Appearance

The Treeing Walker Coonhound is an efficiently built hound with a durable frame. His shoulders are sloping, clean, and muscular, conveying the idea of freedom of action and springiness, with activity and strength. His chest should be deep for lung space. The back is moderately long, muscular and strong, the loins broad and slightly arched. His feet are solid, compact, well padded and cat-like in appearance, with well-arched toes and strong nails for a quick get away. His rather high set tail is moderately long and carried well up in saber-like fashion, curved gracefully up and forward. This Coonhound's muzzle is medium square and rather long, the eyes open, soft, expressive and dark in color. Ears are slightly round or oval, set moderately low and hang gracefully, the inside part tipping toward muzzle. They are soft and velvety. His smooth coat is glossy and fine, yet dense enough for protection; it is a close, hard, hound coat. The preferred coat color is tricolour, which is white black and tan.

Characteristics

This is an energetic, intelligent, active breed with a super-abundance

BREED NOTES

SIZE	GROOMING
✓ ✓ ✓	✓
EXERCISE	**LIFESPAN**
✓ ✓ ✓	✓ ✓

Below: A trailing hound with a treeing instinct.

Right and below: The muzzle is medium square and rather long.

of sense, endurance, trailing, hunting and treeing instinct and ability. He is courteous, composed, confident, fearless and kind. He is generally good with children and other dogs, but has strong hunting instincts where other small animals are concerned! He loves human contact and affection.

Origins and History

From the English Foxhounds that were brought to America the Virginia Hounds evolved, and from them the Walker Foxhound is descended. It is from the Walker Foxhound that the Treeing Walker Coonhound was developed, retaining the same color and similar conformation. This breed was originally classified as an English Coonhound, but in 1945 breeders broke away from the English version to breed in the qualities they desired. Today the breed is occasionally described as a trailing hound with treeing instinct. The Treeing Walker is a sensible hunter; he is fast and hot-nosed with a

A
B
C
D
E
F
G
H
I
J
K
L
M
N
O
P
Q
R
S
T
U
V
W
X
Y
Z

clear, ringing bugle voice, or a steady, clear chop with changeover at the tree. He locates his quarry quickly and has superb treeing ability, as well as endurance. This breed ranges widely and may leave the original track if it picks up a stronger scent. He is used on a variety of game including coon, squirrel, opossum and deer, though deer hunting is illegal in some areas.

Health Issues
The Treeing Walker Coonhound is said to be a very healthy breed with no health issues. This breed's lifespan can be 12 to 13 years.

Exercise and Grooming
This is clearly a working Coonhound and, as such, needs a lifestyle to suit. If not used for hunting, he needs both vigorous exercise and mental stimulation as he can easily become bored. Because of his hunting instinct, his large

yard must be securely fenced. Coat care is minimal, but regular grooming is import to keep skin and coat in healthy condition.

Above and below: The Treeing Walker Coonhound is very clearly a working hound needing a lifestyle to suit, with plenty of exercise and mental stimulation.

Vizsla

Average height: dogs – 22-24 inches; bitches – 21-23 inches
Average weight: dogs – 50-65 pounds; bitches – 40-55 pounds

Appearance

The Viszla is a short-coated hunting dog, of distinguished appearance, robust but fairly lightly built. His head is lean and muscular, the skull moderately wide between the ears with a median line down the forehead. His muzzle is of equal length to the skull, or slightly shorter, gradually tapering to the tip of the nose, which is always brown. The color of the eyes blends with coat color, a solid golden rust in different shadings. The thin ears are silky and proportionately long, with rounded ends and hanging close to

Johnson

Left: A fine example of a top winning Champion.

the cheeks. The Vizsla has moderate angulation in fore and hindquarters, his chest moderately deep and his body strong. Musculature is well developed over the entire body. The tail, which is thicker at the root, has one third docked off and is carried at or near the horizontal. He has a far reaching, light footed gait that is graceful and smooth.

Characteristics

The Vizsla is a natural hunter that has a good nose. He is lively and gentle-mannered, demonstrably affectionate and although sensitive he is fearless with a well developed protective instinct. He can easily be trained but needs a patient, firm hand for he can be somewhat willful. The Vizsla gets along very

A
B
C
D
E
F
G
H
I
J
K
L
M
N
O
P
Q
R
S
T
U
V
W
X
Y
Z

well with children, loving all the play he can get, though he may be a little too excitable for toddlers. He adapts easily to family life and is usually good with other dogs, but must be introduced to cats and smaller pets while he is still young. He does have a tendency to chew and may not be the right choice for owners who want a really calm dog as a pet.

Origins and History

In some countries the Vizsla is called the Hungarian Vizsla, for that is the country from which it hails, having been the hunter and companion of the Magyar hordes that swarmed Central Europe over

Right: Eye color blends with coat color.

Below: 'Didn't I do well? I just won Best in Show!'

1,000 years ago, settling in the country we now know as Hungary. He was a favorite of early barons and warlords who preserved the breed's purity through the years, though it is not known whether this was by design or accident. The Vizsla appears in etchings dating back to the 10th century, and appeared in 14th century manuscripts. Hungary was almost entirely agricultural and pastoral, causing the Vizsla to evolve with an innate hunting instinct, suited to the climatic conditions and available game. He became a swift and cautious dog with superior nose and high-class hunting ability, combining the best assets of pointer and retriever. The breed was imported to the USA in the1950s and admitted to the AKC registry in 1960.

Health Issues
Health problems that may be encountered in the Vizsla are hip dysplasia, congenital heart disease, thyroid disorders, von Willebrand's Disease and eye problems including Progressive Retinal Atrophy (PRA), cataracts and entropion.

Below: A short-coated hunting dog of distinguished appearance.

Above: The head is lean and muscular, the skull moderately wide.

Exercise and Grooming
The Vizsla is an energetic working dog, with an enormous amount of stamina so needs lots of opportunity for exercise. He needs to run off a leash in a safe area and excels at tracking, retrieving, pointing and competitive obedience. The smooth, short-haired coat is easy to keep in good condition, using a firm bristle brush. Bathing should be done only when necessary, using a mild shampoo; alternatively a dry shampoo may be given

Weimaraner

Average height: dogs – 25-27 inches; bitches – 23-25 inches
Average weight: 70-85 pounds

Appearance

The Weimaraner presents a picture of grace, stamina, alertness and balance, his conformation indicating his ability to work with great speed and endurance in the field. His long, aristocratic head conveys a keen, kind, intelligent expression and his eyes, which are shades of light amber, gray or blue-gray, may

BREED NOTES

SIZE	GROOMING
✓	✓
✓	
✓	

EXERCISE	LIFESPAN
✓	✓
✓	✓
✓	

Left: "The grey ghost of Weimar".

appear almost black when dilated with excitement. The strong teeth are well-developed and meet in a scissors bite. His long, lobular ears are slightly folded and set high. The tail is docked and in maturity measure about 8 inches; it is carried in a manner expressing confidence and sound temperament. His strong back is of moderate length, his chest well-developed and deep, while his abdomen is held firmly, with a moderately tucked up flank. His feet are firm and compact, with well-arched, webbed toes. The Weimaraner is well known for his coat color, causing him often to be referred to as "the grey ghost of Weimar". Short, smooth and sleek, it is a solid color in shades of mouse-gray to silver-gray. A small white marking on the chest is permitted, but not elsewhere, unless it is a white spot cause by injury. (In some countries the Longhaired Weimeraner is accepted as another coat variety.)

Characteristics

The Weimaraner's temperament is friendly, fearless, alert and obedient. He is loyal and protective toward his family, with an assertive, bold nature. He thrives on human companionship and is a loyal hunting companion, but this is a breed that should live in a home, not in an outdoor kennel situation.

Origins and History

Compared with many, the Weimaraner is a young breed, dating back only to the early 19th century. He is the product of selective German breeding and it is believed that the Bloodhound has played a part in his makeup,

Right and below: The Weimaraner always presents a picture of grace and alertness.

perhaps indirectly through crosses with various schweisshund breeds. It appears that he has come from stock similar to that of the German Shorthaired Pointer. It is possible that the blood of European brackes and the Spanish Pointer also runs in his veins. In the early days, the Weimaraner was known as the Weimar Pointer, after the court that sponsored the breed. Nobles in the court of Weimar wanted to meld into one breed all the qualities they had found worthwhile in their forays against the abundant game of Germany. They sought speed, good

A
B
C
D
E
F
G
H
I
J
K
L
M
N
O
P
Q
R
S
T
U
V
W
X
Y
Z

scenting ability and courage, coupled with intelligence. Formerly this was a big-game dog used on wolves, wildcats, deer and such like, but by the time these animals had become rare in Germany, fortunately a Weimaraner breed club had been formed, with very strict rules aiming to keep the breed pure. A breed club in the USA was founded in 1929, by which time the Weimaraner had developed into a bird dog, rather than one for big

Right and below: Weimaraner puppies are just enchanting!

game. The breed was granted AKC recognition in 1943.

Health Issues

The Weimaraner Club of America issues a very long list of problems that can affect this breed, amongst them are hypertrophic ostodystrophy in the Weimeraner (HOD), von Willebrand's Disease, bloat, hip

Left: Dam still allowing her pups to suckle.

Below: A show dog conforming to the breed standard.

A
B
C
D
E
F
G
H
I
J
K
L
M
N
O
P
Q
R
S
T
U
V
W
X
Y
Z

dysplasia, corneal dermoid cyst, hypomyelinogenesis, hypothyroidism and Generalized Progressive Retinal Atrophy (GPRA). A small percentage of puppies have an autoimmune reaction following vaccinations with combination modified live virus vaccines.

Exercise and Grooming

The Weimaraner is a powerful working dog with great stamina, so needs regular exercise and frequent opportunities to hike, play and enjoy free run in a field. Coat care is not very demanding, just requiring a through brushing with a firm bristle brush and occasional dry shampoo. Bathing in mild soap may be done when necessary.

Right: The little-known Long-Haired Weimaraner

Welsh Springer Spaniel

Average height: dogs – 18-19 inches; bitches – 17-18 inches
Average weight: 35-45 pounds

Appearance

The compact Welsh Springer Spaniel is obviously built for hard work and endurance; he is well boned, but not in any way coarse. His silhouette is rectangular with a level topline and slightly arched loin. He has a well-developed chest with

BREED NOTES

SIZE	GROOMING
✔ ✔	✔ ✔

EXERCISE	LIFESPAN
✔ ✔ ✔	✔ ✔

Left: This youngster is already willing to learn from his master.

prominent forechest and the brisket reaches to the elbow. His tail is generally docked and displays a lively action, carried nearly horizontal and slightly elevated when excited. Feet are round, tight and well arched, with thick pads. The Welsh Springer's head is in proportion to his body, neither coarse nor narrow and racy. His oval eyes are dark to medium brown and have a soft expression, while his muzzle is about equal to, but never longer than his skull. The ears are set on at eye level and hang close to the cheeks; they are comparatively small and gradually narrow toward the tip, shaped rather like a vine leaf. His coat is naturally straight, flat and soft to the touch,

may be flecked with red ticking.

Characteristics

This is a loyal, affectionate family member who is gentle with children and with other animals. Although he is usually reserved with strangers, he is neither timid, shy, nor unfriendly. He is an active dog, originally bred as a flushing spaniel and he still makes a good hunting companion.

Origins and History

The first hunting dogs were employed by man in around 7,000 BC, these being the likely ancestors of most of today's domestic hunting dogs. By about 250 BC the Welsh Springer's ancestor had developed into the Agassian hunting dog, which belonged to the wild tribes of Roman-occupied Briton. During the Renaissance, the Land Spaniel appeared; this was a Welsh Springer-type dog with red and white markings, used for retrieving. Tapestries dating back to that time show us a dog very similar to the Welsh Springer

Above, below and opposite: This breed has a striking red and white coat, with any pattern acceptable.

sufficiently dense to be waterproof, thornproof and weatherproof. There is moderate feathering on the back of the forelegs, the hind legs above the hocks, chest and underside of the body. Ears and tail are lightly feathered. This breed is a striking rich red and white; any pattern is acceptable and any white area

Above: Show dog displaying the balance of the breed.

Welsh Springer Spaniel is susceptible to hip dysplasia, epilepsy and eye problems.

Exercise and Grooming

This is an active breed so plenty of exercise is important and may include walking, running, hunting or retrieving. The Welsh Springer Spaniel should be combed and brushed with a stiff, bristle brush about three times a week. Extra attention is needed at shedding time. Baths may be given as necessary, or a dry shampoo applied.

Spaniel we know today, although earlier it was called the Welsh Cocker. This dog became very popular in the 18th century and was a favorite hunting dog of the nobles, but in the following century enthusiasm declined and the English Springer Spaniel and other spaniels were more highly favored. Thankfully, in the Victorian era there was a trend for selective breeding and the Welsh Springer returned to the fore, although at shows he had to compete in the same classes as the English Springer, the difference then really being only color. Following the war years it was thought that no Welsh Springers existed in the States, but some were imported and the breed was revived, a specialist breed club being formed in 1961.

Health Issues

Although generally healthy, the

Welsh Terrier

Average height: dogs – 15-15.6 inches; bitches proportionately smaller
Average weight: 20 pounds varying by a few pounds, depending on height of dog and density of bone

A
B
C
D
E
F
G
H
I
J
K
L
M
N
O
P
Q
R
S
T
U
V
W
X
Y
Z

Appearance

A sturdy, compact, rugged fellow, the Welsh Terrier has his tail docked to a length that completes the image of a square dog, roughly as tall as he is long. His body has good substance, with good depth of brisket and moderate width of chest. His loin is strong and moderately short, his topline level. The entire head is rectangular and his small, dark brown eyes are set well in the skull, fairly wide apart and giving a confident, alert

Below and opposite: The breed has a strong muzzle, square outline and traditionally docked tail.

expression so typical of this breed. The foreface is strong, with powerful, punishing jaws and is only slightly narrower than the backskull. His muzzle is strong and squared off, as is his black nose, the furnishings being trimmed to complete the rectangular outline. A scissors bite is preferred, but level is acceptable. His small, V-shaped ears fold just above the topline of the skull and are carried forward, close to the cheek. His hard, wiry coat is dense with a close-fitting thick jacket and he has a short, soft undercoat. The furnishings on muzzle, legs and quarters are dense and wiry. The color of the jacket is

BREED NOTES

SIZE	GROOMING
✓	✓
✓	✓
	✓

EXERCISE	LIFESPAN
✓	✓
✓	✓

black, spreading up onto the neck, down onto the tail and into the

upper thighs. Legs, quarters and head are clear tan, which is a deep reddish color. Slightly lighter tan shades are also acceptable, as is a grizzle jacket.

Characteristics

This game little terrier is alert, aware and spirited, but at the same time he is friendly and shows self control. Intelligence and desire to please are very apparent in his attitude. The Welsh is not so energetic as many of the terrier breeds and makes a very good family companion. Because of his eagerness to please, he is responsive to obedience training and enjoys canine activities such as agility and flyball.

Origins and History

In its early days this breed was more commonly known as the Old English Terrier or Black-and-Tan Wire Haired Terrier. Even as late as 1886 England's Kennel Club allocated a class to "Welsh or Old English Wire Haired Black and Tan Terriers". This is a very old breed the color of which is much as it was over a century ago. Then he was a sporting dog, used in Wales to hunt otter, fox and badger; he therefore has characteristic gameness, but is usually well-mannered and easy to handle. The first classification for the breed under its name of "Welsh Terrier" was at Caernarvon in the mid 1880s when there were 21 dogs entered. Sometimes at shows the same dog was entered as a Welsh Terrier and as an Old English Terrier, depending on the classification offered. The Welsh Terrier first arrived in America in 1888, when Prescott Lawrence imported a dog and bitch and exhibited them in the Miscellaneous class at Madison Square Garden. There was then a lull, but from the first breed classification at Westminster in around 1901, his popularity here has steadily increased.

Health Issues

This is a generally healthy breed, but amongst the problems that can occur are epilepsy, glaucoma, thyroid abnormalities and allergic skin conditions.

Exercise and Grooming

Regular exercise is necessary for the Welsh Terrier, who enjoys a walk on a leash and plenty of time for play. Hand-stripping will bring out the best texture and color in a Welsh Terrier's coat and to present him to perfection, professional expertise is necessary four or five times a year. Between times, he will need a thorough brush and comb once a week, which will bring out the dead

A
B
C
D
E
F
G
H
I
J
K
L
M
N
O
P
Q
R
S
T
U
V
W
X
Y
Z

West Highland White Terrier

Average height: dogs – 11 inches; bitches – 10 inches
Average weight: dogs – 15-22 pounds; bitches – 13-16 pounds

Appearance

The West Highland White Terrier is a well-balanced hardy looking terrier, small and game. He exhibits good showmanship and has an abundance of self-esteem. He is strongly built, deep in chest and with a straight back and powerful hindquarters on muscular legs. His is a great combination of strength and activity. His body between withers and root of tail is slightly shorter than his height at withers. The head is shaped to give a round appearance and his dark, almond-shaped eyes are set widely apart giving a sharp, intelligent look. Overall his expression, aided by his heavy eyebrows, is piercing, inquisitive and pert. The broad skull is slightly domed between the ears and a little longer than the muzzle. The West Highland White Terrier's teeth are large for his size; both a scissors or level bite are equally acceptable. The small, erect ears are set widely apart on the top outer edge of the skull. Hair on the ears is trimmed short and is smooth and velvety, with no fringe at the tips. The relatively short tail (which is never docked), is shaped like a carrot and stands erect. It is covered with hard hair and is as straight as possible, carried gaily, but not over the back. The white coat must be double, consisting of an outer coat of straight hard hair, about two inches long, with shorter coat on neck and shoulders. This is trimmed to blend shorter areas into furnishings, which are longer on stomach and legs.

BREED NOTES

SIZE	GROOMING
✔ ✔	✔ ✔ ✔
EXERCISE	**LIFESPAN**
✔ ✔	✔ ✔

Characteristics

The Westie, as he most commonly known, is a very people-oriented dog, so although he is rather

Above and opposite: The West Highland White is a hardy looking, well-balanced terrier.

independent and self-reliant, he also needs human companionship and attention. He has great stamina, is intelligent and quick in movement, so does well in obedience, agility, flyball, tracking and earthdog tests. Outdoors he a truly sporty, good hunter, with speed and cunning. A Westie will always alert his owners to the approach of a stranger but because of his friendly nature, he does not make a particularly good guard! All terrier, the West Highland White has been described as "a large amount of Scotch spunk, determination and devotion, crammed into a small body".

Origins and History

The West Highland White Terrier descended from similar stock to that of his Scottish cousins, the Scottish Terrier, Skye Terrier, Cairn Terrier and Dandie Dinmont. The Westie is believed to have originated at Poltalloch in Scotland, where he had already been bred for over 100 years before appearing at dog shows. In 1916, Colonel Edward Donald Malcolm of Poltalloch said both his father and grandfather had kept these

Below: 'I just adore relaxing in the garden.'

A
B
C
D
E
F
G
H
I
J
K
L
M
N
O
P
Q
R
S
T
U
V
W
X
Y
Z

A
B
C
D
E
F
G
H
I
J
K
L
M
N
O
P
Q
R
S
T
U
V
W
X
Y
Z

dogs and it is probable that their lineage goes back to the time of King James I, who asked for some "earth-dogges" out of Argyleshire. Legend has it that originally Colonel Malcolm kept a light colored pack of terriers for hunting, but when one of his reddish dogs was mistakenly shot for a fox, he decided only to breed white dogs that could easily been seen in the field. In the past the breed was known as the Roseneath Terrier, also as the Poltalloch Terrier. The breed was first exhibited at Crufts in 1907 and the first AKC registration was in 1908, the name being officially changed to West Highland White Terrier in 1909.

Above: The Westie needs human companionship.

Below: Puppies sharing their toys.

Above: 'What did you say?'

Below: 'Only one of us is interested

Health Issues

Because so much research has been carried out into the health of this breed, the list of problems that may be encountered is exhaustive. It includes Addison's disease, atopic dermatitis, diabetes mellitus, heart disease, hip dysplasia, inflammatory bowel disease (IBD), juvenile cataracts, Legg-Calve Perthes, patella luxation, portosystemic shunt, Westie lung disease and allergy problems.

Exercise and Grooming

The Westie is not greatly demanding from the point of view of exercise, but he should have a regular walk and plenty of play. Being an earth dog, he likes to dig. The Westie's coat requirements if destined for the show ring are much more demanding than those of a Westie kept in pet trim. The former needs much dedication and expertise, for it includes both hand stripping and trimming. In any event, regular grooming is necessary for healthy coat and skin; even pet Westies need a professional "going-over" three or four times each year.

A B C D E F G H I J K L M N O P Q R S T U V **W** X Y Z

Whippet

Average height: dogs – 19-22 inches; bitches – 18-21 inches
Average weight: 25-40 pounds

BREED NOTES

SIZE	GROOMING
✔✔	✔
EXERCISE	**LIFESPAN**
✔✔✔	✔✔✔

Left: A youngster growing up.

Appearance

The Whippet is a thoroughly elegant sighthound of medium size and with moderate bone. He is beautifully balanced, combining muscular power and strength with grace of outline. He is a true sporting hound that covers a maximum of distance with a minimum of lost motion. His long, lean skull is fairly wide between the ears and has a scarcely perceptible stop; the muzzle is long and powerful, denoting great strength of bite, without coarseness. The nose is black and teeth should always meet in a scissors bite. He has a keen, intelligent, alert expression with large, dark eyes. The Whippet has small, rose ears, which are fine in texture, thrown back and folded along the neck in repose. Even when

Above: *A fine example of a Champion, having just won Best in Show.*

Right: *Contemplation on the lawn.*

alert, the fold should be maintained. His long, clean, muscular neck is well arched with no suggestion of throatiness, widening gracefully into the shoulder. The back is broad, firm and well muscled with some length over the loin, the backline running smoothly from the withers with a graceful natural arch beginning over the loin and carrying through over the croup. His brisket is very deep and the ribs well sprung, but with no suggestion of

A
B
C
D
E
F
G
H
I
J
K
L
M
N
O
P
Q
R
S
T
U
V
W
X
Y
Z

Above: The Whippet is the fastest domesticated animal of his weight.

Left: Puppy playing peek-a-boo!

barrel shape. There is a definite tuckup of the underline. The long, tapering tail is carried low with only a gentle upward curve when in motion. The feet are more hare-shaped than cat-shaped, but both are acceptable; they must be well formed with hard, thick pads. Toes are long, close and well arched. The short, close coat, which may be of absolutely any color, is smooth and firm in texture.

Characteristics

The Whippet is the fastest domesticated animal of his weight, capable of speeds up to 35 miles per hour. When racing or coursing, he is extraordinarily keen, but around the home he is quiet, dignified and unobtrusive, not to mention being highly decorative! Although he may look rather delicate, he is by no means fragile, though his skin is thin and can tear easily if caught on barbed wire. He also feels the cold, so always needs a coat when walking outdoors in the winter. This is indeed an ideal dual-purpose small dog for an owner of discrimination; he is amiable, friendly and gentle, making a charming, affectionate and intelligent pet.

Origins and History

The Whippet was developed during the 19th century by breeders whose aim was to produce a dog that was a small, fleet Greyhound, but hardier than the Italian Greyhound;

Right and below: "Gwen" relaxing (above) and with her much adored litter (below).

A
B
C
D
E
F
G
H
I
J
K
L
M
N
O
P
Q
R
S
T
U
V
W
X
Y
Z

Above: A lovely head study of "Nancy" bred and co-owned by the author and Carol Ann Johnson

one that was capable of chasing and capturing small game. For this he needed pluck and tenacity. Several different breeds were used in the Whippet's make-up including the two already mentioned. But there was terrier blood too, the Airedale, Bedlington, Manchester, Yorkshire and English; some of this breeding was evident in the rough-coated Whippets that were found during the breed's early development. In his early days the Whippet was often called the "Snap Dog" because when running along a track or meeting a strange dog they had a tendency to snap at one another, though some say it was because they snapped up the rabbits when chasing them in an enclosure in the days of "snap-dog coursing", in which the unfortunate rabbits had no means of escape. Later they were used for straight racing and were known as "the poor man's racehorse", for keeping the breed was usually purely a gambling proposition, especially favored by miners in the north of England. The breed first appeared on the showbench in 1876 but was not recognized by England's Kennel Club until 1890. In America the breed was recognized in 1888, having been brought here by English mill operators.

Health Issues
The Whippet is generally a very healthy breed but like all sighthounds, is sensitive to

anesthetics, so this must always be discussed with the veterinarian prior to surgery.

Exercise and Grooming

The Whippet needs both walks on a leash and free run. He should have his free exercise in a safely enclosed area, as he tends to run in a straight line and can be almost out of sight in the blink of an eye. Coat care is minimal, but should be brushed regularly to remove dead hair. A rub down with a chamois leather followed by a piece of velvet will put a gleaming finish to the coat, while the Whippet will have enjoyed the massage!

Right and below: Whippets have an abundance of energy as puppies (above) and as adults (below).

White Shepherd

Average height: dogs – 25 inches; bitches – 23 inches
Average weight: dogs – 75-85 pounds; bitches – 60-70 pounds

Appearance

The White Shepherd has a distinct look of intelligence, energy and purpose in life, with something of a regal appearance about him. He is rather longer than tall and has smooth curves, rather than sharp angles. Because he is a working dog, he has to be built with the agility and freedom of movement and endurance that allows him to carry out the tasks required of him. When moving, all parts work in harmony. In males the head shows a certain masculinity but without coarseness, whereas bitches are feminine, without being over-refined. The eyes, dark brown for preference, express a keen intelligent look that is also composed. The ears are moderately pointed and open toward the front; they are carried erect when at attention. The bushy tail hangs at least to the hock and hangs straight down, or in a slight, saber-like curve. The tail is used like a rudder enabling it to keep its balance while turning instantly. The coat is double and weather-resistant, the outer coat medium in length, dense, straight, harsh and close lying, while the undercoat is short, thick and fine in texture. Hair on head and ears is smooth and somewhat softer. The male may carry a thicker ruff than the female. The ideal color is pure white, but other coat markings ranging from very pale cream to light biscuit are acceptable. Nose, lips and eye rims should be fully-pigmented and black; the White Shepherd is not an albino.

Characteristics

This breed has a direct, but not hostile, expression of self-confidence. Eager, alert and ready to serve, the White Shepherd can be a companion, watch dog or service dog. He has an inherent aptitude to guard flocks and is protective toward family members and their property but has a more mellow, soft and sensitive character than the German Shepherd Dog (GSD). He observes strangers carefully and may be rather aloof with them, but is never apprehensive. This breed lacks the serious drive necessary to compete in Schutzhund competition.

Origins and History

The White Shepherd is directly descended from the GSD and because they have similar roots are very similar in many ways. Controversy has surrounded the breed's history as GSD traditionalists consider the white coat a disqualifying fault. The earliest mention of a white coat goes back to 1882, where it appeared in Europe. Some whites were registered with the AKC in 1917 and more in the 1920s, but by the 1930s the color had fallen out of favor. In the 1960s Germans began a serious campaign against the White Shepherd, resulting in its virtual disappearance in Europe; America followed suit. From 1969 things progressed in a more positive fashion as the White German Shepherd Dog Club of America was formed to promote the breed. Several countries have since come to recognise this dog as a breed in its own right. The White Shepherd has evolved from continuous selection for a working companion animal, with a characteristic white color coupled with beauty and elegance. Any extremes have always been discouraged. With his high intelligence, this breed is believed to be one of the most versatile of working dogs.

Health Issues

In 2000 The American White Shepherd Association sponsored a survey of genetic disorders in the breed and retains detailed records.

BREED NOTES

SIZE	GROOMING
✓ ✓ ✓	✓ ✓

EXERCISE	LIFESPAN
✓ ✓ ✓	✓ ✓

The most common problems include hip and elbow dysplasia, von Willebrand's Disease, cardiac problems, malabsorption syndrome, degenerative joint disease, megaesophagus, bloat, allergies and eye problems including corneal inflammation (pannus).

Exercise and Grooming

The White Shepherd is an agile dog so must be given plenty of exercise. His coat is not difficult to manage but daily brushing is recommended to remove dead hair.

Below: A beautiful group, displaying the character of the breed.

A
B
C
D
E
F
G
H
I
J
K
L
M
N
O
P
Q
R
S
T
U
V
W
X
Y
Z

A
B
C
D
E
F
G
H
I
J
K
L
M
N
O
P
Q
R
S
T
U
V
W
X
Y
Z

Wire Fox Terrier

Average height: dogs – 15.5 inches maximum; bitches proportionately lower
Average weight: 16-18 pounds

Appearance

The Wire Fox Terrier is quick and keen, forever on the tip-toe of expectation and ready for the slightest provocation. He has bone and strength in a small bodily frame, but is in no way "cloddy" as speed and endurance are also important to him. He is neither too leggy, nor too short in the leg, standing like a cleverly made, short-backed hunter, covering a lot of ground. Breeders are very specific about the length of his head which bears a relation to the length of the back. His dark eyes are moderately small, deep set and full of fire, life and intelligence; the foreface gradually tapers from eye to muzzle, with a little delicate chiselling. Jaw bones are well developed, armed with a strong set of white teeth, giving the appearance of strength to the foreface, the teeth closing in a vice-like grip. The Wire Fox Terrier's ears are small, V-shaped and moderately thick, their flaps neatly folded over and dropping forward, close to the cheeks. His neck is clean and muscular, the back short and level, the loins muscular and very slightly arched. His chest is deep and not broad, but neither is it too narrow. His tail is set on rather high and carried gaily, but not curled; it is docked to about three-quarters of its length, affording a safe grip when handling a working terrier. His feet are round and compact, not large and with well-cushioned pads. The best coat appears to be broken, the hairs having a tendency to twist; they are dense and of wiry texture, like coconut matting. When the hairs are parted with the fingers, the skin cannot be seen. At their base is a shorter growth of finer, softer hair, which is the undercoat. The predominant color is white; brindle, red, liver or slaty-blue are objectionable, otherwise color is of little importance. When moving, his legs are carried straight forward, the forelegs hanging perpendicular and swinging parallel to the sides, like the pendulum of a clock. The principal propulsive power comes from the hind legs, aided by long thighs, muscular second thighs and well bent stifles.

Characteristics

This is a friendly, devoted and affectionate breed, with a highly

Johnson

Above: Portraying the finest qualities of this cleverly-made breed.

active personality, always ready for a romp. He is generally very good with children and makes a good watchdog because he is so alert by nature. Although fairly friendly with strange people, he has a tendency to be aggressive toward other dogs and has retained his hunting instinct for small prey.

Origins and History

Although for almost 100 years the Wire Fox Terrier was classified with the Smooth Fox Terrier as one breed with two varieties, in 1984 the AKC approved two separate standards, acknowledging them as two distinct breeds. The ancestor of the Wire is believed to be the old rough-coated, black-and-tan working terrier of Wales, Derbyshire and Durham and the breed is considered to be about 20 years younger than the Smooth. Although originally the Smooth and Wire Fox Terriers were bred together, this has not been the case for many years. Like the Smooth, the Wire was used to locate fox, kill vermin and to hunt rabbits and to this day is still used as a hunting companion, although is more frequently a companion of the home.

Health Issues

Problems about which owners should be aware include epilepsy, skin problems, nasal drip, lens luxation, cataracts and shoulder dislocation. Due to this being a predominantly white breed, deafness can occasionally occur.

Exercise and Grooming

The Wire Fox Terrier enjoys regular long walks, coupled with plenty of playtime. He needs freedom to run around in a yard. When walking out he is best kept on a leash, in case his hunting instinct comes into play and he decides to chase a cat! Grooming demands for a pet and show Wire are very different, the latter requiring professional expertise to follow a complex grooming routine. For pet Wires the coat should be brushed with a firm bristle brush and bathed when necessary; an occasional stripping at a parlor will be needed from time to time.

A B C D E F G H I J K L M N O P Q R S T U V **W** X Y Z

Wirehaired Pointing Griffon

Average height: dogs – 22-24 inches; bitches – 20-22 inches
Average weight: 50-60 pounds

He has a double coat, the outer coat of medium length, straight and wiry, its harsh texture providing protection in rough cover. The undercoat, usually lighter in color, is a fine, thick down, providing insulation and water resistance. His legs are covered with denser, shorter hair that is not so coarse. The color is preferably steel gray with brown markings, frequently chestnut brown, or roan, white and brown; white and orange are also acceptable.

BREED NOTES

SIZE	GROOMING
✔ ✔	✔ ✔

EXERCISE	LIFESPAN
✔ ✔ ✔	✔ ✔

Appearance

The strong-limbed Wirehaired Pointing Griffon is bred to cover all terrain covered by the walking hunter. His strong, firm back descends gently to the base of tail, he has moderate spring of rib and his chest reaches the elbow. The loin is strong and his croup and rump are stoutly made for speed. The docked tail is carried straight, or raised slightly. The firm, round feet have tightly closed webbed toes and thick pads. From the side, the muzzle and head are square. His abundant mustache and eyebrows contribute to his friendly expression and rather unkempt appearance. The large eyes range through all shades of yellow and brown. Nose color is always brown, and well open nostrils are essential; teeth meet in a scissors bite. The high-set ears lie flat and close to the head.

Characteristics

Mentally quick and intelligent, the Wirehaired Pointing Griffon is easily trained. Outgoing in character, he is willing to please and utterly trustworthy, making an excellent family dog and fine hunting companion. He is excellent as a pointer in the field, or as a retriever in the water.

Origins and History

This breed was originally called the Korthals Griffon, after Eduard K Korthals, an avid hunter who longed for a dog that could hunt in the marshes and on other terrains too; a robust dog with a keen game-finding nose and a swift, efficient ground covering stride, with endurance for an all day hunt. His ideal dog also needed a co-operative nature, willingness to recover upland game and waterfowl and resistance to heat and cold, needing a harsh,

water repellant coat. He used largely griffon type dogs along with Barbets, Boulets, pointers from France and Germany, spaniels and retrievers, resulting in the Wirehaired Pointing Griffon. The breed first arrived in the USA in 1887 and a specialist club was formed in 1916.

Health Issues

Health problems reported in this breed include hip dysplasia, skin allergies and thyroid diseases.

Exercise and Grooming

He needs regular exercise in a safe, spacious area, with a good run in the park or a swim in the lake. Grooming involves brushing the coat and stripping out dead hair at least a couple of times a month, more frequently for the showring.

A B C D E F G H I J K L M N O P Q R S T U V **W** X Y Z

Xoloitzcuintli

Average height: toy – 11-12 inches; miniature – 12-15 inches; standard – 16-22.5 inches
Average weight: toy – 9-18 pounds; miniature – 13-22 pounds; standard – 22-31 pounds

Appearance

The Xoloitzcuintli, often called Xolo for short, is also known as the Mexican Hairless; there are hairless and coated varieties (both found in the same litter), and three sizes. The hairless has no hair except possibly a tuft of short, coarse hair on head, nape of neck, feet and tail. The coated variety has a short, sleek, flat coat with no bare patches. Color ranges from black to gray, red, liver, or bronze to golden yellow, either a solid color or spotted. His clean, graceful look shows the elegance of a sighthound and the strength and proportions of a terrier. His flexible neck has the grace of an antelope and the strong head is rather broad with a thoughtful, intelligent expression. His almond-shaped eyes can vary from yellow to black and his large, upright, thin-textured ears are expressive.

Characteristics

All three sizes make excellent companions, being reasonably calm but ready to announce the approach of strangers. He is cheerful, attentive, alert and loyal to family members, but naturally protective and rather aloof with strangers. Socialized properly, the Xolo is usually good with children. He learns very quickly, but must be taught to respect his owner. Often he is called a "Velcro dog", because seldom runs off. Xolos are generally good climbers and some can climb trees, so be warned! This primitive breed has great survival skills and will not tolerate abuse or an unstable environment. Those without coat have a higher body temperature than other dogs.

Origins and History

This is reputed to be one of the world's oldest breeds, dating back over 5,700 years. Clay pottery and other artefacts have been found in the tombs of Colima, Mayan and Aztec Indians, the breed was highly prized for its loyalty, intelligence, curative and mystical powers. There are different theories about the actual origin. Some believe they go back to African dogs that developed further in South America, whilst others consider the breed originated in China. Certainly the Aztecs had hairless dogs as pets, bed-warmers, food and sacrificial offerings. The first Xolo were shown in the USA in 1883, but in 1959 the AKC withdrew registration due to lack of numbers. Now the Xoloitzcuitli (pronounced show-low-eets-queent-lee, by the way) is listed under the AKC's

Foundation Stock Service, and has been designated the official dog of Mexico.

Health Issues

The Xolo is a very hardy, healthy breed with no known breed-related health concerns. The hairless variety should, however, wear a sweater in cold weather. This is a very long-lived breed; 15 years is common and 20 years not unusual!

Exercise and Grooming

Both varieties are easy to groom. Coated dogs should be brushed and bathed as normal, but the hairless ones should be bathed and lotioned about twice a month, ideally using hypoallergenic, gentle human products. Over-bathing strips the skin of its natural oils, whereas over-lotioning can clog the pores.

BREED NOTES

SIZE			GROOMING
Min.	St.	Toy	
✓	✓	✓	✓
✓	✓		✓
			✓

EXERCISE	LIFESPAN
✓	✓
✓	✓
✓	✓

Yorkshire Terrier

Average height: 8-9 inches
Average weight: 7 pounds maximum

Appearance

The Yorkshire Terrier must surely be one of the best known Toy breeds, a neat, compact little dog oozing with self-confidence and self-importance. His head is small and rather flat on top, the muzzle not too long and the teeth meet in either a scissors or a level bite. His dark eyes sparkle, with and intelligent expression. The small V-shaped ears are carried erect and set not too far apart. The Yorkshire Terrier's back is rather short and his topline level, with the height at shoulder the same as at the rump. The tail is docked to a medium length and carried higher than the back. In some countries Yorkshire Terriers have natural tails left at their full length. The coat is glossy, fine and silky in texture, the coat on the body it is moderately

Left: '*I should be safe up here with this good find!*'

long and perfectly straight, not wavy. If necessary, it may be trimmed to floor-length for ease of movement and to give a neat appearance. The long headfall is tied with one bow in the center of the head, or parted in the middle and tied with two bows. On the muzzle the hair is very long and should be trimmed on the tips of ears and feet to give a neat appearance. Puppies are born black and tan, usually showing an intermingling of black in the tan hair until they are mature. In adulthood, the Yorkshire Terrier is a dark steel blue and tan, the tan hair being darker at the roots than in the middle and shading to a still lighter shade at the tips.

Left: A puppy with personality plus!

mines and cotton mills, and was also used in competitive rat-killing contests, a sport much enjoyed by miners of the north. The breed we know today first appeared at a show in England in 1861, under the name of "Broken-haired Scotch Terrier". In 1870 it became known as the Yorkshire Terrier, for it was felt that that was the county in which the breed had been improved. There is an early record of a litter born in the USA in 1871 and classes for the breed appeared at shows from 1878, although at that time they were divided into two sizes, under and over 5 pounds. Soon size settled down to an average of 3 to 7 pounds.

Characteristics

Despite his small size, the Yorkshire Terrier is spirited and highly alert; he has never forgotten his terrier ancestry. He makes a devoted companion and is always ready to protect his family, seeming quite unaware of his diminutive size! He is rather independent but ever playful, inquisitive, intelligent, friendly and willing to please. Because he is so active he simply loves participating in dog sports such as obedience, agility, flyball, frisbee, tracking and even earthdog trials. The Yorkie, as he is commonly called, also makes a good therapy dog.

Origins and History

The Yorkshire Terrier can be traced back to the Waterside Terrier, which was a small longish-coated dog of a bluish-gray color. This dog usually weighed about 10 pounds, but could range from 6 to 20. The Waterside Terrier was a result of crossing of the old rough-coated Black-and-Tan English Terrier and the Paisley and Clydesdale Terriers. This little dog was taken to Yorkshire in the mid-19th century by weavers who migrated from Scotland to England. It was a great help in dispatching rats in coal

Health Issues

Amongst the health problems to which the Yorkshire Terrier is susceptible are campylobacteriosis, coccidiotis, collapsing trachea,

Below: A Yorkie is always fun to have around the house.

A
B
C
D
E
F
G
H
I
J
K
L
M
N
O
P
Q
R
S
T
U
V
W
X
Y
Z

Above *This breed is spirited and highly alert.*

Below: *A veteran enjoying the comfort of the armchair.*

Cushing's disease, eclampsia, hemorrhagic gastric enteritis (HE), hypoglycaemia, Legg-Calve Perthes disease, liver shunt, pancreatitis patella luxation and reverse sneezing (pharyngeal gag reflex). Owners should also be aware than the breed can have poor tolerance to anesthesia and risks early tooth decay.

Exercise and Grooming

The Yorkshire Terrier easily adapts to its owner's activity level but appreciates regular opportunities to

run and play. His coat should be brushed on a daily basis, a bow or band used to keep the hair away from the eyes. Maintaining a Yorkshire Terrier's coat in a condition suitable for the showring is a dedicated task, the coat usually being put in wraps to preserve its length and protect against broken ends.

Right: A show Yorkie in full coat.

Below: Stylishly geared out in wraps and jackets to protect the coat.

Cross Breeds

The term "cross breed" can mean many things; it may simply be an accidental mating between two pure-bred dogs, or it may be the result of carefully planned matings that have been carried out specifically to create another breed, in an effort to create a dog with the best attributes of both. Indeed many of the breeds we know today began as cross breeds, but in most cases they were very carefully planned and have long been considered pure-bred.

Sometimes, in order to improve a pure breed, a cross is deliberately introduced. For the sake of example, back in the 1950s, a Pekingese was introduced to Shih Tzu breeding in England. This was a highly controversial move at the time but very careful records were kept and puppies all closely monitored. At first, the offspring that included the Pekingese blood could not be registered with the Kennel Club, but thanks to the careful records that had been kept, fourth generation offspring (always mated back to pure Shih Tzu following that initial outcross) could all be registered as pure-bred Shih Tzu. Still amongst the Shih Tzu fraternity, there is debate as to whether or not this was a wise move, but now it is all in the history books. So, I'm sure, will it be for many of today's cross breeds that a century from now will probably be considered pure-bred dogs.

Planned cross breeds are becoming increasingly popular, especially in America; some are simply "designer dogs" others have a specific purpose. Sometimes a cross breed is created because it especially suitable for allergy sufferers, or maybe particular features of the combination of breeds suits guide dog training for the blind.

Many of today's cross breeds have been given names; perhaps the Labradoodle is one of the most well known. The American Labradoodle is not a pure-bred dog, but a cross between the Labrador and the Poodle and is recognized by the American Canine Hybrid Club, but not by the AKC. The Australian Labradoodle, however, has, since 2004, been registered as a pure breed in Australia. This, too, is a cross between the Labrador and Standard and Miniature Poodles, but through careful and selective breeding for many years, it has reached the stage of becoming classified as a breed in its own right.

American Labradoodles are being bred in slightly differing ways. A straight Labrador-Poodle cross can result in producing a dog with hair that is smooth like that of a Labrador, wiry, wavy or shaggy. Some shed and some do not, and even puppies in the same litter can vary considerably. A Labradoodle that is made up of 25% Labrador and 75% Poodle generally has a wavy/curly shaggy-looking coat and is most likely to be the most allergy-friendly combination. If two first

Left: Lhasa Apso and Poodle cross.

Right: Tibetan Terrier and Cavalier King Charles Spaniel cross.

generation Labradoodles are mated together, there is likely to be as much variety in the puppies as there would be in a straight cross.

It is important to stress that when crossing one breed with another, the attributes of both breeds are not produced automatically. This can only be done by selective breeding, that is to say that over several generations, breeders strive to breed in the good points and breed out the bad ones. In the early stages of any cross breed programme, there will of course be some dogs produced that carry the worst features of both. This means that anyone considering buying a cross breed, should look very carefully not only at the puppies they are viewing, but also at the many characteristics found in both breeds involved.

The number of cross breeds that now exist is frighteningly large, and it is not possible to believe that all of them have been thought out with due care and attention. Certainly many of them make absolutely charming pets and those who have bred them have probably brought up their puppies with all the care and attention they deserve. Sadly other breeders (to use the word loosely) are less careful and have made the cross either just by accident or to make a statement, of whatever sort, maybe simply to create a talking point.

As this book goes to press one American registry service for cross-bred dogs lists over 450 different crosses, amongst them are some very plausible crosses, but some make the mind boggle! To cite just a few examples:

Rottaf =
Afghan Hound x Rottweiler
Bordernese = Bernese Mountain Dog x Border Collie
Brat = American Rat Terrier x Boston Terrier
Aussie-Poo =
Australian Shepherd x Poodle
Ba-Shar = Basset Hound x Shar Pei
English Bull-Walker =
Bulldog x Treeing Walker
Chiweenie =
Chihuahua x Dachshund
Irish Saint =
Irish Terrier x Saint Bernard

… and so the list goes on; one can only wonder in some cases how the matings actually took place!

Some of the more sensible cross breeds, however, have names that are becoming more familiar, such as the Cockapoo. Some Cockapoo clubs are working towards making this a pure breed, with multi-generation crossing, while others are simply sticking to the basic Poodle-Cocker Spaniel mix. If interested in owning this cross breed, it is important top find out which type of Cockapoo breeding has been used. They come in four sizes, "Teacup", which is under 6 pounds; Toy, under 12 pounds; Miniature, 13 to 18 pounds; Maxi, over 19 pounds. Their height varies between 14 and 15 inches.

As the majority of breeds used in cross breeding are covered as individual breeds in this book, the appearance and basic breed characteristics of each can be found under each breed's relevant heading, but prospective cross breed owners should seriously look at both the good and bad points of those breeds that are involved.

Index

D

E

F

G

H

I

J

K

L

M

N

O

P

Acknowledgements

The publishers would like to express their thanks to the following for their help in compiling this book.

Kevin Kingham, Interpet

Pamela O. Kadlec at Just Ducky Kennels, Boykin Spaniel

Patsy Bird, Cirneco del Etna

Doris Meier, Bruenggberghunde, Appenzeller Sennenhund

Jean Wright, A.W.S.C. Judges Education Committee, American Water Spaniel

Kathlen Strunk, American Eskimo Dog

Joyce Maley, Hurricane Chinooks

Pam Peterson, Kai Ken

Debby G. Morris, Star Hound Kennels, Peruvian Inca Orchid

Patricia Leibold Hoover, Xolo

Lorne Durham, Monumental Kennels, South African Boerboel

Ray and Jo Ann Draper, King Pen Kennels, Rat Terrier

Frank and Sandy Mills, Wire Haired Pointing Griffon

Tom Bouma, Stabyhoun

Lars Hammar, Shapendoes

Alex Maldon, Toy Fox Terrier

Amanda Phillips, and Hal Davis of Dabro Photography, White Shepherd

Derek Reich and Glen McDonald,Windriver Beardogs, Karelian Bear Dog

Joe Burkett, White Deer Preserve, Plott Hound

Mrs Temple DaSilva, Secretary, Portuguese Pointer Club of America

Ray and Deborah Matthews, Bluetick 1 Kennels, Bluetick Coonhound

Mahogany Ridge, Black and Tan Coonhound

Homeless Animal Rescue Team, Treeing Tennessee Brindle